TITI LIVI

AB VRBE CONDITA LIBRI

LIBER PRIMVS

TITI LIVI
AB VRBE CONDITA LIBRI

PRAEFATIO
LIBER PRIMVS

Edited by

H. J. EDWARDS

Cambridge :
at the University Press
1968

CAMBRIDGE UNIVERSITY PRESS
Cambridge, New York, Melbourne, Madrid, Cape Town,
Singapore, São Paulo, Delhi, Mexico City

Cambridge University Press
The Edinburgh Building, Cambridge CB2 8RU, UK

Published in the United States of America by Cambridge University Press, New York

www.cambridge.org
Information on this title: www.cambridge.org/9781107621220

First published 1912
Re-issued 1968, 2013

A catalogue record for this publication is available from the British Library

ISBN 978-1-107-62122-0 Paperback

VIRO · OPTIMO

THOMAE · GVLIELMO · DVNN

ARTIVM · LIBERALIVM

MAGISTRO · SEMPER · ADMIRABILI

POTENTI · SEMPER · QVIA · VIDEBATVR · POSSE

HVNC · LIBRVM · QVANTVLVMCVMQVE

ANIMO · GRATISSIMO

D · D · D

DISCIPVLVS

ὥσπερ ἐν ἐσόπτρῳ τῇ ἱστορίᾳ πειρώμενον ἁμωσγεπως
κοσμεῖν καὶ ἀφομοιοῦν πρὸς τὰς ἐκείνων ἀρετὰς τὸν
βίον.

PLUTARCH, *Timoleon*.

PREFACE

AN edition undertaken as a *πάρεργον* in a busy life is apt to delay its appearance: and in the present instance the nine-year canon of Horace has been more than satisfied. Yet in a decade when excavations in the Forum and elsewhere have revealed new evidence for the period with which Livy's first book is concerned a certain delay was not altogether dangerous.

To two friends this book, 'as in private duty bound,' expresses its first and most fervent thanks: to Mr Leonard Whibley, Fellow of Pembroke College, for valued advice and criticism; and to Professor Ridgeway, not only for what his pen has contributed to the study of prehistoric Italy, but for the kindness of his audience, and the keenness of his criticism, at a *recitatio* of the introduction.

The text of W. Weissenborn and H. J. Müller has been generally followed. It seemed undesirable, in an edition of this kind, to provide a regular *apparatus criticus*: the more important questions of reading are therefore considered in the general notes *ad loca*, and a short list of the principal emendations adopted is tabulated for reference on a separate page. A correspondence with Professor R. S. Conway, begun by a fortunate meeting over the Medicean MS. at Florence some years ago, enabled certain points in the text to benefit by his experienced criticism.

No one can study the first book of Livy without appreciating the value of the edition published by Sir John Seeley in 1870: the historical investigations contained in his introduction have still the power to stimulate inquiry and to steady judgment. The Weissenborn-Müller edition of 1908 has been consulted in many places, but chiefly as a means of criticising notes already written, and as a storehouse of references to Livian usage. In questions of syntax frequent use has been made of Riemann's *La Langue et la Grammaire de Tite-Live* and of Kühnast's *Die Hauptpunkte der Livianischen Syntax*.

I treasure in grateful memory a visit to the Forum ten years ago, when Commendatore Boni was kind enough to show and explain the remarkable discoveries which he had recently made. For topographical notes I have chiefly used Professor J. B. Platner's *Topography and Monuments of Ancient Rome* (1904): for Roman religion I am deeply indebted—as who is not?—to Mr Warde Fowler's works.

For the general study of the *origines* of Rome, and of the regal period, the *Storia dei Romani* (*La Conquista del Primato in Italia*) of Professor G. de Sanctis, published in 1907, has been of great assistance and interest. In this admirable work the results of recent investigation, literary and archaeological, are considered side by side with the views of ancient and modern authorities, and conclusions are expressed with equal modesty and sagacity. To Mr J. G. Frazer's *Lectures on the Early History of the Kingship*, used again and again, the pages of this edition acknowledge an indebtedness which in all heartiness I accentuate here.

Last, but by no means least, my thanks are due to the Syndics of the Press for the courtesy of their patience, and to the readers for the detection of many a disfigurement.

H. J. E.

PETERHOUSE,
7 *April* 1912.

CONTENTS

INTRODUCTION

§ 1. Livy and the Augustan Age.

Censetur Apona Livio suo tellus. Martial I. 61. 3.

THE outline of Livy's life is simple but significant. He was born at Patavium (Padua) in 59 or 58 B.C., and died there in A.D. 17; but he spent most of his mature life in Rome, residing there probably throughout the reign of Augustus, so that in point of date his activity may be said to coincide exactly with the Augustan age. Of himself he says scarcely anything[1], and ancient authors say little about him[2]; but mediaeval writers, *more suo*, invent a record sufficiently remarkable to save him from obscurity. Of Patavium, which 'as in private duty bound' he mentions at the very beginning of the first book, we know that it was an ancient city, famous always for its uncompromising love of liberty and integrity, and important in Livy's day for its commerce, its waters, and its oracle. The citizens were strong supporters of Pompey in his struggle with Caesar, the events of which must have impressed themselves upon the boyhood of Livy; indeed, he remained 'Pompeian' all his life, and it is possible that the *Patavinitas* with which some of his critics found fault may be partly connected with this unflinching adherence to republican traditions.

As a natural result of rhetorical studies, he composed several popular dialogues—half-historical, half-philosophical in character—and an epistle on rhetorical training, addressed to his son.

[1] Three passages (I. 19. 3, IV. 20. 7, and XXVIII. 12. 12) contain all that he tells us in this connection.

[2] Suetonius says of Claudius (chapter 41) that in his youth he essayed to write history, on the advice of Livy.

These works seem to have enjoyed a considerable reputation in the first century of the Empire: Seneca sets Livy next to Cicero and Asinius Pollio as a philosopher, and there are those who would place him higher, or highest, among the three for style. Anyhow, we may well believe that his earlier publications declared the author to be a man of uncommon eloquence, and, when he came to Rome, procured him admission to the friendship of Augustus. It is reasonable to suppose that he had at any rate conceived the project of his history independently of any suggestion from the Emperor: and he may have come to Rome in the first instance to study books in the new libraries.

Literature, like politics, was at this time passing through a transition. The Latin prose which had reached its acme of idiom in Caesar and Cicero was adapting itself, under the influence of rhetoric, to a greater variety of culture and interests: the vigorous oratory which had grown to flower and fruit under the Republic was beginning inevitably to droop in an atmosphere which discouraged independence of thought or speech: while poetry, turned and trimmed more and more to suit the taste and win the patronage of Caesar and his court, was employing a number of literary men which increased with the increase of leisure that followed imperial peace. Hitherto, literature had been treated at Rome chiefly as the pastime of a few cultured amateurs, who certainly left the mark of their own individuality on what they wrote, in prose or verse: but now, when literary composition, especially poetry, was at once fashionable and profitable, the number of professional candidates for literary honours raised the standard of style and skill, while it brought under cultivation the whole field of subject-matter.

With all its artificiality, this literary movement had a considerable influence on general study; and here, as in almost everything that belongs to his reign, Augustus supplied a wise initiative. Libraries were formed, and scholars came in from all parts of the Empire to study in Rome. And when Augustus himself sought in a sense to renew the ancient traditions of the

Roman state, it is not surprising that others turned their attention to its history and antiquities. Many men, in their enforced leisure under the new rule, tried to write the record of their own recent experiences in the civil wars; but for others the study—or we may almost call it the cult—of antiquity, with the abundant materials now available, seemed to be more attractive and less contentious. And indeed, the time was peculiarly favourable for a survey of the whole history of Rome and a description of its dramatic unity. The historian might still express, without fear of imperial displeasure, his appreciation of the work and worth of the great Republicans. The time of toleration had not yet passed away, and it was not necessary that a historian of the past should grossly flatter the Emperor of the present.

It was in literary surroundings of this character that Titus Livius of Patavium set himself to compose the history of Rome, from the first-beginnings down to his own times. In what spirit he took up his pen let his own Preface bear witness. He begins[1] by doubting the probable value of his history; his subject is infinite in itself, and may be unattractive to some of his contemporaries: yet he will gladly sacrifice to oblivion his own name and fame, if he may help the history of Imperial Rome, which possesses, in the glory of its antiquity, in the richness of its examples, and in the potency of its philosophy, a fascination that is unique and irresistible. With the enthusiasm of a patriot, Livy could admire the Imperial City, and the men who had made her such; with the independence of a republican, he could declare her virtues, and denounce her vices. Yet for all this he brought the spirit of the Augustan age into the whole of his work, and his 'canonisation of Rome' (as a modern critic[2] has aptly termed it) was—like the *Aeneid* of Virgil—a service to the Principate which no one understood or appreciated better than the Princeps himself. Augustus was wise enough to discern the loyal subject in the avowed republican,

[1] See the analysis given on p. 78.
[2] Mackail, *Latin Literature*, p. 155.

the power of the philosopher in the enthusiasm of the artist; and when Livy disputed the value of Julius Caesar to the commonwealth[1], and praised Pompey so emphatically that Augustus himself could not but call him *Pompeianus*[2], the friendship between them was not impaired.

§ 2. LIVY AS A HISTORIAN AND AS A WRITER.

At non historia cesserit Graecis. nec opponere Thucydidi Sallustium vereor, nec indignetur sibi Herodotus aequari Titum Livium, cum in narrando mirae iucunditatis clarissimique candoris, tum in contionibus supra quam enarrari potest eloquentem: ita quae dicuntur omnia cum rebus tum personis accommodata sunt: adfectus quidem praecipueque eos qui sunt dulciores, ut parcissime dicam, nemo historicorum commendavit magis.

QUINTILIAN, *Institutio Oratoria* X. i. 101.

It was a stupendous task to which Livy addressed himself at the time when Octavian—who had just received the title of Augustus[3]—was engaged in bringing system out of chaos, and (though he concealed the fact) monarchy out of a dead republic. From 27 B.C. to the end of his life Livy laboured on, until his AB VRBE CONDITA LIBRI numbered 142, and his record had reached to the death of Drusus in 9 B.C.[4] He himself[5] spoke of the work as *annales*, the elder Pliny as *historiae*[6]. It was published (like Gibbon's famous work) in sections, *volumina*, which a later generation, not the author himself, marked off into decades: and the work was so vast, for it expanded in treatment as it drew nearer to the time of the writer, that an abridged edition, referred to by Martial in a well-known couplet[7], was found to be more convenient to the bookseller and the purchaser; and *periochae*, or brief summaries of the contents of each book, were compiled, but perhaps not before the fourth century. And

[1] Seneca, *Nat. Qu.* V. 18. 4.
[2] Tacitus, *Ann.* IV. 34.
[3] Livy I. 19. 3.
[4] Livy, *Epitome* CXL.
[5] XLIII. 13. 2.
[6] *Nat. Hist.* XVI. *praef.*
[7] XIV. 190. *Pellibus exiguis artatur Livius ingens,*
quem mea non totum bibliotheca capit.

now, when of the original 142 books only 35 have survived (I to X, and XXI to XLV), these *periochae* remain for us, the melancholy ruins of a monumental achievement.

Livy called his own work *annales*; and the title is not inappropriate, at any rate for those earlier parts of the history in which his record evidently rests upon the Roman annalists. The earliest of them (Q. Fabius Pictor and L. Cincius Alimentus) began to write about the time of the Second Punic War, and the succession lasted till the time of Julius Caesar. They were *narratores rerum non exornatores*[1], and their method of work was to relate the whole of Roman history from its origins to their own day. As authorities they used official documents and records on the one hand, and family memorials on the other: in the former class were treaties (such as that with Gabii), lists of consuls, pontifical books, *libri lintei*; in the latter, funeral orations, poems, pedigrees, personal memoirs. Their sympathies with families or with political parties found frequent expression[2], and they cannot be said to have had any strict or scientific regard for truth.

The earlier annalists seem to have given but a slight account of the origins of Rome and the regal period: the later annalists expanded the tradition, by the incorporation of more material, legendary or imaginary, with no little assistance from Greek sources. The later works were in effect larger editions of the earlier, and tended to replace them in popular acceptance: and investigation seems to prove that Livy adhered mainly to the later annalists as his authorities for the earliest times. Thus Book I appears to be an abridgment of the regal history of Q. Valerius Antias (*fl.* in the age of Sulla), with fairly large excerpts from Q. Aelius Tubero (*fl.* 50 B.C.) in the case of the later reigns, but to have little immediate relationship with L. Calpurnius Piso (consul, 133 B.C.) or C. Licinius Macer (*fl.* 75 B.C.), both of whom, however, are used in the four following books. Livy's method seems to have been to follow one authority at a time, usually without acknowledgment: occasionally he adds at

[1] Cicero, *de Oratore*, II. 12. 54. [2] Cf. Livy VII. 9. 3.

the end of a section some information from another source[1]. If his authorities disagree, he does not attempt to base his own version on criticism, but follows the majority, or the earliest, or the most Roman, according to his own preference[2].

The similarities between Livy and his Greek contemporary Dionysius of Halicarnassus are remarkable, in regard both to form and to subject-matter: and as it cannot be proved that either used the work of the other, we are led to conclude that both had access to the same sources of information—perhaps in the same libraries at Rome. The verbal agreements between them are especially frequent in the chronicle of the last two kings: in fact, the relationship—the synopsis—may be said to begin with the reign of Servius Tullius: but even here they do not use the same authorities, or not in the same way. It would seem that Dionysius, for all his fulness, omits points (*e.g.* state formalities) that might not be intelligible or interesting to Greek readers, while the Roman omits rather what might interfere with the general unity of his subject.

Livy himself tells us in his Preface that the effort of successive historians has been twofold, either to bring more certain information or to improve upon the style of their predecessors: and he has left the impress of his own personality upon the style rather than upon the science of history. And indeed, the influence of rhetoric on the writing of Roman history is beyond dispute. Cicero[3] calls history-writing *opus unum oratorium maxime*, and Quintilian[4] holds the same view. Roman criticism, on the other hand, had no experience, no rules: and thus it was not surprising that rhetoric should prevail over analysis, style over accuracy, in the mind of a historian. In fact, at the time when Livy wrote, the educated Roman was swayed by two dominant influences—patriotism and rhetoric. Livy felt both, and followed both, to the utmost of his capacity: and doubtless he found therein the justification of his task. So history with him was

[1] Soltau, *Livius' Geschichtswerk u. s. w.*, pp. 14 ff.

[2] Mackail, *Latin Literature*, p. 149.

[3] *de Legibus*, I. 2. 6. [4] *Inst. Or.* X. i. 31.

indeed 'philosophy teaching by examples'[1]: and having thus set himself a practical aim—to write a record of Rome from what we may call the Augustan point of view—he showed an indifference about the minute investigation of truth, not only in prehistoric but in historic affairs, which is incompatible with scientific method. Instances can be adduced to show that he adhered pretty closely to the annalists, even in form[2]: but he tried to make their descriptions more pleasing—more presentable, to the taste of his own time—by a periodic style and a nicer choice of expression.

In relating the accepted tradition of Roman *origines* Livy showed sound judgment and a genuine Roman feeling. And though his standard of criticism was not what moderns would call scientific, he had discernment enough to discard much that had been grafted on to an Italian stock by Greek writers: and so his work attained in Rome what might be called a canonical importance[3], and served as a standard authority for the historians of the next centuries—some of whom are useful for us to-day only because they have incidentally preserved from Livy himself a scanty substitute for his lost books.

It is by means of criticism, as an eminent modern writer reminds us, that history purifies and distils separate truths: it is by philosophy that it shapes and coordinates them[4]. In Livy the critic was subordinated to the philosopher, the philosopher to the orator; the analysis of detail to the appreciation of the truth as a whole, the science of unity to the sense of verisimilitude[5]. Thus he can never satisfy critics who hold that the recital of documents is the whole duty of a historian. A mind of his type regarded the earliest ages of Rome as vague generalities,

[1] Cf. *Praefatio* 10.

[2] In many passages in Book I one is tempted to believe that Livy is giving a paraphrase of annals written in verse—*e.g.* of Ennius.

[3] Tacitus (*Ann.* IV. 34) calls him *eloquentiae ac fidei praeclarus in primis.*

[4] Taine, *Essai sur Tite Live*, p. 29.

[5] Cf. Livy V. 21. 9 *In rebus tam antiquis si quae similia veri sint pro veris accipiantur satis habeam.*

and described them in general terms, as an artist might indicate, by a few sweeping strokes, the outlines of a subject which it would take a life-time to fill in. Livy was no archaeologist, and thus he felt no desire to investigate sources of information other than those which literature afforded: he could even leave unread an inscription, close at hand in Rome, which would have saved him from the necessity of stating two alternatives from his authorities[1]. Nor did he exercise any critical judgment of events: and on constitutional questions his words are still the texts of controversy. He was no traveller, like Herodotus, Polybius, and Diodorus: no chronologer, no topographer, no tactician. He had, in fact, no scientific qualifications to write history. We can see from his Preface that he has a certain distrust of his own powers, which was not unnatural when he was immediately confronted with that *crux criticorum*, the origins of Rome: but he had what professed critics too frequently lack, a sense of selection, an intuition sometimes amounting almost to clairvoyance, a 'divination of the truth[2],' which is better than a dull record of events, but which falls far short of the Truth itself. He was a true Roman at heart, and he wrote for Romans their own record; and thus it is that while we can read through Thucydides the canon of history, we learn in Livy the character of Rome[3].

And nowhere more clearly than in the speeches, which naturally afford him the opportunity most suited to his genius, does he express the dominant idea of his political philosophy—'the decline and fall' of Roman character. The ancient critics were inclined to regard the speeches as the best part of his work: yet he probably did not insert them merely to satisfy a sense of rhetoric, for doubtless there were speeches in the annalists whom he followed, and his own merit here as elsewhere consists chiefly of an improvement in form and language. In Book I, if we leave out of consideration short utterances which serve as

[1] Cf. III. 31. [2] Taine, p. 51.

[3] Seneca (*Suas.* VI. 21) says of Livy *candidissimus omnium magnorum ingeniorum aestimator.*

dramatic reliefs to the narrative (such as those of Evander to Hercules, Tanaquil to Servius Tullius, Tullia to Tarquinius, and Lucretia to her husband), and the formalities for making a treaty and declaring war (chapter 32) and for surrender (c. 38), the really significant speeches, in *oratio recta*, are the following: the defence of Horatius by his father (c. 26), and the two speeches of King Tullus Hostilius against the Alban traitor Mettius (c. 28). In these, as in the *orationes obliquae* of L. Tarquinius in the Senate House (c. 47), and of Turnus Herdonius (c. 50) and King Tarquinius Superbus (c. 51), there is something more than mere dramatic relief—there is an attempt to express and emphasize through the utterances of the leading characters the significance, national or political, of an event. Such utterances are more akin to the speeches in Greek historians, though there is no reason to suppose that Livy consciously shaped them upon Greek models.

As a philosopher Livy is no more eminent than as a critic. In both respects he is as it were a divinely gifted amateur, and falls short of supreme excellence. Yet it may well be supposed that had he been more of a critic, more of a philosopher, his style would perforce have lost something of its dominating power. For it is by style that Livy dominates. His heroes speak in a language that is always Roman, passionately, rhetorically Roman; too artistically and sympathetically composed to be monotonous, and yet never allowing the reader to lose sight of the main theme in the particular instance, of the type in the single life. And even in the narrative the orator speaks. It is always 'the rapt oration, flowing free from point to point,' animated and animating, simple yet dramatic, full of the poetical and the picturesque, investing the dry bones of official record with Roman flesh and blood. It is magnificent, but is it history? Is it not the pervading power and personality of Titus Livius—the perfection of a rhetoric which understands exactly how to develop an idea, and to manipulate the passions[1]? We are satisfied more and more as the work progresses with the

[1] Taine, *op. cit.* p. 296.

sense of good style—so good, indeed, that its ample periods, its *lactea ubertas*, almost tire the patience, and set us wishing in perversity for some of the *brevitas*, the *immortalis velocitas*, of Sallust, some of the pungency of Tacitus: just as, in Greek, we might turn from the romance of Herodotus or the straightforwardness of Xenophon to the sheer severity of Thucydides.

What were the chief characteristics of Livy's style may best be gathered from the criticism of Quintilian given at the head of this section[1]. It is obviously more elastic (*e.g.* in the order of words[2]), more poetic, than the Ciceronian idiom: and it did not altogether satisfy the Augustan critics. We do not know exactly what Asinius Pollio meant by the *Patavinitas quaedam* to which he objected in Livy: it may be that the exuberance of rhetoric was too liberal in its admission of expressions that a stricter sense regarded as non-Roman. The charm of Livy, in spite of some adverse criticism (Caligula thought him *verbosus et neglegens*[3]), has remained through the ages: and the enthusiasm of the pilgrim who travelled from Gades to Rome only to see Livy[4] typifies the admiration not only of the Augustan age, but of the civilized world, for a truly Roman genius, for 'the greatest prose style that has ever been written in any age or country[5].'

It is by style, then, that Livy dominates. It may be admitted that other writers—Thucydides, Xenophon, Sallust, Caesar, Tacitus—more strictly fulfil the function of the historian: but it is scarcely just to compare them in this connection with Livy, for they wrote of times not far removed from their own, and it is unfortunately impossible to determine the value of Livy as a historian of the years immediately preceding and containing his own life-time. His genius must be otherwise appraised, in his

[1] Cf. also Quintilian, *I. O.* VIII. I. 3, X. I. 32. Index D *infra* gives references to some of the more frequent Livian constructions in Book I.

[2] One recent critic regards Livy's 'brilliant use of order' as the great feature of his style. H. D. Naylor, *Latin and English Idiom; an object lesson from Livy's Preface.*

[3] Suetonius, *Gaius* 34.

[4] Pliny, *Epistles* II. 38.

[5] Munro, *Criticisms and Elucidations of Catullus*, p. 230.

clear conception of the unity and continuity of his subject, in his all-embracing humanity, his abiding sense of proportion—the genius of generalisation, which is as the moral that adorns the tale.

§ 3. THE LEGENDS CONNECTED WITH THE FOUNDATION OF ROME.

Nil patrium nisi nomen habet Romanus alumnus:
sanguinis altricem non pudet esse lupam.
huc melius profugos misisti, Troia, Penates.
huc quali vecta est Dardana puppis ave!

PROPERTIUS, IV. (V.) i. 37—40.

The story of Trojan migration which Livy gives at the beginning of this book is what has been called above the canonical, that is to say the officially accepted version, of a tradition which had many variants: there is, however, a general agreement, and in certain points a close resemblance, between Livy's account and Virgil's (*Aeneid* V.—X.).

Stesichorus of Himera (*fl.* 600 B.C.), in his 'Destruction of Troy,' is the first author known to us who mentioned wanderings of Aeneas in the West. He brought the hero to Campania, where the promontory of Misenum (near Cumae) took its name from Aeneas' trumpeter. And the Elymi of Sicily stoutly claimed, and in the First Punic War turned to political account with Rome, a Trojan origin. Cumae was full of Trojan associations: and Hecataeus (*fl.* 500 B.C.) traced the name of Capua to Capys, father of Anchises. We do not know what author first brought Aeneas into Latium, but about 400 B.C. the myth of his foundation of a Rome (so called from one of the Trojan women) was generally accepted by Greek writers; and apparently there was as yet no mention of indigenous legends in conjunction with it, and therefore no question of a reconciliation between Greek and Italian elements. It would appear, indeed, that the famous temple of Vesta between Lavinium and Ardea had no share in the most ancient form of the tradition, nothing to do with the movement of Aeneas to Rome. It may be that, once the Trojan origin of Capua was accepted by Greek authorities, the affinity between prehistoric Campanians and Latins suggested a Trojan foundation of Rome[1]. The connection of the temple above-mentioned with the matter may be due to the official sacrifice performed annually by Roman magistrates at Lavinium: and there is no sure indication that even the Laurentine and Alban communities had a common origin in this religious centre.

It is not possible to say how legends, of Greek manufacture, such as those which attributed the foundation of Lanuvium to Diomedes, of Ardea to Danaë, of Rome to Aeneas, came to be adopted among the natives. Perhaps the Sibylline books, which were brought to Rome from Cumae at the time of the Tarquins, may have helped to win acceptance for these foreign fabrics[2]; at any rate, the necessary opposition between Argives and Trojans, and so the acceptance of a Trojan tradition, supplies one explanation of the mysterious sacrifice of the *Argei*, which is an element in the ancient ritual of Rome.

Once the legend of Aeneas had been fully accepted by the Romans, it became necessary to reconcile it with native traditions. Timaeus of Syracuse (*fl.* 275 B.C.) may be said to represent this stage of the development: he, and the fragments of other authors which have to do with this matter, makes Lavinium the original settlement of Aeneas, and gives him only indirect relationship with Rome. But herein no account was taken of Alban legends—and there were leading Roman *gentes* which boasted Alban origin: and so, from Fabius Pictor onwards—*i.e.* from the time of the First Punic War—the Roman annalists traced the foundation of Rome from Aeneas through Lavinium *and* Alba: and this ultimately became the approved tradition thereof[3]. The Latin traditions supplied material for further elaboration: the rivalries of Lavinium and Ardea became those of Aeneas, the founder of Lavinium, and Turnus, the King of

[1] G. de Sanctis, *Storia dei Romani*, vol. I. p. 200.

[2] Dionysius Hal., I. 49 and 55.

[3] The complete fusion of Alban and Trojan legends may belong to the time and work of Cn. Naevius, who was followed by Ennius. De Sanctis, *op. cit.* I. pp. 203 ff.

the Rutuli, whose centre was Ardea; the cult of *Iuppiter Indiges* near the river Numicus was a proper focus for the mystic battle and 'translation' of Aeneas[1]; and the realities of Etruscan tyranny were dramatically embodied in the ferocity of a Mezentius.

The coming of Aeneas to Italy was necessarily dependent in point of time upon the capture of Troy, between which and the traditional date of the foundation of Rome (753 B.C.) there was a gap of about four centuries. This gap the story-makers filled in by expanding what was probably a genuine line of Latin, or rather Alban, kings—the Silvii—into a list of names which illustrated the various elements of the tradition, and betrayed in its very composition the hand of a Greek. With the Alban kings the familiar legend of the foundation of Rome itself is connected. In *Romulus* we have surely no more than a mere adjective, 'the man of Rome,' a variant in fact of *Romanus*. As founder Romulus takes (towards the end of the fourth century B.C.) the place which other traditions had ascribed to Aeneas: and originally he had no twin brother. *Remus* seems to owe his creation to a duplicating tendency, everywhere apparent in the records of Rome—the tendency which is seen in the two Lares, the two sets of Salii, the two consuls, and so on—due perhaps originally to the union of separate communities. The familiar legend, which makes a god the father, and a Vestal[2] the mother of the famous Twins, is entirely in keeping with what seems to have been the regular genealogy of Latin kings. The union of god and Vestal reappears in one story of Servius Tullius' birth, and it is supported by many points in the relationship of Latin kings to Vestals and in the ritual of the Vestals themselves[3].

What, then, is the significance of the she-wolf in the tale of the Twins? It is perhaps simplest to regard the wolf as the representative emblem of one of the tribes which shared in the

[1] Cf. Livy I. 2. 6.

[2] Of the two names by which she is known *Rea Silvia* represents the Latin version of the legend, *Ilia* the Trojan connection.

[3] Cf. Frazer, *Lectures on the Early History of the Kingship*, pp. 218—222.

formation of the Roman community. The antiquity of the Lupercalia, and the presence of the wolf among the old standards of the Roman army, seem to suggest something of the kind. The bronze statue of the she-wolf with the twins as her fosterlings, set up at Rome in 296 B.C.[1], is the earliest record of this emblematic association of the she-wolf with the origins of Rome: but there is evidence elsewhere in Italy of the existence of the emblem at an earlier period. A few years ago I was interested to find and sketch in the Museo Civico at Bologna a large stone stele, one of many brought from the Certosa near by, which shows, in the lower of two panels, a she-wolf suckling one infant[2]. There has been much discussion as to the period and the civilisation to which these stelae belong. We know that the city of Felsina (Bologna) was captured from the Etruscans by the Boian Gauls about 400 B.C., and before the Etruscans there may have been (according to some authorities) a Pelasgian occupation, and before that an Umbrian[3]. There are points of undoubted resemblance between the she-wolf stele and certain slabs discovered at Mycenae; and, while it is impossible to determine as yet the origin of the emblem, it is just conceivable that there lurks in it a secret of the migrations, Pelasgian, Umbrian, Sabine, which were bound up with the first-beginnings of Rome. *Sanguinis altricem non pudet esse lupam.*

Artificial as this legacy of legends seems to be, it probably contains elements of truth. It will scarcely be disputed that Greek poets and story-writers (especially those who belonged to Sicilian cities) helped to make a pedigree for the Romans by blending legends of a type familiar to themselves with traditions of native Italian or other growth. To archaeology, which has

[1] Livy, x. 23.

[2] It is figured in plate CXXXV of Zannoni's work, *Gli Scavi della Certosa di Bologna.*

[3] Zannoni, *op. cit.*, p. 188, regards the ornamentation of the stelae as Umbrian, the composition of the groups and panels as Greek, the faces as Etruscan: and concludes that the art represented is a combination of Umbrian, Graeco-Etruscan, and indigenous elements. Cf. Dennis, *Cities and Cemeteries of Etruria*[3], II., pp. 543 ff.

of late been active in Italian fields, belongs the task of reading the riddles.

Who, then, are the *Aborigines* mentioned at the beginning of Livy's history? It has been argued, with great skill and no mean probability[1], that they are to be regarded as an autochthonous race, identical with the Ligurians; that, partly with Pelasgian assistance, they drove out or merged in themselves the Siculi, who at one time occupied Tibur, Antemnae, Ficulea, Tellenae, Crustumerium, and Aricia; and that the Pelasgian allies, in other words an offshoot of that race which we know elsewhere as 'Mycenaean,' afterwards disappeared, or rather, became absorbed in the more numerous Aborigines, with whom they had probably an affinity of physique and language. Pelasgian influence may well be responsible for the polygonal masonry which is to be seen in walls and gateways both north and south of the Tiber. It is argued, further, that the story of Evander's occupation of the Palatine is probably based on some such Pelasgian migration, associating the Greek and Italian peninsulas; and that the legendary league between Aeneas, Latinus, and Evander, against Turnus and the Rutuli typifies, as has already been suggested, a union of native tribes and kindred immigrants against such racial opponents as the Siculi, who were in effect the advanced guard of the Umbro-Sabellian migrations from the north.

The line of Latin kings seems to represent the existence of a league of towns and communities in Latium, having Alba as its political and religious centre, and *Iuppiter Latiaris* and *Diana* as its patron deities. The gradual increase of the settlements on the Palatine and the neighbouring hills tended to the formation of a single city which should challenge and win the supremacy of this league of Latium. But before this came to pass, the communities by the Tiber were destined to receive into their midst a hostile element, a population that should dominate in all

[1] By Professor W. Ridgeway, in his *Early Age of Greece*, vol. I., and the pamphlet, *Who were the Romans?* read to the British Academy (*Proceedings*, vol. III.).

but language. The advent of the Sabines, a part of the Umbro-Sabellian stock, brought that accession of strength and character which spelt success for Rome. And it is possible to believe[1], by the evidence of religion, of marriage and succession, of armament, of burial or cremation, and of language, that these same Sabines were in effect the *patres* of Rome, who, in themselves and their descendants the *patricii*, evinced towards the Latini, in other words the *plebs*, all the superiority and exclusiveness of a conquering race. That is to say, the essential opposition, through centuries of conflict, between Patricians and Plebeians may conceivably be traced back to racial and not merely to social differences. There is no doubt that this view of the case simplifies and explains many difficult and doubtful points, in the regal period no less than in the earliest ages of the republic.

§ 4. THE BEGINNINGS OF THE CITY: ROMULUS AND TITUS TATIUS: NUMA POMPILIUS.

Non sine causa di hominesque hunc urbi condendae locum elegerunt, saluberrimos collis, flumen opportunum, quo ex mediterraneis locis fruges devehantur, quo maritimi commeatus accipiantur, mare vicinum ad commoditates nec expositum nimia propinquitate ad pericula classium externarum, regionem Italiae mediam, ad incrementum urbis natum unice locum.

LIVY, V. 54. 4.

In this and the following sections it is proposed to trace the growth of the city-state and its institutions during the regal period, and to examine the traditional record of that growth as given by Livy. Annalists and archaeologists are generally agreed—*ea nec adfirmare nec refellere in animo est*—that the earliest settlement of the Rome to be was on the *Palatium* or *mons Palatinus*. From a strategical point of view it was the best hill by the Tiber, and its shape, a rough square with sides of steep rock, about 500 yards long, made it easily capable of defence. Walls, of which fragments still stand, were let into

[1] The theory is ably expounded by Professor Ridgeway in *Who were the Romans?*

the sides, and carried high enough to form battlements. If the foundation of the city conformed, as it was supposed to have done, to ancient ritual, there should be three gates. One gate in the Palatine wall is mentioned by Livy in Book I, the *vetus porta Palati*, near the temple of Jupiter Stator: the other two seem to have been on the west and on the south, the latter perhaps at the foot of the *scalae Caci*.

To this, the earliest settlement, tradition naturally assigns all that belonged to the mythical founder-king—the *Lupercal*, cave of the she-wolf foster-mother; the hut of Faustulus (*tugurium*: Livy's *stabula*), where the Twins were brought up and Romulus afterwards dwelt (hence called *casa Romuli*); the place of his augury. The first *pomerium* must have run round the Palatine[1], perhaps within the wall: yet Tacitus, in a careful description of its supposed circuit, includes ancient land-marks (such as the *forum boarium*, the *ara maxima* of Hercules, the altar of Consus) which imply a wider ring outside the hill, and therefore presumably belong to a stage just after the first.

In the history of Roman religion it is possible to discern various stages of development: and it is not unreasonable to connect with these, to some extent, similar stages in the political growth of the several communities settled by the Tiber. In the beginning the Italian tribes believed that spirits (*numina*) dwelt in everything—sky and thunder, fire and water, stones, trees and animals: examples may be seen in the stone of Terminus, the oak of Feretrius, the fig-tree, the wolf. This 'animism,' as it is called, did not at first endue the spirits of its adoration with definite epithets, much less with definite personality. But the propitiation of the *numina* was all-important to the health, wealth and happiness of those primitive rovers of the wood and the hill; and the type of such worship as they rendered is to be seen in the Lupercalia and the Consualia, in which at first no definite deity is clearly discernible. But

[1] Messalla in Aulus Gellius, *Noctes Atticae* XIII. 14. 2, says *antiquissimum autem pomerium quod a Romulo institutum est Palatini montis radicibus terminabatur.*

though the form of the deity was vague, the ritual of service was most exact; and in such ritual one of the earliest features was the application of a suitable epithet (*e.g. Feretrius*) to the object of worship, and thus it is that many of the earlier titles of Roman deities are adjectives. We may say that in Roman worship the adjective precedes the noun, in time and in importance.

If such was the general character of Roman religion in the age of Romulus, what is the place of a cult of Hercules therein—a cult, too, instituted (as Livy says in c. 7) by Evander, and celebrated *Graeco ritu*? The explanation seems to be twofold. On the one hand we know that Stesichorus of Himera (whose part in the connection of Aeneas with Italy has been mentioned in § 3), wrote a Geryonid, in which were set forth the wanderings of Heracles in the West, and that Timaeus spoke of his passage through Campania. Heracles was, then, one of the characters in the genealogy of Rome which was framed by Hellenic authors: his legend was older in Latium than that of Romulus himself, and he found his proper place by Evander's side as the mythical opponent of Cacus[1]. On the other hand (as is stated in the note on c. 7. 3), we may regard the cult of 'Hercules' here as a native one, in which the spirit of the male genius (the *numen* of virility), the lord of oaths, was worshipped with harvest offerings and a harvest supper at an altar set in the pasturing ground of the Palatine down by the Tiber, but within the *pomerium*. In any case, the name 'Hercules' became the Latin counterpart of 'Heracles,' whose cult was perhaps introduced in the age which we call 'Servius Tullius' (see § 7 below): but the primeval elements were not exterminated, the god Hercules and the *Graecus ritus* did not entirely supplant the *numen*.

The immediate association of Titus Tatius and his Sabines with Romulus in Livy's account is somewhat misleading, for it seems to suggest that the first expansion of the Palatine settlement was on the Capitoline-Quirinal side, the traditional abode of the Sabines; but it is generally believed, both on

[1] De Sanctis, I. pp. 193—4: Pais, *Ancient Italy* (Eng. tr.), p. 236.

topographical and on ritual grounds, that the first development was rather in an eastward and north-eastward direction, over the slopes of the Esquiline and Caelian. The three parts of the Palatine (*Palatium*, *Cermalus*, *Velia*), with three spurs of the Esquiline (*Oppius*, *Cispius*, *Fagutal*), and one of the Caelian (*Sucusa*), make a total of seven: and in the festival of the *Septimontium*, celebrated by the seven groups of settlers, we may see the ritual expression of this expansion, just as in the *Lupercalia* we found the ritual expression of the oldest settlement. Varro[1] describes the *Septimontium* as *feriae non populi sed montanorum modo*. That is to say, the festival implies some sort of religious association, but not a political fusion. The prehistoric struggle for the October horse[2], between the Palatine-men and the rest, seems to belong to this same period.

Then, as we may suppose, the Sabines established themselves on the Quirinal hill, and extended their boundaries gradually to include more and more of the *mons Capitolinus*, with which in ancient days the Quirinal was connected by a ridge[3]. So the northern summit of the Capitoline became their citadel; and the col (called *inter duos lucos*) between it and the southern summit was the traditional situation of the *asylum* where according to one story Romulus harboured runaways. The southern peak—the *Capitolium* proper of later days—was precipitous on one side, where was the famous *saxum Tarpeium*; and there were even those who supposed that the whole hill was once called *mons Tarpeius*. The story of the maid Tarpeia has been variously related and interpreted: Livy's account[4] makes her an example of treachery, but Propertius[5] veils the treachery in her love for Titus Tatius, and Calpurnius Piso, followed by Dionysius of Halicarnassus[6], thought that she pretended treachery to save her country. The fact remains that her sepulchre was erected and her memory honoured by the Romans: and this seems to indicate that she was rather

[1] *de L. L.* VI. 24. [2] Cf. Festus, p. 178.

[3] Platner, *Topography and Monuments of Ancient Rome*, p. 275.

[4] I. II. 6—8. [5] IV. 4. [6] II. 38 ff.

the patron-saint[1], as we may call it, than the betrayer of the Tarpeian height.

The institutions assigned by tradition to the reign of Romulus are the Lictors; the Senate; the *spolia opima*; the thirty *curiae*; and the three *centuriae* of knights. The lictors, in regard to their association with *sacra* as well as with the person of the chief magistrate, undoubtedly date from the regal period: but it is not certain whether the institution was derived from Etruria[2]. The *spolia opima* may well have belonged to the earliest days: but the dedication of them on the Capitol seems rather to belong to the time when Roman and Sabine elements were joined into one community. The question of the Senate and of the *patres* who formed it is discussed in detail in the notes[3]. If we interpret Livy's statement, that the titles *patres* and *patricii* marked the selection of certain heads of families to form the Senate, by connecting *patres* with the Sabines, it follows that the creation of the Senate itself dates from the fusion of Romans (*montani*) and Sabines (*collini*) into one body-politic, the *Quirites*, under Sabine domination. This doubling of the city (*geminata urbe* is Livy's phrase in c. 13. 5) brought the Forum, hitherto a swamp, and the Capitol-Quirinal into the new *pomerium*; and this was accomplished by 'Titus Tatius[4],' that is to say by the Sabine leader, whom we are thus tempted to regard as the real founder of the city, and perhaps as the giver of its name. The Sabines, as belonging to the Umbrian race, burnt their dead; and the cremation-graves in the Forum-cemetery may have been made at this time, after some preliminary draining of the marsh, when the Forum was no longer needed as a neutral ground between rival communities.

The division of the people in *curiae*, different in character from the *gentes*[5], is common to Romans and to Latins, and in

[1] Schwegler, *Röm. Gesch.*, I. p. 486.

[2] See notes on c. 7. 3, *infra*.

[3] On cc. 8. 7, 17. 9.

[4] Cf. Tacitus, *Ann.* XII. 24 *forumque et Capitolium non a Romulo sed a T. Tatio additum urbi credidere: mox pro fortuna pomerium auctum.*

[5] De Sanctis, I. 239, thinks that the *curia* was older than the *gens*:

Rome may belong to the foundation of the first (Palatine) city or to the fusion of Romans and Sabines. The word *cūria* (see note on c. 13. 6) came to mean both a meeting-place for ceremonial purposes[1] and a district or corporation: and though members of the same *curia* may in general have dwelt in the same quarter, it seems that these associations of families, for such they were, like the φρατρίαι in Greece, originated rather in mutual protection and common worship than in any connection of residence. When a larger unit, the state, undertook the duty of protection, the *curiae* contributed each its quota (*centuria*) for the levy (*legio*): and similarly, while the special rites of each *curia* in honour of *Iuno Quiritis* (which seem to suggest a Sabine origin) continued, the whole people celebrated together, according to their *curiae*, certain other rites (*e.g.* the *Fornacalia* and the *Fordicidia*). The *curiae* were, in fact, the formal units of the state until the reorganisation of Servius Tullius. To be enrolled in a *curia* was the warrant of citizenship; and the formalities of adoption (*adrogatio*) and of testament could only be performed before the assembled *curiae*—the *comitia curiata*.

The three centuries of knights (*Titienses*, *Ramnenses*, *Luceres*), included by Livy among the institutions of Romulus' foundation, seem to be identical with the 300 *Celeres*. Livy does not here connect the three centuries with the three traditional tribes bearing the same name, and supposed by ancient writers[2] to have been created by Romulus after the death of Tatius. Discussion has wearied itself over the possible origins of the three tribes[3]—indeed, it is not certain whether *tribus* has

Pelham (*The Roman Curiae*; in his *Essays*, 1911) takes the opposite view. He connects the *curia* with the Sabine conquerors, and considers that it means a threefold organisation—(1) military; (2) territorial, *i.e.* groups of *consortes*, occupying land granted for military service, and forming corporations with *curiones*, *flamines*, and *sacra*; (3) political, *comitia curiata*, *populus Romanus Quiritium*.

[1] So *Curiae Veteres*, at the foot of the eastern slope of the Palatine.

[2] *e.g.* Cicero, *de Rep.* II. 8. 14, Dion. H. II. 7.

[3] See note on c. 13. 8.

anything to do with 'three': and it is unnecessary to treat the matter here. Suffice it to say that the *Titienses* usually stand first, which seems to support the idea of a Sabine conquest; that the association of *Titienses* and *Ramnenses* may express just such a fusion of Sabine and Latin elements as we have been considering; that *Luceres* may represent a third element (*e.g.* the settlers on the Esquiline who had shared in the *Septimontium*) of the same period, or a later addition; that throughout the names are closely connected with the military establishment of the pre-Servian state, each tribe contributing one hundred cavalry, and possibly 1000 infantry. It seems conceivable therefore that we are concerned with what might almost be called regimental names; and this will serve to explain in some degree the reluctance to interfere with them at the bidding of a non-Sabine, non-patrician king at a later date, and their ultimate inclusion, as a distinct unit, a *corps d'élite*, in the Servian establishment.

The life of such a community as is implied by a king, senate, *curiae*, and *centuriae*, represents a civilisation which has progressed beyond the hill-top and the pasture-land to ordered ways of town and farm, and likewise beyond the elemental 'animism' of earliest worship. We are arrived, in fact, at the 'Numa' period in Roman religion. For as Titus Tatius represents the military aspect of the Sabine conquest, so Numa Pompilius may stand for the religious, or rather the ritual, aspect. It is quite conceivable that there was no attempt, because there was no opportunity, to frame a ritual system for the state, as distinct from family and *curia*, until the Sabines became partners, and dominant partners, therein. The *sacra* must have been a strong unifying influence—more than that, the very bond of union—in each *curia*. But when the *patres*, the heads of families, whether exclusively Sabine or including other elements as well, advanced a step in political development by joining to elect a common head, and to supply his council and his army, the state which they formed needed a ritual sanction. *Imperium* was born: it needed the baptism of *sacra* and *auspicia*. Act I (Romulus and Tatius) was naturally followed by Act II (Numa Pompilius). It is a transition from the Palatine to the Septimontium and beyond.

It is interesting to observe, in the case of Numa as almost everywhere else in the regal history, the existence of duplicate traditions, often contaminated. Livy says, but says only to disprove in passing, that Pythagoras was thought by some to have been the source of Numa's training in *ius divinum atque humanum*: and, then, a little later, he attributes the whole of it to the goddess Egeria. Here on the one hand we may see a piece of Greek grafting, more reckless than usual; on the other hand, an incidental reference to the close connection between the King of the State and the Queen of the Wood, which seems to underlie the Latin idea of kingship. If it was proper for the king to be in intimate relationship, to be ritually wedded, with such a queen, was not that marriage the proper source of true ritual for the new state? Ancient ritual depends for its efficacy on a knowledge of the sun and moon in their courses: the nominal founder of Roman religious observance must therefore be responsible also for the calendar. In the priestly offices of his creation the patrician element is clearly marked. He himself performed, among other ritual duties, those of the *flamen Dialis*[1], and evidently regarded them as *sacra regiae vicis*. The other two *flamines* belong to gods—Mars and Quirinus—whom Varro regards as Sabine. The three *flamines* and the *Salii* were always patricians; the Vestal virgins (an institution derived by Livy from Alba, that is to say, of Latin origin, and doubtless far older than 'Numa,' as is already implied in the legend of Rea Silvia, the Vestal mother of Romulus and Remus) were certainly of pure patrician birth so long as it was possible to insist on this qualification.

In the cult of *Fides*, to be celebrated with peculiar care by the *flamines*, Livy records the first instance of the worship of an abstract idea in and for itself. This is probably later in ritual

[1] *i.e.*, in all probability, of *Ianus*: see note on 19. 2. The *Ianus bifrons*, the famous arch in the Forum, is probably one of the gates of the Septimontium.

development than the conception of (*deus*, *Iuppiter*) *Fidius* : and when even *Fides* came to be regarded as a personality and endowed with specific epithets, the abstract idea was lost in the multiplication of concrete attributes[1].

Numa the Sabine stands for the ritual regularity, the jealous conservatism—the Spartan element[2]—of the earliest Roman state: the Sabine conquest, which added this strain to the agricultural community, made it cohesive and, as we might say, conscious of itself, something more than a merely Latin settlement, able so to hold its own in an age of conflict, and to endure without entire self-suppression the domination of an alien dynasty.

§ 5. Rome and Latium: Tullus Hostilius and Ancus Marcius.

Cui deinde subibit
otia qui rumpet patriae residesque movebit
Tullus in arma viros et iam desueta triumphis
agmina. quem iuxta sequitur iactantior Ancus,
nunc quoque iam nimium gaudens popularibus auris.

Virgil, *Aeneid* vi. 813–17.

The precise contribution of these two kings to the regal tradition of Rome cannot be determined: but it is reasonable to regard them as representing a certain stage in the growth of the city-state. Tullus Hostilius was reputed to be the grandson of Hostius Hostilius, a distinguished hero in the wars of Romulus, and Ancus Marcius the son of Numa's daughter: in the latter case certainly, in the former possibly, succession to the kingship through the female line is implied. Between the two reigns there are certain points of similarity which may be the result

[1] J. B. Carter, *Religion of Numa*, p. 25.

[2] The Romans were regarded, by Greek and native writers, as owing much of their constitution and custom to Sparta: cf. Athenaeus, vi. 106 (p. 273), Cicero, *de Rep.* ii. 15. 50, Aul. Gellius, *N. A.* xv. 1, Servius on *Aen.* vii. 176.

of conscious duplication on the part of annalists. Tullus (according to Florus) *omnem militarem disciplinam artemque bellandi condidit*: Cicero attributes to him the institution of the fetial law, but Livy divides that honour, ascribing the formalities of *foedera* to Tullus Hostilius, and of the declaration of war (*res repetere*) to Ancus Marcius. Tullus destroyed Alba, and gave the Albans a home on the Caelian mount, and their chiefs a share in the state, the Senate, and the army. Ancus settled Latins from Politorium, Tellenae, and Ficana on the Aventine, and others near the shrine of Murcia, to connect the Palatine and the Aventine. Tullus built a new *curia*, called after him *Hostilia* (and it is quite probable that the building did belong to the regal period), to accommodate the enlarged Senate: Ancus built the prison hard by, called in later times *carcer Mamertinus*[1]. It was he, moreover, who occupied and fortified the *Ianiculum*, constructing the *pons sublicius* to connect it with the city: and it was he who dug the *Quiritium fossa* to improve the defences of Rome at the weaker points. His defensive scheme was completed by the seizure of the *silva Mesia* from the Veientines, and by the occupation of Ostia.

In this record three points of importance stand out—the destruction of Alba, the fortification of the Janiculum, and the foundation of Ostia. There is no reason to doubt the destruction of Alba: but it is scarcely probable that there was a complete or wholesale transference of the Albans to Rome itself. The records of the close association of Bovillae, a town as ancient as it is historically insignificant, with the *Feriae Latinae* contain evidence which at any rate suggests that some of the evicted Albans may have found a home there. The hegemony of the Latin League, and the responsibilities of its maintenance, passed to Rome: and the occupation and fortification of the Janiculum indicate that Rome realised her responsibilities. In this connection it has been well said that 'No one who has ever stood on the Janiculum, and looked down on the river and the city, and across

[1] Its more classical name, *Tullianum*, has been connected with Tullus Hostilius and Servius Tullius.

the Latin plain to the Alban mountain and the long line of hills—the last spurs of the Apennines—enclosing the plain to the north, can fail to realize that *Rome was originally an outpost of the Latins*, her kinsmen and confederates, against the powerful and uncanny Etruscan race who dwelt in the undulating hill country to the north[1].' The essence of a good defence is counter-attack and security of communications: and both are truly exemplified in the possession of the Silva Mesia and the occupation of Ostia.

This colony is unanimously assigned by tradition to Ancus Marcius: but it is not clear for what reason. A modern view makes another Marcius the founder—C. Marcius Rutilus, dictator in 356 B.C., who defeated the Etruscans at the spot[2]: but the foundation of a colony there in Republican days is not mentioned, and, moreover, probability would suggest that before Veii was conquered the mouth of the Tiber was secured by the Romans[3]. The occupation of Ostia and of the salt-pits indicates a strategical and a commercial shrewdness not unworthy of a king who is the type of all-round competence, in peace and war, and withal perhaps (like some Greek tyrant of the same era) a seeker after popularity, as Virgil thinks in the quotation given at the head of this section[4].

The traditional record follows the lines of topographical probability in filling in the main differences between the 'city of Tatius' and that which was to be enclosed within the Servian wall. We have arrived in fact at the period sometimes known as 'the city of the Four Regions'—*Suburana*[5], *Esquilina*, *Collina*,

[1] Warde Fowler, *Social life at Rome in the age of Cicero*, pp. 4, 5.

[2] Pais, *Storia di Roma*, I. 2, p. 241 n. 2.

[3] Cf. De Sanctis, I. pp. 370–1.

[4] Servius, in his commentary on these lines, preserves a statement of Pompeius Sabinus to the effect that Ancus chafed at the rule of Tullus, *itaque statuerat favore populari Tullum regem cum tota familia occidere.*

[5] The *Suburana* included the *Sucusa*, *Ceroliensis* and *Caelius* itself: it must not be confused with the *Subura*, which in historical times denotes the valley between the Oppian and Cispian mounts. Cf. Platner, p. 40.

Palatina. The order of the regions is somewhat surprising: we do not expect to find the *Suburana*, which roughly corresponded to the Caelian mount, put first, and the Palatine last. Yet the tradition[1] that Tullus Hostilius set his *regia* on the Caelian, to make that district attractive to settlers, seems to indicate that some formal prominence may have been attached to this quarter at such a stage as we are describing. The typical festival of the Four Regions was that connected with the *sacraria Argeorum* (of which Varro[2] says there were 27) and the *pons sublicius*: and though it may have been introduced considerably after the regal period, its stations help to indicate the *pomerium* of the Four Regions (see the plan of Rome), which served also for the Servian city.

The story of Tullus and Ancus may be taken as the typical expression of a period in which the kingly power, firmly established at Rome itself, began to assert itself over the surrounding district: *imperium*, in other words, begins to signify not only authority at home, but sovereignty and empire abroad[3]. The trial of Horatius for the slaying of his sister, which serves to introduce the right of *provocatio* (for it is the usual plan of Livy to found an institution upon a particular instance), illustrates authority at home: the demolition of Alba, and the formalities for declaring war and making a treaty, illustrate authority abroad. This, then, is a convenient point at which to take a brief survey of the relations between Rome and her Latin neighbours.

In the first stages the small communities in the plain of Latium, for all the keenness of cousinly rivalry, were conscious still of cousinship, not shared with Etruscans or Sabines. They began to accept a common worship, and by an annual festival to cement their relationship; and the area of their league extended north to Fidenae, east to Gabii, south to Ardea and perhaps to Suessa Pometia[4]. Lavinium, with its ancient cult of

[1] See c. 30. [2] *L. L.* v. 45—54.

[3] For instances of the word in the two senses in this book see Index A.

[4] De Sanctis, I. p. 380.

Vesta and the Penates, was the religious metropolis, but Alba was the federal centre, and on the Alban mount the *feriae Latinae* were celebrated from the first. The religious association between the communities, perhaps about fifty in number, led naturally to commercial and political understandings: and, with the destruction of Alba, Rome became the guardian of these *prisci Latini*, and so remained, but not without challenge or interruption, till the dissolution of the Latin League in 338 B.C. And Rome was not guardian only, but ruler by right of conquest in a good many instances. The actual conquests cannot of course be traced with any certainty; some, perhaps most, of those which tradition assigns to the kings belong to the republic, in the fifth and fourth century B.C.: but there is no doubt that from very early times the Roman city-state began to be ambitious for the primacy of Latium, and to pursue by separate campaigns and separate treaties the familiar *divide et impera* of later policy.

§ 6. ROME AND ETRURIA: THE TARQUINS.

Iam vero ornamenta Tarquinii et insignia quantam principi populo addiderunt ex ipso habitu dignitatem! actus a Servio census quid effecit, nisi ut ipsa se nosset Romana res publica? postremo Superbi illius importuna dominatio nonnihil, immo vel plurimum profuit. sic enim effectum est, ut agitatus iniuriis populus cupiditate libertatis incenderetur.

FLORI *Epitoma*, I. 2.

With the accession of a Tarquin to the throne the character of the Roman kingship underwent a change. The type of monarch which is represented in the chronicles of the Tarquins is not the *rex* of Latin or Italian tradition, with an *imperium* which implied responsibility, but a 'tyrant' after the pattern familiar in Greek history. It is not improbable that such 'tyrants' may have occupied the throne at Rome in the course of the political transition from monarchy to republic: but whether they were few or many it is not possible to determine.

Among modern critics the opinion is widely held that Tarquinius Priscus and Tarquinius Superbus (his son or grandson, it is not certain which) represent the duplication of a single personality[1]. The names in each case are indeed no more than adjectival. The following analysis will indicate the chief points of similarity and difference between the two reigns as recorded by Livy.

Tarquinius Priscus.	Tarquinius Superbus.
His ambition encouraged by Tanaquil:	His ambition encouraged by Tullia:
Secures the kingdom by an appeal to the people:	Secures the kingdom by a canvass of the *patres minorum gentium* and an appeal to the *iuvenes*:
Creates new *patres—factio haud dubia regis*—a sort of body-guard:	Execution of *primores patrum*: Body-guard: reign of terror (*sine consiliis*):
Successful operations against Latins (e.g. capture of Apiolae) and Sabines:	Conciliation of Latins as supporters against citizens: removal of Turnus Herdonius, and renewal of treaty between Rome and Latins: treaty with Gabii:
Inauguration of a circus and games:	
Erection of private dwellings and shops:	
Fortification of Rome contemplated:	
Increase of cavalry, in opposition to patrician augur, Attus Navius:	Enlargement of the army: War with Volsci (capture of Suessa Pometia[2]):
Cloacae built: spoils of Apiolae[2] used for foundations of Capitoline temple:	Spoils used for building Capitoline temple: Forced labour on public works: Colonies at Signia and Circeii: Deputation to Delphi:
Assassinated.	Exiled.

Here are to be seen all the leading characteristics of such tyrants as Periander of Corinth, Cleisthenes of Sicyon, and Gelo

[1] De Sanctis, *op. cit.* I. 371: Pais, *Ancient Legends of Roman History*, p. 137.

[2] It is believed by some authorities that Apiolae and Suessa Pometia are identical.

of Syracuse—bodyguard, opposition to existing aristocracy, new cults, public works, increased armies, conquests, treaties, colonies. And the reign of Servius Tullius is really of the same type, though ostensibly more beneficent and popular: the confirmation of his kingship (*haud dubius rex*) by successful war with Veii; the census, the new military establishment, the new tribal organisation; the *suovetaurilia* (an old rite used for a state purpose), the temple of Diana; the extension of the city and fortifications beyond the old *pomerium*; the division of captured land on a popular basis; the popular approval of his kingship.

Such government is not *imperium* in the Roman sense; it is Greek tyranny—*dominatio* in the text at the head of this section. The traditional accounts doubtless owe much to the influence of Greek culture in Etruria at the time of the Tarquins (*i.e.* in the seventh and sixth centuries B.C.), and to the Hellenizing tendency of Greek annalists when the story came to be written: but it is just conceivable that the Tarquins may stand for a Greek or a Graeco-Etruscan family settled in the town of the same name, and seizing from thence some opportunity of political unrest at Rome to set up a tyranny of the pattern prevalent about this era in different parts of the Hellenic world[1]. Such tyrannies frequently lasted for more than one generation: and Greek writers who remembered Cypselus and Periander, Orthagoras and Cleisthenes, Peisistratus and Hippias, were not unlikely to expand the tyranny of the Tarquins accordingly, as a necessary chapter in the political history of Rome.

But to admit the possibility that certain Tarquinii set up a tyranny at Rome does not necessarily imply a belief that those Tarquinii were Etruscans. Such, it is true, was the accepted tradition when Livy wrote; and it is accepted also by most modern authorities. On the other hand the rule of an Etruscan dynasty in Rome itself is disputed even by scholars who are prepared to acknowledge that 'Etruscan supremacy in Latium and Campania is one of the most certain facts' in the

[1] Cicero (*de Rep.* II. 19) actually says that Demaratus went to Tarquinii to escape the tyranny of Cypselus at Corinth.

early history of Italy[1]. Such critics believe that the connection between Tarquins and Etruria is due to the identity of their name and that of the Etruscan city, is in fact an etymological myth which serves to explain the introduction into the Roman state of certain emblems, ceremonies, and material improvements generally believed to have come from Etruria[2]. It is urged that, if the Tarquins were Etruscan in origin and sympathy, the elder Tarquin would scarcely be represented in tradition as defeating the Etruscans in two pitched battles and receiving recognition as supreme lord of the twelve cities of Etruria; and the second Tarquin as having continued the supremacy of Rome over Etruria, which Servius Tullius had already confirmed[3]. But jealousy among Etruscan chieftains might account for such warfare, and perhaps it is simplest to suppose that just as there are duplicate traditions—Greek and Latin—for the events preceding the foundation of Rome, so there are duplicate traditions—Etruscan and Latin—for the Tarquin period[4]. The official account, given by Livy, is in both cases a contamination.

The effect of Etruscan domination on Roman religion is to be seen in the introduction of definite images—*e.g.* of the Etruscan trinity, Jupiter (Tinia), Juno, and Minerva—into temples and ritual[5]. But this anthropomorphism was not original in the Etruscans: they owed it to Greek influences, and 'there is no real trace in Italy of an indigenous iconic representation of Jupiter[6].' The new Jupiter of the Capitoline became the central figure of the Roman Pantheon. In the state likewise the Tarquins typified a greater emphasis on the personality of the sovereign—in absolute action and disregard of constitutional limitations at home, in a definite claim to the primacy of Latium outside, supported

[1] Pais, *Ancient Legends of Roman History*, p. 136.

[2] Such as the royal insignia, the triumphal procession, and the construction of *cloacae* and of the Capitoline temple.

[3] De Sanctis, *op. cit.* I. p. 372.

[4] Evidence of such parallel traditions is to be seen in the equation of Tanaquil and Gaia Caecilia, and of Mastarna and Servius Tullius.

[5] Cf. Plutarch, *Numa*, 8. [6] Warde Fowler, *R. F.*, p. 234.

by successful wars and secured by separate treaties with the several cities, Gabii for example.

The *ager Tarquiniorum*—the *campus Martius* of historical times[1]—seems to suggest a royal appropriation of territory; and the existence of a *vicus Tuscus* shows that some Etruscans (employed, perhaps, on the public works) lived once in Rome. But on the Roman character, as on the Latin language, the Etruscans made no impression. In matters of augury, in the formal accompaniments of authority and the embellishments of a triumph, they introduced a certain style—we might almost call it a professional style—of which the Romans recognized the value and retained the practice: but the government of the Tarquin kings, though, like that of the Greek tyrants, it was not altogether or necessarily bad, imposed restraints against which the Roman *patres* struggled until the opposition to monarchy expressed itself in the expulsion of the aliens and the establishment of a republic.

§ 7. THE DEVELOPMENT OF THE CITY-STATE: SERVIUS TULLIUS.

Ancilla natus trabeam et diadema Quirini
et fasces meruit, regum ultimus ille bonorum.

JUVENAL, VIII. 259—60.

In the last section it has been suggested that the record of Servius Tullius corresponds in some respects with that of the Tarquin kings: but the resemblance in form must not be pressed, when the essential difference of character is so unmistakable. To the popular mind Servius Tullius was a favourite of fortune, a good king alive to the true interests of his people[2]—so much so, indeed, that tradition made him the founder, in idea, if not in actual fact, of many cherished institutions of the Republic, the Father of the Plebs, *Tullium qui libertatem civibus stabiliverat*[3].

[1] Livy, II. 5. 2. [2] De Sanctis, I. p. 374.
[3] Accius in Cicero *pro Sestio* 58. 123.

A critical examination of the stories relating to him, though it may discredit our belief in the personality of any such king, yet leaves us convinced that he represents a definite stage in the development of the kingship. He has been identified with that mythical Etruscan Mastarna who freed from bondage his friend Caelius Vibenna (as is seen in the famous wall-painting at Volci), and helped him to establish a company of Etruscans on the Caelian hill, with the consent of Tarquinius Priscus or of some other king[1]; and then (according to the annalists whom the Emperor Claudius, a student of Etruscan antiquities, followed in a well-known speech) took the name of Servius Tullius. This looks suspiciously like a fusion of Etruscan and Latin traditions: and the tale that Servius Tullius was the offspring of a divine father—the Lar or the fire-spirit—and of a slave-mother is entirely in accordance with the old tradition of the Latin kings[2]. The fire that played about his head in infancy is a fitting testimony to so miraculous an origin. Latin, too, is the tale that he succeeded to the kingship by marriage with the daughter of the ruling Tarquin: so Numa, according to tradition, married the daughter of Titus Tatius, and Tarquin the Proud the daughter of Servius. And from a Latin source is probably to be traced the origin of his name and the reason of his place in the kingly series.

Now Roman tradition had a practical aim—to demonstrate that from earliest ages the imperial city became the centre of the Latin league, and assumed the primacy of Latium[3]. Alba Longa had been destroyed before the era of Servius Tullius, but the festival in honour of *Iuppiter Latiaris* on the Alban mount was still the central rite of the Latin League. Meanwhile another city, Aricia, with its cult of Diana, in which some seven other cities joined, had been rising to prominence; and before long the goddess took her place beside the god in the worship of the

[1] Tacitus, *Ann.* IV. 65: Pais, *Ancient Legends of Roman History*, ch. vii.

[2] Cf. Frazer, *History of the Kingship*, pp. 218—222.

[3] Pais, *ib.*, p. 136.

League. Nor is this surprising, for in his elemental characteristics he is a *Ianus*, with none of the attributes of the *Iuppiter Capitolinus* who is to take his place as the sovereign deity of imperial, more than Latin, Rome. Diana is then the feminine expression, *Iuppiter Latiaris* the masculine, of Latin devotion: and it was essential, in the movement of Rome towards the primacy of Latium, that both deities should be ritually propitiated. This is why Servius Tullius was said to have built for Diana a temple in Rome: but it is to be remembered that it stood on the Aventine, *i.e.* outside the *pomerium*, though within the Servian wall, as beseemed a worship not representing the city-state but associated with an outside league[1].

But whether *Servius Tullius rex* at Rome is, or is not, the counterpart of *servus rex* at Aricia, he is the patron of the Latin element in the state, the Father of the Plebs. And the

[1] More than this may be implied in the connection of Servius Tullius with the cult of the Arician Diana. Mated there with the goddess was the masculine spirit Virbius, himself perhaps a local conception of him whom elsewhere we know as Janus. And the priest of Diana at Aricia was an escaped slave, who went about always armed, for whoever killed him succeeded to his office and his title, *rex nemorensis*. He was thus a *servus rex*, regarded as the ritual embodiment of Virbius: and the *clivus Virbius* at Aricia was ever the resort of slaves and beggars. Diana of Aricia was worshipped on the Ides of August: and at a similar August festival of slaves in Rome the dedication of the Aventine temple of Diana by Servius Tullius was commemorated. The *servus rex* at Aricia had often to flee from his would-be successor: and in old age he, the mortal representative of Virbius, would often be caught and slain. So, according to the legend, Servius Tullius tried to flee in Rome, and was slain by the servants of his would-be successor on the *clivus Vrbius* (*Virbius*): hard by was a shrine of Diana, among the oak-groves of the Esquiline, where he himself had lived. This flight of the king (perhaps originally a race for an annual kingship, and then a test of fitness to be king), was ceremonially continued in the *Regifugium*, wherein the *rex sacrorum* fled from the Forum the moment a sacrifice had been offered in the Comitium.

For the whole question see Frazer, *Early History of the Kingship*, especially pp. 264, 274—5; Pais, *Ancient Legends of Roman History*, pp. 145 ff.

general significance of the innovations associated by Livy with his reign—the *census*, the *tributum*, the new army of classes and centuries, the *lustrum*, the four local tribes, the inclusion of the Quirinal and Viminal hills, the extension of the *pomerium*, the fortification of the city, the League of Latins and the Aventine temple of Diana—is that the city-state of Rome was laying upon a broader basis the foundations of sovereignty. The period of Servius Tullius at Rome was then somewhat similar to that of Peisistratus—roughly contemporary—at Athens. The *curia*, in all its senses—military, territorial, political, religious—was replaced by a wiser, because a wider, organisation. The needs and the responsibilities of a nation were beginning to be realised.

We have found it convenient to regard Numa as representative of the older, native-born religious beliefs (*di Indigetes*), and of the sterner Sabine ritual and rule; and we may associate with the age of Servius Tullius the recognition of new cults (*di Novensiles*), introduced to the Romans and accepted by them in consequence of the increase of trade and other dealings with their Sabine, Latin, Greek, and Etruscan neighbours. It is a period, then, of outside influence in religion[1], just as the rise of the plebeians represents the influence of other elements in the state and constitution. The immigrants, or traders, brought their gods, or at any rate their cults, with them: Greek merchants may thus have introduced Heracles, and him the Romans received from them as Hercules, perhaps after he had been localised and Latinised at Tibur[2]: anyhow, his Latinity was so far accepted that his altar was admitted within the *pomerium*, and set up in the *forum boarium*, an altar of altars (*ara maxima*) which tradition connected, as has been seen above (§ 4), with the foundation-days of Rome. The *Graecus ritus* may have been introduced later into this cult of Hercules: it was certainly the rule in a temple of Hercules founded by Sulla near the Circus Flaminius, *i.e.* outside the *pomerium*[3].

[1] Carter, *Religion of Numa*, p. 28.

[2] Carter, *ib.* p. 33.

[3] Warde Fowler, *R. F.*, p. 135.

Religious development and the expansion of the city and the constitution were closely connected. We have explained above that the city of the Four Regions roughly corresponds to the traditions concerning the middle period of the kingship. There may have been further settlements before and during the age which we call that of Servius Tullius; and it is at any rate clear (see the map of Rome) that the area included by the wall ascribed to him was larger on the north-east and the south than that of the Four Regions. But the *pomerium* was not correspondingly extended: and therefore the Aventine, though within the civil boundary, was without the ritual boundary, the *templum* proper, and so remained until the days of Claudius Caesar. This is in itself a significant indication of the fact that the city-state had outgrown, in compass as in constitution, the ritual restrictions of an earlier date. No doubt the line of the Servian wall was in great measure determined by the requirements of defence: the slopes of the Quirinal and the Esquiline, the height of the Aventine, though not as yet required for dwellings, might, if unfortified, offer an attacking force just the *points d'appui* it needed. Therefore, on the side of easiest approach, the east, where nature offered little assistance, the fortifications took the form of an *agger*—ditch, and mound, and wall above the mound. Authorities are disagreed as to whether the portions of 'Servian' wall and *agger* still standing are really those of the regal period: the most recent investigations, however, seem to show a lower and a higher section, and it is at least conceivable that the lower belongs to the sixth century before Christ[1].

Within the wall the Four Regions were recognised and perpetuated by the redistribution of the inhabitants in four local tribes. These may well have been the city's share in a total of some twenty tribes or districts, embracing the territory at this time under Roman control, for Livy (in II. 21) mentions a new tribe, as bringing the total to twenty-one. Livy supposes (c. 43. 13) that these local tribes in Rome were connected with the war-tax

[1] T. Ashby, *Topography of Rome*, in *Companion to Latin Studies*.

(*tributum*), but that they had nothing to do with the total or classification of the centuries in the 'new model' army of Servius. That is to say, they contributed men and money, but not so much nor so many men for each tribe. In other words, the levy of men and money was made, according to the original arrangement, *pro habitu pecuniarum*. In the reconstituted *comitia centuriata*, as Livy knew it,—a voting assembly, not an army, be it remembered—there was a definite connection between tribes and centuries, but in what it consisted is not certain.

The local tribes, the *census*, the *tributum*, and the military establishment according to classes and centuries are alike in this, that they denote a change from a patrician burgess-body, an aristocracy of birth, with individual (*viritim*) responsibilities and privileges, to a *populus* consisting of patricians, their clients, and plebeians, with responsibilities and privileges graduated according to the possession of property, but still practically controlled by a comparatively few richer citizens. There can be no doubt that the need of a larger and more uniform army—for to win and keep the supremacy in Latium the Roman army must be prepared to fight all comers, not Latins only and Volscians, but Etruscans, and Greeks—was the real cause of the new order of things instituted by Servius Tullius. The new *exercitus* might contain within it the possibilities of a great political assembly, but it was not for this cause that Servius needed it: he realised that the patrician privilege of self-sacrifice in continual and hard-fought wars was injurious in itself, and ineffective for the real accomplishment of Rome's ambition. The city was no longer merely a pastoral and agricultural community: trade had come, by land and water, and it was only equitable that those who profited should pay and serve, according to the measure of their ability, for the protection and the assurance of profit.

Livy's account of the Servian army is examined in detail in the notes on chapter 43. There are, however, one or two points which seem to need brief notice here. Hitherto, if they fought at all, the Plebeians had not served in the ranks of the *legio*: henceforth they became liable for legionary service like other citizens, if their property qualification was such as to place them among the *assidui*. But though a general uniformity was aimed at in the new *exercitus*, there is still evidence that the older organisation was not—indeed, could not be—entirely ignored. In the British standing army after the Restoration of 1660, Royalist and Cromwellian elements formed the nucleus of separate regiments: and likewise, of the 18 centuries of *equites* in the army of Servius, six certainly represented the old Patrician cavalry of birth, and twelve were recruited on the new establishment of wealth. Again, the armament of the first *classis* of infantry—the *classis* to which, in an especial sense, the very title was applied—included the *clipeus*, or round shield, while that of the second and third *classes* (according to Livy) included the *scutum*, or half-cylindrical shield: and this difference in the shape of shields implies a difference of military tradition, and even of race[1]. The general fighting formation of the Servian army seems to have been a phalanx of Dorian type, but this is surely an anachronism in an army of the sixth century B.C. Some such formation, however, may have been adopted by the Roman republic for its infantry, when frequent wars brought closer acquaintance with the military systems of the Samnites and the city-states of Magna Graecia: and tradition records that the Romans copied the famous cavalry system of the Tarentines. It is not known how the *equites* of the regal period manœuvred. The presence of war-chariots in the field is, at any rate, implied by such instances as the execution of Mettius Fufetius the Alban dictator[2].

The religious ceremony which completed the census and the inspection-parade of the new army was the *Suovetaurilia*, performed outside the *pomerium* at the altar of Mars, in the plain which bore his name. This sacrifice was not in itself an innovation: from remote antiquity the farmer had thus performed a service of expiation and purification, driving the three animals

[1] Cf. Ridgeway, *Who were the Romans?* p. 18, where the *clipeus* is thought to imply that the first *classis* was composed of Sabines.

[2] Livy I. 28. 10.

thrice round his fields, and then sacrificing them to Mars. Between seed-time and harvest the farmer fought the battles of his community; and Mars was the war-god in whose honour *Salii* danced, spears were moved and *ancilia* beaten. There is then a ritual reason and justification for the adoption by Servius Tullius of the ancient *Suovetaurilia* for the purification of Rome's field of fighting men.

In conclusion, it is to be noted once more that what is related of Servius Tullius is throughout of a plebeian character—not patrician, not Sabine, not Etruscan. In his institutions the good of the Plebs, and through it of the state, is the object in view: the foundations of Rome are broadened and so strengthened.

§ 8. The end of the Monarchy.

Regio imperio duo sunto: eique praeeundo, iudicando, consulendo praetores, iudices, consules appellamino. militiae summum ius habento, nemini parento. ollis salus populi suprema lex esto.

Cicero, *de Legibus*, III. 8.

In the preceding sections an attempt has been made to trace, through the conventional accounts of the regal period, certain stages in the development of Rome. It now remains to consider briefly the causes which may have contributed to the decline and fall of the kingship itself, and to note evidences of the regal principle in the institutions and constitution of the Republic.

According to Livy (I. 60), the last Tarquin king was exiled, after Sextus' deed of shame, and the consulate was substituted for the kingship, in a moment, as it were: the idea of two consuls was taken *ex commentariis Servi Tulli*, and a republic replaced a monarchy as easily as in Portugal a year ago. In this traditional account, however, two points are to be distinguished—the exile of the Tarquins, and the creation of consuls. Why then were the Tarquins expelled? Was it the result of tyrannical oppression and outrage: or was it because

Tarquin the Proud intended to crush the *patres*, and to make a dynasty by changing the rule of succession from the female to the male line? As the husband of Servius' daughter he was qualified to succeed according to Latin usage: but to be truly *rex* he needed formal sanctions of *populus* and *patres*, and he chose to ignore the elective character of the kingship, and to claim the throne by might, as the son or grandson of a former king[1]. It is interesting to notice in this connection that the first two consuls recorded by tradition were both of royal blood; and that one of them, L. Junius Brutus, the son of Tarquin's sister, was really the heir to the throne according to the rule of female succession[2]. But the connection of the change of government with the Tarquins seems to be somewhat irregular and arbitrary: and the traditions differ. On the one hand there is the Roman version—that the exiled Tarquins retired to Caere, and sought Etruscan help, and that Lars Porsenna of Clusium, having conquered the Romans, ignored the Tarquins, and took the kingdom for himself: on the other hand, there is an Etruscan tradition which tells that a Tarquin, king of Rome, was slain and succeeded by the Etruscan Mastarna[3]. And Mastarna, as we have seen above, is identified according to one tradition with Servius Tullius.

Was the end of the kingship sudden at all? The analogy of other histories would seem to suggest that it may have been a gradual process, an evolution rather than a revolution[4]. Yet the reigns of the traditional Roman kings were for the most part ended abruptly. Only two of them, Numa Pompilius and Ancus Marcius, died natural deaths; and these two were of Sabine origin, and scrupulously observed the patrician ritual. Titus Tatius met his end in a local dispute: Romulus was 'translated'—or torn to pieces by the *patres*: Tullus Hostilius was struck by lightning for a ritual offence: the elder Tarquin was slain by the ruffians of the sons of Ancus, Servius Tullius

[1] Frazer, *op. cit.*, p. 253. [2] *Ib.*, p. 251.
[3] De Sanctis, i. p. 329.
[4] *Ib.*, p. 400: Pelham, *Outlines of Roman History*[2], p. 41.

by the servants of L. Tarquinius. This frequency of violence is differently explained: we may see in it a repetition of patrician efforts to remove a king of anti-patrician tendencies[1]; or we may suppose that the Latin kings, and after them the Roman kings, were looked upon as personating a god and put to death in that capacity[2]. Whatever be the explanation, the fact remains that no Roman king really appointed his successor: an *interregnum* was necessary to that end.

The *interregnum* which ensued upon the death of Romulus (c. 17) is doubtless intended by Livy to be typical. There was a *certamen regni ac cupido* in the minds of the *patres*, and a struggle between Roman and Sabine factions: and ultimately there was an understanding between the electing and the confirming bodies. To be complete, then, the election of a Roman king required the civil and the ritual sanction, *imperium* and *auspicia*: the first was conferred by a *lex curiata*, the second was implied in the *patrum auctoritas*[3]. So Numa, Tullus, and Ancus were regularly elected: but not so the three last kings. It is obvious that the *patres*, would not,

[1] Fustel de Coulanges, *La cité antique*, pp. 292 ff.

[2] Frazer, *op. cit.*, p. 269.

[3] Though the *patrum auctoritas* was necessary to complete the election of a Roman king, it is not to be regarded as a mere confirmation of the *imperium*, but rather as the ritual sanction, by which the *auspicia* were entrusted to the king, and afterwards to the consuls. In republican times *imperium* and *auspicia* are so closely associated as to be almost inseparable; but they are distinguishable in the regal period. It is not clear how the high-priesthood of the king (for the true king was also chief priest) was recognized at the beginning of a new reign: possibly it took effect from the *patrum auctoritas*, after a special ceremony of *inauguratio* such as is mentioned by Livy in the case of Numa (c. 18. 9). The title *rex* itself is thought by some authorities to have denoted the king in his priestly capacity, 'the regulator' of ritual and calendar, and to have been conferred before the *imperium*. That there was a distinction between the 'spiritual' and the 'temporal' powers of the king is clear from the fact that when the *imperium* and the *auspicia* passed to the consuls, the spiritualities were committed to a *rex sacrorum*.

because they could not, approve the election of a popular, or non-patrician, king. Tarquinius Priscus seems to have had the popular will on his side at the beginning of his reign[1], and Servius Tullius began his rule in general acquiescence[2]; and both kings may have been duly confirmed in the *imperium* by a *lex curiata*[3]: but Tarquinius Superbus had neither popular nor patrician support. In such cases the *auspicia* remained with the *patres*, in abeyance: and the king himself, though *de facto* and even *de iure* ruler, was in ritual opposition to them, an opposition illustrated by the introduction of new cults (as of Diana by Servius, and of the Capitoline Jupiter by the Tarquins) and the creation of new *patres* by Tarquinius Priscus. So the revolution—or the evolution—which brought the kingship to an end was no popular movement, but a patrician reaction: the keynote of it was *auspicia ad patres redeunt*.

Regio imperio duo sunto. The idea of *imperium*, destined to be the greatest contribution of Rome to politics, can scarcely have attained a full-grown force in the regal period, though the accounts given by the Roman historians might almost lead us to suppose so. Yet even in embryo it stands for magistracy rather than monarchy, for the supreme authority conferred (or confirmed) by a formal act of the burgess-body (*lex curiata*). It is in theory unlimited, but not irresponsible, nor unresponsive to counsel and custom[4]. The king who holds it is at once commander, judge, and president in chief. And the Romans seem to have realised so clearly what this *imperium* implied, without reference to the person of the holder, that they preserved its integrity through the transition from monarchy to republic. The two chief magistrates of the republic possessed the *regium imperium*, unimpaired in idea, though balanced in a sense by duality of persons—the collegiate principle—and

[1] Livy, I. 35. 5 *eum...ingenti consensu populus Romanus regnare iussit.*

[2] *Id.* I. 41. 6 *iniussu populi voluntate patrum.*

[3] Cicero, *de Rep.* II. 20, 21.

[4] Warde Fowler, *City-State of the Greeks and Romans*, pp. 74—78.

limited by annual tenure and by senatorial advice. That is the consulship as we know it in historical times: but this office can scarcely have leapt into being fully developed. There is something to be said for the view which regards the consulship as the cause, and not the effect, of the end of the monarchy[1]. The old name of the consuls, *praetores*, indicates military leaders; and it is not impossible that there may have been more than two at first, for three would naturally be required for the contingents supplied by Titienses, Ramnenses and Luceres. A reconstruction of the military establishment, on a basis of two legions, with two *praetores* to command in the field, may have left the third *praetor* in charge of civil jurisdiction at home—*praetor urbanus*, in fact. A gradual advance of such officers from a subordinate position under a monarch to independence and supreme *imperium* under a republic is as intelligible as a gradual diminution of kingly prerogative until the *rex* is no more than a *rex sacrorum* (but always a patrician), the counterpart of the King-Archon at Athens. The advance of the military commander, and the decline of the priest-king, are alike natural and necessary in an age of conflict such as that through which the Roman state must have passed in the fifth and fourth centuries B.C. The king, then, did not die: but the *patres* gradually effected the transfer of the *imperium*—which, in irresponsible hands, as the Tarquins had shown, might endanger their own position in the state—to magistrates whose limited tenure of office was a reminder and a guarantee of responsibility. And conversely, when any consul or consular showed a tendency in after years to overstep the prescribed limits, even though it were as a benefactor to the state, or at any rate to the plebeians, he was accused by the *patres* of aiming at the kingship: so that *rex* and its cognates became identified in the mind of good republicans with all that was absolute and tyrannical[2].

[1] De Sanctis, I. pp. 403 ff.

[2] Cicero, *de Rep.* II. 30 *expulso Tarquinio tantum odium populum Romanum regalis nominis tenuit, quantum tenuerat post obitum vel potius excessum Romuli desiderium.*

Yet for all the opposition to kingship in any form which appears in the Roman republic of historical times, no Roman doubted, nor can we, that, as Tacitus says[1], *urbem Romam a principio reges habuere.* One cannot mistake the survival of actual names—*rex* (*sacrorum*), *interrex*, *regia*, *regifugium*; the essential unity of *imperium*; the temporary revivals of kingly prerogative in the dictatorship; the insignia of the supreme magistrates, especially on ceremonial occasions such as triumphs. Nor when the earliest constitution of the Roman republic is examined does it reveal any really new elements. The title of the supreme magistrate is changed, but the *imperium* remains: the republican Senate stands in the same advisory relationship as the regal Senate to the holders of *imperium*: the burgess-body has its primary privilege of expressing its voice. To keep whatever was possible, to preserve form even where little or no reality remained; to be conservative, in short, was the true Roman character. The interaction of the forces in the state might and did bring about momentous changes in the relations of magistrates, senate, and citizen-body. A senate which consisted of members serving for life could not but exercise far more control over two annually-elected officers than over a king who was elected for life: and similarly, a burgess-body which was called on to elect its supreme magistrates once a year would thus be frequently and forcibly reminded of its sovereign power, and would realise that its votes were not only competent, but necessary, for the passing of laws and the proper judgment of capital cases. And lastly, the growth of the non-patrician element, in such a state as Rome was in the century 550—450 B.C., brought it about, if not at once upon the end of the kingship, at any rate before long, that the machinery of the popular vote should be exercised in more democratic assemblies such as the *comitia centuriata* and the *concilia plebis*, and not in the more or less patrician *comitia curiata*. The growing experience of a young republic would account for all this development: but the possibility of such development, the germs of political consciousness, were latent in the state while kings

[1] *Annals*, I. 1.

yet ruled. A Servius Tullius may have been, in a sense, the parent of the Republic; and even the Tarquins, by depressing the patricians, incidentally advanced the people.

There was nothing new, then, in the fabric of the republican constitution: but the change in the tenure of the *imperium* made all the difference in the working of the machinery of state.

The traditions which tell of conquests and colonies in the regal period, of a definite assumption of leadership in the Latin League, and a reorganisation of the Roman army on a larger basis, may exaggerate or anticipate the truth: but the state of things which they imply is comprehensible enough. It was an age of frequent, almost continuous, warfare; the Latin communities were striving against one another, and Rome, strengthened, perhaps created, by Sabine chieftains, was beginning to realise her strategic position and her imperial possibilities. Meanwhile, for the kings who had eyes to see beyond the Tiber, the growth of Etruscan wealth and power threatened a far more serious struggle, in which a united Latium might barely hold its own, and a disunited Latium must inevitably be destroyed. What actually happened we cannot tell: it may well be that for a while Rome and the Latin communities of which she was already in some sort the leader fell under Etruscan rule; and when that rule was weakened and withdrawn, probably under pressure from Greeks[1] in the south and Gauls in the north, the city-state of Rome essayed anew, under republican auspices, the task of dividing and conquering its neighbours.

[1] In the battle of Aricia, which probably took place about the end of the sixth century, the Campanian Greeks and the Latins won a decisive victory over the Etruscans. The Romans took no part in it: but this is not surprising, if they were at the time under Etruscan domination. Cf. De Sanctis, I. p. 452. The hold of the Etruscans on Campania was loosened or lost when their sea-power was broken by Hiero, king of Syracuse, in a victory off Cumae in 474 B.C.

TITI LIVI

AB URBE CONDITA LIBRI.

PRAEFATIO.

FACTURUSNE operae pretium sim, si a primordio 1
urbis res populi Romani perscripserim, nec satis scio,
nec, si sciam, dicere ausim, quippe qui cum veterem tum 2
vulgatam esse rem videam, dum novi semper scriptores
5 aut in rebus certius aliquid adlaturos se aut scribendi
arte rudem vetustatem superaturos credunt. utcumque 3
erit, iuvabit tamen rerum gestarum memoriae principis
terrarum populi pro virili parte et ipsum consuluisse; et
si in tanta scriptorum turba mea fama in obscuro sit,
10 nobilitate ac magnitudine eorum me, qui nomini officient
meo, consoler. res est praeterea et immensi operis, ut 4
quae supra septingentesimum annum repetatur, et quae
ab exiguis profecta initiis eo creverit, ut iam magnitudine
laboret sua; et legentium plerisque haud dubito quin
15 primae origines proximaque originibus minus praebitura
voluptatis sint, festinantibus ad haec nova, quibus iam
pridem praevalentis populi vires se ipsae conficiunt. ego 5
contra hoc quoque laboris praemium petam, ut me a
conspectu malorum, quae nostra tot per annos vidit
20 aetas, tantisper certe, dum prisca tota illa mente repeto,
avertam, omnis expers curae, quae scribentis animum
etsi non flectere a vero, sollicitum tamen efficere posset.

Quae ante conditam condendamve urbem poeticis 6
magis decora fabulis quam incorruptis rerum gestarum
25 monumentis traduntur, ea nec adfirmare nec refellere in
animo est. datur haec venia antiquitati, ut miscendo 7

humana divinis primordia urbium augustiora faciat. et
si cui populo licere oportet consecrare origines suas et ad
deos referre auctores, ea belli gloria est populo Romano,
ut, cum suum conditorisque sui parentem Martem
potissimum ferat, tam et hoc gentes humanae ʼpatiantur 5
8 aequo animo quam imperium patiuntur. sed haec et his
similia utcumque animadversa aut existimata erunt, haud
9 in magno equidem ponam discrimine: ad illa mihi pro
se quisque acriter intendat animum, quae vita, qui mores
fuerint, per quos viros quibusque artibus domi militiaeque 10
et partum et auctum imperium sit; ʼlabente deinde
paulatim disciplina velut dissidentis primo mores sequatur
animo, deinde ut magis magisque lapsi sint, tum ire
coeperint praecipites, donec ad haec tempora, quibus
nec vitia nostra nec remedia pati possumus, perventum 15
10 est. hoc illud est praecipue in cognitione rerum salubre
ac frugiferum, omnis te exempli documenta in illustri
posita monumento intueri; inde tibi tuaeque rei publicae
quod imitere capias, inde foedum inceptu, foedum exitu,
11 quod vites. ceterum aut me amor negotii suscepti fallit, 20
aut nulla umquam res publica nec maior nec sanctior
nec bonis exemplis ditior fuit, nec in quam civitatem
tam serae avaritia luxuriaque immigraverint, nec ubi
tantus ac tam diu paupertati ac parsimoniae honos
fuerit: adeo quanto rerum minus, tanto minus cupiditatis 25
12 erat. nuper divitiae avaritiam et abundantes voluptates
desiderium per luxum atque libidinem pereundi perden-
dique omnia invexere. sed querellae, ne tum quidem
gratae futurae, cum forsitan necessariae erunt, ab initio
13 certe tantae ordiendae rei absint: cum bonis potius 30
ominibus votisque et precationibus deorum dearumque,
si, ut poetis, nobis quoque mos esset, libentius incipere-
mus, ut orsis tantum operis successus prosperos darent.

TITI LIVI

AB URBE CONDITA

LIBER I.

[I—III. *The legends of Trojan migration and settlement in Italy.*]

IAM primum omnium satis constat Troia capta in 1 ceteros saevitum esse Troianos; duobus, Aeneae Antenorique, et vetusti iure hospitii et quia pacis reddendaeque Helenae semper 5 auctores fuerunt, omne ius belli Achivos abstinuisse. casibus deinde variis Antenorem cum multitudine Ene- 2 tum, qui seditione ex Paphlagonia pulsi et sedes et ducem rege Pylaemene ad Troiam amisso quaerebant, venisse in intumum maris Adriatici sinum; Euganeisque, 3 10 qui inter mare Alpesque incolebant, pulsis Enetos Troianosque eas tenuisse terras. et in quem primo egressi sunt locum Troia vocatur, pagoque Troiano inde nomen est; gens universa Veneti appellati. Aeneam ab 4 simili clade domo profugum, sed ad maiora rerum initia 15 ducentibus fatis primo in Macedoniam venisse, inde in Siciliam quaerentem sedes delatum, ab Sicilia classe ad Laurentem agrum tenuisse. Troia et huic loco nomen 5

Trojans in Italy: Antenor settles the Eneti,

est. ibi egressi Troiani, ut quibus ab immenso prope errore nihil praeter arma et naves superesset, cum praedam ex agris agerent, Latinus rex Aboriginesque, qui tum ea tenebant loca, ad arcendam vim advenarum armati ex urbe atque agris concurrunt. 5

Aeneas joins King Latinus,

6 duplex inde fama est: alii proelio victum Latinum pacem cum Aenea, deinde adfinitatem iunxisse tradunt, alii, cum 7 instructae acies constitissent, priusquam signa canerent, processisse Latinum inter primores ducemque advenarum evocasse ad colloquium; percunctatum deinde, qui mor- 10 tales essent, unde aut quo casu profecti domo, quidve 8 quaerentes in agrum Laurentem exissent: postquam audierit multitudinem Troianos esse, ducem Aeneam filium Anchisae et Veneris, cremata patria domo profugos sedem condendaeque urbis locum quaerere, et nobilitatem 15 admiratum gentis virique et animum vel bello vel paci paratum dextra data fidem futurae amicitiae sanxisse. 9 inde foedus ictum inter duces, inter exercitus salutationem factam; Aeneam apud Latinum fuisse in hospitio. ibi Latinum apud penates deos domesticum publico 20 adiunxisse foedus filia Aeneae in matrimonium data. 10 ea res utique Troianis spem adfirmat tandem stabili 11 certaque sede finiendi erroris. oppidum condunt; Aeneas ab nomine uxoris Lavinium appellat. brevi stirpis quoque virilis ex novo 25 matrimonio fuit, cui Ascanium parentes dixere nomen.

and founds Lavinium.

2 Bello deinde Aborigines Troianique simul petiti. Turnus rex Rutulorum, cui pacta Lavinia ante adventum Aeneae fuerat, praelatum sibi advenam aegre patiens, simul Aeneae 30 2 Latinoque bellum intulerat. neutra acies laeta ex eo certamine abiit: victi Rutuli, victores

He is attacked by Turnus and Mezentius, but without success.

Aborigines Troianique ducem Latinum amisere. inde 3
Turnus Rutulique diffisi rebus ad florentes opes Etruscorum Mezentiumque regem eorum confugiunt, qui
Caere, opulento tum oppido, imperitans, iam inde ab
5 initio minime laetus novae origine urbis, et tum nimio
plus quam satis tutum esset accolis rem Troianam
crescere ratus, haud gravatim socia arma Rutulis iunxit.
Aeneas, adversus tanti belli terrorem ut animos Aborigi- 4
num sibi conciliaret, nec sub eodem iure solum sed
10 etiam nomine omnes essent, Latinos utramque gentem
appellavit. nec deinde Aborigines Troianis studio ac 5
fide erga regem Aeneam cessere. fretusque his animis
coalescentium in dies magis duorum populorum Aeneas,
quamquam tanta opibus Etruria erat, ut iam non terras
15 solum sed mare etiam per totam Italiae longitudinem ab
Alpibus ad fretum Siculum fama nominis sui implesset,
tamen, cum moenibus bellum propulsare posset, in aciem
copias eduxit. secundum inde proelium Latinis, Aeneae 6
etiam ultimum operum mortalium fuit. situs est, quem-
20 cumque eum dici ius fasque est, super Numicum fluvium;
Iovem Indigetem appellant.

Ascanius founds Alba Longa.

Nondum maturus imperio Ascanius Aeneae filius **3**
erat; tamen id imperium ei ad puberem
aetatem incolume mansit. tantisper tutela
25 muliebri, tanta indoles in Lavinia erat,
res Latina et regnum avitum paternumque puero stetit.
haud ambigam (quis enim rem tam veterem pro 2
certo adfirmet?) hicine fuerit Ascanius, an maior quam
hic, Creusa matre Ilio incolumi natus comesque inde
30 paternae fugae, quem Iulum eundem Iulia gens auctorem nominis sui nuncupat. is Ascanius, ubicumque et 3
quacumque matre genitus (certe natum Aenea constat),

abundante Lavini multitudine florentem iam, ut tum res erant, atque opulentam urbem matri seu novercae reliquit, novam ipse aliam sub Albano monte condidit, quae ab situ porrectae in dorso urbis Longa Alba appellata. 4 inter Lavinium et Albam Longam deductam coloniam 5 triginta ferme interfuere anni. tantum tamen opes creverant maxime fusis Etruscis, ut ne morte quidem Aeneae, nec deinde inter muliebrem tutelam rudimentumque primum puerilis regni movere arma aut Mezentius 5 Etruscique aut ulli alii accolae ausi sint. pax ita con- 10 venerat, ut Etruscis Latinisque fluvius Albula, quem nunc Tiberim vocant, finis esset.

His successors —the Silvian line.

6 Silvius deinde regnat, Ascani filius, casu quodam 7 in silvis natus. is Aeneam Silvium creat; is deinde Latinum Silvium ab eo coloniae 15 aliquot deductae, Prisci Latini appellati. 8 mansit Silviis postea omnibus cognomen, qui Albae regnaverunt. Latino Alba ortus, Alba Atys, Atye Capys, Capye Capetus, Capeto Tiberinus, qui in traiectu Albulae amnis submersus celebre ad posteros nomen flumini 20 9 dedit. Agrippa inde Tiberini filius, post Agrippam Romulus Silvius a patre accepto imperio regnat. Aventino fulmine ipse ictus regnum per manus tradidit. is sepultus in eo colle, qui nunc pars Romanae est urbis, 10 cognomen colli fecit. Proca deinde regnat. is Numi- 25 torem atque Amulium procreat; Numitori, qui stirpis maximus erat, regnum vetustum Silviae gentis legat. plus tamen vis potuit quam voluntas patris aut verecundia 11 aetatis. pulso fratre Amulius regnat. addit sceleri scelus: stirpem fratris virilem interimit, fratris filiae 30 Reae Silviae per speciem honoris, cum Vestalem eam legisset, perpetua virginitate spem partus adimit.

[IV—VII. 3. *The story of Romulus and Remus.*]

Sed debebatur, ut opinor, fatis tantae origo urbis 4 maximique secundum deorum opes imperii principium. vi compressa Vestalis cum 2 geminum partum edidisset, seu ita rata, seu quia deus 5 auctor culpae honestior erat, Martem incertae stirpis 3 patrem nuncupat. sed nec di nec homines aut ipsam aut stirpem a crudelitate regia vindicant. sacerdos vincta in custodiam datur: pueros in profluentem aquam mitti iubet. forte quadam divinitus super ripas Tiberis 4 10 effusus lenibus stagnis nec adiri usquam ad iusti cursum poterat amnis, et posse quamvis languida mergi aqua infantes spem ferentibus dabat. ita velut defuncti regis 5 imperio in proxima alluvie, ubi nunc ficus Ruminalis est (Romularem vocatam ferunt), pueros exponunt. vastae 6 15 tum in his locis solitudines erant. tenet fama, cum fluitantem alveum, quo expositi erant pueri, tenuis in sicco aqua destituisset, lupam sitientem ex montibus qui circa sunt ad puerilem vagitum cursum flexisse; eam summissas infantibus adeo mitem 20 praebuisse mammas, ut lingua lambentem pueros magister regii pecoris invenerit. Faustulo fuisse nomen ferunt. ab eo ad stabula Larentiae 7 uxori educandos datos. sunt qui Larentiam vulgato corpore lupam inter pastores vocatam putent; inde 25 locum fabulae ac miraculo datum. ita geniti itaque 8 educati, cum primum adolevit aetas, nec in stabulis nec ad pecora segnes venando peragrare saltus. hinc robore corporibus animisque sumpto 9 iam non feras tantum subsistere, sed in latrones praeda 30 onustos impetus facere, pastoribusque rapta dividere, et cum his crescente in dies grege iuvenum seria ac iocos celebrare.

The twin sons of Rea Silvia

are exposed in the Tiber,

but rescued by Faustulus,

and educated.

[IV—VII. 3. *The story of Romulus and Remus.*]

5 Iam tum in Palatio monte Lupercal hoc fuisse ludicrum ferunt, et a Pallanteo, urbe Arcadica, Pallantium, 2 dein Palatium montem appellatum. ibi Euandrum, qui ex eo genere Arcadum multis ante tempestatibus tenuerit loca, sollemne adlatum ex Arcadia instituisse, ut 5 nudi iuvenes Lycaeum Pana venerantes per lusum atque lasciviam currerent, quem Romani deinde vocaverunt 3 Inuum. huic deditis ludicro, cum sollemne notum esset, insidiatos ob iram praedae amissae latrones, cum Romulus vi se defen- 10 disset, Remum cepisse, captum regi Amulio 4 tradidisse ultro accusantes. crimini maxime dabant in Numitoris agros ab iis impetum fieri; inde eos collecta iuvenum manu hostilem in modum praedas agere. sic 5 Numitori ad supplicium Remus deditur. iam inde ab 15 initio Faustulo spes fuerat regiam stirpem apud se educari: nam et expositos iussu regis infantes sciebat, et tempus, quo ipse eos sustulisset, ad id ipsum congruere; sed rem immaturam nisi aut per occasionem 6 aut per necessitatem aperiri noluerat. necessitas prior 20 venit. ita metu subactus Romulo rem aperit. forte et Numitori, cum in custodia Remum haberet, audissetque geminos esse fratres, comparando et aetatem eorum et ipsam minime servilem indolem tetigerat animum memoria nepotum; 25 sciscitandoque eodem pervenit, ut haud procul esset 7 quin Remum agnosceret. ita undique regi dolus nectitur. Romulus non cum globo iuvenum, nec enim erat ad vim apertam par, sed aliis alio itinere iussis certo tempore ad regiam venire pastoribus ad regem impetum 30 facit, et a domo Numitoris alia comparata manu **6** adiuvat Remus. ita regem obtruncant. Numitor inter

The capture of Remus by robbers during the Lupercalia

reveals the royal origin of the Twins;

primum tumultum hostis invasisse urbem atque adortos regiam dictitans, cum pubem Albanam in arcem praesidio armisque obtinendam avocasset, postquam iuvenes perpetrata caede 5 pergere ad se gratulantes vidit, extemplo advocato concilio scelera in se fratris, originem nepotum, ut geniti, ut educati, ut cogniti essent, caedem deinceps tyranni seque eius auctorem ostendit. iuvenes per 2 mediam contionem agmine ingressi cum avum regem 10 salutassent, secuta ex omni multitudine consentiens vox ratum nomen imperiumque regi efficit.

by the death of Amulius Numitor becomes King of Alba.

Ita Numitori Albana re permissa Romulum Remum- 3 que cupido cepit in his locis, ubi expositi ubique educati erant, urbis condendae. et 15 supererat multitudo Albanorum Latinorumque; ad id pastores quoque accesserant, qui omnes facile spem facerent parvam Albam, parvum Lavinium prae ea urbe, quae conderetur, fore. intervenit deinde his 4 cogitationibus avitum malum, regni cupido, atque inde 20 foedum certamen coortum a satis miti principio. quoniam gemini essent, nec aetatis verecundia discrimen facere posset, ut di, quorum tutelae ea loca essent, auguriis legerent, qui nomen novae urbi daret, qui conditam imperio regeret, Palatium Romulus, Remus Aventi- 25 num ad inaugurandum templa capiunt. priori Remo 7 augurium venisse fertur sex vultures, iamque nuntiato augurio cum duplex numerus Romulo sese ostendisset, utrumque regem sua multitudo consalutaverat. tempore illi praecepto, at 30 hi numero avium regnum trahebant. inde 2 cum altercatione congressi certamine irarum ad caedem vertuntur. ibi in turba ictus Remus cecidit. vulgatior

The Twins seek a new home.

Remus is slain in a quarrel, and Romulus reigns as king of the new city.

[IV—VII. *The story of Romulus and Remus.*]

fama est ludibrio fratris Remum novos transiluisse muros; inde ab irato Romulo, cum verbis quoque increpitans adiecisset "sic deinde quicumque alius tran-
3 siliet moenia mea!" interfectum. ita solus potitus imperio Romulus; condita urbs conditoris nomine 5 appellata. Palatium primum, in quo ipse erat educatus, muniit. sacra dis aliis Albano ritu, Graeco Herculi, ut ab Euandro instituta erant, facit.

[VII. 4—15. *The story of Hercules in Italy.*]

4 Herculem in ea loca Geryone interempto boves mira specie abegisse memorant, ac prope Tiberim 10 fluvium, qua prae se armentum agens nando traiecerat, loco herbido, ut quiete et pabulo laeto reficeret
5 boves, et ipsum fessum via procubuisse. ibi cum eum cibo vinoque gravatum sopor oppressisset, pastor accola eius loci nomine Cacus, ferox viribus, captus pulchritudine 15 boum cum avertere eam praedam vellet, quia, si agendo armentum in speluncam compulisset, ipsa vestigia quaerentem dominum eo deductura erant, aversos boves, eximium quemque pulchritudine, caudis in speluncam
6 traxit. Hercules ad primam auroram somno excitus 20 cum gregem perlustrasset oculis et partem abesse numero sensisset, pergit ad proximam speluncam, si forte eo vestigia ferrent. quae ubi omnia foras versa vidit nec in partem aliam ferre, confusus atque incertus animi ex
7 loco infesto agere porro armentum occepit. inde cum 25 actae boves quaedam ad desiderium, ut fit, relictarum mugissent, reddita inclusarum ex spelunca boum vox Herculem convertit. quem cum vadentem ad speluncam Cacus vi prohibere conatus esset, ictus clava fidem pastorum nequiquam invocans morte occubuit. 30

Hercules and Cacus.

[VII. 4—15. *The story of Hercules in Italy.*]

Euander tum ea profugus ex Peloponneso auctoritate 8 magis quam imperio regebat loca, venerabilis vir miraculo litterarum, rei novae inter rudes artium homines, venerabilior divinitate credita Carmentae matris, quam 5 fatiloquam ante Sibyllae in Italiam adventum miratae eae gentes fuerant. is tum Euander, concursu pastorum 9 trepidantium circa advenam manifestae reum caedis excitus, postquam facinus facinorisque causam audivit, habitum formamque viri aliquantum ampliorem augustio- 10 remque humana intuens rogitat, qui vir esset. ubi 10 nomen patremque ac patriam accepit, "Iove nate, Hercules, salve" inquit. "te mihi mater, veridica interpres deum, aucturum caelestium numerum cecinit, tibique aram hic dicatum iri, quam 15 opulentissima olim in terris gens maximam vocet tuoque ritu colat." dextra Hercules data accipere 11 se omen impleturumque fata ara condita ac dicata ait. ibi tum primum bove eximia capta de grege sacrum 12 Herculi adhibitis ad ministerium dapemque Potitiis ac 20 Pinariis, quae tum familiae maxime inclitae ea loca incolebant, factum. forte ita evenit, ut Potitii ad tempus 13 praesto essent, hisque exta apponerentur, Pinarii extis adesis ad ceteram venirent dapem. inde institutum mansit, donec Pinarium genus fuit, ne extis sollemnium 25 vescerentur. Potitii ab Euandro edocti antistites sacri 14 eius per multas aetates fuerunt, donec tradito servis publicis sollemni familiae ministerio genus omne Potitiorum interiit. haec tum sacra Romulus una ex omnibus 15 peregrina suscepit, iam tum immortalitatis virtute partae 30 ad quam eum sua fata ducebant, fautor.

Evander institutes the cult of Hercules.

[VIII—XVI. *The reign of Romulus.*]

Romulus gives ordinances, and appoints twelve lictors.

8 Rebus divinis rite perpetratis vocataque ad concilium multitudine, quae coalescere in populi unius corpus nulla re praeterquam legibus 2 poterat, iura dedit, quae ita sancta generi hominum agresti fore ratus, si se ipse 5 venerabilem insignibus imperii fecisset, cum cetero habitu se augustiorem, tum maxime lictoribus duodecim 3 sumptis fecit. alii ab numero avium, quae augurio regnum portenderant, eum secutum numerum putant; me haud paenitet eorum sententiae esse, quibus et 10 apparitores hoc genus ab Etruscis finitimis, unde sella curulis, unde toga praetexta sumpta est, et numerum quoque ipsum ductum placet; et ita habuisse Etruscos, quod ex duodecim populis communiter creato rege singulos singuli populi lictores dederint. 15

The city grows, and becomes a Refuge.

4 Crescebat interim urbs munitionibus alia atque alia appetendo loca, cum in spem magis futurae multitudinis quam ad id, quod tum hominum 5 erat, munirent. deinde ne vana urbis magnitudo esset, adiciendae multitudinis causa 20 vetere consilio condentium urbes, qui obscuram atque humilem conciendo ad se multitudinem natam e terra sibi prolem ementiebantur, locum, qui nunc saeptus 6 escendentibus inter duos lucos est, asylum aperit. eo ex finitimis populis turba omnis sine discrimine, liber an 25 servus esset, avida novarum rerum perfugit, idque primum 7 ad coeptam magnitudinem roboris fuit. cum iam virium haud paeniteret, consilium deinde viribus parat: centum creat senatores, sive quia is numerus satis erat, sive quia soli centum erant, qui creari patres possent: patres certe 30 ab honore, patriciique progenies eorum appellati.

9 Iam res Romana adeo erat valida, ut cuilibet

finitimarum civitatum bello par esset; sed penuria mulierum hominis aetatem duratura magnitudo erat, quippe quibus nec domi spes prolis nec cum finitimis conubia essent. 5 tum ex consilio patrum Romulus legatos circa vicinas gentes misit, qui societatem conubiumque novo populo peterent: urbes quoque ut cetera ex infimo nasci; dein, quas sua virtus ac di iuvent, magnas opes sibi magnumque nomen 10 facere. satis scire origini Romanae et deos adfuisse et non defuturam virtutem. proinde ne gravarentur homines cum hominibus sanguinem ac genus miscere. nusquam benigne legatio audita est: adeo simul spernebant, simul tantam in medio crescentem molem sibi 15 ac posteris suis metuebant; ac plerisque rogitantibus dimissi, ecquod feminis quoque asylum aperuissent: id enim demum compar conubium fore. aegre id Romana pubes passa, et haud dubie ad vim spectare res coepit. cui tempus locumque aptum ut daret Romulus, aegri 20 tudinem animi dissimulans ludos ex industria parat Neptuno Equestri sollemnis; Consualia vocat. indici deinde finitimis spectaculum iubet, quantoque apparatu tum sciebant aut poterant concelebrant, ut rem claram exspectatamque facerent. multi mortales convenere, studio 25 etiam videndae novae urbis, maxume proximi quique, Caeninenses Crustumini Antemnates; iam Sabinorum omnis multitudo cum liberis ac coniugibus venit. invitati hospitaliter per domos cum situm moeniaque et fre quentem tectis urbem vidissent, mirantur tam brevi rem 30 Romanam crevisse. ubi spectaculi tempus venit, deditaeque eo mentes cum oculis erant, tum ex composito orta vis, signoque dato iuventus Romana ad rapiendas

In their want of women, the Romans make overtures to their neighbours, but without success.

2 3 4 5 6 7 8 9 10

11 virgines discurrit. magna pars forte, in quem quaeque inciderat, raptae; quasdam forma excellentes primoribus patrum destinatas ex plebe homines, quibus datum negotium erat, domos deferebant.
12 unam longe ante alias specie ac pulchritudine insignem 5 a globo Talassii cuiusdam raptam ferunt, multisque sciscitantibus, cuinam eam ferrent, identidem, ne quis violaret, Talassio ferri clamitatum: inde nuptialem hanc
13 vocem factam. turbato per metum ludicro maesti parentes virginum profugiunt, incusantes violati hospitii 10 foedus deumque invocantes, cuius ad sollemne ludosque
14 per fas ac fidem decepti venissent. nec raptis aut spes de se melior aut indignatio est minor. sed ipse Romulus circumibat, docebatque patrum id superbia factum, qui conubium finitimis negassent. illas tamen in matri- 15 monio, in societate fortunarum omnium civitatisque, et,
15 quo nihil carius humano generi sit, liberum fore. mollirent modo iras, et quibus fors corpora dedisset, darent animos. saepe ex iniuria postmodum gratiam ortam, eoque melioribus usuras viris, quod adnisurus pro se 20 quisque sit, ut, cum suam vicem functus officio sit,
16 parentium etiam patriaeque expleat desiderium. accedebant blanditiae virorum factum purgantium cupiditate atque amore, quae maxime ad muliebre ingenium efficaces preces sunt. 25

The Rape of the Sabines.

10 Iam admodum mitigati animi raptis erant. at raptarum parentes tum maxime sordida veste lacrimisque et querellis civitates concitabant. nec domi tantum indignationes continebant, sed congregabantur undique ad Titum Tatium, regem 30 Sabinorum, et legationes eo, quod maximum Tatii
2 nomen in iis regionibus erat, conveniebant. Caeninenses

The indignation of the Sabine states.

Crustuminique et Antemnates erant, ad quos eius iniuriae pars pertinebat. lente agere his Tatius Sabinique
visi sunt; ipsi inter se tres populi communiter bellum
parant. ne Crustumini quidem atque Antemnates pro 3
5 ardore iraque Caeninensium satis se impigre movent:
ita per se ipsum nomen Caeninum in agrum Romanum
impetum facit. sed effuse vastantibus fit obvius cum 4
exercitu Romulus, levique certamine docet vanam sine
viribus iram esse. exercitum fundit fugatque, fusum
10 persequitur; regem in proelio obtruncat et
spoliat; duce hostium occiso urbem primo
impetu capit. inde exercitu victore reducto 5
ipse, cum factis vir magnificus tum factorum ostentator
haud minor, spolia ducis hostium caesi suspensa fabricato
15 ad id apte ferculo gerens in Capitolium escendit, ibique
ea cum ad quercum pastoribus sacram deposuisset, simul
cum dono designavit templo Iovis finis, cognomenque
addidit deo. "Iuppiter Feretri," inquit "haec tibi victor 6
Romulus rex regia arma fero, templumque
20 his regionibus, quas modo animo metatus
sum, dedico sedem opimis spoliis, quae
regibus ducibusque hostium caesis me auc-
torem sequentes posteri ferent." haec templi est origo, 7
quod primum omnium Romae sacratum est. ita deinde
25 dis visum, nec irritam conditoris templi vocem esse, qua
laturos eo spolia posteros nuncupavit, nec multitudine
compotum eius doni vulgari laudem. bina postea inter
tot annos, tot bella opima parta sunt spolia: adeo rara
eius fortuna decoris fuit.

Romulus routs the men of Caenina,

and offers the first *spolia opima* to Jupiter Feretrius.

30 Dum ea ibi Romani gerunt, Antemnatium exer- **11**
citus per occasionem ac solitudinem hostiliter in fines Romanos incursionem facit.

Further Sabine defeats.

raptim et ad hos Romana legio ducta palatos in agris
2 oppressit. fusi igitur primo impetu et clamore hostes,
oppidum captum; duplicique victoria ovantem Romulum Hersilia coniunx precibus raptarum fatigata orat,
ut parentibus earum det veniam et in civitatem acci- 5
piat: ita rem coalescere concordia posse. facile im-
3 petratum. inde contra Crustuminos profectus bellum
inferentes. ibi minus etiam, quod alienis cladibus ceci-
4 derant animi, certaminis fuit. utroque coloniae missae,
plures inventi, qui propter ubertatem terrae in Crustumi- 10
num nomina darent. et Romam inde frequenter migratum est, a parentibus maxime ac propinquis raptarum.

5 Novissimum ab Sabinis bellum ortum, multoque id
maximum fuit: nihil enim per iram aut cupiditatem
actum est, nec ostenderunt bellum prius quam intulerunt. 15
6 consilio etiam additus dolus. Spurius Tarpeius Romanae
praeerat arci. huius filiam virginem auro
corrumpit Tatius, ut armatos in arcem accipiat (aquam forte ea tum sacris extra moenia pe-
7 titum ierat); accepti obrutam armis necavere, seu ut 20
vi capta potius arx videretur, seu prodendi exempli
causa, ne quid usquam fidum proditori esset. ad-
8 ditur fabulae, quod vulgo Sabini aureas armillas magni
ponderis brachio laevo gemmatosque magna specie anu-
los habuerint, pepigisse eam quod in sinistris manibus 25
9 haberent; eo scuta illi pro aureis donis congesta. sunt
qui eam ex pacto tradendi quod in sinistris manibus esset
derecto arma petisse dicant, et fraude visam agere sua
ipsam peremptam mercede.

The story of Tarpeia.

12 Tenuere tamen arcem Sabini, atque inde pos- 30
tero die, cum Romanus exercitus instructus quod inter
Palatinum Capitolinumque collem campi est complesset,

non prius descenderunt in aequum, quam ira et cupiditate recuperandae arcis stimulante animos in adversum Romani subiere. principes utrimque pugnam ciebant: ab Sabinis Mettius Curtius, ab Romanis Hostius Hostilius. hic rem Romanam iniquo loco ad prima signa animo atque audacia sustinebat. ut Hostius cecidit, confestim Romana inclinatur acies, fusaque est ad veterem portam Palatii: Romulus et ipse turba fugientium actus arma ad caelum tollens "Iuppiter, tuis" inquit "iussus avibus hic in Palatio prima urbi fundamenta ieci. arcem iam scelere emptam Sabini habent; inde huc armati superata media valle tendunt. at tu, pater deum hominumque hinc saltem arce hostes, deme terrorem Romanis fugamque foedam siste. hic ego tibi templum Statori Iovi, quod monumentum sit posteris tua praesenti ope servatam urbem esse, voveo." haec precatus, velut si sensisset auditas preces, "hinc," inquit "Romani, Iuppiter optimus maximus resistere atque iterare pugnam iubet." restitere Romani tamquam caelesti voce iussi: ipse ad primores Romulus provolat. Mettius Curtius ab Sabinis princeps ab arce decucurrerat, et effusos egerat Romanos toto quantum foro spatium est, nec procul iam a porta Palatii erat, clamitans "vicimus perfidos hospites, imbelles hostes. iam sciunt longe aliud esse virgines rapere, aliud pugnare cum viris." in eum haec gloriantem cum globo ferocissimorum iuvenum Romulus impetum facit. ex equo tum forte Mettius pugnabat; eo pelli facilius fuit. pulsum Romani persecuntur, et alia Romana acies audacia regis accensa fundit Sabinos. Mettius in paludem sese strepitu sequentium trepidante equo coniecit; averteratque ea res etiam Sabinos tanti

A Roman reverse is stayed by Romulus' vow to Jupiter Stator.

periculo viri. et ille quidem adnuentibus ac vocantibus suis favore multorum addito animo evadit: Romani Sabinique in media convalle duorum montium redintegrant proelium; sed res Romana erat superior.

13 Tum Sabinae mulieres, quarum ex iniuria bellum 5 ortum erat, crinibus passis scissaque veste victo malis muliebri pavore ausae se inter tela volantia inferre, ex transverso impetu facto dirimere infestas acies, dirimere iras,

The intervention of the Sabine women restores peace and amity.

2 hinc patres hinc viros orantes, ne se sanguine nefando 10 soceri generique respergerent, ne parricidio macularent 3 partus suos, nepotum illi, hi liberum progeniem. "si adfinitatis inter vos, si conubii piget, in nos vertite iras. nos causa belli, nos vulnerum ac caedium viris ac parentibus sumus. melius peribimus quam sine alteris 15 vestrum viduae aut orbae vivemus." movet res cum mul-4 titudinem tum duces. silentium et repentina fit quies; inde ad foedus faciendum duces prodeunt, nec pacem modo sed civitatem unam ex duabus faciunt, regnum 5 consociant, imperium omne conferunt Romam. ita ge- 20 minata urbe, ut Sabinis tamen aliquid daretur, Quirites a Curibus appellati. monumentum eius pugnae, ubi primum ex profunda emersus palude equom Curtius in vado statuit, Curtium lacum appellarunt.

6 Ex bello tam tristi laeta repente pax cariores Sabinas 25 viris ac parentibus et ante omnes Romulo ipsi fecit. itaque, cum populum in curias

The thirty Curiae.

7 triginta divideret, nomina earum curiis imposuit. id non traditur, cum haud dubie aliquanto numerus maior hoc mulierum fuerit, aetate an dignitatibus suis virorumve 30 an sorte lectae sint, quae nomina curiis darent. eodem tempore et centuriae tres equitum conscriptae sunt:

Ramnenses ab Romulo, ab T. Tatio Titienses appellati; Lucerum nominis et originis causa incerta est. inde non modo commune sed concors etiam regnum duobus regibus fuit.

5 Post aliquot annos propinqui regis Tatii legatos **14** Laurentium pulsant, cumque Laurentes iure gentium agerent, apud Tatium gratia suorum et preces plus poterant. igitur illorum poenam in se vertit: nam Lavini, cum ad 10 sollemne sacrificium eo venisset, concursu facto interficitur. eam rem minus aegre quam dignum erat 3 tulisse Romulum ferunt, seu ob infidam societatem regni, seu quia haud iniuria caesum credebat. itaque bello quidem abstinuit: ut tamen expiarentur legatorum 15 iniuriae regisque caedes, foedus inter Romam Laviniumque urbes renovatum est.

Tatius is killed, and Romulus becomes sole king. 2

Et cum his quidem insperata pax erat: aliud multo 4 propius atque in ipsis prope portis bellum ortum. Fidenates nimis vicinas prope se 20 convalescere opes rati, priusquam tantum roboris esset, quantum futurum apparebat, occupant bellum facere. iuventute armata immissa vastatur agri quod inter urbem ac Fidenas est. inde ad laevam versi, quia 5 dextra Tiberis arcebat, cum magna trepidatione agres- 25 tium populantur; tumultusque repens ex agris in urbem illatus pro nuntio fuit. excitus Romulus (neque enim 6 dilationem pati tam vicinum bellum poterat) exercitum educit, castra a Fidenis mille passuum locat. ibi 7 modico praesidio relicto egressus omnibus copiis partem 30 militum locis circa densissima ob virgulta obscuris subsidere in insidiis iussit; cum parte maiore atque omni equitatu profectus, id quod quaerebat, tumultuoso et

War with Fidenae.

minaci genere pugnae adequitando ipsis prope portis hostem excivit. fugae quoque, quae simulanda erat, eadem equestris pugna causam minus mirabilem dedit. 8 et cum velut inter pugnae fugaeque consilium trepidante equitatu pedes quoque referret gradum, plenis repente 5 portis effusi hostes impulsa Romana acie studio instandi 9 sequendique trahuntur ad locum insidiarum. inde subito exorti Romani transversam invadunt hostium aciem; addunt pavorem mota e castris signa eorum, qui in praesidio relicti fuerant: ita multiplici terrore perculsi 10 Fidenates prius paene quam Romulus quique cum eo equites erant circumagerent frenis equos, terga vertunt 10 multoque effusius, quippe vera fuga, qui simulantes paulo 11 ante secuti erant, oppidum repetebant. non tamen eripuere se hosti: haerens in tergo Romanus priusquam 15 fores portarum obicerentur velut agmine uno irrumpit.

15 Belli Fidenatis contagione irritati Veientium animi et consanguinitate (nam Fidenates quoque Etrusci fuerunt), et quod ipsa propinquitas loci, si Romana arma omnibus infesta 20 finitimis essent, stimulabat, in fines Romanos excucur- 2 rerunt populabundi magis quam iusti more belli. itaque non castris positis, non exspectato hostium exercitu raptam ex agris praedam portantes Veios rediere. Romanus contra, postquam hostem in agris non invenit, 25 dimicationi ultimae instructus intentusque Tiberim transit. 3 quem postquam castra ponere et ad urbem accessurum Veientes audivere, obviam egressi, ut potius acie decernerent, quam inclusi de tectis moenibusque dimicarent. 4 ibi viribus nulla arte adiutis tantum veterani 30 robore exercitus rex Romanus vicit, persecutusque fusos ad moenia hostes urbe valida muris ac

The men of Veii are involved:

their defeat.

situ ipso munita abstinuit; agros rediens vastat ulciscendi magis quam praedae studio. eaque clade haud minus 5 quam adversa pugna subacti Veientes pacem petitum oratores Romam mittunt. agri parte multatis in centum 5 annos indutiae datae.

Haec ferme Romulo regnante domi militiaeque 6 gesta, quorum nihil absonum fidei divinae originis divinitatisque post mortem creditae fuit, non animus in regno avito recuperando, 10 non condendae urbis consilium, non bello ac pace firmandae. ab illo enim profecto viribus datis tantum 7 valuit, ut in quadraginta deinde annos tutam pacem haberet. multitudini tamen gratior fuit quam patribus, 8 longe ante alios acceptissimus militum animis; trecentosque armatos ad custodiam corporis, quos Celeres 15 appellavit, non in bello solum sed etiam in pace habuit.

The character of Romulus.

16 His immortalibus editis operibus cum ad exercitum recensendum contionem in campo ad Caprae paludem haberet, subito coorta tempestas 20 cum magno fragore tonitribusque tam denso regem operuit nimbo, ut conspectum eius contioni abstulerit. nec deinde in terris Romulus fuit. Romana 2 pubes sedato tandem pavore, postquam ex tam turbido die serena et tranquilla lux rediit, ubi vacuam sedem 25 regiam vidit, etsi satis credebat patribus, qui proxumi steterant, sublimem raptum procella, tamen velut orbitatis metu icta maestum aliquamdiu silentium obtinuit. deinde a paucis initio facto deum deo natum, regem 3 parentemque urbis Romanae salvere universi Romulum 30 iubent; pacem precibus exposcunt, uti volens propitius suam semper sospitet progeniem. fuisse credo tum 4 quoque aliquos, qui discerptum regem patrum manibus

The translation of Romulus.

[VIII—XVI. *The reign of Romulus.*]

taciti arguerent (manavit enim haec quoque sed perobscura fama); illam alteram admiratio viri et pavor
5 praesens nobilitavit. Et consilio etiam unius hominis addita rei dicitur fides. namque Proculus Iulius, sollicita civitate desiderio regis et infensa patribus, gravis, ut 5 traditur, quamvis magnae rei auctor in contionem prodit.
6 "Romulus," inquit "Quirites, parens urbis huius, prima hodierna luce caelo repente delapsus se mihi obvium dedit. cum perfusus horrore venerabundus adstitissem,
7 petens precibus, ut contra intueri fas esset: 'abi, nuntia' 10 inquit 'Romanis, caelestes ita velle, ut mea Roma caput orbis terrarum sit: proinde rem militarem colant, sciantque et ita posteris tradant nullas opes humanas
8 armis Romanis resistere posse.' haec" inquit "locutus sublimis abiit." mirum quantum illi viro nuntianti haec 15 fides fuerit, quamque desiderium Romuli apud plebem exercitumque facta fide immortalitatis lenitum sit.

[XVII. *An Interregnum.*]

17 Patrum interim animos certamen regni ac cupido versabat. necdum ad singulos, quia nemo magnopere eminebat in novo populo, pervenerat; factionibus inter ordines certabatur. 20

A disputed succession results in an Interregnum.

2 oriundi ab Sabinis, ne, quia post Tati mortem ab sua parte non erat regnatum, in societate aequa possessionem imperii amitterent, sui corporis creari regem volebant; Romani veteres peregrinum 25
3 regem aspernabantur. in variis voluntatibus regnari tamen omnes volebant libertatis dulcedine nondum
4 experta. timor deinde patres incessit, ne civitatem sine imperio, exercitum sine duce, multarum circa

civitatium irritatis animis vis aliqua externa adoriretur. et esse igitur aliquod caput placebat, et nemo alteri concedere in animum inducebat. ita rem inter se centum 5 patres decem decuriis factis singulisque in singulas 5 decurias creatis, qui summae rerum praeessent, consociant. decem imperitabant, unus cum insignibus imperii et lictoribus erat; quinque dierum spatio finie- 6 batur imperium ac per omnes in orbem ibat; annuumque intervallum regni fuit. id ab re, quod nunc quoque 10 tenet nomen, interregnum appellatum. fremere deinde 7 plebs, multiplicatam servitutem, centum pro uno dominos factos; nec ultra nisi regem et ab ipsis creatum videbantur passuri. cum sensissent ea moveri patres, 8 offerendum ultro rati quod amissuri erant, ita gratiam 15 ineunt summa potestate populo permissa, ut non plus darent iuris quam detinerent. decreverunt enim, ut, 9 cum populus regem iussisset, id sic ratum esset, si patres auctores fierent. hodie quoque in legibus magistratibusque rogandis usurpatur idem ius vi adempta: 20 priusquam populus suffragium ineat, in incertum comitiorum eventum patres auctores fiunt. tum interrex contione 10 advocata "quod bonum faustum felixque sit," inquit "Quirites, regem create: ita patribus visum est. patres deinde, si dignum qui secundus ab Romulo numeretur 25 crearitis, auctores fient." adeo id gratum plebi fuit, 11 ut, ne victi beneficio viderentur, id modo sciscerent iuberentque, ut senatus decerneret qui Romae regnaret.

[XVIII—XXI. *The reign of Numa Pompilius.*]

18 Inclita iustitia religioque ea tempestate Numae Pompili erat. Curibus Sabinis habitabat, consultissimus vir, ut in illa quisquam esse aetate poterat, omnis divini atque humani iuris.

Numa Pompilius.

2 auctorem doctrinae eius, quia non exstat alius, falso 5 Samium Pythagoram edunt, quem Servio Tullio regnante Romae centum amplius post annos in ultima Italiae ora circa Metapontum Heracleamque et Crotonam iuve-
3 num aemulantium studia coetus habuisse constat. ex quibus locis, etsi eiusdem aetatis fuisset, quae fama in 10 Sabinos? aut quo linguae commercio quemquam ad cupiditatem discendi excivisset? quove praesidio unus per tot gentes dissonas sermone moribusque pervenisset?
4 suopte igitur ingenio temperatum animum virtutibus fuisse opinor magis, instructumque non tam peregrinis 15 artibus quam disciplina tetrica ac tristi veterum Sabinorum, quo genere nullum quondam incorruptius fuit.

5 Audito nomine Numae patres Romani, quamquam inclinari opes ad Sabinos rege inde sumpto videbantur, tamen neque se quisquam nec 20 factionis suae alium nec denique patrum aut civium quemquam praeferre illi viro ausi ad unum omnes Numae Pompilio regnum deferendum decernunt.

His election is confirmed by auspices.

6 accitus, sicut Romulus augurato urbe condenda regnum adeptus est, de se quoque deos consuli iussit. inde ab 25 augure, cui deinde honoris ergo publicum id perpetuumque sacerdotium fuit, deductus in arcem in lapide ad
7 meridiem versus consedit. augur ad laevam eius capite velato sedem cepit, dextra manu baculum sine nodo aduncum tenens, quem lituum appellarunt. inde ubi 30 prospectu in urbem agrumque capto deos precatus regiones ab oriente ad occasum determinavit, dextras ad

meridiem partes, laevas ad septemtrionem esse dixit, signum contra, quoad longissime conspectum oculi 8 ferebant, animo finivit; tum lituo in laevam manum translato dextra in caput Numae imposita precatus ita 5 est: "Iuppiter pater, si est fas hunc Numam Pompilium, 9 cuius ego caput teneo, regem Romae esse, uti tu signa nobis certa adclarassis inter eos fines, quos feci." tum peregit verbis auspicia, quae mitti vellet; quibus missis declaratus rex Numa de templo descendit.

10 Qui regno ita potitus urbem novam, conditam vi **19** et armis, iure eam legibusque ac moribus de integro condere parat. quibus cum 2 inter bella adsuescere videret non posse, quippe efferari militia animos, mitigandum ferocem populum armorum 15 desuetudine ratus Ianum ad infimum Argiletum indicem pacis bellique fecit, apertus ut in armis esse civitatem, clausus pacatos circa omnes populos significaret. bis 3 deinde post Numae regnum clausus fuit, semel T. Manlio consule post Punicum primum perfectum bellum, 20 iterum, quod nostrae aetati di dederunt ut videremus, post bellum Actiacum ab imperatore Caesare Augusto pace terra marique parta. clauso eo cum omnium circa 4 finitimorum societate ac foederibus iunxisset animos, positis externorum periculorum curis ne luxuriarent otio 25 animi, quos metus hostium disciplinaque militaris continuerat, omnium primum rem ad multitudinem imperitam et illis saeculis rudem efficacissimam, deorum metum iniciendum ratus est. qui cum descendere ad animos 5 sine aliquo commento miraculi non posset, simulat sibi 30 cum dea Egeria congressus nocturnos esse; eius se monitu, quae acceptissima dis essent, sacra instituere, sacerdotes suos cuique deorum praeficere.

A policy of peace.

[XVIII—XXI. *The reign of Numa Pompilius.*]

6 Atque omnium primum ad cursus lunae in duodecim menses discribit annum; quem, quia tricenos dies singulis mensibus luna non explet, desuntque dies solido anno, qui solstitiali circumagitur orbe, intercalariis mensibus interponendis 5 ita dispensavit, ut vicesimo anno ad metam eandem solis, unde orsi essent, plenis omnium annorum spatiis 7 dies congruerent. idem nefastos dies fastosque fecit, quia aliquando nihil cum populo agi utile futurum erat.

The arrangement of the calendar.

20 Tum sacerdotibus creandis animum adiecit, quam- 10 quam ipse plurima sacra obibat, ea maxime quae nunc 2 ad Dialem flaminem pertinent. sed quia in civitate bellicosa plures Romuli quam Numae similes reges putabat fore, iturosque ipsos ad bella, ne sacra regiae vicis desererentur, flaminem 15 Iovi adsiduum sacerdotem creavit, insignique eum veste et curuli regia sella adornavit. huic duos 3 flamines adiecit, Marti unum, alterum Quirino; virginesque Vestae legit, Alba oriundum sacerdotium et genti conditoris haud alienum. iis, ut adsiduae templi antistites 20 essent, stipendium de publico statuit, virginitate aliisque 4 caerimoniis venerabiles ac sanctas fecit. Salios item duodecim Marti Gradivo legit, tunicaeque pictae insigne dedit et super tunicam aeneum pectori tegumen, caelestiaque arma, quae ancilia appel- 25 lantur, ferre ac per urbem ire canentes carmina cum 5 tripudiis sollemnique saltatu iussit. pontificem deinde Numam Marcium Marci filium ex patribus legit, eique sacra omnia exscripta exsignataque attribuit, quibus hostiis, quibus diebus, ad quae 30 templa sacra fierent, atque unde in eos sumptus pecunia 6 erogaretur. cetera quoque omnia publica privataque

The institution of the Flamens,

the Salii,

the Pontifex.

sacra pontificis scitis subiecit, ut esset, quo consultum plebes veniret, ne quid divini iuris neglegendo patrios ritus peregrinosque adsciscendo turbaretur; nec caelestes 7 modo caerimonias sed iusta quoque funebria placandosque manes ut idem pontifex edoceret, quaeque prodigia fulminibus aliove quo visu missa susciperentur atque curarentur. ad ea elicienda ex mentibus divinis Iovi Elicio aram in Aventino dicavit, deumque consuluit auguriis, quae suscipienda essent.

21 By moral improvement the state wins the respect of its neighbours.

Ad haec consultanda procurandaque multitudine omni a vi et armis conversa et animi aliquid agendo occupati erant, et deorum adsidua insidens cura, cum interesse rebus humanis caeleste numen videretur, ea pietate omnium pectora imbuerat, ut fides ac ius iurandum proximo legum ac poenarum metu civitatem regerent. et cum 2 ipsi se homines in regis, velut unici exempli, mores formarent, tum finitumi etiam populi, qui antea castra non urbem positam in medio ad sollicitandam omnium pacem crediderant, in eam verecundiam adducti sunt, ut civitatem totam in cultum versam deorum violari ducerent nefas. lucus erat, quem medium ex opaco 3 specu fons perenni rigabat aqua. quo quia se persaepe Numa sine arbitris velut ad congressum deae inferebat, Camenis eum lucum sacravit, quod earum ibi concilia cum coniuge sua Egeria essent. et soli Fidei sollemne instituit. ad id sacrarium flamines bigis curru arcuato 4 vehi iussit, manuque ad digitos usque involuta rem divinam facere, significantes fidem tutandam sedemque eius etiam in dexteris sacratam esse. multa alia sacri- 5 ficia locaque sacris faciendis, quae Argeos pontifices vocant, dedicavit. omnium tamen maximum eius operum

[XVIII—XXI. *The reign of Numa Pompilius.*]

fuit tutela per omne regni tempus haud minor pacis quam regni.

6 Ita duo deinceps reges, alius alia via, ille bello hic pace, civitatem auxerunt. Romulus septem et triginta regnavit annos, Numa tres et quadraginta. cum valida 5 tum temperata et belli et pacis artibus erat civitas.

[XXII—XXXI. *The reign of Tullus Hostilius.*]

22 Numae morte ad interregnum res rediit. inde Tullum Hostilium, nepotem Hostili, cuius in infima arce clara pugna adversus Sabinos fuerat, regem populus iussit: patres auctores 10

Tullus Hostilius is chosen king.

2 facti. hic non solum proximo regi dissimilis sed ferocior etiam quam Romulus fuit. cum aetas viresque tum avita quoque gloria animum stimulabat. senescere igitur civitatem otio ratus undique materiam excitandi belli

3 quaerebat. forte evenit, ut agrestes Romani 15 ex Albano agro, Albani ex Romano praedas

4 in vicem agerent. imperitabat tum Gaius Cluilius Albae. utrimque legati fere sub idem tempus ad res repetendas missi. Tullus praeceperat suis, ne quid prius quam mandata agerent. satis sciebat nega- 20

Quarrels and parleys between Rome and Alba

5 turum Albanum: ita pie bellum indici posse. ab Albanis socordius res acta: excepti hospitio ab Tullo blande ac benigne comi fronte regis convivium celebrant. tantisper Romani et res repetiverant priores et neganti

6 Albano bellum in tricesimum diem indixerant. haec 25 renuntiant Tullo. tum legatis Tullus dicendi potestatem, quid petentes venerint, facit. illi omnium ignari primum purgando terunt tempus: se invitos quicquam, quod minus placeat Tullo, dicturos, sed imperio subigi: res

repetitum se venisse; ni reddantur, bellum indicere iussos. ad haec Tullus "nuntiate" inquit "regi vestro, 7 regem Romanum deos facere testes, uter prius populus res repetentes legatos aspernatus dimiserit, ut in eum 5 omnes expetant huiusce clades belli." haec nuntiant **23** domum Albani. et bellum utrimque summa ope parabatur, civili simillimum bello, prope inter parentes natosque, Troianam utramque prolem, cum Lavinium ab Troia, ab Lavinio Alba, ab Albanorum 10 stirpe regum oriundi Romani essent. eventus tamen 2 belli minus miserabilem dimicationem fecit, quod nec acie certatum est, et tectis modo dirutis alterius urbis duo populi in unum confusi sunt.

result in war.

Albani priores ingenti exercitu in agrum Romanum 3 15 impetum fecere. castra ab urbe haud plus quinque milia passum locant, fossa circumdant: fossa Cluilia ab nomine ducis per aliquot saecula appellata est, donec cum re nomen quoque vetustate abolevit. in his castris 4 Cluilius Albanus rex moritur; dictatorem Albani Mettium 20 Fufetium creant. interim Tullus ferox praecipue morte regis magnumque deorum numen, ab ipso capite orsum, in omne nomen Albanum expetiturum poenas ob bellum impium dictitans, nocte praeteritis hostium castris infesto exercitu in agrum Albanum pergit. ea res ab stativis 5 25 excivit Mettium. ducit quam proxume ad hostem potest. inde legatum praemissum nuntiare Tullo iubet, priusquam dimicent, opus esse colloquio: si secum congressus sit, satis scire ea se allaturum, quae nihilo minus ad rem 30 Romanam quam ad Albanam pertineant. haud asper- 6 natus Tullus, tamen, si vana adferantur, in aciem educit. exeunt contra et Albani. postquam instructi utrimque

A conference is proposed by the Alban dictator Mettius Fufetius,

stabant, cum paucis procerum in medium duces proce-
7 dunt. ibi infit Albanus: "iniurias et non redditas res
ex foedere quae repetitae sint, et ego regem nostrum
Cluilium causam huiusce esse belli audisse videor, nec
te dubito, Tulle, eadem prae te ferre. sed si vera potius 5
quam dictu speciosa dicenda sunt, cupido imperii duos
8 cognatos vicinosque populos ad arma stimulat. neque,
recte an perperam, interpretor; fuerit ista eius delibe-
ratio, qui bellum suscepit: me Albani gerendo bello
ducem creavere. illud te, Tulle, monitum velim: 10

who lays stress on the Etruscan danger.

Etrusca res quanta circa nos teque maxime
sit, quo propior es Tuscis, hoc magis scis.
multum illi terra, plurimum mari pollent.
9 memor esto, iam cum signum pugnae dabis, has duas
acies spectaculo fore, ut fessos confectosque simul victo- 15
rem ac victum adgrediantur. itaque si nos di amant,
quoniam non contenti libertate certa in dubiam imperii
servitiique aleam imus, ineamus aliquam viam, qua, utri
utris imperent, sine magna clade, sine multo sanguine
10 utriusque populi decerni possit." haud displicet res 20
Tullo, quamquam cum indole animi tum spe victoriae
ferocior erat. quaerentibus utrimque ratio initur, cui et
fortuna ipsa praebuit materiam.

24 Forte in duobus tum exercitibus erant trigemini

Romans and Albans agree to refer the question of supremacy to a contest of champions;

fratres nec aetate nec viribus dispares. 25
Horatios Curiatiosque fuisse satis constat,
nec ferme res antiqua alia est nobilior.
tamen in re tam clara nominum error
manet, utrius populi Horatii, utrius Curiatii
fuerint. auctores utroque trahunt; plures tamen in- 30
venio, qui Romanos Horatios vocent; hos ut sequar,
2 inclinat animus. cum trigeminis agunt reges, ut pro

sua quisque patria dimicent ferro: ibi imperium fore, unde victoria fuerit. nihil recusatur. tempus et locus con- 3 venit. priusquam dimicarent, foedus ictum inter Romanos et Albanos est his legibus, ut, cuius populi cives eo certa- 5 mine vicissent, is alteri populo cum bona pace imperitaret.

Foedera alia aliis legibus, ceterum eodem modo omnia fiunt. tum ita factum accepimus nec ullius vetustior foederis memoria est. fetialis regem Tullum ita rogavit: "iubesne me, rex, 10 cum patre patrato populi Albani foedus ferire?" iubente rege "sagmina" inquit "te, rex, posco." rex ait "puram tollito." fetialis ex arce graminis herbam 5 puram attulit. postea regem ita rogavit: "rex, facisne me tu regium nuntium populi Romani Quiritium, vasa 15 comitesque meos?" rex respondit: "quod sine fraude mea populique Romani Quiritium fiat, facio." fetialis 6 erat M. Valerius. is patrem patratum Spurium Fusium fecit verbena caput capillosque tangens. pater patratus ad ius iurandum patrandum, id est sanciendum fit foedus, 20 multisque id verbis, quae longo effata carmine non operae est referre, peragit. legibus deinde recitatis 7 "audi," inquit "Iuppiter, audi, pater patrate populi Albani, audi tu, populus Albanus: ut illa palam prima postrema ex illis tabulis cerave recitata sunt sine dolo 25 malo, utique ea hic hodie rectissime intellecta sunt, illis legibus populus Romanus prior non deficiet. si prior 8 defexit publico consilio dolo malo, tum, ille Diespiter, populum Romanum sic ferito, ut ego hunc porcum hic hodie feriam, tantoque magis ferito, quanto magis potes 30 pollesque." id ubi dixit, porcum saxo silice percussit. 9 sua item carmina Albani suumque ius iurandum per suum dictatorem suosque sacerdotes peregerunt.

but a treaty is first made.

[XXII—XXXI. *The reign of Tullus Hostilius.*]

25 Foedere icto trigemini sicut convenerat arma capiunt. cum sui utrosque adhortarentur, deos patrios patriam ac parentes, quidquid civium domi, quidquid in exercitu sit, illorum tunc arma, illorum intueri manus, feroces et suopte 5 ingenio et pleni adhortantium vocibus in medium inter

Fight between the Horatii and the Curiatii.

2 duas acies procedunt. consederant utrimque pro castris duo exercitus periculi magis praesentis quam curae expertes: quippe imperium agebatur in tam paucorum virtute atque fortuna positum. itaque ergo erecti suspen- 10 sique in minime gratum spectaculum animo incenduntur.
3 datur signum, infestisque armis, velut acies, terni iuvenes magnorum exercituum animos gerentes concurrunt. nec his nec illis periculum suum, publicum imperium servitiumque obversatur animo futuraque ea deinde patriae 15
4 fortuna, quam ipsi fecissent. ut primo statim concursu increpuere arma micantesque fulsere gladii, horror ingens spectantis perstringit, et neutro inclinata spe torpebat
5 vox spiritusque. consertis deinde manibus cum iam non motus tantum corporum agitatioque anceps telorum 20 armorumque, sed vulnera quoque et sanguis spectaculo essent, duo Romani super alium alius vulneratis tribus
6 Albanis exspirantes corruerunt. ad quorum casum cum conclamasset gaudio Albanus exercitus, Romanas legiones iam spes tota, nondum tamen cura deseruerat, exanimes 25
7 vicem unius, quem tres Curiatii circumsteterant. forte is integer fuit, ut universis solus nequaquam par, sic adversus singulos ferox. ergo ut segregaret pugnam eorum, capessit fugam, ita ratus secuturos, ut quemque
8 vulnere adfectum corpus sineret. iam aliquantum spatii 30 ex eo loco, ubi pugnatum est, aufugerat, cum respiciens videt magnis intervallis sequentes, unum haud procul ab

sese abesse. in eum magno impetu rediit; et dum 9
Albanus exercitus inclamat Curiatiis, uti opem ferant
fratri, iam Horatius caeso hoste victor secundam pugnam
petebat. tunc clamore, qualis ex insperato faventium
5 solet, Romani adiuvant militem suum, et ille defungi
proelio festinat. prius itaque quam alter, qui nec procul 10
aberat, consequi posset, et alterum Curiatium conficit.
iamque aequato Marte singuli supererant, sed nec spe 11
nec viribus pares. alterum intactum ferro corpus et
10 geminata victoria ferocem in certamen tertium dabat,
alter fessum vulnere, fessum cursu trahens corpus,
victusque fratrum ante se strage victori obicitur hosti.
nec illud proelium fuit. Romanus exsultans "duos" 12
inquit "fratrum Manibus dedi, tertium causae belli
15 huiusce, ut Romanus Albano imperet, dabo." male
sustinenti arma gladium superne iugulo defigit, iacentem
spoliat. Romani ovantes ac gratulantes Horatium acci- 13
piunt eo maiore cum gaudio, quo prope metum res
fuerat. ad sepulturam inde suorum nequaquam paribus
20 animis vertuntur, quippe imperio alteri aucti, alteri
dicionis alienae facti. sepulcra exstant quo quisque loco 14
cecidit, duo Romana uno loco propius Albam, tria
Albana Romam versus, sed distantia locis, ut et pugnatum est.

25 Priusquam inde digrederentur, roganti Mettio, ex **26**
foedere icto quid imperaret, imperat Tullus, uti iuventutem in armis habeat, usurum se eorum opera, si bellum
cum Veientibus foret. ita exercitus inde domos abducti.

Princeps Horatius ibat trigemina spolia prae se gerens. 2
30 cui soror virgo, quae desponsa uni ex
Curiatiis fuerat, obvia ante portam Capenam fuit; cognitoque super umeros fratris paludamento

Horatius slays his sister;

sponsi, quod ipsa confecerat, solvit crines et flebiliter
3 nomine sponsum mortuum appellat. movet feroci iuveni
animum comploratio sororis in victoria sua tantoque
gaudio publico. stricto itaque gladio simul verbis
4 increpans transfigit puellam. "abi hinc cum immaturo 5
amore ad sponsum," inquit "oblita fratrum mortuorum
vivique, oblita patriae. sic eat quaecumque Romana
5 lugebit hostem." atrox visum id facinus patribus plebi-
que, sed recens meritum facto obstabat. tamen raptus
in ius ad regem. rex, ne ipse tam tristis ingratique 10
ad vulgus iudicii ac secundum iudicium supplicii auctor
esset, concilio populi advocato "duoviros" inquit
"qui Horatio perduellionem iudicent secundum legem
6 facio." lex horrendi carminis erat: "duoviri perduellionem iudicent. si a duoviris provocarit, provocatione 15
certato. si vincent, caput obnubito, infelici arbori
reste suspendito, verberato vel intra pomerium vel
7 extra pomerium." hac lege duoviri creati,
qui se absolvere non rebantur ea lege ne
innoxium quidem posse, cum condemnassent, tum alter 20
ex his "Publi Horati, tibi perduellionem iudico" inquit.
8 "i, lictor, colliga manus." accesserat lictor iniciebatque
laqueum. tum Horatius auctore Tullo, clemente legis
interprete, "provoco" inquit. ita de provocatione certa-
9 tum ad populum est. moti homines sunt in eo iudicio 25
maxime Publio Horatio patre proclamante, se filiam
iure caesam iudicare; ni ita esset, patrio iure in filium
animadversurum fuisse. orabat deinde, ne se, quem
paulo ante cum egregia stirpe conspexissent,
10 orbum liberis facerent. inter haec senex 30
iuvenem amplexus, spolia Curiatiorum fixa
eo loco, qui nunc Pila Horatia appellatur,

he is condemned,

but subsequently acquitted, after the eloquent appeal of his father.

ostentans, "huncine," aiebat "quem modo decoratum ovantemque victoria incedentem vidistis, Quirites, eum sub furca vinctum inter verbera et cruciatus videre potestis, quod vix Albanorum oculi tam deforme specta-
5 culum ferre possent? i, lictor, colliga manus, quae 11 paulo ante armatae imperium populo Romano pepererunt. i, caput obnube liberatoris urbis huius; arbore infelici suspende, verbera vel intra pomerium, modo inter illa pila et spolia hostium, vel extra pomerium, modo inter
10 sepulcra Curiatiorum. quo enim ducere hunc iuvenem potestis, ubi non sua decora eum a tanta foeditate supplicii vindicent?" non tulit populus nec patris 12 lacrimas nec ipsius parem in omni periculo animum; absolveruntque admiratione magis virtutis quam iure
15 causae. itaque, ut caedes manifesta aliquo tamen piaculo lueretur, imperatum patri, ut filium expiaret pecunia publica. is quibusdam piacularibus sacrificiis factis, 13 quae deinde genti Horatiae tradita sunt, transmisso per viam tigillo capite adoperto velut sub iugum misit
20 iuvenem. id hodie quoque publice semper refectum manet; sororium tigillum vocant. Horatiae sepulcrum, 14 quo loco corruerat icta, constructum est saxo quadrato.

Nec diu pax Albana mansit. invidia vulgi, quod **27**
25 tribus militibus fortuna publica commissa fuerit, vanum ingenium dictatoris corrupit, et, quoniam recta consilia haud bene evenerant, pravis reconciliare popularium animos coepit. igitur ut prius in bello pacem, sic in 2 pace bellum quaerens, quia suae civitati animorum plus
30 quam virium cernebat esse, ad bellum palam atque ex edicto gerundum alios concitat populos, suis per speciem societatis proditionem reservat. Fidenates, colonia 3

Romana, Veientibus sociis consilii adsumptis pacto transitionis Albanorum ad bellum atque arma incitantur. 4 cum Fidenae aperte descissent, Tullus Mettio exercituque eius ab Alba accito contra hostes ducit. ubi Anienem transiit, ad 5 confluentis collocat castra. inter eum locum et Fidenas 5 Veientium exercitus Tiberim transierat. hi et in acie prope flumen tenuere dextrum cornu, in sinistro Fidenates propius montes consistunt. Tullus adversus Veientem hostem derigit suos; Albanos contra legionem 10 Fidenatium collocat. Albano non plus animi erat quam fidei. nec manere ergo nec transire aperte ausus sensim ad montes succedit. 6 inde, ubi satis subisse sese ratus est erigit totam aciem, fluctuansque animo, ut tereret tempus, ordines 15 explicat. consilium erat, qua fortuna rem daret, ea 7 inclinare vires. miraculo primo esse Romanis, qui proximi steterant, ut nudari latera sua sociorum digressu senserunt; inde eques citato equo nuntiat regi, abire Albanos. Tullus in re trepida duodecim vovit Salios 20 8 fanaque Pallori ac Pavori. equitem clara increpans voce, ut hostes exaudirent, redire in proelium iubet, nihil trepidatione opus esse; suo iussu circumduci Albanum exercitum, ut Fidenatium nuda terga invadant. idem 9 imperat, ut hastas equites erigerent. id factum magnae 25 parti peditum Romanorum conspectum abeuntis Albani exercitus intersaepsit; qui viderant, id quod ab rege auditum erat rati, eo acrius pugnant. terror ad hostes transit: et audiverant clara voce dictum, et magna pars Fidenatium, ut qui coloni additi Romanis essent, Latine 30 10 sciebant. itaque, ne subito ex collibus decursu Albanorum intercluderentur ab oppido, terga vertunt. instat

War with Veii and Fidenae.

Disloyalty of the Albans.

[XXII—XXXI. *The reign of Tullus Hostilius.*]

Tullus fusoque Fidenatium cornu in Veientem alieno pavore perculsum ferocior redit. nec illi tulere impetum, sed ab effusa fuga flumen obiectum ab tergo arcebat. quo postquam fuga inclinavit, alii arma foede iactantes 11
5 in aquam caeci ruebant, alii, dum cunctantur in ripis, inter fugae pugnaeque consilium oppressi. non alia ante Romana pugna atrocior fuit.

28 Tum Albanus exercitus, spectator certaminis, deductus in campos. Mettius Tullo devictos
10 hostes gratulatur, contra Tullus Mettium benigne adloquitur. quod bene vertat, castra Albanos Romanis castris iungere iubet; sacrificium lustrale in diem posterum parat. ubi illuxit, paratis omnibus, ut 2 adsolet, vocari ad contionem utrumque exercitum iubet.

The punishment of the traitor Mettius.

15 praecones ab extremo orsi primos excivere Albanos. ii novitate etiam rei moti, ut regem Romanum contionantem audirent, proximi constitere. ex composito armata 3 circumdatur Romana legio. centurionibus datum negotium erat, ut sine mora imperia exsequerentur. tum 4
20 ita Tullus infit: "Romani, si umquam ante alias ullo in bello fuit, quod primum dis immortalibus gratias ageretis, deinde vestrae ipsorum virtuti, hesternum id proelium fuit. dimicatum est enim non magis cum hostibus quam, quae dimicatio maior atque periculosior est, cum
25 proditione ac perfidia sociorum. nam, ne vos falsa opinio 5 teneat, iniussu meo Albani subiere ad montes, nec imperium illud meum sed consilium et imperii simulatio fuit, ut nec vobis, ignorantibus deseri vos, averteretur a certamine animus, et hostibus circumveniri se ab tergo
30 ratis terror ac fuga iniceretur. nec ea culpa, quam arguo, 6 omnium Albanorum est: ducem secuti sunt, ut et vos, si quo ego inde agmen declinare voluissem, fecissetis.

Mettius ille est ductor itineris huius, Mettius idem huius machinator belli, Mettius foederis Romani Albanique ruptor. audeat deinde talia alius, nisi in hunc insigne 7 iam documentum mortalibus dedero." centuriones armati Mettium circumsistunt. rex cetera ut orsus erat 5 peragit: "quod bonum faustum felixque sit populo Romano ac mihi vobisque, Albani, populum omnem Albanum Romam traducere in animo est, civitatem dare plebi, primores in patres legere, unam urbem, unam rem publicam facere. ut ex uno quondam in duos populos 10 8 divisa Albana res est, sic nunc in unum redeat." ad haec Albana pubes inermis ab armatis saepta in variis voluntatibus communi tamen metu cogente silentium 9 tenet. tum Tullus "Metti Fufeti," inquit "si ipse discere posses fidem ac foedera servare, vivo tibi ea 15 disciplina a me adhibita esset: nunc, quoniam tuum insanabile ingenium est, at tu tuo supplicio doce humanum genus ea sancta credere, quae a te violata sunt. ut igitur paulo ante animum inter Fidenatem Romanamque rem ancipitem gessisti, ita iam corpus passim 20 10 distrahendum dabis." exinde duabus admotis quadrigis in currus earum distentum illigat Mettium, deinde in diversum iter equi concitati lacerum in utroque curru corpus, qua inhaeserant vinculis membra, portantes. aver-11 tere omnes ab tanta foeditate spectaculi oculos. primum 25 ultimumque illud supplicium apud Romanos exempli parum memoris legum humanarum fuit. in aliis gloriari licet, nulli gentium mitiores placuisse poenas.

29 Inter haec iam praemissi Albam erant equites, qui multitudinem traducerent Romam. legiones 30 2 deinde ductae ad diruendam urbem. quae ubi intravere portas, non quidem fuit tumultus

Alba Longa is demolished, and the inhabitants are removed to Rome,

ille nec pavor, qualis captarum esse urbium solet, cum effractis portis stratisve ariete muris aut arce vi capta clamor hostilis et cursus per urbem armatorum omnia ferro flammaque miscet; sed silentium triste ac tacita maestitia 3
5 ita defixit omnium animos, ut prae metu obliti, quid relinquerent, quid secum ferrent, deficiente consilio rogitantesque alii alios nunc in liminibus starent, nunc errabundi domos suas ultimum illud visuri pervagarentur. ut vero 4 iam equitum clamor exire iubentium instabat, iam fragor
10 tectorum quae diruebantur ultimis urbis partibus audiebatur, pulvisque ex distantibus locis ortus velut nube inducta omnia impleverat, raptim quibus quisque poterat elatis, cum larem ac penates tectaque, in quibus natus quisque educatusque esset, relinquentes exirent, iam continens
15 agmen migrantium impleverat vias. et conspectus aliorum 5 mutua miseratione integrabat lacrimas; vocesque etiam miserabiles exaudiebantur mulierum praecipue, cum obsessa ab armatis templa augusta praeterirent ac velut captos relinquerent deos. egressis urbem Albanis Ro- 6
20 manus passim publica privataque omnia tecta adaequat solo, unaque hora quadringentorum annorum opus, quibus Alba steterat, excidio ac ruinis dedit: templis tamen deum (ita enim edictum ab rege fuerat) temperatum est.

25 Roma interim crescit Albae ruinis: duplicatur civium **30** numerus; Caelius additur urbi mons, et quo frequentius habitaretur, eam sedem Tullus regiae capit, ibique deinde habitavit.

where they are incorporated in the state.

principes Albanorum in patres, ut ea quoque pars rei 2
30 publicae cresceret, legit: Tullios Servilios Quinctios Geganios Curiatios Cloelios; templumque ordini ab se aucto curiam fecit, quae Hostilia usque ad patrum

3 nostrorum aetatem appellata est. et ut omnium ordinum viribus aliquid ex novo populo adiceretur, equitum decem turmas ex Albanis legit, legiones et veteres eodem supplemento explevit et novas scripsit.

4 Hac fiducia virium Tullus Sabinis bellum indicit, 5 genti ea tempestate secundum Etruscos opulentissimae viris armisque. utrimque

War with the Sabines.

5 iniuriae factae ac res nequiquam erant repetitae: Tullus ad Feroniae fanum mercatu frequenti negotiatores Ro-
6 manos comprehensos querebatur; Sabini suos prius in 10 lucum confugisse ac Romae retentos. hae causae belli ferebantur. Sabini, haud parum memores et suarum virium partem Romae ab Tatio locatam et Romanam rem nuper etiam adiectione populi Albani auctam,
7 circumspicere et ipsi externa auxilia. Etruria erat vicina, 15 proximi Etruscorum Veientes. inde ob residuas bellorum iras maxime sollicitatis ad defectionem animis voluntarios traxere, et apud vagos quosdam ex inopi plebe etiam merces valuit: publico auxilio nullo adiuti sunt, valuitque apud Veientes (nam de ceteris minus 20
8 mirum est) pacta cum Romulo indutiarum fides. cum bellum utrimque summa ope pararent, vertique in eo res videretur, utri prius arma inferrent, occupat Tullus
9 in agrum Sabinum transire. pugna atrox ad silvam Malitiosam fuit, ubi et peditum quidem robore, ceterum 25 equitatu aucto nuper plurimum Romana acies valuit.
10 ab equitibus repente invectis turbati ordines sunt Sabinorum; nec pugna deinde illis constare nec fuga explicari sine magna caede potuit.

31 Devictis Sabinis cum in magna gloria magnisque 30 opibus regnum Tulli ac tota res Romana esset, nuntiatum regi patribusque est in monte Albano lapidibus

pluisse. quod cum credi vix posset, missis ad id visen- 2
dum prodigium in conspectu haud aliter,
quam cum grandinem venti glomeratam in
terras agunt, crebri cecidere caelo lapides.
5 visi etiam audire vocem ingentem ex summi 3
cacuminis luco, ut patrio ritu sacra Albani facerent, quae
velut dis quoque simul cum patria relictis oblivioni
dederant, et aut Romana sacra susceperant aut fortunae,
ut fit, obirati cultum reliquerant deum. Romanis quoque 4
10 ab eodem prodigio novendiale sacrum publice susceptum
est, seu voce caelesti ex Albano monte missa—nam id
quoque traditur—seu aruspicum monitu: mansit certe
sollemne, ut, quandoque idem prodigium nuntiaretur,
feriae per novem dies agerentur.

Miraculous stone-showers on the Alban Mount.

15 Haud ita multo post pestilentia laboratum est. unde 5
cum pigritia militandi oreretur, nulla tamen
ab armis quies dabatur a bellicoso rege,
salubriora etiam credente militiae quam domi iuvenum
corpora esse, donec ipse quoque longinquo morbo est
20 implicitus. tunc adeo fracti simul cum 6
corpore sunt spiritus illi feroces, ut, qui
nihil ante ratus esset minus regium quam sacris dedere
animum, repente omnibus magnis parvisque superstitionibus obnoxius degeret, religionibusque etiam populum
25 impleret. vulgo iam homines, eum statum rerum, qui 7
sub Numa rege fuerat, requirentes, unam opem aegris
corporibus relictam, si pax veniaque ab diis impetrata
esset, credebant. ipsum regem tradunt volventem com- 8
mentarios Numae, cum ibi quaedam occulta sollemnia
30 sacrificia Iovi Elicio facta invenisset, operatum iis sacris
se abdidisse; sed non rite initum aut curatum id sacrum
esse, nec solum nullam ei oblatam caelestium speciem,

The plague.

A religious revival.

[XXII—XXXI. *The reign of Tullus Hostilius.*]

sed ira Iovis sollicitati prava religione fulmine ictum cum domo conflagrasse. Tullus magna gloria belli regnavit annos duos et triginta.

[XXXII—XXXIV. *The reign of Ancus Marcius.*]

Ancus Marcius becomes king: he restores religious observances,

32 Mortuo Tullo res, ut institutum iam inde ab initio erat, ad patres redierat, hique interregem 5 nominaverant. quo comitia habente Ancum Marcium regem populus creavit; patres fuere auctores. Numae Pompili regis nepos 2 filia ortus Ancus Marcius erat. qui ut regnare coepit, et avitae gloriae memor, et quia proximum regnum, cetera 10 egregium, ab una parte haud satis prosperum fuerat aut neglectis religionibus aut prave cultis, longeque antiquissimum ratus sacra publica ut ab Numa instituta erant facere, omnia ea ex commentariis regis pontificem in album relata proponere in publico iubet. inde et 15 civibus otii cupidis et finitimis civitatibus facta spes in 3 avi mores atque instituta regem abiturum. igitur Latini, cum quibus Tullo regnante ictum foedus erat, sustulerant animos; et, cum incursionem in agrum Romanum fecissent, repetentibus res Romanis superbe responsum 20 reddunt, desidem Romanum regem inter sacella et aras 4 acturum esse regnum rati. medium erat in Anco ingenium, et Numae et Romuli memor; et praeterquam quod avi regno magis necessariam fuisse pacem credebat cum in novo tum feroci populo, etiam quod illi contigisset 25 otium, sine iniuria id se haud facile habiturum: temptari patientiam et temptatam contemni, temporaque esse 5 Tullo regi aptiora quam Numae. ut tamen, quoniam Numa in pace religiones instituisset, a se bellicae caerimoniae proderentur, nec gererentur solum sed etiam 30 indicerentur bella aliquo ritu, ius ab antiqua gente Aequiculis, quod nunc fetiales habent, descripsit, quo res repetuntur.

Legatus ubi ad fines eorum venit, unde res repetuntur, 6
5 capite velato filo (lanae velamen est) "audi, Iuppiter" inquit, "audite fines" (cuiuscumque gentis sunt, nominat), "audiat fas! ego sum publicus nuntius populi Romani; iuste pieque legatus venio verbisque meis fides
10 sit." peragit deinde postulata. inde Iovem testem facit: 7 "si ego iniuste impieque illos homines illasque res dedier mihi exposco, tum patriae compotem me numquam siris esse." haec, cum fines suprascandit, haec, quicumque 8 ei primus vir obvius fuerit, haec portam ingrediens, haec
15 forum ingressus paucis verbis carminis concipiendique iuris iurandi mutatis peragit. si non deduntur quos 9 exposcit, diebus tribus et triginta (tot enim sollemnes sunt) peractis bellum ita indicit: "audi Iuppiter et tu 10 Iane Quirine dique omnes caelestes vosque terrestres
20 vosque inferni audite! ego vos testor, populum illum" (quicumque est, nominat) "iniustum esse, neque ius persolvere. sed de istis rebus in patria maiores natu consulemus, quo pacto ius nostrum adipiscamur." cum iis nuntius Romam ad consulendum redit. confestim 11
25 rex his ferme verbis patres consulebat: "quarum rerum litium causarum condixit pater patratus populi Romani Quiritium patri patrato Priscorum Latinorum hominibusque Priscis Latinis, quas res nec dederunt nec solverunt nec fecerunt, quas res dari fieri solvi oportuit, dic,"
30 inquit ei, quem primum sententiam rogabat, "quid censes?" tum ille: "puro pioque duello quaerendas 12 censeo, itaque consentio consciscoque." inde ordine

and institutes certain formalities in regard to the declaration of war.

alii rogabantur, quandoque pars maior eorum qui aderant in eandem sententiam ibat, bellum erat consensum. fieri solitum, ut fetialis hastam ferratam aut sanguineam praeustam ad fines eorum ferret, et non minus tribus 13 puberibus praesentibus diceret: "quod populi Priscorum 5 Latinorum hominesque Prisci Latini adversus populum Romanum Quiritium fecerunt deliquerunt, quod populus Romanus Quiritium bellum cum Priscis Latinis iussit esse, senatusque populi Romani Quiritium censuit consensit conscivit, ut bellum cum Priscis Latinis fieret, ob 10 eam rem ego populusque Romanus populis Priscorum Latinorum hominibusque Priscis Latinis bellum indico facioque." id ubi dixisset, hastam in fines eorum 14 emittebat. hoc tum modo ab Latinis repetitae res ac bellum indictum, moremque eum posteri acceperunt. 15

33 Ancus demandata cura sacrorum flaminibus sacerdotibusque aliis exercitu novo conscripto profectus Politorium urbem Latinorum vi cepit, secutusque morem regum priorum, qui rem Romanam auxerant hostibus in 20 civitatem accipiendis, multitudinem omnem 2 Romam traduxit. et cum circa Palatium, sedem veterum Romanorum, Sabini Capitolium atque arcem, Caelium montem Albani implessent, Aventinum novae multitudini datum. additi eodem haud ita multo post Tellenis 25 3 Ficanaque captis novi cives. Politorium inde rursus bello repetitum, quod vacuum occupaverant Prisci Latini. eaque causa diruendae urbis eius fuit Romanis, ne 4 hostium semper receptaculum esset. postremo omni bello Latino Medulliam compulso aliquamdiu ibi Marte 30 incerto varia victoria pugnatum est: nam et urbs tuta munitionibus praesidioque firmata valido erat, et castris

Ancus defeats the Latins, and removes a large number to Rome, where they occupy the Aventine.

in aperto positis aliquotiens exercitus Latinus comminus cum Romanis signa contulerat. ad ultimum omnibus 5 copiis conisus Ancus acie primum vincit, inde ingenti praeda potens Romam redit, tum quoque multis milibus 5 Latinorum in civitatem acceptis, quibus, ut iungeretur Palatio Aventinum, ad Murciae datae sedes. Ianiculum 6 quoque adiectum, non inopia loci, sed ne quando ea arx hostium esset. id non muro solum, sed etiam ob commoditatem itineris ponte Sublicio, tum primum in 10 Tiberim facto, coniungi urbi placuit. Quiritium quoque 7 fossa, haud parvum munimentum a planioribus aditu locis, Anci regis opus est. ingenti incremento rebus 8 auctis cum in tanta multitudine hominum discrimine recte an perperam facti confuso facinora clandestina 15 fierent, carcer ad terrorem increscentis audaciae media urbe imminens foro aedificatur. nec urbs tantum hoc rege crevit sed etiam ager finesque: silva Mesia Veientibus adempta usque ad mare imperium prolatum, et in ore Tiberis Ostia urbs condita, salinae circa factae; egregieque rebus bello gestis aedis Iovis Feretrii amplificata. 20

34 Anco regnante Lucumo, vir impiger ac divitiis potens, Romam commigravit cupidine maxime ac spe magni honoris, cuius adipiscendi Tarquiniis (nam ibi quoque peregrina stirpe oriundus erat) facultas non fuerat. Demarati 25 2

Lucumo and Tanaquil leave Tarquinii for Rome:

Corinthii filius erat, qui ob seditiones domo profugus cum Tarquiniis forte consedisset, uxore ibi ducta duos filios genuit. nomina his Lucumo atque Arruns fuerunt. Lucumo superfuit patri bonorum omnium heres, Arruns 30 prior quam pater moritur uxore gravida relicta. nec diu 3 manet superstes filio pater; qui cum ignorans nurum ventrem ferre immemor in testando nepotis decessisset,

puero post avi mortem in nullam sortem bonorum nato
4 ab inopia Egerio inditum nomen. Lucumoni contra
omnium heredi bonorum cum divitiae iam animos facerent, auxit ducta in matrimonium Tanaquil summo loco
nata, et quae haud facile his, in quibus nata erat, 5
5 humiliora sineret ea, quo innupsisset. spernentibus
Etruscis Lucumonem exule advena ortum, ferre indignitatem non potuit, oblitaque ingenitae erga patriam
caritatis, dummodo virum honoratum videret, consilium
6 migrandi ab Tarquiniis cepit. Roma est ad id potissi- 10
mum visa: in novo populo, ubi omnis repentina atque
ex virtute nobilitas sit, futurum locum forti ac strenuo
viro; regnasse Tatium Sabinum, arcessitum in regnum
Numam a Curibus, et Ancum Sabina matre ortum
7 nobilemque una imagine Numae esse. facile persuadet 15
ut cupido honorum, et cui Tarquinii materna tantum
patria esset.

8 Sublatis itaque rebus amigrant Romam. ad Ianiculum forte ventum erat. ibi ei carpento
sedenti cum uxore aquila suspensis demissa 20
leviter alis pilleum aufert, superque carpentum cum magno clangore volitans rursus, velut ministerio
divinitus missa, capiti apte reponit, inde sublimis abit.
9 accepisse id augurium laeta dicitur Tanaquil, perita, ut
vulgo Etrusci, caelestium prodigiorum mulier. excelsa 25
et alta sperare complexa virum iubet: eam alitem, ea
regione caeli et eius dei nuntiam venisse, circa summum
culmen hominis auspicium fecisse, levasse humano super-
10 positum capiti decus, ut divinitus eidem redderet. has
spes cogitationesque secum portantes urbem ingressi 30
sunt, domicilioque ibi comparato L. Tarquinium Priscum
11 edidere nomen. Romanis conspicuum eum novitas

an eagle by the way gives an omen of success.

divitiaeque faciebant, et ipse fortunam benigno alloquio, comitate invitandi beneficiisque quos poterat sibi conciliando adiuvabat, donec in regiam quoque de eo fama perlata est. notitiamque eam brevi apud regem libera- 12
5 liter dextreque obeundo officia in familiaris amicitiae adduxerat iura, ut publicis pariter ac privatis consiliis bello domique interesset, et per omnia expertus postremo tutor etiam liberis regis testamento institueretur.

[XXXV–XL. *The reign of Lucius Tarquinius.*]

Lucius Tarquinius secures the kingdom.

Regnavit Ancus annos quattuor et viginti, cuilibet **35**
10 superiorum regum belli pacisque et artibus et gloria par. iam filii prope puberem aetatem erant. eo magis Tarquinius instare, ut quam primum comitia regi creando fierent; quibus 2 indictis sub tempus pueros venatum ablegavit. isque
15 primus et petisse ambitiose regnum et orationem dicitur habuisse ad conciliandos plebis animos compositam: cum se non rem novam petere, quippe qui non primus, 3 quod quisquam indignari mirarive posset, sed tertius Romae peregrinus regnum adfectet; et Tatium non ex
20 peregrino solum sed etiam ex hoste regem factum, et Numam ignarum urbis non petentem in regnum ultro accitum: se, ex quo sui potens fuerit, Romam cum 4 coniuge ac fortunis omnibus commigrasse; maiorem partem aetatis eius, qua civilibus officiis fungantur
25 homines, Romae se quam in vetere patria vixisse; domi 5 militiaeque sub haud paenitendo magistro, ipso Anco rege, Romana se iura, Romanos ritus didicisse; obsequio et observantia in regem cum omnibus, benignitate erga

6 alios cum rege ipso certasse. haec eum haud falso memorantem ingenti consensu populus Romanus regnare iussit. ergo virum cetera egregium secuta, quam in petendo habuerat, etiam regnantem ambitio est; nec minus regni sui firmandi quam augendae rei publicae 5 memor centum in patres legit, qui deinde minorum gentium sunt appellati, factio haud dubia regis, cuius beneficio in curiam venerant.

The Circus Maximus is laid out.

7 Bellum primum cum Latinis gessit, et oppidum ibi Apiolas vi cepit, praedaque inde maiore, 10 quam quanta belli fama fuerat, revecta ludos opulentius instructiusque quam priores 8 reges fecit. tunc primum circo, qui nunc maximus dicitur, designatus locus est. loca divisa patribus equitibusque, ubi spectacula sibi quisque facerent, fori appellati. 15 9 spectavere furcis duodenos ab terra spectacula alta sustinentibus pedes. ludicrum fuit equi pugilesque ex 10 Etruria maxime acciti. sollemnes, deinde annui mansere ludi, Romani magnique varie appellati. ab eodem rege et circa forum privatis aedificanda divisa sunt loca, 20 **36** porticus tabernaeque factae. muro quoque lapideo

For a Sabine war, the king meditates an increase of the cavalry:

circumdare urbem parabat, cum Sabinum bellum coeptis intervenit. adeoque ea subita res fuit, ut prius Anienem transirent hostes, quam obviam ire ac prohibere exer- 25 2 citus Romanus posset. itaque trepidatum Romae est. et primo dubia victoria magna utrimque caede pugnatum est. reductis deinde in castra hostium copiis datoque spatio Romanis ad comparandum de integro bellum, Tarquinius, equitem maxime suis deesse viribus ratus, ad 30 Ramnes Titienses Luceres, quas centurias Romulus scripserat, addere alias constituit, suoque insignes relinquere

nomine. id quia inaugurato Romulus fecerat, negare 3
Attus Navius, inclitus ea tempestate augur, neque mutari neque novum constitui, nisi aves addixissent, posse. ex eo ira regi 4
5 mota, eludensque artem, ut ferunt, "age dum," inquit "divine tu, inaugura, fierine possit, quod nunc ego mente concipio." cum ille in augurio rem expertus profecto futuram dixisset, "atqui hoc animo agitavi," inquit "te novacula cotem discissurum: cape
10 haec et perage, quod aves tuae fieri posse portendunt." tum illum haud cunctanter discidisse cotem ferunt. statua Atti capite velato, quo in loco res acta est, in 5
comitio, in gradibus ipsis ad laevam curiae fuit, cotem quoque eodem loco sitam fuisse memorant, ut esset ad
15 posteros miraculi eius monumentum. auguriis certe 6
sacerdotioque augurum tantus honos accessit, ut nihil belli domique postea nisi auspicato gereretur, concilia populi, exercitus vocati, summa rerum, ubi aves non admisissent, dirime-
20 rentur. neque tum Tarquinius de equitum 7
centuriis quicquam mutavit, numero alterum tantum adiecit, ut mille et octingenti equites in tribus centuriis essent. posteriores modo sub isdem nominibus qui additi erant appellati sunt, quas nunc, quia geminatae sunt, sex
25 vocant centurias.

Attus Navius the augur opposes the project,

with the result that augury is officially recognised.

Hac parte copiarum aucta iterum cum Sabinis **37**
confligitur. sed praeterquam quod viribus creverat Romanus exercitus, ex occulto etiam additur dolus, missis qui magnam vim lignorum
30 in Anienis ripa iacentem ardentem in flumen conicerent; ventoque iuvante accensa ligna et pleraque in ratibus impacta sublicis cum haererent pontem incendunt. ca 2

Overthrow of the Sabines.

quoque res in pugna terrorem attulit Sabinis, effusis eadem fugam impedit, multique mortales, cum hostes effugissent, in flumine ipso periere; quorum fluitantia arma ad urbem cognita in Tiberi prius paene, quam 3 nuntiari posset, insignem victoriam fecere. eo proelio 5 praecipua equitum gloria fuit: utrimque ab cornibus positos, cum iam pelleretur media peditum suorum acies, ita incurrisse ab lateribus ferunt, ut non sisterent modo Sabinas legiones ferociter instantes cedentibus, sed subito 4 in fugam averterent. montes effuso cursu Sabini pete- 10 bant; et pauci tenuere, maxima pars, ut ante dictum est, 5 ab equitibus in flumen acti sunt. Tarquinius instandum perterritis ratus, praeda captivisque Romam missis, spoliis hostium (id votum Vulcano erat) ingenti cumulo accensis, pergit porro in agrum Sabinum exercitum 15 6 inducere; et quamquam male gestae res erant, nec gesturos melius sperare poterant, tamen, quia consulendi res non dabat spatium, iere obviam Sabini tumultuario milite; iterumque ibi fusi perditis iam prope rebus pacem **38** petiere. Collatia et quidquid citra Collatiam agri erat 20 Sabinis ademptum, Egerius (fratris hic filius erat regis) Collatiae in praesidio relictus. deditosque Collatinos ita accipio eamque deditionis 2 formulam esse: rex interrogavit "estisne vos legati oratoresque missi a populo Collatino, ut vos populumque 25 Collatinum dederetis?" "sumus." "estne populus Collatinus in sua potestate?" "est." "deditisne vos populumque Collatinum, urbem agros aquam terminos delubra utensilia, divina humanaque omnia in meam populique Romani dicionem?" "dedimus." "at ego 30 3 recipio." bello Sabino perfecto Tarquinius triumphans 4 Romam redit. inde Priscis Latinis bellum fecit. ubi

The surrender of Collatia.

nusquam ad universae rei dimicationem ventum est ad singula oppida circumferendo arma omne nomen Latinum domuit. Corniculum, Ficulea vetus, Cameria, Crustumerium, Ameriola, 5 Medullia, Nomentum, haec de Priscis Latinis aut qui ad Latinos defecerant capta oppida. pax deinde est facta.

Capture of Latin towns.

Maiore inde animo pacis opera incohata quam 5 quanta mole gesserat bella, ut non quietior 10 populus domi esset, quam militiae fuisset: nam et muro lapideo, cuius exordium operis Sabino 6 bello turbatum erat, urbem, qua nondum munierat, cingere parat; et infima urbis loca circa forum aliasque interiectas collibus convalles, quia ex planis locis haud 15 facile evehebant aquas, cloacis fastigio in Tiberim ductis siccat; et aream ad aedem in Capitolio Iovis, quam 7 voverat bello Sabino, iam praesagiente animo futuram olim amplitudinem loci occupat fundamentis.

Public works.

Eo tempore in regia prodigium visu eventuque **39** 20 mirabile fuit: puero dormienti, cui Servio Tullio fuit nomen, caput arsisse ferunt multorum in conspectu. plurimo igitur cla- 2 more inde ad tantae rei miraculum orto excitos reges, et, cum quidam familiarium aquam ad 25 restinguendum ferret, ab regina retentum, sedatoque iam tumultu moveri vetuisse puerum, donec sua sponte experrectus esset. mox cum somno et flammam abisse. 3 tum abducto in secretum viro Tanaquil "viden tu puerum hunc," inquit "quem tam humili cultu educa- 30 mus? scire licet hunc lumen quondam rebus nostris dubiis futurum praesidiumque regiae afflictae: proinde materiam ingentis publice privatimque decoris omni

The miracle which happened to Servius Tullius:

4 indulgentia nostra nutriamus." inde puerum liberum loco coeptum haberi erudirique artibus, quibus ingenia ad magnae fortunae cultum excitantur. evenit facile, quod dis cordi esset. iuvenis evasit vere indolis regiae, nec, cum quaereretur gener Tarquinio, quisquam Ro- 5 manae iuventutis ulla arte conferri potuit, filiamque ei 5 suam rex despondit. hic quacumque de causa tantus illi honos habitus credere prohibet serva natum eum parvumque ipsum servisse. eorum magis sententiae sum, qui Corniculo capto Servi 10 Tulli, qui princeps in illa urbe fuerat, gravidam viro occiso uxorem, cum inter reliquas captivas cognita esset, ob unicam nobilitatem ab regina Romana prohibitam ferunt servitio partum Romae edidisse Prisci Tarquini 6 domo. inde tanto beneficio et inter mulieres familiari- 15 tatem auctam, et puerum, ut in domo a parvo eductum, in caritate atque honore fuisse; fortunam matris, quod capta patria in hostium manus venerit, ut serva natus crederetur fecisse.

his uncertain origin.

40 Duodequadragesimo ferme anno, ex quo regnare 20 coeperat Tarquinius, non apud regem modo sed apud patres plebemque longe maximo 2 honore Servius Tullius erat. tum Anci filii duo, etsi antea semper pro indignissimo habuerant se patrio regno tutoris fraude pulsos, regnare Romae 25 advenam non modo vicinae sed ne Italicae quidem stirpis, tum impensius iis indignitas crescere, si ne ab 3 Tarquinio quidem ad se rediret regnum, sed praeceps inde porro ad servitia caderet, ut in eadem civitate post centesimum fere annum quam Romulus, deo prognatus, 30 deus ipse, tenuerit regnum, donec in terris fuerit, id Servius, serva natus, possideat. cum commune Romani

His preferment vexes the sons of Ancus,

[XXXV—XL. *The reign of Lucius Tarquinius.*]

nominis tum praecipue id domus suae dedecus fore, si Anci regis virili stirpe salva non modo advenis sed servis etiam regnum Romae pateret. ferro igitur eam arcere 4 contumeliam statuunt. sed et iniuriae dolor 5 in Tarquinium ipsum magis quam in Servium eos stimulabat, et quia gravior ultor caedis, si superesset, rex futurus erat quam privatus; tum Servio occiso quemcumque alium generum delegisset, eundem regni heredem facturus videbatur:—ob haec 10 ipsi regi insidiae parantur. ex pastoribus duo ferocissimi 5 delecti ad facinus, quibus consueti erant uterque agrestibus ferramentis, in vestibulo regiae quam potuere tumultuosissime specie rixae in se omnes apparitores regios convertunt. inde, cum ambo regem appellarent 15 clamorque eorum penitus in regiam pervenisset, vocati ad regem pergunt. primo uterque vociferari et certatim 6 alter alteri obstrepere. coerciti ab lictore et iussi in vicem dicere tandem obloqui desistunt; unus rem ex composito orditur. dum intentus in eum se rex totus 7 20 averteret, alter elatam securim in caput deiecit, relictoque in vulnere telo ambo se foras eiciunt.

who plot the assassination of Tarquinius.

[XLI—XLVIII. *The reign of Servius Tullius.*]

41 Tarquinium moribundum cum qui circa erant excepissent, illos fugientes lictores comprehendunt. clamor inde concursusque populi 25 mirantium, quid rei esset. Tanaquil inter tumultum claudi regiam iubet, arbitros eiecit; simul quae curando vulneri opus sunt, tamquam spes subesset, sedulo comparat, simul, si destituat spes, alia praesidia molitur. Servio propere accito cum paene 2

Tanaquil secures the kingdom for Servius.

exsanguem virum ostendisset, dextram tenens orat, ne inultam mortem soceri, ne socrum inimicis ludibrio esse 3 sinat. "tuum est," inquit "Servi, si vir es, regnum, non eorum, qui alienis manibus pessimum facinus fecere. erige te deosque duces sequere, qui clarum hoc fore 5 caput divino quondam circumfuso igni portenderunt. nunc te illa caelestis excitet flamma, nunc expergiscere vere. et nos peregrini regnavimus. qui sis, non unde natus sis, reputa. si tua re subita consilia torpent, at tu 4 mea consilia sequere." cum clamor impetusque multi- 10 tudinis vix sustineri posset, ex superiore parte aedium per fenestras in novam viam versus (habitabat enim rex 5 ad Iovis Statoris) populum Tanaquil adloquitur. iubet bono animo esse: sopitum fuisse regem subito ictu, ferrum haud alte in corpus descendisse, iam ad se 15 redisse; inspectum vulnus abterso cruore, omnia salubria esse. confidere prope diem ipsum eos visuros; interim Servio Tullio iubere populum dicto audientem esse, eum iura redditurum obiturumque alia regis munia esse. 6 Servius cum trabea et lictoribus prodit, ac sede regia 20 sedens alia decernit, de aliis consulturum se regem esse simulat. itaque per aliquot dies, cum iam exspirasset Tarquinius, celata morte per speciem alienae fungendae vicis suas opes firmavit. tum demum palam factum est comploratione in regia orta. Servius praesidio firmo 25 munitus primus iniussu populi voluntate patrum regnavit. 7 Anci liberi iam tum comprensis sceleris ministris, ut vivere regem et tantas esse opes Servi nuntiatum est, Suessam Pometiam exsulatum ierant.

42 Nec iam publicis magis consiliis Servius quam privatis 30 munire opes, et ne, qualis Anci liberum animus adversus Tarquinium fuerat, talis adversus se Tarquini liberum esset, duas filias iuvenibus regiis Lucio atque Arrunti Tarquiniis iungit. nec rupit tamen fati necessitatem humanis consiliis, qui in invidia regni etiam inter domesticos infida 5 omnia atque infesta faceret. peropportune ad praesentis quietem status bellum cum Veientibus (iam enim indutiae exierant) aliisque Etruscis sumptum. in eo bello et virtus et fortuna enituit Tulli; 3 fusoque ingenti hostium exercitu haud dubius rex, seu 10 patrum seu plebis animos periclitaretur, Romam rediit. 2

Servius strengthens his position by domestic ties, and by a successful war with Veii.

Adgrediturque inde ad pacis longe maximum opus, 4 ut, quem ad modum Numa divini auctor iuris fuisset, ita Servium conditorem omnis in civitate discriminis ordinumque, quibus inter gradus dignitatis fortunaeque 15 aliquid interlucet, posteri fama ferrent. censum enim 5 instituit, rem saluberrimam tanto futuro imperio, ex quo belli pacisque munia non viritim ut ante, sed pro habitu pecuniarum fierent. tum classes centuriasque et hunc ordinem ex censu 20 discripsit vel paci decorum vel bello. ex iis, qui centum **43** milium aeris aut maiorem censum haberent, octoginta confecit centurias, quadragenas seniorum ac iuniorum: prima classis omnes 2 appellati; seniores ad urbis custodiam ut 25 praesto essent, iuvenes ut foris bella gererent. arma his imperata galea clipeum ocreae lorica, omnia ex aere—haec ut tegumenta corporis essent: tela in hostem hastaque et gladius. additae huic classi duae 3 fabrum centuriae, quae sine armis stipendia facerent; 30 datum munus ut machinas in bello ferrent. secunda 4 classis intra centum usque ad quinque et septuaginta milium censum instituta, et ex iis, senioribus

He institutes the Census;

and redistributes the citizens according to property, upon a military basis of Classes and Centuries,

iunioribusque, viginti conscriptae centuriae. arma imperata scutum pro clipeo, et praeter loricam omnia eadem.
5 tertiae classis in quinquaginta milium censum esse voluit. totidem centuriae et haec, eodemque discrimine aetatium factae; nec de armis quicquam mutatum, ocreae tantum 5
6 ademptae. in quarta classe census quinque et viginti milium; totidem centuriae factae; arma mutata, nihil
7 praeter hastam et verutum datum. quinta classis aucta, centuriae triginta factae. fundas lapidesque missiles hi secum gerebant. in his accensi, cornicines tubicines- 10
8 que in tres centurias distributi. undecim milibus haec classis censebatur. hoc minor census reliquam multitudinem habuit: inde una centuria facta est immunis militia. ita pedestri exercitu ornato distributoque equitum ex primoribus civitatis duodecim scripsit centurias. 15
9 sex item alias centurias, tribus ab Romulo institutis, sub isdem, quibus inauguratae erant, nominibus fecit. ad equos emendos dena milia aeris ex publico data, et quibus equos alerent, viduae attributae, quae bina milia aeris in annos singulos penderent. haec omnia in dites 20
10 a pauperibus inclinata onera. deinde est honos additus:

increasing at once the burdens and the privileges of the rich.

non enim, ut ab Romulo traditum ceteri servaverant reges, viritim suffragium eadem vi eodemque iure promisce omnibus datum est; sed gradus facti, ut neque exclusus 25 quisquam suffragio videretur, et vis omnis penes primores
11 civitatis esset. equites enim vocabantur primi, octoginta inde primae classis centuriae primum peditum vocabantur; ibi si variaret, quod raro incidebat, ut secundae classis vocarentur, nec fere umquam infra ita descende- 30
12 rent, ut ad infimos pervenirent. nec mirari oportet hunc ordinem, qui nunc est post expletas quinque et

triginta tribus duplicato earum numero centuriis iuniorum seniorumque, ad institutam ab Servio Tullio summam non convenire. quadrifariam enim urbe divisa regioni- 13 bus collibusque, qui habitabantur, partes eas tribus 5 appellavit, ut ego arbitror a tributo (nam eius quoque aequaliter ex censu conferendi ab eodem inita ratio est); neque eae tribus ad centuriarum distributionem numerumque quicquam pertinuere.

44 Censu perfecto, quem maturaverat metu legis de 10 incensis latae cum vinculorum minis mortisque, edixit, ut omnes cives Romani, equites peditesque, in suis quisque centuriis in campo Martio prima luce adessent. ibi 2 instructum exercitum omnem suovetaurilibus lustravit, 15 idque conditum lustrum appellatum, quia is censendo finis factus est. milia LXXX eo lustro civium censa dicuntur. adicit scriptorum antiquissimus Fabius Pictor eorum, qui arma ferre possent, eum numerum fuisse. ad eam multitudinem urbs quoque amplificanda visa 3 20 est. addit duos colles, Quirinalem Viminalemque; inde deinceps auget Esquilias, ibique ipse, ut loco dignitas fieret, habitat. aggere et fossis et muro circumdat urbem: ita pomerium profert. pomerium, verbi vim solam intuentes, postmoerium 4 25 interpretantur esse: est autem magis circamoerium locus, quem in condendis urbibus quondam Etrusci, qua murum ducturi erant, certis circa terminis inaugurato consecrabant, ut neque interiore parte aedificia moenibus continuarentur, quae nunc vulgo etiam coniungunt, et 30 extrinsecus puri aliquid ab humano cultu pateret soli. hoc spatium, quod neque habitari neque arari fas erat, 5 non magis quod post murum esset, quam quod murus

Purification of the army by the Suovetaurilia.

Extension of the city.

post id, pomerium Romani appellarunt, et in urbis incremento semper, quantum moenia processura erant, tantum termini hi consecrati proferebantur.

45 Aucta civitate magnitudine urbis, formatis omnibus domi et ad belli et ad pacis usus, ne semper 5 armis opes acquirerentur, consilio augere imperium conatus est, simul et aliquod addere urbi

The temple of Diana.

2 decus. iam tum erat inclitum Dianae Ephesiae fanum. id communiter a civitatibus Asiae factum fama ferebat. eum consensum deosque consociatos laudare mire Servius 10 inter proceres Latinorum, cum quibus publice privatimque hospitia amicitiasque de industria iunxerat. saepe iterando eadem perpulit tandem, ut Romae fanum Dianae populi Latini cum populo Romano facerent.

3 ea erat confessio caput rerum Romam esse, de quo 15 totiens armis certatum fuerat. id quamquam omissum iam ex omnium cura Latinorum ob rem totiens infeliciter temptatam armis videbatur, uni se ex Sabinis fors dare

4 visa est privato consilio imperii recuperandi. bos in Sabinis nata cuidam patri familiae dicitur miranda 20 magnitudine ac specie. fixa per multas aetates cornua in vestibulo templi Dianae monumentum ei fuere mira-

5 culo. habita, ut erat, res prodigii loco est; et cecinere vates, cuius civitatis eam cives Dianae immolassent, ibi

6 fore imperium; idque carmen pervenerat ad antistitem 25 fani Dianae, Sabinusque, ut prima apta dies sacrificio visa est, bovem Romam actam deducit ad fanum Dianae et ante aram statuit. ibi antistes Romanus, cum eum magnitudo victimae celebrata fama movisset, memor responsi Sabinum ita adloquitur: "quidnam tu hospes 30 paras?" inquit "inceste sacrificium Dianae facere? quin tu ante vivo perfunderis flumine? infima valle

praefluit Tiberis." religione tactus hospes, qui omnia, 7
ut prodigio responderet eventus, cuperet rite facta,
extemplo descendit ad Tiberim. interea Romanus im-
molat Dianae bovem. id mire gratum regi atque
5 civitati fuit.

Servius quamquam iam usu haud dubie regnum **46**
possederat, tamen, quia interdum iactari
voces a iuvene Tarquinio audiebat se iniussu
populi regnare, conciliata prius voluntate
10 plebis agro capto ex hostibus viritim diviso,
ausus est ferre ad populum, vellent iuberentne se
regnare; tantoque consensu, quanto haud quisquam
alius ante, rex est declaratus. neque ea res Tarquinio 2
spem adfectandi regni minuit: immo eo impensius, quia
15 de agro plebis adversa patrum voluntate
senserat agi, criminandi Servi apud patres
crescendique in curia sibi occasionem datam
ratus est, et ipse iuvenis ardentis animi et domi uxore
Tullia inquietum animum stimulante. tulit enim et 3
20 Romana regia sceleris tragici exemplum, ut taedio regum
maturior veniret libertas, ultimumque regnum esset,
quod scelere partum foret. hic L. Tarquinius (Prisci 4
Tarquini regis filius neposne fuerit, parum liquet; pluribus tamen auctoribus filium ediderim) fratrem habuerat
25 Arruntem Tarquinium, mitis ingenii iuvenem. his duo- 5
bus, ut ante dictum est, duae Tulliae regis filiae
nupserant, et ipsae longe dispares moribus. forte ita
inciderat, ne duo violenta ingenia matrimonio iunge-
rentur, fortuna credo populi Romani, quo diuturnius
30 Servi regnum esset, constituique civitatis mores possent.
angebatur ferox Tullia nihil materiae in viro neque ad 6
cupiditatem neque ad audaciam esse; tota in alterum

Servius' kingship is confirmed by a popular declaration.

The ambition of L. Tarquinius and Tullia minor.

aversa Tarquinium eum mirari, eum virum dicere ac regio sanguine ortum; spernere sororem, quod virum 7 nacta muliebri cessaret audacia. contrahit celeriter similitudo eos, ut fere fit malum malo aptissimum; sed initium turbandi omnia a femina ortum est. ea secretis 5 viri alieni adsuefacta sermonibus nullis verborum contumeliis parcere de viro ad fratrem, de sorore ad virum; et se rectius viduam et illum caelibem futurum fuisse contendere quam cum impari iungi, ut elanguescendum 8 aliena ignavia esset. si sibi eum, quo digna esset, di 10 dedissent virum, domi se prope diem visuram regnum fuisse, quod apud patrem videat. celeriter adulescentem 9 suae temeritatis implet. Arruns Tarquinius et Tullia minor prope continuatis funeribus cum domos vacuas novo matrimonio fecissent, iunguntur nuptiis magis non 15 prohibente Servio quam adprobante. tum vero in dies

47 infestior Tulli senectus, infestius coepit regnum esse.

Tullia incites Tarquinius to usurp the throne.

iam enim ab scelere ad aliud spectare mulier scelus, nec nocte nec interdiu virum conquiescere pati, ne gratuita praeterita 20 2 parricidia essent: non sibi defuisse, cui nupta diceretur, nec cum quo tacita serviret; defuisse, qui se regno dignum putaret, qui meminisset se esse Prisci Tarquini filium, qui habere quam sperare regnum 3 mallet. "si tu is es, cui nuptam esse me arbitror, et 25 virum et regem appello: sin minus, eo nunc peius mutata res est, quod istic cum ignavia est scelus. quin 4 accingeris? non tibi ab Corintho nec ab Tarquiniis, ut patri tuo, peregrina regna moliri necesse est; di te penates patriique et patris imago et domus regia et in 30 domo regale solium et nomen Tarquinium creat vocatque 5 regem. aut si ad haec parum est animi, quid frustraris civitatem? quid te ut regium iuvenem conspici sinis? facesse hinc Tarquinios aut Corinthum, devolvere retro ad stirpem, fratris similior quam patris." his aliisque 6 increpando iuvenem instigat, nec conquiescere ipsa 5 potest, si, cum Tanaquil, peregrina mulier, tantum moliri potuisset animo, ut duo continua regna viro ac deinceps genero dedisset, ipsa, regio semine orta, nullum momentum in dando adimendoque regno faceret. his 7 muliebribus instinctus furiis Tarquinius circumire et 10 prensare minorum maxime gentium patres, admonere paterni beneficii, ac pro eo gratiam repetere; adlicere donis iuvenes; cum de se ingentia pollicendo tum regis criminibus omnibus locis crescere. postremo, ut iam 8 agendae rei tempus visum est, stipatus agmine armatorum 15 in forum irrupit. inde omnibus perculsis pavore in regia sede pro curia sedens patres in curiam per praeconem ad regem Tarquinium citari iussit. convenere 9 extemplo, alii iam ante ad hoc praeparati, alii metu, ne non venisse fraudi esset, novitate ac miraculo attoniti et 20 iam de Servio actum rati. ibi Tarquinius maledicta ab 10 stirpe ultima orsus, servum servaque natum post mortem indignam parentis sui, non interregno, ut antea, inito, non comitiis habitis, non per suffragium populi, non auctoribus patribus, muliebri dono regnum occupasse. 25 ita natum, ita creatum regem, fautorem infimi generis 11 hominum, ex quo ipse sit, odio alienae honestatis ereptum primoribus agrum sordidissimo cuique divisisse; omnia onera, quae communia quondam fuerint, inclinasse 12 in primores civitatis; instituisse censum, ut insignis ad 30 invidiam locupletiorum fortuna esset, et parata unde, ubi vellet, egentissimis largiretur. huic orationi Servius **48** cum intervenisset trepido nuntio excitatus, extemplo a vestibulo curiae magna voce "quid hoc," inquit "Tarquini, rei est? qua tu audacia me vivo vocare ausus es patres aut in sede considere mea?" cum ille ferociter ad haec: se patris sui tenere sedem, multo quam servum 5 potiorem, filium regis, regni heredem, satis illum diu per licentiam eludentem insultasse dominis; clamor ab utriusque fautoribus oritur, et concursus populi fiebat in curiam, apparebatque regnaturum qui vicisset. tum Tarquinius, necessitate iam etiam ipsa cogente ultima 10 audere, multo et aetate et viribus validior medium arripit Servium, elatumque e curia in inferiorem partem per gradus deiecit; inde ad cogendum senatum in curiam rediit. fit fuga regis apparitorum atque comitum. ipse prope exsanguis ab iis, qui missi ab Tarquinio fugientem 15 consecuti erant, interficitur. creditur, quia non abhorret a cetero scelere, admonitu Tulliae id factum. carpento certe, id quod satis constat, in forum invecta nec reverita coetum virorum evocavit virum e curia, regemque prima appellavit. a quo facessere 20 iussa ex tanto tumultu cum se domum reciperet, pervenissetque ad summum Cuprium vicum, ubi Dianium nuper fuit, flectenti carpentum dextra in Vrbium clivum, ut in collem Esquiliarium eveheretur, restitit pavidus atque inhibuit frenos is qui iumenta 25 agebat, iacentemque dominae Servium trucidatum ostendit. foedum inhumanumque inde traditur scelus monumentoque locus est: Sceleratum vicum vocant, quo amens agitantibus furiis sororis ac viri Tullia per patris corpus carpentum egisse fertur, partemque 30 sanguinis ac caedis paternae cruento vehiculo contaminata ipsa respersaque tulisse

Servius protests, but is ejected from the Senate-house, and slain.

Tullia congratulates her husband,

and drives over her father's body.

[XLI—XLVIII. *The reign of Servius Tullius.*]

ad penates suos virique sui, quibus iratis malo regni principio similes prope diem exitus sequerentur.

Servius Tullius regnavit annos IIII et XL ita, ut 8 bono etiam moderatoque succedenti regi difficilis aemu-5 latio esset. ceterum id quoque ad gloriam accessit, quod cum illo simul iusta ac legitima regna occiderunt. id ipsum tam mite ac tam moderatum imperium tamen, 9 quia unius esset, deponere eum in animo habuisse quidam auctores sunt, ni scelus intestinum liberandae 10 patriae consilia agitanti intervenisset.

[XLIX—LX. *The reign of Tarquinius Superbus.*]

The tyranny of Tarquinius.

Inde L. Tarquinius regnare occepit, cui Superbo **49** cognomen facta indiderunt, quia socerum gener sepultura prohibuit, Romulum quoque insepultum perisse dictitans; primoresque patrum, quos 2 15 Servi rebus favisse credebat, interfecit: conscius deinde male quaerendi regni ab se ipso adversus se exemplum capi posse, armatis corpus circumsaepsit. neque enim 3 ad ius regni quicquam praeter vim habebat, ut qui neque populi iussu neque auctoribus patribus regnaret. eo 4 20 accedebat, ut in caritate civium nihil spei reponenti metu regnum tutandum esset. quem ut pluribus incuteret, cognitiones capitalium rerum sine consiliis per se solus exercebat, perque eam causam occidere, in 5 exsilium agere, bonis multare poterat non suspectos modo 25 aut invisos, sed unde nihil aliud quam praedam sperare posset. praecipue ita patrum numero imminuto statuit 6 nullos in patres legere, quo contemptior paucitate ipsa ordo esset, minusque per se nihil agi indignarentur. hic enim regum primus traditum a prioribus morem de omnibus senatum consulendi solvit, domesticis consiliis rem publicam administravit, bellum pacem foedera societates per se ipse cum quibus voluit iniussu populi 8 ac senatus fecit diremitque. Latinorum sibi maxime gentem conciliabat, ut peregrinis quoque opibus tutior 5 inter cives esset, neque hospitia modo cum primoribus 9 eorum sed adfinitates quoque iungebat. Octavio Mamilio Tusculano (is longe princeps Latini nominis erat, si famae credimus, ab Vlixe deaque Circa oriundus), ei Mamilio filiam nuptum dat, perque eas nuptias multos 10 sibi cognatos amicosque eius conciliat.

50 Iam magna Tarquini auctoritas inter Latinorum proceres erat, cum in diem certam ut ad lucum Ferentinae conveniant indicit: esse quae agere de rebus communibus velit. 15 2 conveniunt frequentes prima luce. ipse Tarquinius diem quidem servavit, sed paulo ante quam sol occideret venit. multa ibi toto die in 3 concilio variis iactata sermonibus erant. Turnus Herdonius ab Aricia ferociter in absentem Tarquinium erat 20 invectus: haud mirum esse Superbo inditum Romae cognomen (iam enim ita clam quidem mussitantes, volgo tamen eum appellabant); an quicquam superbius 4 esse quam ludificari sic omne nomen Latinum? principibus longe a domo excitis ipsum, qui concilium 25 indixerit, non adesse. temptari profecto patientiam, ut, 5 si iugum acceperint, obnoxios premat. cui enim non apparere, adfectare eum imperium in Latinos? quod si sui bene crediderint cives, aut si creditum illud et non raptum parricidio sit, credere et Latinos, quamquam ne 30 6 sic quidem alienigenae, debere: sin suos eius paeniteat, quippe qui alii super alios trucidentur, exsulatum eant,

At a conference of Latin chiefs, Turnus of Aricia protests against the absent Tarquinius.

bona amittant, quid spei melioris Latinis portendi? si se audiant, domum suam quemque inde abituros neque magis observaturos diem concilii quam ipse, qui indixerit, observet. haec atque alia eodem pertinentia seditiosus 7
5 facinerosusque homo iisque artibus opes domi nactus cum maxime dissereret, intervenit Tarquinius. is finis 8 orationi fuit. aversi omnes ad Tarquinium salutandum; qui silentio facto monitus a proximis, ut purgaret se, quod id temporis venisset, disceptatorem ait se sumptum
10 inter patrem et filium cura reconciliandi eos in gratiam moratum esse; et quia ea res exemisset illum diem, postero die acturum quae constituisset. ne id quidem 9 ab Turno tulisse tacitum ferunt; dixisse enim nullam breviorem esse cognitionem quam inter patrem et filium,
15 paucisque transigi verbis posse: ni pareat patri, habiturum infortunium esse. haec Aricinus in regem Romanum **51** increpans ex concilio abiit. quam rem Tarquinius aliquanto quam videbatur aegrius ferens confestim Turno necem machinatur,

Tarquinius plots his destruction,

20 ut eundem terrorem, quo civium animos domi oppresserat, Latinis iniceret. et quia pro imperio palam 2 interfici non poterat, oblato falso crimine insontem oppressit. per adversae factionis quosdam Aricinos servum Turni auro corrupit, in deversorium eius vim
25 magnam gladiorum inferri clam sineret. ea cum una 3 nocte perfecta essent, Tarquinius paulo ante lucem accitis ad se principibus Latinorum quasi re nova perturbatus, moram suam hesternam, velut deorum quadam providentia illatam, ait saluti sibi atque illis
30 fuisse. ab Turno dici sibi et primoribus populorum 4 parari necem, ut Latinorum solus imperium teneat. adgressurum fuisse hesterno die in concilio; dilatam

rem esse, quod auctor concilii afuerit, quem maxime
5 peteret. inde illam absentis insectationem esse natam,
quod morando spem destituerit. non dubitare, si vera
deferantur, quin prima luce, ubi ventum in concilium sit,
instructus cum coniuratorum manu armatusque venturus 5
6 sit. dici gladiorum ingentem esse numerum ad eum
convectum. id vanum necne sit, extemplo sciri posse.
7 rogare eos, ut inde secum ad Turnum veniant. suspectam
fecit rem et ingenium Turni ferox et oratio hesterna et
mora Tarquini, quod videbatur ob eam differri caedes 10
potuisse. eunt inclinatis quidem ad credendum animis,
tamen nisi gladiis deprehensis cetera vana existimaturi.
8 ubi est eo ventum, Turnum ex somno excitatum circumsistunt custodes; comprehensisque servis, qui caritate
domini vim parabant, cum gladii abditi ex omnibus locis 15
deverticuli protraherentur, enimvero manifesta res visa,
iniectaeque Turno catenae; et confestim Latinorum
9 concilium magno cum tumultu advocatur. ibi tam atrox
invidia orta est gladiis in medio positis, ut indicta causa
novo genere leti deiectus ad caput aquae Ferentinae 20
crate superne iniecta saxisque congestis mergeretur.
52 revocatis deinde ad concilium Latinis Tarquinius col-
laudatisque, qui Turnum novantem res pro manifesto
2 parricidio merita poena adfecissent, ita verba fecit: posse
quidem se vetusto iure agere, quod, cum 25
omnes Latini ab Alba oriundi sint, in eo
foedere teneantur, quo ab Tullo res omnis
Albana cum coloniis suis in Romanum
3 cesserit imperium; ceterum se utilitatis id magis omnium
causa censere, ut renovetur id foedus, secundaque potius 30
fortuna populi Romani ut participes Latini fruantur,
quam urbium excidia vastationesque agrorum, quas Anco

and persuades the Latins to renew the treaty with Rome,

prius, patre deinde suo regnante perpessi sint, semper aut exspectent aut patiantur. haud difficulter persuasum 4 Latinis, quamquam in eo foedere superior Romana res erat. ceterum et capita nominis Latini stare ac sentire 5 cum rege videbant, et Turnus sui cuique periculi, si adversatus esset, recens erat documentum. ita renovatum 5 foedus, indictumque iunioribus Latinorum, ut ex foedere die certa ad lucum Ferentinae armati frequentes adessent. qui ubi ad edictum 6 10 Romani regis ex omnibus populis convenere, ne ducem suum neve secretum imperium propriave signa haberent, miscuit manipulos ex Latinis Romanisque, ut ex binis singulos faceret binosque ex singulis; ita geminatis manipulis centuriones imposuit.

securing thereby an increase of the army.

15 Nec, ut iniustus in pace rex, ita dux belli pravus **53** fuit: quin ea arte aequasset superiores reges, ni degeneratum in aliis huic quoque decori offecisset. is primus Volscis bellum in 2 ducentos amplius post suam aetatem annos 20 movit, Suessamque Pometiam ex his vi cepit. ubi cum 3 divendita praeda quadraginta talenta argenti refecisset, concepit animo eam amplitudinem Iovis templi, quae digna deum hominumque rege, quae Romano imperio, quae ipsius etiam loci maiestate esset. captivam pecu-25 niam in aedificationem eius templi seposuit.

A capable general, Tarquinius engages in war with the Volsci.

Excepit deinde eum lentius spe bellum, quo Gabios 4 propinquam urbem, nequiquam vi adortus, cum obsidendi quoque urbem spes pulso a moe ibus adempta esset, postremo minime 30 arte Romana, fraude ac dolo, adgressus est. nam cum velut posito bello fundamentis templi faciendis 5 aliisque urbanis operibus intentum se esse simularet,

His youngest son Sextus treacherously wins influence at Gabii;

[XLIX—LX. *The reign of Tarquinius Superbus.*]

Sextus filius eius, qui minimus ex tribus erat, transfugit ex composito Gabios, patris in se saevitiam intolerabilem 6 conquerens: iam ab alienis in suos vertisse superbiam, et liberorum quoque eum frequentiae taedere, ut quam in curia solitudinem fecerit, domi quoque faciat, ne 5 7 quam stirpem, ne quem heredem regni relinquat. se quidem inter tela et gladios patris elapsum nihil usquam sibi tutum nisi apud hostes L. Tarquini credidisse. nam ne errarent, manere iis bellum, quod positum simuletur, et per occasionem eum incautos invasurum. 10 8 quod si apud eos supplicibus locus non sit, pererraturum se omne Latium, Volscosque se inde et Aequos et Hernicos petiturum, donec ad eos perveniat, qui a patrum crudelibus atque impiis suppliciis tegere liberos 9 sciant. forsitan etiam ardoris aliquid ad bellum armaque 15 se adversus superbissimum regem ac ferocissimum popu- 10 lum inventurum. cum, si nihil morarentur, infensus ira porro inde abiturus videretur, benigne ab Gabinis excipitur. vetant mirari, si, qualis in cives, qualis in 11 socios, talis ad ultimum in liberos esset. in se ipsum 20 postremo saeviturum, si alia desint. sibi vero gratum adventum eius esse, futurumque credere brevi, ut illo adiuvante a portis Gabinis sub Romana moenia bellum

54 transferatur. inde in consilia publica adhiberi. ubi cum de aliis rebus adsentire se veteribus 25 Gabinis diceret, quibus eae notiores essent; ipse identidem belli auctor esse, et in eo sibi praecipuam prudentiam adsumere, quod utriusque populi vires nosset, sciretque invisam profecto superbiam regiam civibus esse, quam ferre ne liberi quidem potuis- 30 2 sent. ita cum sensim ad rebellandum primores Gabinorum incitaret, ipse cum promptissimis iuvenum praedatum

receives the chief command there;

atque in expeditiones iret, et dictis factisque omnibus ad fallendum instructis vana accresceret fides, dux ad ultimum belli legitur. ibi cum inscia multitudine, quid 3 ageretur, proelia parva inter Romam Gabiosque fierent, 5 quibus plerumque Gabina res superior esset, tum certatim summi infimique Gabinorum Sex. Tarquinium dono deum sibi missum ducem credere. apud milites vero 4 obeundo pericula ac labores pariter, praedam munifice largiendo tanta caritate esse, ut non pater Tarquinius 10 potentior Romae quam filius Gabiis esset. itaque 5 postquam satis virium collectum ad omnes conatus videbat, tum ex suis unum sciscitatum Romam ad patrem mittit, quidnam se facere vellet, quando quidem, ut omnia unus per se Gabiis posset, ei di dedissent. 15 huic nuntio, quia, credo, dubiae fidei videbatur, nihil 6 voce responsum est. rex velut deliberabundus in hortum aedium transit sequente nuntio filii; ibi inambulans tacitus summa papaverum capita dicitur baculo decussisse. interrogando exspectandoque responsum nuntius fessus, 7 20 ut re imperfecta, redit Gabios, quae dixerit ipse quaeque viderit, refert: seu ira seu odio seu superbia insita ingenio nullam eum vocem emisisse. Sexto ubi, quid 8 vellet parens, quidve praeciperet tacitis ambagibus, patuit, primores civitatis criminando alios apud populum, alios sua ipsos 25 invidia opportunos interemit. multi palam, quidam, in quibus minus speciosa criminatio erat futura, clam interfecti. patuit quibusdam volentibus fuga, aut 9 in exsilium acti sunt, absentiumque bona iuxta atque 30 interemptorum divisui fuere. largitiones inde praedaeque; et dulcedine privati commodi sensus malorum publicorum adimi, donec orba consilio auxilioque Gabina

removes the leading citizens, and delivers Gabii to his father.

res regi Romano sine ulla dimicatione in manum traditur.

55 Gabiis receptis Tarquinius pacem cum Aequorum gente fecit, foedus cum Tuscis renovavit. inde ad negotia urbana animum convertit; 5 quorum erat primum, ut Iovis templum in monte Tarpeio monumentum regni sui nominisque relinqueret: Tarquinios reges ambos, patrem vovisse, filium 2 perfecisse. et ut libera a ceteris religionibus area esset tota Iovis templique eius, quod inaedificaretur, exaugurare 10 fana sacellaque statuit, quae aliquot ibi a T. Tatio rege primum in ipso discrimine adversus Romulum pugnae 3 vota, consecrata inaugurataque postea fuerant. inter principia condendi huius operis movisse numen ad indicandam tanti imperii molem traditur deos; nam cum 15 omnium sacellorum exaugurationes admitterent aves, in 4 Termini fano non addixere. idque omen auguriumque ita acceptum est, non motam Termini sedem unumque eum deorum non evocatum sacratis sibi finibus firma 5 stabiliaque cuncta portendere. hoc perpetuitatis auspicio 20 accepto secutum aliud magnitudinem imperii portendens prodigium est: caput humanum integra facie aperientibus 6 fundamenta templi dicitur apparuisse, quae visa species haud per ambages arcem eam imperii caputque rerum fore portendebat; idque ita cecinere vates, quique in 25 urbe erant, quosque ad eam rem consultandam ex Etruria acciverant. augebatur ad impensas regis animus. 7 itaque Pomptinae manubiae, quae perducendo ad culmen operi destinatae erant, vix in fundamenta suppeditavere. 8 eo magis Fabio, praeterquam quod antiquior 30 est, crediderim quadraginta ea sola talenta 9 fuisse, quam Pisoni, qui quadraginta milia

The temple of Jupiter is begun,

with great expenditure of treasure

pondo argenti seposita in eam rem scribit, quippe summam pecuniae neque ex unius tum urbis praeda sperandam, et nullius ne horum quidem magnificentia operum fundamenta non exsuperaturam. intentus per- **56**
5 ficiendo templo fabris undique ex Etruria accitis non pecunia solum ad id publica est usus, sed operis etiam ex plebe. qui cum haud parvus et ipse militiae adderetur labor, minus tamen plebs gravabatur se templa deum exaedificare manibus
10 suis, quam postquam et ad alia, ut specie minora sic 2 laboris aliquanto maioris, traducebantur opera, foros in circo faciendos cloacamque maximam, receptaculum omnium purgamentorum urbis, sub terram agendam; quibus duobus operibus vix nova haec magnificentia
15 quicquam adaequare potuit. his laboribus exercita plebe, 3 quia et urbi multitudinem, ubi usus non esset, oneri rebatur esse, et colonis mittendis occupari latius imperii fines volebat, Signiam Circeiosque colonos misit, praesidia urbi futura terra marique.

and of labour.

20 Haec agenti portentum terribile visum: anguis ex 4 columna lignea elapsus cum terrorem fugamque in regia fecisset, ipsius regis non tam subito pavore perculit pectus quam anxiis implevit curis. itaque cum ad publica pro- 5
25 digia Etrusci tantum vates adhiberentur, hoc velut domestico exterritus visu Delphos ad maxime inclitum in terris oraculum mittere statuit. neque re- 6 sponsa sortium ulli alii committere ausus duos filios per ignotas ea tempestate terras, ignotiora maria, in Graeciam
30 misit. Titus et Arruns profecti. comes iis additus L. 7 Iunius Brutus, Tarquinia, sorore regis, natus, iuvenis longe alius ingenio, quam cuius simulationem induerat.

On account of a portent the king sends his sons, with Brutus, to Delphi.

is cum primores civitatis in quibus fratrem suum ab avunculo interfectum audisset, neque in animo suo quicquam regi timendum neque in fortuna concupiscendum relinquere statuit, contemptuque tutus esse, ubi in iure
8 parum praesidii esset. ergo ex industria factus ad 5 imitationem stultitiae cum se suaque praedae esse regi sineret, Bruti quoque haud abnuit cognomen, ut sub eius obtentu cognominis liberator ille populi Romani
9 animus latens opperiretur tempora sua. is tum ab Tarquiniis ductus Delphos, ludibrium verius quam 10 comes, aureum baculum inclusum corneo cavato ad id baculo tulisse donum Apollini dicitur, per ambages
10 effigiem ingenii sui. quo postquam ventum est, perfectis patris mandatis cupido incessit animos iuvenum sciscitandi, ad quem eorum regnum Romanum esset venturum. 15 ex infimo specu vocem redditam ferunt: "imperium summum Romae habebit qui vestrum primus, o iuvenes,
11 osculum matri tulerit." Tarquinius Sextus, qui Romae relictus fuerat, ut ignarus responsi expersque imperii esset, rem summa ope taceri iubent; ipsi inter se, uter 20 prior, cum Romam redissent, matri osculum daret, sorti
12 permittunt. Brutus alio ratus spectare Pythicam vocem, velut si prolapsus cecidisset, terram osculo contigit, scilicet quod ea communis mater omnium mortalium
13 esset. reditum inde Romam, ubi adversus Rutulos 25 bellum summa vi parabatur.

57 Ardeam Rutuli habebant, gens, ut in ea regione atque in ea aetate, divitiis praepollens. eaque ipsa causa belli fuit, quod rex Romanus cum ipse ditari exhaustus magnificentia 30 publicorum operum, tum praeda delenire popularium
2 animos studebat, praeter aliam superbiam regno infestos

Rutulian War. The siege of Ardea,

etiam quod se in fabrorum ministerio ac servili tam diu habitos opere ab rege indignabantur. temptata res est, si primo impetu capi Ardea posset. ubi id parum 3 processit, obsidione munitionibusque coepti premi hostes. 5 in his stativis, ut fit longo magis quam acri bello, satis 4 liberi commeatus erant, primoribus tamen magis quam militibus; regii quidem iuvenes interdum otium conviviis 5 comissationibusque inter se terebant. forte potantibus 6 his apud Sex. Tarquinium, ubi et Collatinus cenabat 10 Tarquinius Egerii filius, incidit de uxoribus mentio; suam quisque laudare miris modis. inde certamine 7 accenso Collatinus negat verbis opus esse, paucis id quidem horis posse sciri, quantum ceteris praestet Lucretia sua. "quin, si vigor iuventae inest, conscendimus equos, 15 invisimusque praesentes nostrarum ingenia? id cuique spectatissimum sit, quod necopinato viri adventu occurrerit oculis." incaluerant vino. "age sane!" omnes. citatis 8 equis avolant Romam. quo cum primis se intendentibus 20 tenebris pervenissent, pergunt inde Collatiam, ubi 9 Lucretiam haudquaquam ut regias nurus, quas in convivio luxuque cum aequalibus viderant tempus terentes, sed nocte sera deditam lanae inter lucubrantes ancillas in medio aedium sedentem inveniunt. muliebris certaminis 10 25 laus penes Lucretiam fuit. adveniens vir Tarquiniique excepti benigne; victor maritus comiter invitat regios iuvenes. ibi Sex. Tarquinium mala libido Lucretiae per vim stuprandae capit; cum forma tum spectata castitas incitat. et tum quidem ab nocturno iuvenali ludo in 11 30 castra redeunt.

whence the Tarquinii ride on a surprise visit to their wives.

58 Paucis interiectis diebus Sex. Tarquinius inscio Collatino cum comite uno Collatiam venit. ubi exceptus benigne ab ignaris consilii cum post cenam in hospitale cubiculum deductus esset, amore ardens, postquam satis tuta circa sopitique omnes videbantur, stricto gladio ad dormientem Lucretiam venit, sinistraque manu mulieris pectore oppresso "tace Lucretia" inquit; "Sex. Tarquinius sum; 3 ferrum in manu est, moriere, si emiseris vocem." cum pavido ex somno mulier nullam opem, prope mortem imminentem videret, tum Tarquinius fateri amorem, orare, miscere precibus minas, versare in omnes partes mulie- 4 brem animum. ubi obstinatam videbat et ne mortis quidem metu inclinari, addit ad metum dedecus; cum mortua iugulatum servum nudum positurum ait, 5 ut in sordido adulterio necata dicatur. quo terrore cum vicisset obstinatam pudicitiam violatrix libido, profectusque inde Tarquinius ferox expugnato decore muliebri esset, Lucretia maesta tanto malo nuntium Romam eundem ad patrem Ardeamque ad virum mittit, ut cum singulis fidelibus amicis veniant: ita facto matu- 6 ratoque opus esse; rem atrocem incidisse. Spurius Lucretius cum P. Valerio Volesi filio, Collatinus cum L. Iunio Bruto venit, cum quo forte Romam rediens ab nuntio uxoris erat conventus. Lucretiam sedentem maestam in cubiculo inveniunt. adventu suorum la- 7 crimae obortae. quaerentique viro "satin salve?" "minime" inquit: "quid enim salvi est mulieri amissa pudicitia? vestigia viri alieni, Collatine, in lecto sunt tuo. ceterum corpus est tantum violatum, animus insons: mors testis erit. sed date dexteras fidemque haud 8 impune adultero fore. Sex. est Tarquinius, qui hostis pro hospite priore nocte vi armatus mihi sibique, si vos 9 viri estis, pestiferum hinc abstulit gaudium." dant

Sextus Tarquinius' deed of shame.

ordine omnes fidem; consolantur aegram animi avertendo noxam ab coacta in auctorem delicti: mentem peccare non corpus, et unde consilium afuerit, culpam abesse. "vos" inquit "videritis, quid illi debeatur: ego 10
5 me etsi peccato absolvo, supplicio non libero; nec ulla deinde impudica Lucretiae exemplo vivet." cultrum, 11 quem sub veste abditum habebat, eum in corde defigit, 12 prolapsaque in vulnus moribunda cecidit. conclamat vir paterque. Brutus illis luctu occupatis cultrum ex **59**
10 vulnere Lucretiae extractum manante cruore prae se tenens "per hunc" inquit "castissimum ante regiam iniuriam sanguinem iuro, vosque, di, testes facio, me L. Tarquinium Superbum cum scelerata coniuge et omni liberorum
15 stirpe ferro igni, quacumque dehinc vi possim, exsecuturum, nec illos nec alium quemquam regnare Romae passurum." cultrum deinde Collatino tradit, inde Lu- 2 cretio ac Valerio, stupentibus miraculo rei, unde novum in Bruti pectore ingenium. ut praeceptum erat, iurant;
20 totique ab luctu versi in iram Brutum, iam inde ad expugnandum regnum vocantem, secuntur ducem. elatum 3 domo Lucretiae corpus in forum deferunt, concientque miraculo, ut fit, rei novae atque indignitate homines. pro se quisque scelus regium ac vim queruntur. movet 4
25 cum patris maestitia, tum Brutus castigator lacrimarum atque inertium querellarum auctorque, quod viros, quod Romanos deceret, arma capiendi adversus hostilia ausos. ferocissimus quisque iuvenum cum armis voluntarius 5 adest, sequitur et cetera iuventus. inde pari praesidio
30 relicto Collatiae ad portas, custodibusque datis, ne quis eum motum regibus nuntiaret, ceteri armati duce Bruto Romam profecti. ubi eo ventum est, quacumque incedit 6

Brutus rouses the Romans against the reigning house.

armata multitudo, pavorem ac tumultum facit. rursus ubi anteire primores civitatis vident, quidquid sit, haud
7 temere esse rentur. nec minorem motum animorum Romae tam atrox res facit, quam Collatiae fecerat. ergo ex omnibus locis urbis in forum curritur. quo 5 simul ventum est, praeco ad tribunum Celerum, in quo tum magistratu forte Brutus erat, populum advocavit.
8 ibi oratio habita nequaquam eius pectoris ingeniique, quod simulatum ad eam diem fuerat, de vi ac libidine Sex. Tarquinii, de stupro infando Lucretiae et miserabili 10 caede, de orbitate Tricipitini, cui morte filiae causa
9 mortis indignior ac miserabilior esset. addita superbia ipsius regis miseriaeque et labores plebis in fossas cloacasque exhauriendas demersae: Romanos homines, victores omnium circa populorum, opifices ac lapicidas 15
10 pro bellatoribus factos. indigna Servi Tulli regis memorata caedis et invecta corpore patris nefando vehiculo
11 filia, invocatique ultores parentum di. his atrocioribusque credo aliis, quae praesens rerum indignitas haudquaquam relatu scriptoribus facilia subicit, memo- 20 ratis incensam multitudinem perpulit, ut imperium regi abrogaret, exsulesque esse iuberet L. Tarquinium cum
12 coniuge ac liberis. ipse iunioribus, qui ultro nomina dabant, lectis armatisque ad concitandum inde adversus regem exercitum Ardeam in castra est profectus; impe- 25 rium in urbe Lucretio, praefecto urbis iam ante ab rege
13 instituto, relinquit. inter hunc tumultum Tullia domo profugit execrantibus quacumque incedebat invocantibusque parentum furias viris mulieribusque.

60 Harum rerum nuntiis in castra perlatis cum re nova 30 trepidus rex pergeret Romam ad comprimendos motus, flexit viam Brutus (senserat enim adventum), ne obvius fieret; eodemque fere tempore diversis itineribus Brutus Ardeam, Tarquinius Romam venerunt. Tarquinio clau- 2 sae portae exsiliumque indictum; liberatorem urbis laeta castra accepere, exactique inde liberi regis. duo patrem 5 secuti sunt, qui exsulatum Caere in Etruscos ierunt; Sextus Tarquinius Gabios tamquam in suum regnum profectus ab ultoribus veterum simultatium, quas sibi ipse caedibus rapinisque concierat, est interfectus.

Banishment of the Tarquinii.

10 L. Tarquinius Superbus regnavit annos quinque et 3 viginti. regnatum Romae ab condita urbe ad liberatam annos ducentos quadraginta quattuor. duo 4 consules inde comitiis centuriatis a praefecto urbis ex commentariis Servi Tulli creati sunt, L. Iunius 15 Brutus et L. Tarquinius Collatinus.

Election of the first consuls.

NOTES

[References are made in the notes to 'Roby,' i.e. the School Latin Grammar of H. J. Roby (stereotyped edition); and to 'W.-M.,' i.e. to the 1908 edition of Book I. by W. Weissenborn and H. J. Müller.]

THE PREFACE.

p. 1. Analysis: (§ 1) *Will my history prove worth the making? I know not.* (§§ 2, 3) *Among rivals so numerous and so eminent, my name may be overshadowed and obscured; but what matter, if, in this labour of love, I may further the history of the Imperial Nation?* (§ 4) *It is true that the retrospect of seven centuries is an infinite task, and unattractive to many a modern reader:* (§ 5) *yet for myself it will bring its own reward in diverting attention from the troubles of to-day.*

(§ 6) *Prehistoric traditions I do not propose to support or to subvert:* (§ 7) *remote antiquity must be allowed a certain poetic licence, and the martial glory of the Imperial Nation may well justify a pedigree that dates from Mars.* (§§ 8, 9) *But, opinions apart, I would invite the student to contemplate the men and the measures of our Imperial history, the transition from the strictness of the past to the laxity of the present;* (§ 10) *for History teaches by types of good and ill.* (§§ 11, 12) *My experience tells me that the Roman state has avoided longer than the rest those evils of luxury and extravagance which waste its energies to-day. But mine be no key-note of complaint:* (§ 13) *rather let me begin my task with prayers to heaven for success.*

The first paragraph sets forth the literary and political environment of the author, the second, his historical attitude. The tone is extremely modest throughout, free at once from pedantry, flattery, and partisanship. See the Introduction, §§ 1, 2.

1 § 1. **facturusne...sim**] As Quintilian has remarked (*Inst. Or.* IX. 4. 74), *T. Livius hexametri exordio coepit.*

operae pretium] 'something worth the trouble.' In c. 24. 6 *operae* occurs alone, but see note there.

2 **res...perscripserim**] 'succeed in completing the history': subjunctive, because dependent on a subjunctive, cf. Roby § 760 (2).

3 **ausim**] 'would I dare.' In origin this form seems to be an aorist optative (cf. 18. 9 *adclarassis*): it occurs again in Livy, in negative sentences. The ordinary perf. subj. is not common in apodosis: but we may compare VII. 10. 2 *iniussu tuo, imperator, extra ordinem numquam pugnaverim, non si certam victoriam videam*, and the use in assertions qualified by an implied condition, e.g. IX. 24. 7 *hoc quidem ascensu vel tres armati quamlibet multitudinem arcuerint.*

3 § **2. veterem...vulgatam**] 'old...over-done': 'stale...stereotyped.'

4 **rem**] 'the subject.'

dum...credunt] The phrase explains *veterem...vulgatam* in reverse order. *dum* has a quasi-causal sense here, 'as,' 'inasmuch as.'

novi semper scriptores] 'fresh authors in continual succession.' Notice the position of the adverb, which Livy frequently adopts, more especially in descriptions of time and place. Sometimes (as here) the adverb has almost the force of an adjective, as epithet or predicate (cf. the use of adverbs with the article in Greek, e.g. ἡ ἄνω πόλις): sometimes it serves to emphasize the preceding word. This looser use of adverbs is a characteristic of Silver Latin.

5 **in rebus**] 'subjects,' 'matter' as opposed to *arte* 'style,' 'manner.'

aliquid adlaturos] a phrase for an original contribution to a subject: cf. Cic. *de Off.* I. 44. 155 *quidquid ad rem publicam attulimus, si modo aliquid attulimus.*

7 § **3. memoriae**] dat. after *consuluisse* ('to have laboured for the historical record'): the word serves to break an awkward succession of genitives.

principis...populi] 'the Imperial Nation.'

8 **et ipsum**] (= καὶ αὐτόν) 'personally,' 'likewise,' more emphatic than *ipsum* alone would have been. Cicero uses *et ipse* rarely, Livy very often, e.g. 7. 4, 12. 3, 46. 2 in Book I. The phrase, usually found towards the end of a sentence, serves to couple a particular case or a personal climax with the remarks that have suggested or introduced it. Cf. Propertius, II. 16. 54 *deceptus quoniam flevit et ipse deus.*

9 **in...turba**] 'amid so vast a crowd of authors.' This is a common use of *in*, drawing attention to the circumstances, whether favourable or unfavourable: it may often be best rendered by an affirmative or adversative phrase. Cf. 17. 1 *in novo populo*; 17. 3 *in variis voluntatibus.*

fama] Cf. Martial's Preface to his first book of Epigrams—*mihi fama vilius constet et probetur in me novissimum ingenium.*

in obscuro] = *obscura*, but avoids assonance: Livy affects this use of *in* with a neuter adjective in predicates.

10 **nobilitate**] 'renown,' 'distinction'—of birth or authorship.

officient] 'obstruct,' 'obliterate': cf. Cic. *Tusc. D.* V. 32. 92 *offecerat videlicet apricanti.*

11 § **4**. **res**] 'my subject'; in other words, the Roman Empire, to which the two relative clauses seem properly to refer.

et] answered by *et legentium...*

immensi] 'infinite,' 'boundless,' in its literal sense, for Livy cannot foresee the extent to which his work will be developed.

ut quae...repetatur] 'implying as it does a retrospect of more than seven centuries.' The verb *repetere* means 'go back to seek,' and so 'trace from the beginning' (so again in l. 20 below): the English word 'research' is similar. *ut* (like *quippe*, *utpote*) gives a personal emphasis to the reason expressed by the relative clause; cf. 1. 5 *ut quibus... superesset.*

12 **et quae**] The relative pronoun is repeated, to indicate a different aspect of the subject—the growth of the Empire. The transition may be thus expressed: 'wherein a state, starting from slender beginnings, has grown until it is oppressed by its own immensity.'

15 **origines**] 'elements,' 'genesis.' Cato's work upon the early history of the Italian cities was so called; cf. Cic. *Planc.* 27. 66 *populi origines: libenter enim etiam verbo utor Catonis.* **proxima originibus**, 'the next stages.'

16 **festinantibus ad haec nova**] 'as they hurry on to these modern questions,' i.e. the civil wars. **iam pridem** probably goes with *conficiunt*; i.e. the troubles are still continuing, or scarcely over. The Preface thus seems to be a little earlier than the date of Book I. (i.e. 27—25 B.C.), as indicated by events mentioned in c. 19. 3 (see note). Not a few historians of the early Augustan age wrote monographs on certain characters and aspects of their own times, or memoirs of their own careers, and these works must often have caused a renewal of party feelings. From these reminiscences Livy seeks to dissociate himself by the study of Roman antiquity.

19 § **5**. **tot per annos**] More than 20, if we regard Caesar's invasion of Italy in 49 B.C. as the starting-point, and 28—7 B.C. as the date of this Preface.

20 **dum prisca...repeto**] i.e. *dum prisca illa* (as opposed to *haec nova*) *tota mente repeto*, 'in a whole-hearted study of that glorious past.'

21 **curae**] 'concern' i.e. 'ulterior motive,' 'partisanship'; alluding to the attitude of contemporary writers: see n. on l. 16 above.

22 **posset**] The tense refers to an anxiety which 'might have been,'

but is avoided by *omnis expers curae*: the emendation *possit* would indicate a prospective anxiety, which is not so effective. Livy is not describing a future, but a present state of mind.

23 § **6. ante...urbem]** 'before the foundation of the city in fact or fancy,' 'before the foundation was completed or contemplated': *ante conditam = ante quam condita est, ante condendam = ante quam conderetur*, i.e. the one anticipates the fact, the other the intention. W. compares XXI. 21. 8 *inter labores aut iam exhaustos aut mox exhauriendos*.

quae...traduntur] 'traditions.'

poeticis...monumentis] 'more appropriate to poetic fiction than to the genuine records of historical fact.' The adjective *decora* (with its two dependent datives, *fabulis* and *monumentis*) forms a second predicate.

25 **adfirmare...refellere]** 'support'...'subvert.'

26 § **7. antiquitati]** 'ancient story,' almost 'the prehistoric period.'

p. 2. 1 **humana divinis**, i.e. history and mythology.

augustiora] 'more imposing.'

2 **et ad deos referre auctores]** 'by a reference to divine authorship.' The whole sentence *si cui...auctores* is intended to lead up to what follows, from the general principle to the special case.

3 **ea...ut...patiantur]** 'such as to make the nations accept': a result, probably, not a hope, is here expressed. Rome's career of war was a justification to the world of this mythical connexion with the war-god. Notice the contrast here between *populus Romanus* and *gentes humanae*.

4 **cum...potissimum ferat]** 'when (or perhaps *cum* = 'although,' 'even when') they choose to declare Mars as the father of themselves and their founder': cf. 42. 4 *ut Servium conditorem...posteri fama ferrent*.

7 § **8. animadversa aut existimata]** 'regarded or reviewed.'

haud in magno...discrimine] 'I shall attach no great importance thereto,' lit. 'reckon as a great difference.' Cf. Virg. *Aen.* X. 108 *Tros Rutulusve fuat, nullo discrimine habebo*.

8 § **9. mihi]** 'I would have...' 'in my view.' The dat. is 'ethic,' i.e. it expresses the person interested in the statement, and helps to describe an ideal case: cf. Virg. *Georg.* I. 43 *depresso incipiat iam tum mihi taurus aratro ingemere*; Cic. *de Or.* II. 20 (§ 85) *oratorem...sit enim mihi tinctus litteris*.

pro se quisque] = *pro virili parte* (§ 3), 'according to his individual ability': the verb follows in the singular, emphasizing the individuality of each student. **intendat** 'concentrate.'

10 **domi militiaeque**] locatives, 'at home and abroad.' The two words are regularly used to express the distinction between internal and external affairs: so *imperium domi, imperium militiae*. Cf. 36. 6 *belli domique*.

11 **et partum et auctum**] 'acquired and advanced.'

labente...] The whole sentence is controlled by *sequatur animo*, and expresses stages of dissolution, by metaphors taken from building. Regularity (*disciplina*), the cement of character (*mores*), lapses (*labente*), and the first crack (*dissidentes primo*) is started: this gradually enlarges, and at last the structure collapses.

12 **dissidentis**] (acc. pl.) 'starting asunder': so the best MSS. The word is very rare and poetical, but may be justified in this poetical description: if *desidentes* (from *desīdo*) be read, it means 'subsiding.'

13 **ut**] 'how': the construction after *sequatur* is slightly changed.

15 **remedia**] Cf. XXXIV. 49. 3 *intermori vehementioribus, quam quae pati posset, remediis civitatem sinere.*

16 § **10. hoc...frugiferum**] 'The one preeminently healthful and fruitful characteristic of historical study is...'

17 **te...tibi...tuae**] Addressed to an imaginary reader, and so to the public.

omnis...documenta] 'lessons (examples) of every type': so *exemplis* below.

in illustri...monumento] 'set luminously upon record': the adjective expresses the result rather than the attribute, i.e. it is proleptic.

19 **quod imitere...vites**] 'models for imitation'...'for avoidance.'

foedum...exitu] 'foul in origin and consequence,' i.e. from beginning to end.

20 § **11. ceterum**] (= δ' οὖν) 'for the rest': to resume the main subject.

aut...aut] The first alternative is merely a foil to bring out the second.

sanctior] 'more moral.'

22 **in quam civitatem**] i.e. *civitas in quam*: a restatement of *res publica*.

23 **serae**] The adjective has a predicative force; cf. *primus*, 10. 5 *novissimum*, 16. 2 *sublimis*.

immigraverint] i.e. from Greece and the East, in this case.

25 **adeo**] 'for in truth,' 'as a matter of fact,' introduces an adequate reason for the assertion just made: cf. 9. 5; II. 27. 3 *movebant consulem haec: sed tergiversari res cogebat. adeo in alteram causam non collega solum praeceps ierat, sed omnis factio nobilium.* So *ita* often in Plautus,

e.g. *Most.* 996 *sum circum vectus: ita ubi nunc sim nescio*: cf. also *tanta* in c. 3. 1 of this book.

27 § **12. desiderium...omnia**] 'a craving for the ruin of oneself and one's environment by wilful waste.' *luxuria* is the spirit of extravagance which manifests itself in *luxus*. Tacitus tells the contrary tale of the Germans (*Germ.* 19): *nemo enim illic vitia ridet, nec corrumpere et corrumpi saeculum vocatur.*

29 **cum forsitan necessariae erunt**] *cum* is temporal, and answers *tum quidem*: *forsitan* expresses an afterthought, or parenthesis ('as perhaps they will be') to the sentence, and has no effect on the mood of *erunt*: nor has it in 53. 9 below, where it occurs at the head of a sentence in *oratio obliqua*. Cf. IX. 11. 13 *et illi quidem, forsitan et publica, sua certe liberata fide, ab Caudio in castra Romana inviolati redierunt*; Cic. *Fam.* I. 8. 2 *ut quibusdam forsitan videor* (where *forsitan* = 'and perhaps I do'); Sall. *Iug.* 114 *incertae ac forsitan paulo post interiturae vitae parcere*; Propertius, II. 15. 54 *forsitan includet crastina fata dies.* The use of *quamvis* with adjectives is similar.

ab initio...rei] 'at least from the beginning of this mighty undertaking.'

30 § **13. potius**] is renewed in **libentius**: 'far sooner, far more willingly would I have begun.'

31 **precationibus**] So Demosthenes begins his speech 'On the Crown' πρῶτον μέν, ὦ ἄνδρες 'Αθηναῖοι, τοῖς θεοῖς εὔχομαι πᾶσι καὶ πάσαις: and the Roman orators, as we see in several of Cicero's speeches, made similar appeals; so that Servius says (on *Aen.* XI. 301) *maiores nullam orationem nisi invocatis numinibus incohabant.*

33 **tantum**] So the best MSS.: some editors read *tanti*, which would make *orsis* a substantive (= 'beginnings'), a later usage except in the sense of 'words.'

CHAPTER I.

(On the traditions contained in chapters I.—VII. see Introduction, § 3.)

p. 3. 1 § **1. iam...omnium**] The phrase expresses both the transition from the Preface to the History, and the first point which Livy wishes to introduce, 'To begin at the beginning,'....

satis constat] 'it is commonly agreed' (as a tradition, not as a certainty).

in ceteros] qualified by **duobus**, 'in two cases.' The dat. after *abstinuisse* is unusual.

3 **Aeneae**] Various reasons were given for his escape—advocacy of peace, enmity towards Paris and Priam, betrayal of the city, covenant with the Greeks after the capture.

Antenori] He had entertained Menelaus and Odysseus when they came on an embassy (*Iliad* III. 203), and thus gained his salvation *vetusti iure hospitii*: his house was saved from pillage by a panther-skin hung before the door. As the traditional founder of Patavium (cf. Virgil, *Aeneid*, I. 242—9), the birthplace of Livy, he has a special claim to a place in this record. Tacitus (*Ann.* XVI. 21) mentions games at Patavium founded by Antenor.

5 **fuerunt**] *fuerint* might have been expected, under the influence of the *oratio obliqua*, introduced by *constat*, but *fuerunt* (in fact, all the clause from *et vetusti*) is Livy's own statement.

omne ius belli abstinuisse] 'waived the full right of war,' i.e. destruction of the men, enslavement of the women and children. Cf. Cicero, *de Off.* I. 11. 35 *parta autem victoria, conservandi ii qui non crudeles in bello, non immanes fuerunt.*

6 § **2**. **Enetum**] gen. pl. Livy gives here that account of the Veneti which is parallel to the Trojan traditions of early Rome: other authorities believed the Veneti to be connected with the Gallic tribe of the same name, while Herodotus (V. 9) regarded them as Illyrians. It is possible that the connection of Antenor and Trojans with this part of Italy represents (as in the case of Aeneas) a Pelasgian migration.

8 **Pylaemene**] He is mentioned as the leader of the Paphlagonians in Iliad II. 851, and as slain by Menelaus in V. 579. **ad Troiam**, 'by,' 'near Troy.'

9 § **3**. **Euganeis**] In the time of the elder Pliny they were still a separate people; and the hills between Patavium (Padua) and Verona are still known as Colli Euganei. Sidonius Apollinaris calls Livy's writings *Euganeae chartae.*

11 **in quem...locum...vocatur**] The relative has attracted its substantive into its own case: cf. Ter. *Eun.* 653 *eunuchum quem dedisti nobis, quas turbas dedit!* Virg. *Aen.* I. 573 *urbem quam statuo, vestra est.* See Roby, § 450.

12 **Troiano**] This dative is usual in the case of names, and is best explained as due to attraction. Servius says: *dicimus et 'nomen mihi est Cicero' et 'Ciceronis' et 'Ciceroni': melius tamen dativo.* Below in § 5, *Troia* is an instance of the nominative.

13 **universa**] 'as a whole.'

§ 4. **ab**] gives the occasion of the departure, implying both sequence and consequence (cf. ἐξ).

15 **ducentibus fatis**] Aeneas is always the 'Man of Destiny.'

in Macedoniam] i.e. to Aenea, on the west coast of Chalcidice.

17 **tenuisse**] intransitive, 'steered for': so elsewhere in Livy (e.g. XXXI. 45. 14 *Cassandream petentes, primo ad Mendin tenuere*), and in Ovid (e.g. *Met.* II. 140 *medio tutissimus ibis...inter utrumque tene*). Cf. Soph. *Phil.* 220 τίνες ποτ' εἰς γῆν τήνδε...κατέσχετε;

p. 4. 1 § 5. **ut quibus**] See n. on *ut quae*, Praef. 4.

ab immenso prope] For *ab* see n. above. *prope=fere*, an apology for the use of *immenso* in a figurative sense: the same adjective needs no apology in Praef. 4, where it has its literal meaning.

2 **superesset**] Most MSS. have *superessent*, which, if accepted, would be a construction to suit the sense, i.e. *nihil praeter arma et naves=arma et naves.*

4 **Aborigines**] The name suggests its own derivation from *ab origine*—ὥσπερ ἂν ἡμεῖς εἴποιμεν γενεάρχας ἢ πρωτογόνους, as Dionysius says (I. 10), or more simply οἱ ἀπ' ἀρχῆς. The usual Greek spelling of the name is Ἀβοριγῖνες, but a variant form Ἀβερριγῖνες (i.e. wanderers), is given by Dionysius. On the question of their identity, see the Introduction.

6 § 6. **inde**] 'from this point.' The first version is given in the *Aeneid* (last six books): Livy agrees with Virgil for the most part in this opening chapter.

8 § 7. **canerent**] Probably the subjunctive here is due to the *oratio obliqua*: but Livy affects it with *prius quam*, even where little or no notion of anticipation is implied. The verb is probably intransitive: 'sounded.'

9 **primores**] 'the front ranks.'

11 **profecti**] *essent* may be understood from the previous clause, or (better) the phrase *unde...profecti* may be taken as qualifying *exissent*. For the contracted form cf. 7. 7 *mugissent.*

13 § 8. **audierit**] This use of a primary tense in the midst of an *oratio obliqua*, and following historic tenses (*essent*, *exissent*), is an example of *repraesentatio*, or a reproduction of the tense of the *oratio recta*—in this case *audiit*. Livy frequently admits such variations from the hard and fast 'rule' of *oratio obliqua*: in all probability he desired to retain the tenses of the *oratio recta*, but was hampered by the limited tense-capacities of the subjunctive mood. This is the view of Dr R. S. Conway, set forth in a useful appendix to his edition of Book II., from which the following general principles are quoted:

A. *In passages of Oratio Obliqua in which Livy is using Primary Tenses after a past governing Verb, the Primary Tenses appear, as a rule, only where they are actually retained from the Oratio Recta;* i.e. (1) *all retainable Tenses are retained with great regularity; but* (2) *where a change of Tense is unavoidable (as in converting the Imperative and the Future of the Oratio Recta), there Livy's usage varies, but the Tense chosen is most often Secondary.*

B. (1) *The Subjunctives which depend directly upon the Main Verb which introduces the Oratio Obliqua, take the regular Sequence; thus, they are Secondary after a Past Tense, whether or not the Primary Tenses are retained in the body of the speech itself.*

(2) *Similarly the Imperfect Subjunctive which is regularly used to give a Past Command throws any Verbs that may depend upon it into Secondary Tenses; and this influence sometimes extends even into the next sentence.*

15 **condendaeque urbis locum**] a genitive of description: cf. 15. 6; 47. 8; 48. 9; IX. 45. 18 *oratores pacis petendae.* *urbi* is also read, in which case the dative expresses a notion of object or of 'work contemplated' (Roby § 481): cf. V. 54. 4 *urbi condendae locum elegerunt*; XXX. 22. 6 *locum condendo oppido ceperunt.*

nobilitatem] 'renown.'

16 **bello...paratum**] dat. of indirect object: cf. XXVI. 12. 13 *dixit se et Campanos paratos eruptioni fore.*

18 § **9. ictum**] Strictly speaking it was the victim, not the treaty, which was 'struck,' but the object of the action passes into the result: cf. 'strike (hands upon) a bargain.'

20 **penates deos**] 'household gods' (perhaps connected with *penus*, 'store-room': cf. *penetralia*). Livy thus admits a prehistoric origin for the very ancient rites of the Penates (and Vesta) at Lavinium, which every consul, dictator, and praetor, at the beginning and the end of his office, was bound to celebrate. Lavinium was in effect the religious metropolis of the Latin communities and of Rome, and retained its importance as such until the fall of paganism.

22 § **10. utique**] 'undoubtedly,' 'at any rate': implying previous uncertainty.

stabili...sede] 'in a sure and certain settlement': the two epithets are often found together.

finiendi erroris] objective genitive, after *spem.*

23 § **11. oppidum**] 'town': the *urbs* was yet to come.

25 **stirpis**] This alternative form for *stirps* (cf. *plebs* and *plebis*) occurs

again in 3. 10, being used in both cases to denote a *male* child. The word is masculine as well as feminine in ordinary use: cf. Virg. *Aen.* XII. 208 *imo de stirpe recisum.*

26 **Ascanium**] He was the son of Aeneas and Creusa, according to Virgil and the ordinary accounts.

dixere nomen] 'assigned the name': cf. Hor. *Od.* IV. 8. 12 *pretium dicere muneri.*

CHAPTER II.

28 § **1. Rutulorum**] Their centre-point (cf. c. 57. 1 of this book) was Ardea.

pacta fuerat] Does this mean that the act of betrothal had taken place, or that the state of betrothal was over? Probably the latter: Riemann, in his *Études sur la langue et la grammaire de Tite-Live* (pp. 213 and foll.), has indicated clearly that the use of *fuerat* with a pf. part. in Livy denotes in most cases a state which had existed previously to the given moment: cf. 26. 2 *desponsa fuerat*; 27. 1; 45. 3; 55. 2; 59. 8. In 7. 8, 14. 9, 29. 6, 56. 11, however, he considers that *fueram* is simply equivalent to *eram*.

p. 5. 1 § **2. Latinum amisere**] The legend thus conveniently removed Latinus out of the way of any possible rivalry with Aeneas.

2 § **3. diffisi rebus**] 'mistrusting their strength.'

ad florentes opes Etruscorum] For the Etruscan power cf. n. on *Etruria* below (§ 5).

3 **Mezentium**] The name is of Etruscan or Oscan origin; the variant spellings *Medientius*, *Messentius* are Latin attempts to render the *z* of the Italic dialects.

4 **Caere**] 'at Caere.' The word is indeclinable (except for Virgil's *Caeritis*, *Caerete*): cf. *Reate*, which has the same form for nom., acc., and abl.

The ancient name of Caere was Agylla, and according to Dionysius (I. 20) it was one of the primitive towns connected with the Pelasgi and Aborigines, before the Etruscan occupation: other authorities agree with this statement, which is supported by the discovery of an alphabet differing in arrangement from the Etruscan. Strabo (p. 220) gives a story connecting the change of name with the Etruscan capture: cf. Ridgeway, *Early Age of Greece*, I. pp. 244—7.

When Rome was attacked by the Gauls in 390 B.C., the Caerites showed kindness to the Vestals, and received the partial franchise, *civitas sine suffragio* (Aul. Gellius, XVI. 13): afterwards the phrase *in tabulas Caeritum referri* became equivalent to partial disfranchisement.

5 **nimio plus**] 'far more': cf. II. 37. 4 *nimio plus quam velim:* XXIX. 33. 4 *multitudine, quae nimio maior erat.* A colloquial use, common in Plautus: cf. our 'far and away.'

7 **haud gravatim**] 'without reluctance': the form *gravatim* (rare for *gravate*) is due to a false analogy with old fem. accusatives like *partim, statim.*

9 § **4. conciliaret**] 'win,' 'secure': cf. 46. 1; 27. 1 (*reconciliare*).

10 **Latinos**] If *Latium* comes from a root *prat*, 'smoothe' (cf. πλατύς), it means 'Broadland,' 'Lowland': so *Latini* = Lowlanders, Plain-men; cf. πεδιεῖς, πεδιακοί.

12 § **5. his animis**] i.e. *studio ac fide erga regem.*

14 **Etruria**] The evidence of archaeology supports the statement here made. Traces of Etruscan occupation have been discovered in the Po valley, on the Adriatic sea-board, in the territory of the Volsci, in Campania, in Rome itself, in Corsica, and perhaps in Sardinia. It is not certain whether they expanded from the north after a land-migration to Italy, or came to Etruria by sea, and thence moved outwards, north and south. The ancient authorities, Herodotus (I. 94), Strabo (p. 219) and Velleius Paterculus (I. 1), hold the latter view, which seems the more probable. Their history is made up of conflicts with their neighbours —Ligurians, Umbrians, Greek settlers, Gauls, and Romans. To themselves they were *Rasennas* (cf. Dion. Hal. I. 30. 3 αὐτοὶ μέντοι σφᾶς αὐτοὺς ἐπὶ τῶν ἡγεμόνων τινὸς Ῥασέννα τὸν αὐτὸν ἐκείνῳ τρόπον ὀνομάζουσι), from which by some such form as *Tu-Rasena, Tarsena,* Τυρσηνοί may have come: to the Umbrians they were Strangers (*Etruscus, Etruria* are supposed to be derived from Umbrian *etru* = *alter*). They were, as Livy states, a maritime power; they developed a sea-trade, and fought as allies of Carthage against the Phocaeans (536 B.C.) and against Cumae (474).

16 **implesset**] Livy uses many such contracted forms, e.g. 7. 7 *mugissent*; 11. 9 *petisse.*

17 **cum...posset**] 'although he might have repelled the war by (or from) his city-walls,' i.e. fought on the defensive: cf. III. 69. 5 *bellum ab urbe ac moenibus propulsari.* For the tactics, cf. 15. 3; 33. 4.

18 § **6. secundum**] 'successful.'

Aeneae] For the significance of this end, see the Introduction, and the note on 15. 6 *creditae*, below. As Varro drily put it: *sed Aeneam, quoniam non comparuit, deum sibi fecerunt Latini.*

19 **quemcumque]** It was customary in Roman prayer to avoid all possible offence by giving a deity all his titles (e.g. *Matutine pater, seu Iane libentius audis*), and adding even then some such phrase as *aut quocumque alio nomine rite vocaris*: the same idea seems to be present in Aesch. *Ag.* 160 Ζεύς, ὅστις ποτ' ἐστίν, εἰ τόδ' αὐτῷ φίλον κεκλημένῳ. Here Livy follows the custom, giving Aeneas the benefit of the generalisation: moreover Paulus, p. 106, says, *Indigetes di, quorum nomina vulgari non licet.*

20 **super Numicum]** 'beyond the N.,' i.e. on the further side from Rome, on which Lavinium was situated. According to one tradition, Aeneas fell into the Numicus (Numicius) in his flight from Mezentius, and Ascanius slew the latter in revenge.

21 **Iovem Indigetem]** The word *Indiges* means 'local' in abode or activity, ἐπιχώριος, χθόνιος: so Dionysius (I. 64) says that the inscription in this case ran πατρὸς θεοῦ χθονίου. As *Iuppiter Indiges, Pater Indiges,* or *Deus Indiges* (and afterwards *Aeneas Indiges* also), Aeneas became closely connected with the ancient sanctuary of Latin unity, the home of the Penates at Lavinium.

CHAPTER III.

22 § **1. imperio]** For the dat., expressing remote object, cf. II. 5. 3 *seges matura messi*; Hor. *Od.* I. 23. 12 *tempestiva viro.*

25 **tanta...erat]** explains *muliebri*, and gives a reason for the whole sentence: cf. Praef. 11 *adeo.*

26 **puero stetit]** 'was assured to the lad': so Virg. *Aen.* I. 268 *dum res stetit Ilia regno.*

27 § **2. quis...pro certo adfirmet?]** Hypothetical subjunctive, a protasis being understood. The same phrase occurs again in XXVII. 1. 13: it expresses the attitude adopted by Livy in the Preface (§ 6).

29 **comes inde]** For the order cf. 6. 1 *caedem deinceps tyranni.*

30 **Iulum]** cf. Virg. *Aen.* I. 267—8 *at puer Ascanius, cui nunc cognomen Iulo additur—Ilus erat, dum res stetit Ilia regno. Iulus* probably means 'little Jupiter'; and the traditional connection of the Julii with *Iulus* is supported by their family worship of Veiovis (the little Jupiter). Between Iulus and Silvius (see § 6) there was, according to one tradition, a division of prerogatives, Iulus being invested with the chief priesthood. (Cf. Frazer, *Early History of the Kingship*, p. 202.)

eundem] A certain antithesis lies hidden here: 'whom as Iulus, though one and the same.' Cf. Aurelius Victor, *Orig. Gent. Rom.* IV. 7 *hunc Faunum plerique eundem Silvanum a silvis esse dixerunt.*

31 § **3. ubicumque...genitus**] 'no matter where or of what mother born.' The adverb and pronoun are used absolutely.

p. 6. 1. **ut**] restrictive: cf. Dion. Hal. II. 8 χρήμασιν ὡς ἐν τοῖς τότε καιροῖς εὐπόρους. For similar uses of *ut* see Praef. 4 *ut quae*; 34. 7 *ut cupido.*

multitudine] 'population,' as often in this book.

2 **matri seu novercae**] i.e. according as we believe him to have been her son, or not.

3 **sub Albano monte**] 'at the foot of': see Virg. *Aen.* I. 269—271.

ab situ] 'after,' 'because of': cf. 17. 6 *id ab re interregnum appellatum.*

4 **urbis**] is used loosely after *quae*, referring to the preceding *urbem*: cf. Praef. 11 *res publica...in quam civitatem*: § 9 below *colle...colli.*

Longa] The same epithet is applied to many straggling villages in England.

5 **Lavinium**] sc. *conditum.*

7 § **4. maxime**] 'especially after the rout of the Etruscans.'

morte] abl. = occasion.

8 **inter**] 'during,' 'in the course of': used with reference to time or circumstances: cf. 10. 7 *inter tot annos, tot bella.*

rudimentum] 'attempt,' 'essay': cf. XXXI. 11. 15 *rudimenta adulescentiae ponere.*

10 **ausi sint**] The tense reproduces the *ausi sunt* (not *audebant*) of direct narrative: see note on 1. 8 *audierit.*

11 § **5. Albula**] So Virgil, *Aen.* VIII. 330—2 *tum reges asperque immani corpore Thybris, a quo post Itali fluvium cognomine Thybrim diximus: amisit verum vetus Albula nomen.* Pliny, *Nat. H.* III. 5. 9, *Tiberis antea Tybris appellatus et prius Albula.* The traditional cause of the change in the name of the river is given in § 8 below: cf. Ovid, *Fasti* II. 389 *Albula, quem Tibrim mersus Tiberinus in unda reddidit*; also *Fasti* IV. 47, *Met.* XIV. 614.

13 § **6. Silvius**] This list of kings, which serves to make up the discrepancy of about four hundred years between the fall of Troy and the foundation of Rome, may have been composed under Greek influence in the first half of the last century B.C., when the chronology was seen to be erratic. Dionysius (I. 74) fills up neatly the 432 years which Cato reckoned to be the interval. It is probable that in the *Silvii* there is a genuine Latin tradition of a dominant woodland clan—the basis of subsequent elaboration. In their crowns of oak (cf. Virg. *Aen.* VI. 772) the *Silvii* may have symbolised their identification with the Latin Jupiter,

the god of the sky, the thunder and the oak (cf. Frazer, *op. cit.*, p. 201).

The names are drawn from various sources. *Alba*, for instance, was a Roman surname (cf. Aemilius Alba, a friend of Verres), and likewise *Agrippa*: *Atys* looks like an attempt to connect the *gens Atia* with the Phrygian Atys, when Phrygian pedigrees were fashionable: *Capys* was the Homeric father of Anchises. The story of *Tiberinus* was, according to Servius, derived by Livy from Alexander Polyhistor, who wrote in the time of Sulla: *Aventinus* belongs to the same class.

16 § 7. **Prisci Latini**] In historical times this expression denoted the older members of the Latin League, the *triginta populi*, or settlements supposed to be of Alban origin, as opposed to the Latin colonies, sent out in conjunction with Rome. Cf. 32. 11.

17 § 8. **Silviis**] For the dat. cf. n. on 1. 3 *Troiano*.

20 **celebre ad posteros**] 'famous among the posterities.' *ad* (= *apud*), cf. 36. 5 *ut esset ad posteros miraculi eius monumentum*.

22 § 9. **Aventino**] dat. with *tradidit*.

25 § 10. **Numitorem**] connected (like *Numa*) with a root *nam* 'assign,' so = 'dispenser': cf. Νέμεσις, νόμος.

28 **patris...aetatis**] The first gen. is subjective, the second objective, i.e. 'regard for seniority,' cf. 6. 4. For the combination of genitives cf. 23. 10 *cum indole animi tum spe victoriae ferocior*.

31 § 11. **Reae Silviae**] dat. after *adimit* ('tried to take away'). *Rea* is probably the original spelling, and may be either a proper name, or a noun, 'the dedicated,' i.e. *rea voti* (so Preller, *Römische Mythologie*, I. 133 n.): the spelling *Rhea* is due to Greek influence, connecting the mother of the Twins with the Great Mother of Phrygia (cf. also the name *Ilia*, given to *Rea Silvia* by Horace, Ovid and others), or with the legend that she plunged into the Anio and became a river-goddess.

31 **per speciem honoris...legisset**] 'by the pretended compliment of choosing her as a Vestal.' *cum...legisset* explains *species honoris*.

Vestalem] The significance of this priesthood goes back to the primitive ages when the maintenance of a central fire was vital to the comfort of the community. Originally the duty of tending the fire belonged to the maiden daughters of the chief: then the office became more religious, and was entrusted to a special guild, who still retained the characteristic of virginity. There were Vestals in Lavinium, Tibur, and probably in all the Latin communities. Numa (cf. 20. 3) was regarded as the formal founder of the order at Rome. It is important to remember in connection with *Rea Silvia* that the Vestal Virgins were originally believed to be the wives of the fire-god, and the old Latin kings were accordingly regarded as born of this divine father and these human mothers. (Cf. Frazer, *op. cit.*, p. 221.)

CHAPTER IV.

p. 7. 1 § **1. debebatur fatis**] 'was destined by fate.' *fatis* is probably ablative: cf. Virg. *Aen.* VII. 120 *fatis mihi debita tellus.* For *fata* cf. 1. 4; 7. 11; 7. 15.

2 **secundum**] 'next to.'

3 § **2. vi...edidisset**] 'had suffered violence, and become the mother of twins.'

4 **seu...seu...**] Notice that neither alternative *admits* the divine paternity—a touch of scepticism on Livy's part.

5 **incertae**] 'disputed,' 'unassigned': the epithet belongs not to *stirps* but to the circumstances of the sentence, being really equivalent to *quod incerta res erat.*

6 § **3. · nec di nec homines**] i.e. the father, whether divine or human: 'no divine or human agency.'

9 § **4. forte quadam divinitus**] 'by a divine dispensation, as we may say'—a translation of θείᾳ τινὶ τύχῃ in Livy's own style, adjective + adverb.

Tiberis...dabat] *Tiberis* is the subject throughout. The phrase *ad iusti...amnis*, 'to the regular water-way,' is not awkward if the personality of the river is borne in mind. *spem* governs *posse...infantes*: the king's servants were anxious to fulfil the letter and not the spirit of his orders. *nec...et*: the two clauses are like in character, but the first is cast in a negative form: cf. 23. 2; 28. 5. *quamvis languida*, 'however sluggish,' cf. 16. 5 *quamvis magnae*; for the epithet cf. Hor. *Od.* II. 14. 17 *ater flumine languido Cocytus errans.*

13 § **5. alluvie**] 'pool'; nowhere else so used. *eluvie* ('overflow') has been suggested.

ficus Ruminalis...Romularem] So Ovid, *Fasti* II. 411—2 *arbor erat: remanent vestigia, quaeque vocatur Rumina nunc ficus Romula ficus erat.* According to Festus (p. 270) *Ruminalis* means '*quod sub arbore ea lupa mammam dedit Romulo et Remo, mamma autem rumis dicitur*': and there was a goddess *Rumīna*, the guardian of nursing mothers. More probably the word is connected (like *ruma*, *rumis*) with the root *sru* (= 'stream,' 'flow'); and so means '(the fig) by the stream': in this connection it may be noted that *Rūmōn* was an ancient name of the Tiber (cf. Servius on *Aen.* VIII. 63 and 90), and *Roma* probably comes from the same source, meaning 'Stream-city' (cf. Στρύμη, *Reate*). If so, *Rōmulus* and *Rĕmus* (Gk Ῥῶμος) are simply two forms for the inhabitant thereof. The form *Romularem* was probably due to two causes: (1) the derivation of an earlier spelling *Rumularem* from *rumis*; (2) the desire to connect the tree with Romulus. The fig-tree was closely associated with the *Fauni* (called sometimes *ficarii*).

nunc] Cf. the lines of Ovid quoted above. It was situated near the Lupercal, on the W. side of the Palatine.

14 **exponunt**] The exposure of the children reminds us of the stories of Moses and of Cyrus.

15 **tenet fama**] Cf. κατέχει λόγος, Thuc. I. 10.

16 § **6. alveum**] 'basket,' 'tray': used for a boat also (cf. Virg. *Aen.* VI. 412 *accipit alveo Aeneam*), and for the bed of a river.

17 **tenuis**] has practically the force of a separate clause, 'because it was shallow': cf. 7. 9 *manifestae*, 50. 3 *in absentem*. For the epithet, cf. Cicero *de Repub.* II. 34 *influxit enim non tenuis quidam e Graecia rivulus in hanc urbem*; and Propertius, I. 11. 11.

19 **summissas**] probably predicate with *praebuisse*, 'stooped and gave.'

20 **lingua lambentem**] Cf. Ovid, *Fasti* II. 418 *et fingit lingua corpora bina sua*; Virg. *Aen.* VIII. 634 *corpora fingere lingua.* The dam (it is thought) aids with her tongue the development of new-born limbs: from which comes the phrase 'lick into shape.'

21 **Faustulo**] For the dat. see n. on I. 3 *Troiano.* Here (as in 50. 3) *ei* is to be supplied.

The name *Faustulus* here is an attempt to connect the origins of Rome with the worship of *Faunus. Faustulus* (like *Faustus*) is connected with *favere*, and means therefore 'the kind one': *Faunus* is by some traced to the same source, by others connected with *fari* (i.e. 'the prophet'), or with *Favonius* (from a root *pu*, 'purify'). There were many *Fauni*, spirits of the wood—perhaps an ancient woodland race themselves—who could help or hurt crops and cattle; prophetic sometimes in warning or encouragement. This ancient *numen* of the country was utilised for their own purposes by priests and annalists: for the former he became Pan, the god of the Lupercalia: for the latter a mythical king of Latium, connected with the mythical Evander—identical with him, if we may accept one modern view which regards Evander as a translation of the Latin Faunus, made to suit the graecizing tendency of the earliest Roman archaeologists. Fowler, *Roman Festivals*, pp. 257—265.

22 § 7. **ad stabula**] 'in his cottage.'

Larentiae] i.e. *Acca Larentia* (? 'mother of the Lares'). In all the most ancient cults of Italy the nature of the deity is veiled in divers names and epithets: thus *Acca Larentia* was one variety of the Dea Dia worshipped by the Arval Brethren—a guild probably as old as the state itself. Here she seems to be a sort of *Fauna*, or feminine to Faunus: in another aspect she is the she-wolf itself. The sinister sense of *lupa* ('harlot') which Livy gives in the rationalising view of the next sentence found some justification in the legend of an amour between Acca Larentia and Hercules. It is not certain how the she-wolf came into the tale—as it did at least as early as 296 B.C.—whether as the sacred animal of Mars, the Palatine god, or because of the Lupercal, or otherwise. See Introduction, § 3.

23 **vulgato corpore**] 'because she made herself common property.'

26 § 8. **nec in stabulis...segnes**] 'no sluggards in the cottage or with the cattle.'

29 § 9. **subsistere**] 'stand up to'—a Livian word, cf. IX. 31. 6 *praepotentem armis Romanum subsistere*: Gk ὑφιστάναι.

31 **seria ac iocos**] 'tasks and sports': 'grave moods and gay.' *ludicrum* in the next chapter seems to be an instance of the latter, while the former may allude to the raids and the plot against the king.

CHAPTER V.

p. 8. 1 § 1. **Palatio**] a substantive: *monte* is in apposition, unless it be a gloss.

Lupercal] This word denotes (1) a place—the grotto at the foot (W.) of the Palatine, where tradition set the sacred fig-tree of the Twins: (2) as here, a festival, i.e. the Lupercalia, celebrated in historical times on 15 February. The name *Lupercal* seems to be made up of *lupus* and *arcere*, so = 'wolf-fence,' but whether this refers to a wolf-stronghold or to a fending off of wolves is not clear, though we may believe there is some connection with the wolf of Mars. The festival may have taken its title from the spot, or from the celebrants, called *Luperci*: the creation of a deity *Lupercus* is of later date. The festival was of extreme antiquity, probably pre-Roman. First of all goats and a dog were sacrificed, and sacred cakes were offered: next, two youths of rank were smeared on the forehead with blood, and wiped with wool: then, clad only in the skins of the goats, they feasted: and lastly, they and their companies ran round the Palatine, striking with strips of goat-skin all the women who came in their way. It is not clear in honour of what god these rites were performed: the name *Inuus*, mentioned below by Livy, is probably one epithet of that spirit who reappears as Faunus, Silvanus and Pan. The significance of the ceremony seems to have been a renewal of life by the life-blood of sacrifice, and by the wearing of the skin of the victims: the last act, in which the Luperci (or *creppi*, as they were commonly called) ran a regular course round the Palatine, i.e. the *pomerium* or boundary of the city, was meant to be both a purification and a fertilisation. The two guilds of Luperci (like the *Salii*: see n. on 20. 4) belonged to two separate communities, subsequently united. See Fowler, *Roman Festivals*, pp. 310—321.

Lupercal hoc fuisse ludicrum] This may be translated in two ways: (1) 'our festival of the Lupercalia was celebrated,' *hoc ludicrum* being in apposition to *Lupercal*: (2) 'our Lupercalia existed as a festival.' Livy is speaking of his own day (*hoc*); the feast lasted on till the end of the 5th century of our era. *ludicrum*: the word is especially appropriate here for a 'festival' where the sportive character (*per lusum atque lasciviam*) is so remarkable: cf. XXVIII. 7. 14 *Olympiorum sollemne ludicrum*.

2 **Pallanteo**] The Greek form is Παλλάντιον or Παλάντιον: its reputed founder was Pallas son of Lycaon. This fanciful derivation of *Palatium* is a link in the chain which connects Arcadia with the origins of Rome: the word is probably derived from a root *pa* 'protect' (cf. *Pales*), and so = 'a fenced place.'

3 § **2. Euandrum**] The story of Evander, and the resemblance between the Arcadian Λύκαια, or rites of *Pan Lycaeus*, and the *Lupercalia*, give support to the theory of a Pelasgian settlement in Latium. The mother of Evander, Carmenta (7. 9), is a being unmistakably Italian, connected in all probability with the group of primitive spirits of which Mars and Faunus are the dominant types.

4 **ex eo genere**] i.e. from the stock of Pallanteum.

tempestatibus] 'ages': so again in the singular in 18. 1; 30. 4; 36. 3; 56. 6. The plural is not so used by Cicero: it occurs in Plautus and Sallust.

5 **tenuerit loca**] 'was lord of those quarters.'

sollemne] 'ceremony': the word originally means 'annual,' and thence passes naturally to 'custom' and 'rite.'

instituisse] The word has here a double government (1) *sollemne*, (2) *ut...currerent*.

6 **venerantes...currerent]** 'worship by running.'

per lusum atque lasciviam] 'in boisterous sport': so in II. 18. 2, *per ludos...per lasciviam.*

8 **Inuum]** See n. on *Lupercal* above.

11 **§ 3. cepisse, captum]** Livy (unlike his predecessors in prose) affects this repetition to express rapid succession of events: the usage is common enough in poets. Cf. 10. 4 *fundit...fusum*; 12. 9 *pelli... pulsum.*

12 **ultro]** 'actually,' i.e. one would rather have expected to see *latrones* as accused than as accusers.

§ 4. crimini] predicative dative. **fieri** 'was being made,' 'meditated.'

15 **Numitori]** To N., as the aggrieved party (according to the accusation) Remus is delivered by Amulius for punishment.

16 **§ 5. spes]** in a neutral sense, 'notion,' 'fancy': with *fuerat* it = ἤλπισεν.

18 **sustulisset]** subjunctive, because it expresses part of the *oratio obliqua* introduced by *sciebat*, and represents Faustulus' view.

19 **immaturam]** 'too soon,' 'before the time': the adjective is quasi-adverbial, cf. 16. 2 *sublimem.*

20 **aperiri]** The infin. passive is regularly used in cases like this after verbs of wishing: cf. Cic. *de Sen.* 2 *et te et me ipsum levari volo.*

22 **§ 6. Numitori]** Livy very frequently uses the dative in such cases as this, and often at the head of the sentence, to express a close relationship with some noun; the genitive might in most instances have been used, but the dative adds a peculiar emphasis to the person or object concerned: cf. 9. 14 *raptis spes*, 12. 4 *urbi fundamenta ieci*, 39. 1 *puero...caput arsisse.*

24 **comparando]** 'as he considered.' The ablative of the gerund is loosely connected with the real subject (Numitor), expressing a notion both of instrument and of attendant circumstances; in many cases (e.g. *sciscitando* below, 54. 7 *interrogando exspectandoque responsum*) it does duty for the nominative of the present participle. The word *comparando* means 'putting two and two together,' and here indicates that Numitor, by means of circumstantial evidence, had been reminded of his grandsons: it is in fact completed by *memoria nepotum.*

ipsam] 'actual.'

26 **sciscitando]** i.e. reflection prompted inquiry: the result was anticipated, however, by the revelations of Faustulus to Romulus.

haud procul esset] probably impersonal, making a periphrase with *quin.*

§ **7.** **regi**] dat. of indirect object.

28 **Romulus**] He had grasped the situation, and foreseen the necessity of forcible measures in support of Numitor.

30 **ad regem**] i.e. Amulius. *ad* (for the commoner *in*) *regem* expresses the object of attack: cf. 'aim at.'

Chapter VI.

32 § **1.** **inter primum tumultum**] 'at the beginning of the uproar.' For *inter*, expressing the circumstances, cf. 3. 4 *inter muliebrem tutelam*.

p. 9. 1 **urbem...regiam**] By representing that the city was in danger, he had been able to concentrate the men-at-arms for the defence of the citadel, leaving the palace at the mercy of Romulus and Remus.

3 **in obtinendam**] The preposition expresses both place and purpose.

praesidio armisque] 'by an armed garrison.'

5 **ad se**] Numitor took command of the citadel, and there received the Twins.

7 **deinceps**] has almost an adjectival force 'the subsequent assassination,' cf. 15. 7 *in quadraginta deinde annos*. See n. on *novi semper*, Praef. 2.

9 § **2.** **agmine**] 'in column': they marched at the head of their armed followers, as concealment was no longer necessary. For the abl. (manner) cf. XXII. 30. 1 *agmine incedentes*.

regem] 'as king': so 7. 1.

11 **ratum...efficit**] 'secured the king in his title and his throne.' Numitor was *de facto* king already, but not *de iure*: *consentiens vox* is a sort of prehistoric type of the popular elections of kings mentioned later in the book.

12 § **3.** **Albana re**] 'the state of Alba': so in 54. 10 *Gabina res*.

13 **cupido**] Cicero would have said *cupiditas*, which Livy uses rather in the sense of 'passion.'

16 **ad id**] 'thereto': used loosely to express the sense of the previous clause.

pastores] i.e. the followers of the Twins.

qui...spem facerent] 'in all, a body numerous enough readily to create the expectation.' *qui*='so that.'

18 **conderetur**] 'which was to be founded.'

20 § **4.** **quoniam essent...posset...essent**] The subjunctives are intended to express the thoughts of the Twins themselves.

21 **aetatis verecundia**] See n. on 3. 10.

22 **di**] i.e. the spirits of field and wood.

tutelae] gen. of secondary predicate : cf. 25. 13 *dicionis alienae facti* ; XXI. 41. 12 *tutelae nostrae duximus*.

auguriis legerent] 'might choose through the medium of auguries,' 'declare their choice by omens.' The gods did not *choose* by omens, but they could control a human choice by that means.

23 **qui...daret**] i.e. *qui det* of *oratio recta*. Either 'which was to give,' (reported question) where *qui* = *uter* : or final, 'one who should give.'

24 **Aventinum**] Is it possible that the whole story of the augury may have been founded on a fancied connexion of *Aventinus* with *aves*?

25 **ad inaugurandum templa**] 'stations (enclosures) for taking auguries.' See notes on 18. 9.

capiunt] historic present, and thus associated with historic dependents *legerent...daret...regeret*.

CHAPTER VII.

26 § **1**. **vultures**] were technically *alites*, i.e. they gave their augury by manner of flight, as opposed to *oscines*, 'singing-birds.'

28 **regem**] 'as king': so above, 6. 2. **sua**] 'their own,' 'their proper,' referring to and emphasizing the central figures of the scene. This use of *suus* is common in Livy : cf. 7. 15; 25. 1; 26. 11 ; 50. 6; 58. 7.

29 **tempore...numero**] The ablatives express the ground of claim. *praecepto* is to be taken with *tempore* only, meaning 'for priority of time,' 'because they were first in time.'

30 **trahebant**] 'sought to claim,' 'appropriate': cf. 24. 1.

31 § **2**. **certamine irarum**] 'by passionate rivalry.' Livy is fond of plurals in the case of abstract nouns ; but possibly the plural here describes the anger of the two parties.

32 **ibi**] 'there,' 'thereupon,' a frequent use in Livy : so in 54. 3.

p. 10. 1 **ludibrio fratris**] 'in derision of his brother.'

2 **ab...Romulo**] Ovid (*Fasti*, IV. 843) attributes the murder to Celer, to whom Romulus (he says) had entrusted the care of the walls.

3 **sic**] sc. *pereat* or *peribit*.

5 § **3**. **condita**] i.e. founded before the quarrel: it is not part of the predicate.

7 **muniit**] 'enclosed': so *munitionibus*, *munirent* in 8. 4.

8 **aliis**] = *ceteris*: cf. 1. 1; 12. 9; 57. 2. The sentence is like a Greek model—*τοῖς μὲν ἄλλοις, τῷ δὲ Ἡρακλεῖ.*

Albano] i.e. Latin, native, as opposed to *Graeco*: notice the chiasmus. The Romans sacrificed *capite velato*: but in this rite of Hercules the chief celebrant (the *praetor urbanus*) was bare-headed and laurel-wreathed, according to Greek rule.

Herculi] The name of the Roman Hercules may have come from the Greek through the Etruscan *Hercle*, or it may have a native origin, and have been afterwards connected by resemblance with Ἡρακλῆς: in any case the character and attributes of Hercules are distinct. He is to be identified with the deity otherwise known as *Dius Fidius* and *Semo Sancus*; *me dius fidius* = *me hercule*. He is then a lord of oaths, closely related to Jupiter; and oaths were taken at the *ara maxima*, the centre of the worship of Hercules and of the legends which Livy here relates. He is further the Genius of the man, the male principle: so Romans swore by Hercules, Dius Fidius, or their Genius; women by their Juno.

This worship of a male deity dated from a remote age: one indication of its antiquity is seen in the round *aedes Herculis* which was near neighbour to the *ara maxima* in the Forum Boarium. A ritual reconstruction, at some time or other, may have introduced certain Greek characteristics, known to have existed, and alluded to here by Livy (*Graeco ritu*): but much that was ancient, and probably native, survived, e.g. the sacrificial meal, and the exclusion of women (as from a festival of the male Genius). An especially remarkable feature in the worship was the offering of tithes paid to the *ara maxima* in cases of victory or discovered treasure. This tithe-giving accompanied the cult of Hercules in Italy, and may have begun in an offering of first-fruits at harvest-time: but it is unique in Italian ritual.

The *ara maxima* and the Aventine were closely connected with the myth of Hercules and Cacus. Here again we seem to have something un-Italian in character and personages, and yet familiar enough in the East. It is possible that the tale may have come from Phoenicia through Greek traders to Sicily or Cumae, and thence to the Tiber, and that the cult indicates a foreign worship furnished with an Italian home and name. In Căcus (connected with *caecus*) we may see a demon of darkness and the underworld, overcome by the genius of life, truth, and manhood—a type, as the Romans conceived it, of triumph: the Greek mythologists regarded him as a wicked one (κακός), who opposed the good chieftain (εὔανδρος), and was overcome by the hero of strength on his way back from one of his labours. Fowler, *Rom. Fest.*, pp. 138—144, 193—197. See also Introduction, §§ 4, 7.

Livy's account should be compared with those of Virgil (*Aen.* VIII. 186—251), Propertius (IV. 9. 1—20), and Ovid (*Fasti*, I. 543—584).

8 **Euandro]** See n. on 5. 2. Here, as before, he serves as the authority for introducing a Greek cult.

9 § 4. **Geryone]** a three-headed king who lived in Spain, according to the common legend. By a strange coincidence there was a *Geryonis oraculum* at Patavium, Livy's birth-place (cf. Suet. *Tib.* 14), which may indicate that according to another legend Geryon belonged to Italy.

mira specie] 'of rare beauty': cf. 45. 4 *bos...miranda...specie.*

11 **qua]** 'at a point where.'

12 **laeto]** 'rich': cf. Juv. XII. 13 *laeta Clitumni pascua.*

13 **et ipsum]** = *καὶ αὐτόν*, implying here something unusual, and leading up to the next point: see n. on Praef. 3. Propertius (IV. 9. 4) has *et statuit fessos fessus et ipse boves.*

14 § 5. **oppressisset]** 'came upon' = *κατέλαβεν*. *sopor*, the deep sleep of the weary.

15 **Cacus]** See n. on *Herculi* above.

16 **avertere]** here 'raid,' 'lift': below *aversos* has the literal meaning, 'tail first.' Cf. Propertius, IV. 9. 12 *aversos cauda traxit in antra boves*: Virgil, *Aen.* VIII. 209, 210 *atque hos, ne qua forent pedibus vestigia rectis, cauda in speluncam tractos.* The trick was practised by Hermes when he stole the cattle of the gods: cf. Hom. *Hymn.* 4. 76 *ἴχνι' ἀποστρέψας.*

17 **quaerentem...erant]** 'must have brought the owner to the cave in his search.' The fut. part. with *sum* contains all the meanings of *μέλλω*.

18 **deducere]** here, as often, connotes 'to the proper place.'

boves, eximium quemque] The plural is immediately restricted by a singular in apposition. *eximium* is in sense a superlative, and thus naturally coupled with *quemque*: cf. Cic. *in V.* IV. 142 *egregium quemque.*

21 § 6. **numero]** dative: *abesse* is used by Livy with the sense and government of *deesse*, 'to be wanting.'

22 **si forte]** = *εἴ πως*, '(to see) if,' 'in case': cf. 57. 2. **eo...ferrent]** 'led thither,' i.e. tended in the direction of the cave: not 'led him thither,' which would be nonsense with *pergit ad proximam speluncam.* *eo* may connote here, as in line 18 above, the place desired, i.e. where the oxen were.

23 **foras]** 'outwards.' **nec in partem aliam]** 'and only in the one direction' (i.e. towards his resting-place).

24 **incertus animi]** *animi* is locative: cf. 58. 9 *aegram animi*, also IV. 57. 3 *incertus sententiae*, and XXXVI. 42. 6 *incertus consilii.*

25 **porro]** 'on,' 'farther.'

26 § 7. **ad desiderium**] Cf. XLII. 67. 12 *ad horum preces in Boeotiam duxit.* **ut fit**] is practically an epithet—'with the usual craving.'

27 **mugissent**] Livy affects the contracted forms *-issem*, *-isse* throughout: cf. II. 9; 27. 6 *subisse*; 35. 2 *petisse*; 39. 3 *abisse*; 41. 5 *redisse*.

reddita] 'answering': so Virg. *Aen.* VIII. 218 *reddidit una boum vocem.*

29 **fidem**] 'help,' 'protection': cf. Cic. *pro Mur.* 40. 86 *fidem vestram oro atque obsecro*; Plaut. *Capt.* II. 3. 58 *di vostram fidem!*

30 **morte occubuit**] This, not *mortem*, is probably the right reading.

p. 11. 1 § 8. **ea...loca**] i.e. the Palatium.

auctoritate] 'influence,' i.e. a moral rather than an absolute control: for *imperio* cf. 6. 4 above.

2 **venerabilis...litterarum**] 'he won respect for the wonderful gift of letters.' So Dionysius (I. 33. 4) attributes the introduction of letters into Italy to the Arcadian colonists. The mother alphabet of ancient Italy was probably like that of Euboea, and thus the old Italian scripts are commonly called Chalcidian. Perhaps Cumae (where the Chalcidian type obtained) may have been one of the original points of connection between Greece and Italy in this respect. But it is possible to believe that the gift of letters to Italy came through Pelasgian settlements (e.g. of Caere, see note on c. I. 3 above), independently of Chalcidian colonists. Cf. W. Ridgeway, *Early Age of Greece*, vol. I. pp. 245, 246. In the Italian dialects an earlier and a later stratum are to be seen, the first dating before, the second in most cases after, the Etruscan invasion. Cf. R. S. Conway, *Atti del Congresso Internaz. di Scienze Storiche*, 1903, vol. II. § 1.

3 **rudes artium**] 'ignorant of arts': the gen. expresses the thing lacked, as in III. 7. 7 *inops auxilii humani*; IX. 9. 6 *omnium egena corpora.*

4 **Carmentae**] (connected with *carmen*, *Camenae*) 'the chantress,' i.e. prophetess: so (according to Servius) prophets were once called *carmentes*, and their utterances were set down in *libri carmentarii*. Carmenta was the patron-goddess of Roman matrons.

5 **fatiloquam**] 'as a prophetess.'

ante Sibyllae...adventum] i.e., in other words, before the introduction of the Sibylline books into the Roman state. These books were of Greek origin, acquired probably from Cumae (according to the legend, from a Sibylla, or prophetess, of that place, who sold them to Tarquinius Superbus), whither they may have come from Erythrae, the traditional home of prophecy.

7 § **9. trepidantium circa**] 'bustling about': the preposition (cf. *περί*) expresses both position and relation.

manifestae] (cf. *tenuis*, 4. 6) has the force of a subordinate clause, i.e. 'now made manifest': cf. 26. 12 *caedes manifesta*.

9 **habitum...humana**] *ampliorem* belongs to *formam*, *augustiorem* to *habitum*.

aliquantum] rare for *aliquanto* with comparatives: cf. Ter. *Eun.* I. 2. 51 *aliquantum ad rem est avidior*.

11 § **10. Iove nate**] Διογενές: the Italian Hercules was not the son of Jupiter.

12 **interpres deum**] 'mouthpiece of heaven': cf. Cic. *Phil.* XIII. 5 *Iovis interpretes nuntiique* (of augurs); Virg. *Aen.* IV. 356 *interpres divom* (Mercury).

14 **cecinit**] 'chanted,' i.e. 'prophesied': the word implies that the prophecy was in rhythmic form, and is frequently found in this sense; cf. 55. 6. So *carmen* is used of anything uttered in rhythmic form—a prophecy, charm, formula; cf. 24. 6, 26. 6, 45. 5.

aram...maximam] i.e. the *ara maxima* in the Forum Boarium, just to the W. of the N.W. end of the Circus Maximus. See n. on *Herculi* above. The whole story here given is centred in this ancient altar, which was perhaps the oldest (*maxima*) in Rome.

15 **opulentissima**] an implied prophecy.

olim] 'hereafter': cf. Virg. *Aen.* I. 203 *forsan et haec olim meminisse iuvabit*.

16 **vocet...colat**] These seem to be indirect jussives, answering to the *vocato*, *colito* of the prophecy.

tuoque ritu] i.e. with Greek ritual: cf. § 3 above, and n. on *Herculi*.

17 § **11. fata**] 'destiny'—as foretold by the *fatiloqua*.

ara...dicata] may be explanatory of *impleturum fata*, 'in the foundation and dedication of an altar,' i.e. by Hercules; or supplementary, 'so soon as an altar had been founded and dedicated.' The second is more probable, as Hercules could scarcely build an altar for the worship of himself, which follows. In the first case *fata*='destiny,' in the second, 'his destiny.'

18 § **12. bove eximia**] A heifer was in historical times the regular victim in this rite.

19 **dapemque**] i.e. the *polluctum Herculis*; see n. on *Herculi* above (§ 3).

Potitiis ac Pinariis] Of these two old Patrician families, connected from the earliest times with this worship of Hercules (cf. Virg. *Aen.* VIII. 268—70), the Pinarii, for some reason or another, dropped out, and the

Potitii, according to Livy (IX. 29. 9), were induced by Appius Claudius, censor in 312 B.C., to forego their rights in favour of the *servi publici*; but their *gens* was punished with extinction.

22 § **13. exta**] 'the sacrificial meal,' i.e. the parts of the victim consumed by the sacrificers (cf. Plautus, *Mil. Gl.* III. 1. 117 *abducunt me ad exta*); as opposed to *ceteram dapem*, 'the rest of the banquet,' i.e. the other food and drink of the feast.

23 **institutum**] 'it was ordained,' introducing *ne...vescerentur*, an indirect prohibition, of which *ne...vescantur* would be the direct form.

25 § **14. antistites**] 'chief celebrants': cf. 20. 3.

28 § **15. haec tum sacra**] For the order see note on *novi semper*, Praef. 2. *tum* refers back to § 3.

una] 'the only': cf. Caes. *B.G.* IV. 7 *Ubii, qui uni legatos miserant.*

29 **immortalitatis...partae**] Romulus felt sympathy and admiration for the 'immortality'—the place among the immortals, and the immortal fame—which Hercules won by prowess; for he too was a subject of Destiny. The whole sentence anticipates the *immortalia opera* and *immortalitas* of c. 16, and echoes the *impleturum fata* of § 12 above.

30 **eum sua fata**] *sua*='his proper,' with reference to *Romulus*, the main subject (cf. note on § 1 *sua multitudo*): *eum* is the object of *ducebant*, with reference to the historian.

CHAPTER VIII.

(For the reign of Romulus see Introduction, § 4.)

p. 12. 2 § **1. coalescere...corpus**] 'unite in a single body politic.'

4 **iura dedit**]=νόμους ἔθηκεν, 'made ordinances.'

§ **2. ita, si**] 'only if,' 'not unless.' **fecisset**]=the fut. perf. of *oratio recta*: cf. 31. 7 *meam opem relictam, si pax...impetrata esset.*

6 **cetero habitu**] 'general state' (cf. Suet. *Calig.* 52 *vestitu calciatuque et cetero habitu*): the arrangement of the clauses here is in the Greek manner.

7 **lictoribus**] These officers (originally deputed, if the derivation from *licere* be correct, to summon assemblies) appear from the earliest time onwards as the attendants of authority, religious and secular. The bundles of rods (*fasces*) and axes which they carried denoted the power of life and death, and to them at first was committed the execution of the death penalty. Under the Republic, a section of them (varying in strength according to the dignity of the office) acted as constables to each of the higher magistrates, attending him at home and in public.

8 § **3. ab numero**] 'in consequence of,' 'after': cf. § 7 *ab honore*; 17. 6 *id ab re...interregnum appellatum.*

9 **eum**] with *numerum*: understand *Romulum* with *secutum.*

10 **haud paenitet**] 'I am satisfied.'

sententiae] gen. of secondary predicate; cf. 39. 5; 25. 13 *dicionis alienae facti.*

11 **apparitores**] Cf. 40. 5; 48. 4: this word (from *appareo*, 'attend') denotes the free attendants of Roman officials, as opposed to *servi publici.* The *apparitores* were paid and privileged: they were divided into five classes or corporations—*scribae, accensi, lictores, viatores, praecones.*

hoc genus] acc. of description (Roby § 462): cf. XXVI. 47. 1 *liberorum capitum virile secus* ('of the male sex') *ad decem millia capta.*

Etruscis] It was the Roman fashion to derive any usage of uncertain origin from the Etruscans, and in this case the sacred Etruscan number twelve afforded some probability of connection. Strabo, Dionysius and Diodorus Siculus agree with Livy in ascribing the lictors to Etruria, and there is evidence of similar officials on Etruscan monuments.

sella curulis] a square-topped stool with curved legs, the official seat of all Roman magistrates possessing *imperium*; movable (*curulis* probably denotes 'portable in a chariot'), to indicate that the *imperium* was not confined to a single place, cf. 20. 2.

12 **toga praetexta**] the outer garment, purple-bordered, of curule magistrates, and certain priests; worn also by free-born boys (XXIV. 7. 2) until they came of age (when they assumed the *toga virilis*).

13 **ductum**] sc. *esse.* This use of the pf. infin. pass. is not infrequent with verbs denoting wish or view, where the realisation is put for the anticipation: cf. Ter. *Ad.* 214 *adulescenti morem gestum oportuit.* The infin. in such cases resembles the Greek construction of the article and infin.: the sense here is, 'those who approve the view that the number also was derived' (in the first case).

14 **duodecim populis**] The following are supposed to have been the twelve 'communities' of Etruria proper: Volaterrae, Arretium, Cortona, Perusia, Clusium, Rusellae, Vetulonia, Volsinii, Volci, Tarquinii, Caere, Veii.

15 **dederint**] For tense see n. on 1. 8 *audierit.*

16 § **4. munitionibus...appetendo**] Livy affects this combination of ablatives: cf. 14. 7 *genere pugnae, adequitando*; 47. 6 *his aliisque increpando.* In such cases the abl. of gerund (=circumstances) serves to

expand and explain the other ablative (=means). For the use of the gerund see n. on 5. 6.

17 **in spem**] 'in anticipation,' 'in accordance with their hope': cf. 21. 2 *in mores*. **futurae multitudinis**] 'of a population to be'—a favourite Livian use of the future participle.

18 **ad id, quod...erat**] 'to suit the present number of persons.' *hominum*, gen. of divided whole: cf. 25. 1 *quidquid civium domi...sit*.

19 § **5.** **vana**] in literal sense, 'empty.'

21 **vetere consilio**] 'in accordance with the established policy.'

obscuram atque humilem] 'mean and lowly': cf. Cic. *in Verr.* II. 5. 70, § 181 *Pompeius humili atque obscuro loco natus*.

23 **qui nunc...est**] 'which is seen on descent, an enclosure to this day, the Two-Grove Clearing.' Livy omits to state that this spot called *Inter Duos Lucos* (cf. Dion. H. II. 15. 4 *μεθόριον δυεῖν δρυμῶν*) was on the Capitoline; it was in fact the col between the two eminences of that hill, on which woods were believed once to have existed. *lucus* itself originally meant 'a clearing,' a sense which may have survived in *Lucus Asyli*, another title of this spot. **escendentibus**] The dat. gives the point of view (i.e. the 'person judging,' Roby, § 477); it is like the Greek usage, cf. Thuc. I. 24. 1 *Ἐπίδαμνός ἐστι πόλις ἐν δεξιᾷ ἐσπλέοντι τὸν Ἰόνιον κόλπον*, also 23. 10 *quaerentibus*, and Plin. *N. H.* XVIII. 35 *verum confitentibus latifundia perdidere Italiam*.

If *descendentibus* is the right reading, Livy's account must be taken from an authority who has just described the Capitol. But perhaps we ought to read *escendentibus* (*escendo* and *descendo* are again confused in VIII. 10. 12), which may have been a word specially appropriate for climbing the Capitol: cf. 10. 5 below.

24 **asylum**] 'as a refuge,' in apposition to *locum*: cf. Virg. *Aen.* VIII. 342 *hinc lucum ingentem, quem Romulus acer Asylum rettulit... monstrat*.

25 § **6.** **sine discrimine...esset**] 'without distinction whether bond or free.' *discrimine* implies a question, and therefore takes (*utrum*)...*an*: cf. 33. 8.

26 **primum...roboris**] 'the first element of strength towards the greatness essayed.' *coepta magnitudo* is an echo of *futura multitudo* above.

28 § **7.** **consilium...parat**] 'provided a council for his forces.' The dat. expresses indirect object, with a sense also of close relationship: cf. 12. 4 *urbi fundamenta ieci*. For *consilium*, cf. 49. 7.

centum] Dionysius Hal. (II. 12) gives the composition thus: 1 king's deputy +9 (3 × 3) tribal representatives +90 (3 × 30) gentile representatives = 100. **ab honore**] Cf. § 3 *ab numero*; 17. 6 *id ab re... interregnum appellatum.*

centum...appellati. These sentences introduce the problem of the *patres*, which recurs in c. 17. Livy here ascribes the creation of a Senate to Romulus, and attributes the titles *patres*, *patricii* to the privilege of membership thereof: Dionysius states that Romulus formed his Senate on a representative basis, ἐκ τῶν πατρικίων ἄνδρας ἑκατὸν ἐπιλεξάμενος. In other words, Livy says they were *patres* because they were *senatores*, and Dionysius *vice versa*. Possibly the truth may rest in part with both views. The *patres familias*, i.e. chiefs of clans, united to form the original state, must have met for the conduct of common affairs before a king was chosen: he continued the council, but controlled its composition by his own choice, i.e. he formed an order from the *patres familias* and their families, *patricii* (= those who possessed a chief or *pater familias*), 'clansmen.' The members of this order, supplemented perhaps from time to time by a fresh choice of senators (*lectio senatus*) on the part of the King, naturally appropriated the titles *patres*, *patricii* for themselves and their descendants: in this sense Livy may be right in saying *patres certe ab honore, patriciique progenies eorum appellati.* Cicero (*de Rep.* II. 23) holds the same view. For the further development of the question, see notes on *patres* in c. 17.

CHAPTER IX.

p. 13. 1 § 1. **finitimarum...bello**] 'war against, upon'; objective genitive.

penuria] 'for want of': abl. of cause.

2 **hominis...erat**] 'was destined to last but one man's lifetime,' 'for a single generation.'

5 § 2. **ex consilio patrum**] 'on the advice of the Fathers.' Romulus put to immediate use the council of his creation.

7 § 3. **urbes...miscere**] The arguments of the envoys are thrown into *oratio obliqua*, loosely introduced by the previous sentence.

10 § 4. **origini Romanae**] 'the birth of Rome,' i.e. 'Rome at her birth,' from which *Romae* must be carried on to the second half of the sentence. Even as (*et*) the gods had begun, so (*et*) would manly worth (*virtus*) continue the work.

12 **sanguinem...miscere**] 'blend their blood and stock': cf. IV. 4. 6 *sanguinem sociare.*

13 § 5. **adeo**] 'indeed'; see n. on Praef. 11.

14 **sibi...metuebant]** The dat. expresses the completion of the sense: but the use of *metuo* with direct and indirect objects together is rare.

15 **plerisque rogitantibus]** abl. abs. 'with the frequent enquiry.'

16 **id...demum]** 'that nothing else would be a fitting form of wedlock': the clause drifts into *or. obl.* after the sense contained in *rogitantibus*.

19 **§ 6. aegritudinem animi]** 'personal annoyance': the word echoes *aegre* just above.

21 **Neptuno Equestri...Consualia]** Held afterwards on 21 August. *Consus* is probably connected with *condere*, i.e. 'the god of the (harvest) store'—whether kept above or below ground. So this is a harvest-home festival—a holiday for all country-folk, in which horses and mules shared. At one of the two Consualia horse-races took place in the Circus Maximus, which may owe its origin to the festival. So *Consus* (whose altar was at one end of the Circus) came to be identified with Poseidon Hippius (Dion. H. II. 31), Latinized into *Neptunus Equester*. It would be natural to invite neighbours to such a merry-making, and possibly the capture of wives in the course of it was not infrequent. Fowler, *R. F.* pp. 206—9.

22 **§ 7. quantoque...poterant]** 'with all the magnificence then known or possible.' **concelebrant]** is a present of anticipation, 'prepared to celebrate.'

23 **claram exspectatamque]** The two epithets are inter-dependent; 'famous by expectancy,' 'by the anticipation thereof.'

24 **§ 8. mortales]** not uncommon in the sense of 'souls,' 'persons.'

25 **proximi quique]** 'all the nearest communities.'

26 **Caeninenses]** of Caenina, E. of Rome. **Crustumini]** of Crustumeria or Crustumium, about 12 miles N. of Rome, beyond Fidenae. **Antemnates]** of Antemna (or -ae), at the junction of the Anio and the Tiber.

28 **§ 9. per domos]** 'in every house.'

frequentem tectis] 'close-packed with houses.'

31 **§ 10. ex composito]** 'as agreed,' 'according to the plan': the phrase recurs in 53. 5.

32 **vis]** 'the violence'—explained by what follows, and expected after the statement *ad vim spectare res coepit* in § 6.

p. 14. 1 **§ 11. magna pars...raptae]** (sc. *sunt*): the construction suits the sense.

forte] 'indiscriminately,' just as they were (ὡς ἔτυχον).

in quem] i.e. *ab eo* (*eis*), *in quem*. **inciderat]** 'fell in with,' 'encountered': the pluperfect expresses frequency; cf. n. on *nuntiaretur* 31. 4.

2 **excellentes...destinatas**] The first point gives the reason for the second.

3 **ex plebe**] is practically an adjective 'of the populace,'=*plebeii*: cf. 17. 4 *sine imperio*.

6 § **12. Talassii**] The real meaning of this word is still undecided. We know that *Talasse* or *Talassio* was the regular Roman cry of salutation to a bride as she passed to the bridegroom's house; and it is probable that the word is an invocation of some old marriage-god, associated with the primitive form of marriage by capture of which the 'Rape of the Sabines' is here made a type. The word *Talus* is an old Sabine name, and the marriage-god *Talassius* or *Talassio* may have been of Sabine origin. Another marriage-custom which survived from the days of wife-capture was the parting of the bride's hair with the point of a spear (called *hasta caelibaris*) to indicate that she was the prize of the spear (cf. Gk. δορίληπτος).

raptam ferunt] 'was being carried off, they say': the *or. obl.* reproduces *rapiebatur*.

8 **inde**] Note that Livy, by using *oratio obliqua*, leaves the responsibility for this explanation with his informants.

10 § **13. incusantes...foedus**] either (1) 'denouncing a treaty where hospitality had been outraged': gen. of quality, cf. IX. 45. 18 *miserunt Romam oratores pacis petendae amicitiaeque*; or (2) 'accusing the treaty of violated hospitality,' i.e. regarding the treaty as responsible for the outrage. It is proposed by some commentators to read *violatum* for *violati*, or *scelus* for *foedus*.

12 **per fas ac fidem**] (1) 'by religion and honour' (which they expected the Romans to observe): cf. Plaut. *Most.* 500 *per fidem deceptus sum*, 'under promise of protection': or (2) *per*=παρά, 'contrary to': cf. *perfidus*, *periurus*, *perdo*.

raptis] For the position and case see n. on 5. 6 *et Numitori*. There were 683 of the *raptae*, according to Dionysius (II. 30); and they were paraded next day, and allotted by Romulus.

14 § **14. patrum**] i.e. of the Sabine women.

15 **in matrimonio**] They would have the position of wives, not of concubines, in spite of their parents' refusal to accept *conubium* with Rome: cf. Dion. H. II. 30. 5 ὡς οὐκ ἐφ' ὕβρει τῆς ἁρπαγῆς ἀλλ' ἐπὶ γάμῳ γενομένης. *in matrimonio* gives the legal position, the rest of the sentence its characteristics.

17 **liberum**] gen. pl.: the form occurs again in 39. 4. **fore**] emphatic, 'would live.'

17 § **15. mollirent, darent]** in *oratio recta mollite, date.*

19 **animos]** 'affections.'

20 **usuras]** 'they would find.'

22 **parentium...desiderium]** 'satisfy their craving for parents and homeland.' **expleat]** The tense reproduces the original statement.

23 § **16. factum purgantium]** *factum* is either (1) a substantive; 'seeking to excuse the deed on the ground of passion'; or (2) = *factum esse*, 'pleading the excuse that it was done in passion.'

24 **ad]** 'to deal with,' 'in reference to': cf. 26. 5 *ingrati ad vulgus iudicii*; IX. 16. 14 *invicti ad laborem corporis.*

CHAPTER X.

26 § **1. raptis]** 'of the stolen women.' Dat. of close relationship; see n. on 5. 6 *Numitori.*

30 **Titum Tatium]** *Tatius* is probably connected with *tata*, 'father.' The whole name suits the early Latin taste for alliteration: cf. Ennius, *o Tite tute Tati tibi tanta tiranne tulisti*; and our phrases 'tit for tat,' 'tittle-tattle,' 'tick-tack.'

31 **eo]** 'to his court.'

p. 15. 4 § **3. pro ardore]** 'to satisfy the zeal.'

6 **nomen Caeninum]** i.e. all persons called of Caenina, 'the whole state of Caenina': cf. 23. 4 *Albanum*, 52. 4 *Latinum.*

9 § **4. fundit...fusum]** See n. on 5. 3 *cepisse...captum.*

13 § **5. cum...minor]** 'splendid in prowess, and no less splendid in his display of the same.'

15 **gerens]** Rare in prose in this literal sense; it occurs again in 26. 2, there also in connection with *spolia.*

Capitolium] i.e. the hill afterwards so called, the S. end of the Capitoline: the N. end was called *Arx.*

escendit] This word, which denotes climbing to the top of some high object, with some exertion, is appropriate here. It is found with *in Capitolium* (in some MSS. at any rate) in XXXVIII. 48. 16, and 51. 12: and with *in arcem* of another city in XXXVII. 37. 2.

16 **quercum...sacram]** As the tree of Jupiter—regarded perhaps as his dwelling-place—the oak was naturally sacred to the shepherds; and in this dedication of spoils to Jupiter of the oak, we see an interesting prototype of the triumphal procession of historical times, which led the oak-crowned victor to the temple of Jupiter on the Capitol. Cf. Fowler, *R. F.* pp. 229 foll.: Frazer, *Kingship*, p. 199.

17 **designavit...finis**] Cf. 35. 8. The seclusion of a small enclosure (*sacellum*) would be a natural step in the development of a primitive worship: the connection of the act with Romulus is of a piece with traditional custom.

cognomen] 'special title,' i.e. a special epithet for the particular cult.

18 § **6. Feretri**] here connected with *feretrum*, the frame (cf. *ferculum* above) on which trophies were carried: so 'the Carrier,' i.e. receiver of spoils hung upon his tree, i.e. upon himself. Notice *fero...ferent* also in the form of dedication. But it may with perhaps greater probability be connected with *ferire*, thus making Jupiter 'the Striker,' an appropriate epithet of a god who wields the lightning: and Propertius (IV. 10. 46 *omine quod certo dux ferit ense ducem*) gives this first of the two derivations.

19 **templum**] 'a close': **regionibus**] 'boundaries': **animo metatus**] (cf. 18. 8 *animo finivit*) 'measured in fancy.' These are all terms of augury: see the notes on 18. 7—8.

21 **sedem...spoliis**] *sedem* is in apposition to *templum*: cf. 30. 2 *templum...curiam*. *spolia opima* = 'spoils in chief,' 'spoils of honour,' taken personally by a Roman commander from the commander of the enemy, slain in single combat. It is interesting to note in this connection the following clause of an ancient law, said to belong to the kingly period: *cui suo auspicio classe procincta opima spolia capiuntur dari aeris* CCC *oporteat et bovem caedito Iovi Feretrio* (Festus, *opima*, p. 189). There were three recorded instances of *spolia opima*: (1) this one; (2) in 428 B.C., when A. Cornelius Cossus won them from Lars Tolumnius, king of Veii (IV. 20): (3) in 222 B.C., when Marcellus won them from Viridomarus, king of the Insubrian Gauls.

22 **me auctorem**] 'my example.'

24 § **7. primum**] Romulus is represented as choosing an ancient worship and making it, by means of a temple, the religious centre and focus of his new state.

25 **visum**] 'was ordained,' 'seemed good' (=ἔδοξε): the two clauses *nec...esse*, *nec...laudem* are its dependents.

26 **nuncupavit**] 'solemnly stated' (as part of the act of dedication): indicative, because the statement comes from the historian.

nec...laudem] 'and that the honour of such a gift should not be made common because of the number of those who achieved success.' *eius doni* explains both *compotum* and *laudem*. *eius doni laudem*, 'the renown of the particular gift,' or 'the honour of such a gift' (to the god):

in IV. 32. 11 a Dictator exhorts his Master of the Horse to be *memor opimi doni, Romulique ac Iovis Feretrii.*

27 **bina**] 'on two occasions.' *spolia opima* is like *castra*, a plural with a special meaning: so *bina* not *duo*.

inter] 'in the course of': cf. 29. 1 *inter haec iam praemissi Albam erant equites*, 55. 3 *inter principia condendi huius operis.*

29 **eius fortuna decoris**] 'the happiness of that distinction.' *fortuna* = τὸ εὔδαιμον, implying at once that to win the *spolia opima* was a rare piece of luck, and also that it was vouchsafed from heaven (cf. *dis visum*).

CHAPTER XI.

31 § **1. per occasionem ac solitudinem**] is a hendiadys, 'took advantage of the absence of defenders.'

hostiliter] 'as an act of war.' **ad hos**] 'to meet them.'

p. 16. 1 **legio**] 'levy.'

2 **oppressit**] 'caught.'

§ **2. impetu et clamore**] 'charge and cheer.'

3 **ovantem**] See 26. 10 *n*.

4 **Hersilia**] The name belongs originally to a Sabine deity, the mate of Quirinus: then, when Quirinus and Romulus were identified, Hersilia took human form as chief of the Sabine women, and was associated with Romulus. She was supposed to have taken the lead (which as a Sabine patron-saint of marriage she would naturally do) in making peace after the battle mentioned by Livy in c. 12.

precibus fatigata] 'importuned by the prayers'—just as Queen Esther was importuned by the prayers of Mordecai (Esther, iv.).

8 § **3. ceciderant**] 'were already depressed.'

9 § **4. utroque**] i.e. to Antemnae and Crustumerium.

coloniae] Here Livy assumes that the conquests of Rome were colonized in the fashion of a later time, and thus carries the system back to Romulus.

10 **in Crustuminum...darent**] 'gave in their names for (offered to go to) the Crustumine territory.' *nomina dare* is properly a military phrase, 'to enlist': and this was practically enlistment for colonial service.

11 **migratum**] Romulus did not object to this, as he wanted a settled population.

13 § **5. novissimum**] 'last of all': for the predicative use of the adjective cf. *Praef.* 11 *tam serae...immigraverint.*

ab Sabinis ortum] 'arose on the Sabine side,' or 'was begun by the Sabines,' *ortum* being regarded as equivalent to *coeptum*.

14 **per iram aut cupiditatem**] (cf. 12. 1 below) 'for motives of passion or greed.

16 § **6. consilio**] 'strategy': the word sums up the sense of *nihil... intulerunt*.

Tarpeius] The personal name is probably formed from an ancient designation of part of the Capitoline Hill. *arci* here would seem to mean the whole hill: in later times *Arx* was the name of the N. height, but the *Saxum Tarpeium* is usually placed at the S. end, commonly called *Capitolium*. A recent authority, however, places it on the *Arx*. Cf. Ettore Pais, *Ancient Legends of Roman History*, chap. vi. 1.

18 **accipiat...accepti**] See n. on 5. 3 *cepisse.. captum*.

19 **sacris**] dat. of 'work contemplated' (Roby, § 481). Cf. 21. 5 *loca sacris faciendis*, 35. 1 *comitia regi creando*.

20 § **7. armis**] 'shields': so again in 25. 5.

21 **prodendi...causa**] 'to make a public example.' The *proditori* which follows seems almost to require that *prodendi* should be taken in its other sense of 'betray,' but the construction scarcely permits this.

22 **ne quid...esset**] *fidum* is predicative: 'that nothing on earth should trust a traitor.'

23 § **8. quod...habuerint**] 'because they had': subjunctive, because in *oratio obliqua* as part of the *fabula*.

24 **magna specie**] 'of massive form.'

25 **pepigisse**] 'covenanted for.'

manibus] = 'hands' or 'arms': the ambiguity enabled the Sabines to evade the spirit, by keeping the letter, of their promise.

quod...haberent] 'what they had' (she said).

26 **eo**] = *ea re* 'therefore': cf. such uses as *eo melius*.

27 § **9. ex pacto tradendi**] 'by the terms of surrender.' This version of the story is that of L. Calpurnius Piso, who added that Tarpeia communicated her scheme to Romulus, and that her tomb was honoured by the Romans. Cf. Dion. H. II. 38; Florus, I. I. 12. Propertius (IV. 4) makes Tarpeia a Vestal, who betrays the Capitol to Tatius in her love for him.

28 **derecto**] 'outright.' **petisse**] For contracted form see note on 7. 7 *mugissent*.

sua...mercede] 'was done to death instead (*ipsam*) by the payment of her own choice.'

CHAPTER XII.

30 § **1. tamen**] = δ' οὖν, 'as a matter of fact' (no matter what the legends are).

31 **quod...est**] The indicative is used to describe a permanent fact, not affected by the clause *cum...complessent*. *campi* gen. of divided whole, cf. 14. 4 *agri quod...est*; Caes. *B.G.* III. 16 *navium quod ubique fuerat in unum locum coegerant*.

p. **17.** 4 **ab Sabinis**] 'on the side of': cf. § 8 below; 17. 2 *ab sua parte;* and Plautus, *Rud.* 1100 *omnia ego istaec facile patior, dum hic hinc a me sentiat. Tr. atqui nunc a te stat, verum hinc cibit testimonium.*

§ **2. Mettius Curtius**] The first name reappears in 23. 4, assigned to the Alban dictator, just as Hostilius reappears in his opponent, Tullus Hostilius. Perhaps *Mettius* is to be connected with *medix* or *meddix*, an Alban magistrate. *Curtius* is probably the same as *curtus* 'short': it is the title of a Roman gens.

5 **Hostius Hostilius**] For the alliteration and duplication cf. *Titus Tatius*.

6 **ad prima signa**] 'in the forefront of the battle.'

8 **ad veterem...Palatii**] Dionysius calls it Μουγωνίδες πύλαι: it was on the N.E. side of the Palatium, opening on the Via Nova, near the site of the temple of Jupiter Stator. See plan.

9 § **3. et ipse**] See n. on Praef. 3.

13 § **4. superata**] combines the notions of 'pass' and 'seize.'

16 § **6. templum**] No actual temple was built till 294 B.C.: but the dedication of the spot as a *templum* of Jupiter Stator may well have been traceable to the regal period.

Statori] 'as the Stayer': Ζεὺς ὀρθώσιος, Dion. H. II. 50.

17 **praesenti**] 'prompt,' 'powerful': cf. 'a very present help in trouble' Psalm 46, 1.

19 § **7. optimus maximus**] standing epithets of Jupiter, frequently found in inscriptions.

20 **tamquam**] (= ὡς, ἅτε) expresses *their* view of the command.

22 § **8. princeps**] 'first,' 'at their head': cf. 26. 2.

23 **toto...est**] 'throughout the whole area now belonging to the Forum': *spatio* must be supplied with *toto*.

25 § **9. perfidos...hostes**] 'our faithless friends, our faint-hearted foes.'

30 **alia**] = *cetera*: cf. 7. 3 *aliis*.

31 **sese...coniecit**] He saw that this was his only chance of escape. Cf. Dion. Hal. II. 42.

p. 18. 1 **adnuentibus suis favore...animo**] Livy is fond of accumulating ablatives in this fashion to introduce all the attendant circumstances of an action. Examples will be found in 13. 1; 14. 8; 15. 4; 33. 1; 46. 1.

CHAPTER XIII.

6 § **1. crinibus...pavore**] For the accumulation of ablatives, see note above. Here the first two describe the appearance of the women, the third explains their intervention.

8 **ex transverso**] 'across': cf. *transversam* 14. 9.

11 § **2. soceri generique**] nom. pl.

parricidio] 'the slaughter of kindred.' The word is variously derived: *parens*, *pater*, or *par* (preposition) + *caedo*. The meaning seems to have been gradually extended, from the murder of parents (as in 47. 1 below) to that of relatives (as here), of magistrates (as 'fathers' in office), of citizens generally: then to have denoted murderous (i.e. treasonable) action towards one's country (as in 52. 1 below). For the first extension of meaning cf. **αὐτοκτόνος**, which is applied to Medea's murder of her children, and to the mutual murder of Eteocles and Polynices.

12 **nepotum**] 'their babes, born to be grandchildren of the one party, and children of the other.'

13 § **3. adfinitatis**] 'connexion': **conubii**] 'intermarriage.'

15 **melius peribimus**] 'it will be better for us to perish': cf. 50. 5 *quod si sui bene crediderint cives*.

sine...vestrum] 'by losing one or other of you.'

17 § **4. quies**] 'cessation of hostilities': cf. *ἡσυχία*.

20 **consociant**] 'agree to concentrate': Dionysius (II. 4. 6) says *ἱερὰ συνενεγκάμενοι*. **imperium**] 'government,' 'sovereignty.'

21 § **5. tamen**] 'after all,' i.e. in spite of seeming advantages to the Romans.

Quirites a Curibus] 'they (the new body of citizens) were called Q. after Cures'—the ancient capital of the Sabines, situated on a tributary of the Tiber, in the S. of the Sabine territory. The tradition that a body of Sabine raiders successfully established itself on the Quirinal Hill and even the Capitoline, and subsequently became united with the Latin tenants of the Palatine, is probably sound; and the name

Quirites dates back to this fusion. Cf. Festus, p. 254, *Quirites autem dicti post foedus a Romulo et Tatio percussum communionem et societatem populi factam indicant*; and the formal title *populus Romanus Quiritium* (which occurs in 24. 5 and 32. 11 below). But whence came this title of *Quirites* we know not for certain: besides the local derivation which Livy offers, there are those from *quiris* (*curis*), a Sabine word for 'spear,' and from *curia* 'ward,' the organisation mentioned below. The connection with *curis* is hard to reconcile with the civil, non-military character which very early became attached to the word *Quirites*, and was made use of by Caesar in addressing his mutinous legionaries: on the other hand, *curia* would supply just that basis of definite political organisation required, and would indicate that this fusion of Latins and Sabines was the real foundation of the state.

24 **statuit**] 'halted,' 'brought up.'

Curtium...appellarunt] A different story is told in VII. 6 to account for the name of the *lacus Curtius*: according to the version there given M. Curtius mounted his horse, and leaped into a cavity which had suddenly opened.

25 **§ 6. ex bello...pax**] a chiasmus, which serves to throw special emphasis on the word *pax*. For *laeta repente pax* ('the gratification of unexpected peace') cf. note on Praef. 2 *novi semper scriptores*. Peace was valuable to Rome because it gave time for the further solidification of the civic system.

27 **curias**] 'wards.' The word (probably connected with *curare*, from a root *sku*, shelter) has two meanings: (1) a building for religious purposes (like 'church'); (2) a district (like 'parish'), whose inhabitants dwell near the building, and meet therein for periodical services and feasts (e.g. the *Fornacalia*), under the supervision of a *curio*. In both senses the word became less religious and more political in course of time. Legend attributes the political organisation of *curiae* to a person (Romulus), as usual, but more probably it was a gradual development: perhaps the formation of the thirty here mentioned represents a time somewhat later than the union of Roman and Sabine communities—the era of 'Tullus Hostilius' in fact, commemorated in the common court-house called after him *curia Hostilia*, and in the *comitium*.

28 **nomina earum**] This account (rejected by Plutarch and Varro) is probably based on the accidental appropriateness of some of the existing names (e.g. *Titia, Rapta*): it does not suit such titles as *Veliensis, Foriensis*, which seem to have had a local origin.

29 **§ 7. cum...fuerit]** 'although as a matter of fact the number of women must have been considerably greater than this' (30).

30 **aetate...sint]** The possible methods of selection are given—seniority, rank, lot. *lectae sint* represents *lectae sunt* of direct narration, just as *fuerit=fuit*. *darent* follows the past sense implied in *lectae sint*, and represents the *dabunt* of direct narration.

31 **§ 8. eodem tempore]** Here, as in 30. 1—3 and again in cc. 35—36, the developments in political and military organisations are closely connected.

32 **centuriae]** 'squadrons': mentioned again in 36. 2. According to the account of Dionysius (II. 13), the 30 *curiae* each chose 10 men: it appears also that there was a military organisation in 10 *turmae* of 30 men each (10 *Ramnenses*, 10 *Titienses*, 10 *Luceres*). This arrangement, though supported by the mention of *decem turmae* in c. 30. 3 below, does not agree very well with the three *centuriae*, unless we regard these as administrative and not tactical units, each under its own officer, who in turn was responsible to the *Tribunus Celerum*.

p. 19. 1 **Ramnenses...Titienses...Lucerum]** All that is certain about these names is their extreme antiquity. Probably the first two indicate the Roman and Sabine elements of that fusion described above (n. on *Quirites*): *Ramnes* (as the word appears in 36. 2) may be connected with *Roma*, or with a root *rap*='harry,' 'hurry'; *Titienses* may have some relation to a Sabine name or worship, for the *sodales Titii* were appointed *retinendis Sabinorum sacris* (cf. Tac. *Ann.* I. 54). The *Luceres* are still, as in Livy's day, shrouded in obscurity: they have sometimes been traced to an Etruscan origin, by connecting the word with *lucumo*, an Etruscan title, but there is no evidence to show that Etruscans had a share in the political origins of Rome. There may be some truth in the view of Lange which connects the *Luceres* with Alba, and believes that an Alban element was incorporated in the Quirites, at a somewhat later date—the period of 'Tullus Hostilius' abovementioned. Derived (like *lucumo*) from the root *luk* 'shine,' the word may have meant 'brilliant lords' (cf. *splendidi, illustrissimi*)—the *principes Albanorum* mentioned in 30. 2: if so, the completion of the senate of 300, the 30 *curiae*, and the 3 *centuriae* all came perhaps at the conclusion of a struggle with Alba. In Propertius IV. 1. 31 there is authority for the reading *hinc Titiens Ramnesque viri Luceresque Soloni*; and Dionysius (II. 37. 2) states that Lucumo brought from Solonium a band of Etruscans to help Romulus against Titus Tatius, and that an Alban contingent came for the same purpose. Now Solonium was close to Lanuvium and Ardea (from which place, according to Festus, the Luceres came under their king Lucerus): and it is possible that the third element in the Roman polity is to be traced to that district, where, as we have seen already, the early struggles of the Aborigines and their Trojan (Pelasgian) allies took place.

2 **non...concors**] 'not united only, but unanimous.'

CHAPTER XIV.

6 § **1. pulsant**] 'beat.' Dionysius (II. 51, 52) gives in detail the story of the raid. Romulus was willing to deliver up the culprits, but Tatius refused: the followers of Tatius attacked the Laurentine envoys, and brought matters to the verge of war. Romulus then surrendered the offenders, but Tatius rescued them.

iure...agerent] 'proceeded according to the law of nations': i.e. the usages commonly observed by the various Italian *gentes* with whom the Romans early came in contact. Of these usages the Roman lawyers formed a system which should operate in cases where non-Romans were concerned, as opposed to the *ius civile* by which the Romans themselves were judged.

9 § **2. Lavini...ad sollemne sacrificium**] See notes on 1. 9 *penates*, 2. 6 *Iovem Indigetem*.

12 § **3. ob...regni**] 'because the dual kingship could not be trusted': cf. Ennius *nulla sancta societas nec fides regni est*; Tac. *Ann.* XIII. 17 *insociabile regnum aestimantes*.

13 **haud iniuria**] Romulus (acc. to Dion. H.) opposed the action of Tatius, and had no personal quarrel with the Laurentines.

19 § **4. nimis vicinas**] Fidenae was about 5 miles N. of Rome.

20 **opes**] 'a power.'

esset] The subj. implies anticipation: 'before it could be.'

21 **occupant...facere**] 'began war first': for this use of *occupo*, with infinitive, not uncommon in Livy, cf. 30. 8.

25 § **5. tumultus repens**] 'the sudden disorder': cf. Ov. *M.* V. 5 *inque repentinos convivia versa tumultus*.

28 § **6. mille passuum**] For the acc. cf. 23. 3 n.

30 **locis...obscuris**] 'in stations here and there hidden by reason of the very thick brushwood-growth.' The MSS. here have *circa densa obsita virgulta*, which must surely be wrong. I am of opinion that the reading adopted in the text may have been corrupted thus: *densissima* (with *ob* written above)

virgulta, *densis ob sima v.*, *densa obsita v.* If *densa obsita virgulta* is allowed to stand, *densa* must be regarded as qualifying the compound word *obsita-virgulta*: cf. 31. 8 *quaedam occulta sollemnia-sacrificia*, 57. 11 *ab nocturno iuvenali-ludo*.

§ **7**. **subsidĕre**] 'crouch.' **id quod quaerebat**] refers to *hostem excivit*.

p. 20. 1 **genere...adequitando**] For the combination of ablatives see n. on 8. 4 *munitionibus...appetendo*. **portis**] Cf. IX. 22. 4 *adequitare Samnites vallo*.

2 **quae...erat**] 'which was to be feigned' according to the stratagem.

3 **mirabilem**] 'remarkable,' 'noticeable.' In a cavalry engagement there are always charges and countercharges.

4 § **8**. **inter...trepidante**] 'wavering between the thought of fight or of flight': cf. 27. 11.

5 **plenis...portis**] For the order cf. n. on *novi* etc. Praef. 2. Here *repente* belongs both to *plenis* and to *effusi*. 'On a sudden, the gates were crowded, and the enemy streamed out.'

6 **impulsa...studio**] For the accumulation of ablatives see note on 12. 9. *impulsa* 'broken.'

8 § **9**. **transversam**] 'in flank,' 'enfiladed,' as we should say now. So *ex transverso* 13. 1.

9 **pavorem**] i.e. the panic caused by the flank attack.

12 **circumagerent**] 'could turn.' The subjunctive with *priusquam* expresses anticipated intention; the indicative, anticipated action.

terga vertunt] The historic present is associated with a historic tense (*circumagerent*); cf. *obicerentur...irrumpit* in § 11 below.

13 **effusius**] 'in greater disorder' than the *simulantes* (acc. pl.), i.e. 'feigning fugitives,' 'a feigned flight' (the Romans).

15 § **11**. **in tergo**] 'at their heels.'

CHAPTER XV.

17 § **1**. **Veientium animi**] = *Veientes*, the real subject of *excucurrerunt*. The V. had three reasons for interference—political, racial, local.

20 **si...essent**] This clause amplifies the notion of *propinquitas loci*: 'if (as they felt) the arms of Rome were (or were to be) a danger to all their neighbours.' *essent* in direct narration might be either *sunt* or *futura sunt*. For *si* cf. the Greek use of εἰ after words of emotion.

22 **populabundi** (nom. pl.)...**belli**] 'in the fashion of a raid, rather than

of regular warfare.' What advantage they expected from this marauding is not clear: it would naturally seem to be the readiest way of exciting the Romans to energetic action.

25 § **2. Romanus**] used collectively for 'the Romans': cf. 25. 12 (*Romanus Albano*), 27. 10 (*Veientem*).

26 **dimicationi...intentusque**] 'equipped and eager for a final struggle.' Dat. of 'work contemplated' (Roby, § 481): cf. 21. 5 *loca sacris faciendis*.

28 § **3. potius**] implies that they preferred an open fight: for the tactics cf. 2. 5 *cum moenibus bellum propulsare posset, in aciem copias eduxit.*

29 **de**] 'from,' i.e. 'down from.'

30 § **4. viribus...adiutis**] 'his forces unaided by strategy,' in contrast to c. 14 above: the sense is repeated by *tantum...robore*. For *arte* many MSS. read *parte*, i.e. 'in no respect.' For the accumulation of ablatives in this sentence see n. on 12. 9.

32 **fusos...hostes**] The participle adds a separate predicate: *vicit —fudit—persecutus est.*

urbe valida] 'stronghold,' amplified by the clause *muris...munita*. The final struggle with Veii came later, in historical times (405—396 B.C.).

p. 21. 4 **oratores**] 'envoys,' lit. 'speakers' of oral instructions: so Virg. *Aen.* VII. 153.

§ **5. agri**] This is in effect the beginning of the *ager publicus* of Rome: *publicatur enim ille ager qui ex hostibus captus est, Digest* XLIX. 45. 20. The portion of territory, acquired by conquest (cf. 33. 8), or *deditio* (cf. c. 38), which was not appropriated by the king or devoted to sacred use or incorporated in *ager privatus* (cf. 46. 1), became *ager publicus*.

multatis] dative, scil. *Veientibus*: 'mulcted,' 'condemned to lose'; a judicial word for punishment, especially used in the case of fines. Cf. 49. 5.

in centum annos] But in c. 27 the Fidenates and Veientes renew the war.

6 § **6. haec ferme**]=τοιαῦτα καὶ παραπλήσια, 'such, more or less.'

domi militiaeque] See n. on Praef. 9.

7 **absonum fidei**] 'out of harmony with a belief in,' 'inconsistent with the credibility of.' The dat. expresses the thing affected, and is used loosely in such cases as this by Augustan and later writers, where a preposition would be required by the Ciceronian idiom (Roby, § 474). Cf. Horace, *A.P.* 112 *si dicentis erunt fortunis absona dicta*; *Ep.* I. 18. 5 *est huic diversum vitio vitium prope maius.*

8 **creditae**] 'accredited,' 'accepted.' It is possible that in this departure and deification of Romulus, as in the decease of Aeneas (c. 2. 6) and the destruction of Tullus Hostilius (c. 31. 8), we have evidences of the close connection between the kingship and Jupiter, the god of the sky, of the thunder, and of the oak. As *Quirinus*, if we derive it from the same root as *quercus*, Romulus *was* in effect the oak god. Cf. A. B. Cook, 'Zeus, Jupiter, and the oak, *Classical Review*, xviii. (1904), pp. 368 foll.; Frazer, *op. cit.* p. 206.

Ovid (*Fasti*, II. 477—480) gives the three usual explanations of the name: *sive quod hasta curis priscis est dicta Sabinis, bellicus a telo venit in astra deus: sive suo regi nomen posuere Quirites; seu quia Romanis iunxerat ille Cures*. Quirinus is held to be a Sabine deity by Varro; and it is noteworthy that his *flamen*, down to imperial times, must needs be a Patrician. If *Quirinus* is derived from *Cures*, the form may be due to Plebeian pronunciation: for the Greek writers transliterate it as Κύριvος. See Prof. W. Ridgeway's paper, *Who were the Romans?* read before the British Academy on 24 April, 1907.

With the mythical exception of Romulus the Romans raised none of their heroes to divine estate until the latter end of the Republic, when Greek and Oriental notions began to possess the minds of all classes. When Livy wrote this account of the apotheosis of Romulus, Julius Caesar had been deified, and Augustus was receiving divine honours at Rome and abroad.

10 **non...firmandae**] The three clauses are an expansion of *nihil. condendae...firmandae* are genitives of definition.

11 § **7. profecto**] 'assuredly,' i.e. no one will gainsay: the word throws an added emphasis on *ab illo*, cf. 36. 4. **valuit**] i.e. the Roman state.

12 **in quadraginta deinde annos**] Cf. 6. 1 *caedem deinceps tyranni*.

14 § **8. ante alios**] This may be taken in two ways: (1) 'more than other (kings),' referring to Romulus: (2) 'to the sympathies of soldiers, far more than others,' where it stands for *magis quam aliorum* (*animis*). The character described suits Julius Caesar as well as Romulus: possibly Livy had the former in his mind.

trecentosque...corporis] Here is assigned to Romulus one of the regular adjuncts of the Greek tyrant, the body-guard granted by his supporters to protect him against political opponents.

15 **Celeres**] This word is either derived from a root *kal*, i.e. 'speedy,' 'excellent,' so 'champions': or connected with κέλης, 'a cavalier.' Celer is mentioned as their eponymous chief in Ovid, *Fasti*, IV. 837.

CHAPTER XVI.

(See Introduction, § 4: and compare the account given by Ovid, *Fasti*, II. 475—512.)

17 § 1. **immortalibus**] 'undying,' with a notion of 'fit for immortality,' i.e. divinity: cf. 7. 15 n.

18 **ad...paludem**] (called in Ovid, *Fasti*, II. 491 *Caprea palus*) i.e. the part of the Campus Martius in which the Circus Flaminius was afterwards laid out.

20 **fragore tonitribusque**] 'thunder-claps,' a hendiadys.

22 **nec...fuit**] 'And afterwards Romulus was not on earth': a conventional phrase for the disappearance of a hero; cf. Genesis, v. 24 (of Enoch) 'He was not.' For the significance of the sudden disappearance in a storm, see n. on c. 15. 6 above.

23 § 2. **ex tam turbido die**] 'after this disturbance of the day,' 'hour of tempest.' For this use of *dies* as a part of itself cf. Virg. *Ec.* III. 57 *nunc formosissimus annus.*

25 **satis...patribus**] 'was quite prepared to believe the Fathers.'

26 **sublimem raptum**] sc. *esse Romulum*, 'whirled away on high.' *sublimis* is predicative here and in § 7. The phrase is poetical, and occurs frequently in Plautus and Terence: Virgil too is fond of *sublimis*, cf. *Aen.* I. 415 *ipsa Paphum sublimis abit.*

27 **aliquamdiu**] Note the position of the adverb.

28 § 3. **deum**] For the significance of this deification see note on *creditae* in c. 15. 6 above. **parentem urbis**] Cicero was hailed as *parens patriae* after the discomfiture of the Catilinarian conspiracy; and the title *pater patriae* was accepted by Julius Caesar, Augustus, and Vespasian.

29 **salvere...iubent**] 'saluted.' **precibus**] i.e. they at once accepted the deification.

30 **volens propitius**] 'of his grace and favour': the two words occur in a form of prayer to Mars in Cato, *de Re Rustica*, 141, 2. For the asyndeton cf. *prima postrema* 24. 7, *vellent iuberentne* 46. 1.

31 **sospitet**] is also an old religious word.

§ 4. **tum quoque**] 'even then'—as there are rationalists to-day, Livy means.

p. 22. 1 **manavit**] 'spread,' 'leaked out': cf. II. 49. 1 *manat tota urbe rumor.*

4 § 5. **Proculus Iulius**] The legend said that he was an Alban; his

second name may have been added as a compliment to the *gens Iulia*, which proudly traced its origin to Alba.

5 **gravis...auctor**] 'a weighty authority, according to tradition, however great the event.'

quamvis magnae] 'however (no matter how) great': cf. 4. 4 *quamvis languida*.

7 § **6**. **Quirites**] See n. on 13. 5.

prima...luce] 'at dawn to-day.'

10 **ut contra...esset**] 'that it might be lawful to regard him face to face' —as a mark of divine favour. The Roman custom in prayer was to cover the head and prostrate the body to the earth.

15 § **8**. **abiit**] Livy omits to state that Romulus (according to the legend) here announced his divinity as Quirinus: cf. Ovid, *Fasti*, II. 507 *tura ferant, placentque novum pia turba Quirinum*.

mirum (*est*) **quantum...fuerit**] The construction here is normal, *fuerit* denoting the *fuit* of direct narration: *quantum* is adverbial. Sometimes *mirum quantum*, regarded as one word (like θαυμάσιον ὅσον), takes indicative: cf. II. I. II *id mirum quantum profuit ad concordiam civitatis*.

haec] neut. pl. after *nuntianti*.

17 **facta...immortalitatis**] 'by the establishment of a belief in his immortality': cf. 15. 6.

CHAPTER XVII.

(See Introduction, § 4.)

18 § **1**. **Patrum**] The word, placed thus at the head of the chapter, is in direct contrast to *plebem exercitumque* just above.

certamen...cupido] 'an ambitious struggle for the kingdom': how protracted it was is expressed by *versabat* and the following imperfects.

20 **in...populo**] i.e. 'because it was a new nation.'

pervenerat] i.e. *certamen...cupido*. In this sentence the MSS. have *a singulis* (emended into *ad singulos*), which would mean that the contest had its origin in individuals.

21 **factionibus inter ordines**] See n. on *patres*, § 9.

22 § **2**. **oriundi**] Common in Livy, cf. 20. 3; 23. 1. Translate 'the Sabine stock.'

23 **ab sua parte...regnatum**] 'There had been no king on their side,' 'from their point of view.' For this use of *a*, 'on the side of,' cf. 12. 1.

25 **veteres peregrinum**] 'original')('alien': notice the chiasmus, which

brings the two adjectives into strong contrast. So new was the fusion of communities that the Romans still regarded the Sabines as aliens.

26 § 3. **in variis...tamen**] Here *in* = 'in spite of,' and is answered by *tamen*: the same phrase, with *tamen*, recurs in 28. 8.

regnari] is probably impersonal (like *regnatum* above and in 60. 3 below), i.e. 'that there should be a king'; not personal, 'to be under a king.'

29 § 4. **sine imperio**] 'masterless'; the phrase (like *sine duce*) is equivalent to an adjective. The sentiment expressed is that of the men of Israel in 1 Samuel, viii. 19, 20.

p. 23. 1 **externa**] 'foreign'—a different sense from that of *peregrinus* above: perhaps the Etruscan power is alluded to.

3 **in animum inducebat**] 'would bring himself to': Livy uses *in animum* (rather than *animum*) *inducere*.

§ 5. **centum patres**] Cf. 8. 7.

4 **factis**] 'formed' (by arrangement, or perhaps according to some accepted classification, e.g. the *curiae*). **creatis**] 'elected' (as representatives). **in singulas**] 'for (to represent) each ten.'

5 **qui...praeessent**] 'to direct the administration,' as distinct from *imperitabant*, 'exercised the sovereignty' (cf. 22. 4).

consociant] Here, as often, the historic present is associated with a historic tense (*praeessent*).

8 § 6. **in orbem ibat**] 'went the round.' **annuum**] 'for a year.'

9 **ab re**] Cf. *ab numero avium* 8. 3.

10 **interregnum**] Notice that in this case each whole decury had the *imperium* in turn, the order of decuries being determined by lot (Dion. H. II. 57): inside the decury one person had for five days the insignia of royalty. In republican times *interregnum* resulted on occasions when there were no consuls, and no one qualified to conduct a consular election: the *auspicia* lapsed *ad patres*, who appointed an *interrex*, who in turn appointed another (there must be at least two, for the first could not hold an election of consuls), and so on for periods of five days each, till the proper order of government was restored. For the distinctively *patrician* character of the *interregnum* see n. on *patres auctores fiunt* below.

§ 7. **fremere**] hist. inf.: for the sentiment cf. *Il.* II. 204 οὐκ ἀγαθὸν πολυκοιρανίη· εἷς κοίρανος ἔστω.

12 **et...creatum**] 'and a king, too, of their own creation.'

videbantur passuri] 'looked like allowing,' 'seemed likely to allow.'

14 § 8. **ultro**] 'in anticipation.'

quod...erant] 'what they were bound to lose.' The fut. part. with *sum* in Livy has all the meanings of μέλλω with the infinitive.

15 **potestate**] i.e. not *imperium*.

ita...ut non] (μὲν...δ' οὐ...) 'without giving more prerogative.' So afterwards, in the struggle between the orders, the Patricians successively conceded what seemed to be the less important prerogatives of the magistracies, retaining the greater by means of a new and exclusive office, e.g. the praetorship and the censorship.

populo] i.e. the *comitia curiata*.

17 § **9. iussisset**] 'had designated': this constitutional use of *iubeo* occurs in 22. 1 and elsewhere in this book.

sic...fierent] 'should be ratified (valid) only on condition that the fathers gave confirmation.' For *sic...si* cf. 8. 2 *ita, si*; 31. 7 *unam spem, si*.

The meaning of *patres auctores fiunt* has been much disputed. The evidence shows that these *patres* cannot be identified (1) with the (Republican) Senate, because in the struggle concerning the Licinian Rogations the Senate were overcome, but *patricii se auctores futuros negabant* (VI. 42. 10): nor (2) with the Comitia Curiata, which (at least in Republican times) was not exclusively Patrician, and itself needed the *patrum auctoritas* for its resolutions (VI. 41. 10). Moreover, Servius Tullius (cf. Cic. *de Rep.* II. 21) obtained the lesser, but not the greater sanction—*non commisit se patribus sed Tarquinio sepulto populum de se ipse consuluit, iussusque regnare legem de imperio suo curiatam tulit.*

In another passage of Cicero (*pro Domo*, 14. 38) a list of peculiarly Patrician offices and privileges is given: *ita populus Romanus brevi tempore neque regem sacrorum, neque flamines, neque Salios habebit, nec ex parte dimidia reliquos sacerdotes, neque auctores centuriatorum et curiatorum comitiorum: auspiciaque populi Romani, si magistratus patricii creati non sint, intereant necesse est, cum interrex nullus sit, quod et ipsum patricium esse et a patriciis prodi necesse est.* There would seem, then, to have been a recognised body of *patres* or *patricii* who had originally the power of conducting and confirming the most important religious and state procedure.

The simplest explanation of the problem is undoubtedly that of Professor Ridgeway, who (in the paper referred to in the note on 15. 6 *creditae* above), from the evidence afforded by material remains, tradition, priesthoods, marriage rites, disposal of the dead, and language, argues that the Patricians are Sabines (who had conquered Rome), the Plebeians Ligurians.

Now Livy speaks here of *centum patres*, and in 8. 7 (see note) he told us that Romulus chose that number to be his *senatores*; of whom it was said *patres certe ab honore, patriciique progenies eorum appellati*. He thus bases on privilege what Professor Ridgeway bases on ethnology. Nor is Livy far wrong in speaking of *ordines* in this connection, for these senatorial *patres* and *patricii* may well have constituted a distinct *ordo*, a privileged nobility, apart from other *patres familias* of the *gentes* forming the state: so in 18. 5 *patres* and *cives* are mentioned separately, and probably *factionibus inter ordines certabatur* (§ 1 above) means that there was a contest between the privileged and non-privileged families for the choice of a king. The *patres* proper regard with a jealous eye any action on the part of the king which was 'popular,' i.e. tended to break down the barrier of their exclusiveness, or to increase the importance of any members of the state outside their class; and, when the Tarquins were expelled, the *patres* resumed the *imperium* as of right, in the person of magistrates selected from the *patricii*.

So long as the Senate remained identical with this privileged class (i.e. until the end of the Regal period), it retained the final sanctions of the chief acts of state. But when, with the development of the Plebeian party, the Senate ceased to be 'Patrician,' the privileged order pursued exactly the same policy as in the case of the chief magistracies—they conceded the lesser powers, but retained the greater: they abandoned the Senate as their own sphere of political influence, and appropriated the powers of final sanction to their own body. This was the last barrier of exclusiveness which the Plebeian reformers had to pass: they passed it not by abolishing the *patrum auctoritas*, but by making it a preliminary and not a final sanction. This was achieved by the Lex Publilia of 339 B.C., and by the Lex Maenia of a later date: to this Livy alludes here in the words *hodie quoque...fiunt*, into which is condensed by anticipation the whole story of the struggle between Patricians and Plebeians.

19 **rogandis**] 'propose': lit. 'ask' the assembly to approve, a measure (*rogatio*) or a magistrate.

vi adempta] 'deprived of its vitality, significance.' For the reform which thus reduced the *patrum auctoritas* to a mere formality, see n. on *patres* above.

20 **priusquam...ineat**] 'before the people can proceed to voting': the subj. denotes anticipation. In VIII. 12. 15 (where the reform is mentioned) the phrase is *ante initum suffragium*.

in...eventum] 'upon an issue still undecided by the electorate.' *in* expresses the state of things contemplated by those acting: cf. XLIII. 12. 2 *priusquam id sors cerneret, in incertum...in utramque provinciam decerni.*

21 § **10.** **contione**] i.e. the *comitia curiata.*

22 **quod...sit**] A form of prayer, regularly inserted as a preamble in public proclamations (cf. 28. 7): *fortunatum* is sometimes added. The Greek equivalent is ἀγαθῇ τύχῃ.

24 **secundus ab Romulo**] 'second after R.,' 'as a successor to R.'

25 **crearitis**] Notice the stages in the election: (1) *contio* summoned by *interrex*; (2) *creatio*, election of a candidate; (3) *patrum auctoritas*; (4) *inauguratio*, cf. 18. 6—9. (1) Implies a continuity in the succession; (2) and (3) the conferment of *imperium* by the *populus*, and confirmation of the same by the *patres*; (4) the admission to priestly supremacy.

26 § **11.** **victi beneficio**] 'outdone in obligation.'

id...iuberentque] 'ordained and required no more than that.' In historical times *scisco* is used technically with *plebs* (so *plebiscitum*), *iubeo* with *populus* (cf. Cic. *Flacc.* VII. 15 *quae scisceret plebs, aut quae populus iuberet*). Here the expression means that the whole body-politic concurred in the matter.

27 **regnaret**] The tense represents the dubitative *regnet* of direct narration, i.e. 'who is to rule.'

CHAPTER XVIII.

(For the reign of Numa see Introduction, § 4.)

p. 24. 1 § **1.** **Numae Pompili**] The first name is apparently connected with a root *nam*, 'regulate,' 'dispose': cf. νόμος, *numerus*, *Numitor.* The second comes (like Pompeius) from a root *pankan* meaning 'five' (cf. πέμπτος); the Sabines labialized, unlike the Latins (cf. *Quinctius*, *Quinctilius*). So the whole title may signify 'king of law and order, fifth of his line.'

2 **Curibus**] See n. on 13. 5.

3 **ut...quisquam**] 'so far as any mortal.' *ut* is restrictive: *quisquam*, properly employed in negative clauses, is here extended to a clause wherein a certain restriction is implied; cf. 22. 6 *invitos quicquam dicturos.*

5 § **2.** **doctrinae eius**] i.e. *omnis...iuris.* **exstat**] 'is available.'

6 **Samium Pythagoram**] P. was born in Samos, and subsequently

migrated to the S. of Italy (Magna Graecia): he flourished about 530 B.C. Numa's traditional date was 714—762 B.C.

edunt] i.e. men generally.

7 **centum amplius**] For the omission of *quam* (the regular rule till the post-Augustan period) cf. 23. 3 *plus quinque*.

8 **Metapontum...Crotonam**] Greek colonies on the S. coast of Italy. The form *Crotona* comes from the accus. of the Greek Κρότων: cf. *statera* and στατήρ.

9 **aemulantium studia**] 'striving to copy his studies.' **coetus**] 'classes.'

10 § **3**. **quae fama**] sc. *pervenisset*. If *qua fama* be read, *Pythagoras pervenisset* must be supplied.

11 **linguae commercio**] 'interchange of language,' 'common tongue.'

14 § **4**. **temperatum...fuisse**] 'that his (Numa's) mind was regulated by (or 'tempered to') good qualities': the same word occurs again in 21. 6.

15 **magis**] 'rather' than the view that Pythagoras had trained him.

peregrinis] 'alien'; the right word for the Greeks settled in Italy—the Ἰταλιῶται.

16 **tetrica et tristi**] 'strict and solemn.' Cf. Ovid *Am.* III. 8. 61 *exaequet tetricas licet illa Sabinas*.

18 § **5**. **patres Romani...quisquam...ausi**] The general subject is subdivided in the two clauses *neque se...alium* (best turned by a parenthesis), and resumed in the third, *nec denique...ausi*.

24 § **6**. **augurato**] 'after augury,' an adverbial use (cf. *explorato*, *optato*, *inconsulto*) which has grown out of an ablative absolute, expressing attendant circumstances. *augurato* is emphatic, influencing both *urbe condenda* ('at the foundation of the city') and *regnum*.

26 **cui**] 'to whom (as augur),' 'to whose office.'

honoris ergo] 'in virtue of the privilege.' *ergo* is an archaic word, fairly common in Livy, but used mostly in formal phrases like this.

publicum...fuit] 'was officially secured in perpetuity.' In other words, Numa (according to Livy) founded the College of Augurs: Cicero, however (*de Rep.* II. 9), says that Romulus *ex singulis tribubus singulos cooptavit augures*.

27 **deductus in arcem**] 'inducted to the citadel': the force of *de-* here is not 'down' but 'to the proper destination.' *arcem*, i.e. the N. eminence of the Capitoline, where was (in historical times) the spot called *auguraculum*.

in lapide] 'on the Stone': probably Livy refers to some particular stone associated with this ceremony of *inauguratio*, which was continued in Republican days in the case of the *rex sacrorum* and other priests. It may have been an aërolite, associated with Jupiter or Terminus: St Augustine speaks of a *lapis Capitolinus*. The oath *per Iovem lapidem* (cf. Cicero, *ad Fam.* VII. 12, and Polybius, IV. 25. 6 Δία λίθον) is an evidence of the sanctity of a particular stone of this kind.

ad meridiem versus] 'with his face towards the south.'

28 § **7. capite velato**] 'with his head covered'—by means of a fold of his robe, the *toga praetexta* (or *trabea*): see 36. 5, and note. The usage may have originated at a time when the worshippers dreaded the sight of deities or departed spirits. The Greek custom, on the other hand, was to perform religious duties bareheaded.

29 **sedem cepit**] Where there was no special enclosure like the *auguraculum*, the augur sat in a square tent with one opening, commanding a view of the *templa* (see below).

30 **lituum**] 'a crook': the word is possibly of Etruscan origin, and seems to be connected with a root *lik*; cf. *obliquus*.

32 **regiones...determinavit**] 'defined the boundaries,' i.e. divisions of the sky for purposes of augury. This he did with his *lituus*, marking across the sky one imaginary line (*decumanum*) from E. to W., and another (*cardo*) from N. to S. The space of sky thus intersected was called *templum*, i.e. a precinct cut off (from root *tam*, 'cut,' cf. τέμενος). Then a similar *templum* was marked off on the earth by a certain formula (*conceptis verbis*), i.e. by naming definite objects (trees or land-marks) as limits.

Notice the augural significance of the *templum*, which Festus (v. 157) describes as *locus ita effatus* (i.e. *conceptis verbis*) *aut ita saeptus* (by enclosure) *ut una parte pateat angulosque adfixos habeat ad terram*. *fanum*, on the other hand, means a locality consecrated by *pontifices*: and the claims of any *fana* or *sacella* had to be satisfied by *exauguratio* before the *inauguratio* and *consecratio* of a *templum* on the same spot could take place. Thus a *fanum* was not necessarily a *templum*, nor a *templum* a *fanum*.

dextras...dixit] 'appointed the right sections to be towards the south, the left towards the north.'

p. 25. 2 **signum contra...animo finivit**] (cf. 10. 6 *animo metatus*) 'in front of him he set an imaginary (*animo*) limit-mark.' This would be one of the four land-marks of the *templum* on earth.

4 § **8. translato**] 'passed,' 'shifted': as a bishop would pass his staff from his right hand to his left before giving a blessing.

6 § **9. uti...adclarassis**] 'O vouchsafe to reveal'; evidently a formula

of the augurs, which explains the archaic form *adclarassis*, really an aorist optative: cf. n. on *ausim*, Praef. 1.

8 **peregit verbis**] 'formally recited'—using a form of words: cf. 32. 8.

auspicia] Auspices granted thus in answer to prayer were known as *impetrita* or *impetrativa*. By associating the auspices with the accession of Numa, Livy emphasizes their importance in the life of Rome. They were indeed one of the most jealously guarded privileges of the Patricians, who did nothing, private or public, *nisi auspicato*. So *auspicium* represents, here and elsewhere, the divine sanction of *imperium*.

9 **declaratus**] an official word, 'returned,' 'declared' as elected.

templo] i.e. 'the enclosure,' as explained above.

CHAPTER XIX.

11 § 1. **eam**] resumptive, to contrast the Rome of war and the Rome of peace. For this use of the demonstrative *is*, to reestablish a sentence after pause or interruption, cf. 49. 9 *ei Mamilio*, 58. 11 *cultrum, quem... habebat, eum....*

iure...moribus] 'law (the whole system), ordinances (the several enactments) and usages' (religious and social).

13 § 2. **adsuescere**] sc. *eam*.

quippe] 'in fact,' 'nay rather' = μὲν οὖν. **efferari**] 'brutalised: infinitive after *videret*.

15 **Ianum**] The word has generally been referred to a root *ja* = 'go,' or 'come': if so, Janus is the 'door-god,' 'god of entrances,' just as Vesta is the 'hearth-goddess'—the one representing the first approach of the house, the other its last or inmost sanctity. Thus explained, Janus is the god of beginning, mentioned first in prayer (as Vesta is mentioned last); his favour was sought at the outset of all enterprises, and his door was left open in war, that his watchful eye might follow the fortunes of his worshippers. Cf. Fowler, *R. F.* pp. 282—289.

But this explanation of the form and attributes of *Ianus* is rejected by those who see in him the partner and consort of Diana, and regard the pair as duplicates of Jupiter and Juno, deriving all four words from the root *di*, 'bright,' from which come also Zeus and Dione. When the various Latin tribes were associated to form one city, their various cults were associated also. Those who hold this view go on to derive *ianua* from *Ianus*; thus a *ianua foris* is a door guarded by a *Ianus*, or perhaps, in its lintel and two side-posts, the door represents a triple Janus. Cf. A. B. Cook, *op. cit.* p. 369; Frazer, *op. cit.* p. 289.

The arch of *Ianus geminus* (*bifrons*), with the double-headed figure above, was situated to the N.E. of the Forum.

Argiletum] the region N.E. of the Forum, which afterwards became the Booksellers' Row of Rome. The word, fancifully connected by Virgil (*Aen.* VIII. 346) with the death of an Argive in Evander's day, is perhaps derived from *argilla*, 'white clay,' the termination being collective, like *olivetum*, *buxetum*.

indicem] 'an ensign.' **apertus...clausus**] Notice the emphatic position.

19 § **3**. **post Punicum...bellum**] in 235 B.C.—but opened again the same year.

21 **post bellum Actiacum**] 'after the campaign of Actium,' in 29 B.C. Augustus had the door closed again in 25 B.C. and in 4 B.C., so that this statement of Livy gives us one clue to the date of this book.

Augusto] Octavian received this title in 27 B.C.—another clue.

23 § **4**. **societate ac foederibus**] The two words are often found side by side, and the relation between them is indicated in Cic. *Phil.* II. 35. 89 *societatem foedere confirmare*.

iunxisset] i.e. Numa.

24 **luxuriarent**)(**continuerat**] 'might run wild')('had curbed, kept in hand.'

26 **rem...efficacissimam**] 'a most effective instrument for the treatment of a populace unlearned and unpolished in those early times.' For *ad* see n. on 9. 16.

28 § **5**. **qui**] i.e. *metus*.

descendere ad animos] 'sink into their hearts.'

29 **commento miraculi**] 'fictitious miracle.'

30 **Egeria**] i.e. 'the Deliverer,' a nymph, or Camena, connected with sources and bubbling streams (cf. Curtius VII. 5 *aqua, quae egeritur ex terra*), who can aid prophets or teachers in delivering their burden: cf. n. on *Camenis*, 21. 3. Egeria was also a tree-spirit, and her name may be etymologically connected with the oak: thus she may be a duplicate of Diana. We see from Virgil, *Aen.* VII. 763, that she was associated at Aricia with Virbius and Diana. The mystical union of Numa (as an impersonation of the oak god, in virtue of his kingship) and Egeria is in this case to be interpreted as a duplicate of the union between the King and Queen of the Wood. Cf. Frazer, *op. cit.* pp. 196, 217.

31 **essent**] i.e. so he said: therefore subjunctive.

32 **suos cuique**] The possessive pronoun here refers not to the subject, but to the remoter object of the sentence: cf. 52. 4 *sui cuique periculi*; Cic. *de Off.* I. 5. 14 *in tribuendo suum cuique.*

p. 26. 1 § 6. **omnium primum**] A definite calendar was a necessary preliminary to a detailed worship. **ad**] 'to suit,' 'according to' (κατά).

2 **discribit**] 'marks off,' 'distributes' (this spelling of the word is to be preferred in all cases where the notion of 'distribution' is implied): cf. 42. 5 and XLV. 15. 1 *in quattuor urbanas tribus discripti erant libertini.*

tricenos singulis] The distributive sense of the words is emphasized.

4 **desunt dies...anno**] either (1) 'the days fail to make up (fall short of) a full (i.e. a solar) year; or (2) 'days are wanting for....' For *solidus* cf. Hor. *Od.* I. 1. 20 *partem solido demere de die.*

qui...orbe] either (1) 'which is the circuit of a solar revolution,' i.e. *solstitiali* is used loosely for *solari*; or (2) 'which is formed by (represents) a revolution from solstice to solstice,' i.e. from summer to summer.

5 **intercalariis**] lit. 'proclaimed between,' so 'inserted by proclamation,' 'supernumerary.' The proclamation of such alterations in the calendar was made (in Republican times) by the Pontiffs, who summoned the *comitia curiata* (called in this case *comitia calata*, i.e. 'summoned') for the purpose.

6 **dispensavit**] 'arranged,' 'regulated.'

ut vicesimo anno...dies congruerent] 'that in the twentieth year the periods of all the years should be filled up, and the days should coincide with the same point of the sun's course from which they had started'; i.e. Numa introduced a pure lunar year, reconciling it with the solar year by inserting a certain number of months in every cycle. The length of his cycle (*vicesimo anno*=every 19 years) is the same as that of Meton, who reformed the Greek calendar in 432 B.C.: it is possible therefore that Livy here attributes to Numa what belongs to another time and place, following the pious fraud of some pontiff, who wished to give the traditional founder of the calendar the credit of astronomical accuracy. In Meton's cycle each period of seven years received one intercalary month.

It was commonly believed that the earliest Roman year, called the 'Year of Romulus,' consisted of 304 days, arranged in 10 months, beginning with March, and ending with December. Now this number of days agrees neither with the sun nor with the moon; the next arrangement, however, ascribed to Numa, consisted of 12 lunar months, or

355 days. This method, in use after the reforms of the Decemvirs, was reconciled with the solar system by intercalating 22 or 23 days every other year: in four years this brings the average of days in a year to 366¼ or one day too much. Subsequent intercalary reforms served only to produce hopeless confusion, and the calendar was not set right until its reformation by Julius Caesar.

8 § 7. **nefastos**] 'days of no business.' **fastos**] 'days of business,' i.e. when it was lawful for judgment to be pronounced (*fastus* being connected with *fari*).

9 **nihil...agi**] 'that no business should be discussed in popular assembly.' Cf. Aul. Gell. XIII. 15. 10 *cum populo agere est rogare quid populum, quod suffragiis suis aut iubeat aut vetet.*

futurum erat] 'was sure to be.' Livy somewhat cynically credits Numa with a desire of reducing the political tumults of subsequent centuries by a reduction of the days available.

CHAPTER XX.

11 § 1. **ipse**] The king was high priest *ex officio*, and after the establishment of the Republic certain priestly duties were carried out by a *rex sacrorum*: cf. the ἄρχων βασιλεὺς at Athens.

12 **Dialem flaminem**] 'the chaplain of Jupiter'; or possibly 'of Janus' (see n. on *Ianum*, 19. 2). The word *flamen* is connected with *flare*, and thus means 'the blower,' i.e. one who fans the flame (for sacrifice). The *flamines* may originally have been sons of the chief (as the *vestales* were daughters), deputed to keep up the sacred fire: in the later sense they were sacrificing priests of particular gods.

14 § 2. **ipsos**] 'in person.'

15 **vicis**] 'office.'

16 **adsiduum**] 'perpetual,' almost = 'resident'; cf. § 3 and 21. 1.

17 **veste**] i.e. the toga praetexta, which he was obliged always to wear: when he went out he wore a special *apex* (*albogalerus*) and a cloak (*laena*) made by his wife, the *flaminica*; he carried a sacrificial knife, and a wand to keep off the profane crowd. Up to the Imperial period, he was always a patrician.

curuli regia sella] See note on 8. 3.

18 **Marti...Quirino**] For Quirinus as the deified Romulus see notes on 15. 6 above. Quirinus, like Mars, was regarded as a Sabine God by Varro, and may be a duplicate of Mars: the one was patron of the Quirinal, the other of the Palatine (Septimontium), and the two thus

associated represent the association of the two separate communities originally occupying these hills. Further evidence of this association is seen in the two sets of Salii (see note below). Cf. Fowler, *R. F.* pp. 237, 322—3.

19 § 3. **Vestae**] 'for (the service of) Vesta,' dat. of indirect object. For the significance of the Vestals see n. on 3. 11.

Alba oriundum] 'of Alban origin': cf. 17. 2.

genti...haud alienum] 'not unconnected with the stock of the founder' (of Alba). For the dative see n. on 15. 6 *nihil absonum fidei.*

20 **antistites**] 'priestesses in chief,' 'chief celebrants.'

21 **aliisque caerimoniis**] 'and by ceremonies as well.' The maiden was transferred by a special ceremony (*captio*) from the *potestas* of her father into that of the *pontifex maximus*: then she was taken to the *atrium Vestae*: her hair was cut off and dedicated: then she put on the white clothes of her office, and was sworn in.

22 § 4. **Salios**] i.e. 'dancers.' This was an ancient guild of priest-warriors, belonging to a primitive cult. Such guilds existed in many places in Italy; in Rome itself there were 12 Palatini, for the worship of Mars Gradivus, and 12 Collini (cf. 27. 7 below), for that of Quirinus. Probably their solemn dance in procession with the *ancilia*, which took place in March, represented the protection of the corn-spirit from hostile demons. Cf. Fowler, *R. F.* pp. 41—2.

23 **Gradivo**] is differently explained: (1) from *gradior*, 'the strider'; (2) from *gravi-divus*, 'the forceful'; and (3) Festus, p. 97 *quia gramine sit ortus.* The first explanation, by which Mars is the 'God of Marching,' a good soldierly epithet, seems to be the right one.

tunicae pictae insigne] 'the distinction of the embroidered doublet.' The Salii wore also the *trabea* and *apex*, and a sword, and carried in the right hand a short stick, with which they struck the *ancilia.*

25 **ancilia**] 'sacred shields.' The word is derived from *amb-* and *caedo*, denoting that the shields had two curved indentations in the rim, which made them like violins in shape. The tradition was that one shield fell from heaven, and eleven more were made exactly like it, that it might not be known and stolen.

The shape of the shield is identical with those of the Mycenaean age, and is perhaps (like the *scutum*) to be traced to the Pelasgians or Aborigines. The Umbro-Latins had a round shield. Ridgeway, *Early Age of Greece*, I. p. 455.

27 **tripudiis...saltatu**] 'with triple tread, in ceremonial dance': the second phrase explains the first. *tripudium* is to be derived from

ter and *pes*, or from *terripavium* (*pavīre*, 'beat') acc. to Cicero *de Div.* II. 34, 72.

§ **5. pontificem**] This official (as were the pontiffs of the Republic) was concerned with the state religion as a whole, not associated (like the *flamines*, *Vestales* and *Salii*) with a particular deity or rite. The usual derivation connects the word with *pons* and *facio*, and supposes that bridges (e.g. the Pons Sublicius—see 33. 6 below) were connected with certain acts of worship or propitiation. According to x. 6, the original number of pontiffs was four: Cicero (*de Rep.* II. 14, 26) says five. There was probably no *pontifex maximus* under the Kings, as these themselves were chief priests *ex officio*.

Is it possible that *pontifices* is to be derived from a root *pont-* or *pompt-* (i.e. five, cf. *Pontius*, *Pompilius*) and *fac-*, and that it means 'five doers,' i.e. 'sacrificers,' 'celebrants'? This would agree with the view that there were five pontiffs originally: and it is known that they were closely associated with formalities of real and personal transfer (wills and adoptions), in which they may well have been the five witnesses required for a transaction *per aes et libram*. In the earlier regal period they seem to have formed the king's court before which a civil suit (*lis*) was settled; and the *legis actio sacramenti* certainly suggests that there was a sacral element in such procedure which the *pontifices* may have introduced. Cf. Muirhead, *Roman Law*, pp. 72, 73.

28 **Numam Marcium**] Possibly we ought to read *Numa Marcium*, and to suppose that Marcius was the husband of Numa's daughter and the father of Ancus Marcius: this would be an indication of succession in the female line. (See Introduction, §§ 5, 7.) Like many other names in this book Marcius was probably introduced into the tradition to glorify a noble Roman house.

29 **exscripta exsignataque**] 'exactly copied and recorded'—probably from Sabine originals. The record so made may well be the *commentarii* mentioned in 32. 2 below. [Weissenborn-Müller.]

31 **fierent**] This subj. (like *erogaretur*, *susciperentur atque curarentur* below) expresses a deliberative sense, in a dependent clause: cf. 17. 11 *decerneret qui regnaret*, 29. 3 *obliti quid relinquerent*.

32 **erogaretur**] 'was to be disbursed': *erogare* is the technical term for paying out money from the public treasury (cf. *de publico*, § 3 above) with the consent of the people.

§ **6. publica...sacra**] There were two general divisions of *sacra*—*publica*, those performed at public expense for the public benefit, or for mountains, hamlets, and the like; *privata*, rites performed for individuals, households, or clans.

p. 27. 1 **scitis**] 'ordinances.'

2 **patrios...peregrinos**] 'national,' 'alien.' Numa must be speaking here for the united Roman and Sabine populations: in 17. 2 the Romans regarded the Sabines as *peregrini*. For *peregrinus* see also 7. 15.

3 § **7**. **nec...modo...ut**]=*et ut non modo*. The whole clause is still dependent on *subiecit* above.

caelestes caerimonias] 'services of the gods in heaven,' as opposed to the infernal deities and spirits.

4 **iusta**] 'proper,' 'orthodox,' in accordance with *ius divinum*.

placandos manes] 'the duty of propitiating departed spirits.'

5 **prodigia...missa**] 'vouchsafed in lightning-flashes or other manifestations.'

6 **susciperentur atque curarentur**] 'were to be taken up and treated.' *curarentur* is for *procurarentur*: cf. *procuranda* just below. The technical phrase *suscipere procurationem* is found. For the subjunctive see n. on *fierent* above.

8 **Elicio**] This name (i.e. 'enticer,' 'revealer') was applied to Jupiter because he could call down lightning and rain, and convey signs and omens. It is possible that the particular cult associated with the altar on the Aventine included the rite of *Aquaelicium*, i.e. the procuring (*elicere*) of rain. Cf. Fowler, *R. F.* p. 232.

CHAPTER XXI.

10 § **1**. **procuranda**] a technical word: ='to avert or expiate by sacrifice.'

13 **cura**] is explained by *cum...videretur*, 'ever-present indwelling (*insidens*) thought of the gods, with the feeling that the influence of heaven intervened in the affairs of men.'

15 **imbuerat**] 'impressed,' 'inspired' (for the first time).

proximo...metu] (1) 'with fear ready to hand,' or (2) 'with fear in second place,' 'as a next resort.' Positive loyalty (*fides ac ius iurandum*) is backed by negative.

17 § **2**. **in mores**] 'to copy the character': cf. *in spem*, 8. 4.

20 **verecundiam**] 'sense of restraint.' **totam**] 'entirely.'

21 **violari**] Our English sense seems to require the act. infin. in such

cases as this, but the passive is equally idiomatic in Latin: cf. the use of pass. infin. after verbs of wishing, e.g. Cic. *de Senect.* § 2 *me ipsum levari volo.*

22 **nefas**] 'a religious crime,' not *iniuria*.

§ **3.** **lucus**] It was near the Porta Capena.

quem medium] 'the heart of which.'

24 **arbitris**] 'eye-witnesses,' the original meaning of the word: it occurs again in 41. 1.

velut] 'as he said,' 'ostensibly': cf. ὡς, δῆθεν in Greek.

25 **Camenis**] (sometimes spelt *Casmenae*, and generally derived from a root *kas*, whence come *carmen*, *Carmenta*; so equivalent to) 'chantresses,' and therefore, because divinations would be given in rhythmic form, 'enchantresses' or 'prophetesses.' They were nymphs of the water-springs, of a lesser degree than Egeria, and were supposed to have a power of bringing prophetic utterance (like other things) to birth.

quod...essent] The subjunctive shows that this was the reason given by Numa.

concilia] 'meetings.' **coniuge**] 'consort.'

26 § **4.** **soli Fidei**] *solus* has probably its original meaning of 'whole,' 'unimpaired' (derived from a root *sar*, 'protect,' 'cherish,' and connected with *salvus*, *solidus*, ὅλος). Seeley suggested the reading *solus*, as a close equivalent of Dionysius' πρῶτος ἀνθρώπων (II. 75). *Fides* represents the sense of obligation for which the Romans in their earlier history were so distinguished: *Punica fides* ('treachery') gives the other side of the picture.

sollemne] 'a regular festival,' on 1st October.

27 **sacrarium**] 'shrine': it was on the Capitol, close by the temple of Jupiter.

flamines] i.e. the three above-mentioned. "The presence of the *flamines* at any rite is always evidence of its antiquity; and in this case they may have represented the union of the two communities of Septimontium and Quirinal in a common worship on the Capitol, the central point being represented by the Flamen Dialis": Fowler, *R. F.*, p. 237.

arcuato] 'hooded.' **bigis**] has the force of a second epithet to *curru*, 'two-horsed'; or, as we say, 'in a covered coach and pair.' The *currus arcuatus* is probably identical with the *carpentum*, for which see n. on 34. 8.

28 **involuta**] This practice of wrapping is clearly ancient, and seems to denote that the seat and the service of truth and obligation cannot be

too minutely and carefully protected. The goddess herself is described as *albo Fides velata panno*, Hor. *Od.* I. 35, 21.

30 **in dexteris**] The right hand, given and taken, has been in all times and most places the pledge of obligation.

31 § **5. sacris faciendis**] dat. of work contemplated: cf. 15. 2 *dimicationi ultimae instructus*.

Argeos] These spots were probably 24 in number (acc. to Varro, 27), six in each of the four Regions of Rome connected with Servius Tullius. On 17 March a procession went round to these *Argeorum sacella*, but what to do is not clear. Tradition said that Argive heroes were buried in these places: the derivation of the word is undecided, and is made still more difficult by the other meaning of *Argei*, 'dummies' of rushes, thrown into the Tiber on 15 May in each year. The whole question is well discussed in Warde Fowler's *Roman Festivals*, p. 111 ff.

p. 28. 1 **tutela...regni**] 'an equal maintenance of peace and of prerogative.'

3 § **6. duo deinceps reges**] For the order of words see n. on Praef. 2 *novi semper auctores*.

4 **auxerunt**] 'advanced.'

6 **temperata**] 'tempered to,' or 'regulated by.' Cf. 18. 4.

CHAPTER XXII.

(For the reign of Tullus Hostilius see Introduction, § 5.)

7 § **1. interregnum**] See c. 17 above.

9 **in infima arce**] 'at the foot of the citadel': see 12. 2 above.

10 **iussit...auctores facti**] See n. on 17. 9 above.

13 § **2. senescere**] 'languish,' 'decline': cf. 25. 7. The word is a favourite with Livy.

17 § **4. imperitabat**] 'was sovereign'; cf. 17. 5. In 23. 3 he is called *dux*, in 22. 7 and 23. 4, 7 *rex*; his successor is *dictator* in 23. 4.

18 **Cluilius**] (another form is *Cloelius*) was the name of a Roman gens (cf. n. on *Marcius*, 20. 5): the word comes from a root *clu*, and denotes 'the Famous' (cf. *inclutus*, *Cluentius*), and thus in its origin is scarcely a proper name, but an epithet.

19 **ad res repetendas**] 'to require restitution.' For the formalities see 32. 5—14 below.

21 **pie**] 'with a good conscience,' 'without scruple.'

23 § **5. blande ac benigne**] 'graciously and generously,' referring to

Tullus. **comi fronte**, probably refers to the envoys, 'with a smiling countenance,' i.e. there was civility on both sides, with design on the one hand, without it on the other. In some MSS. *comiter* (a word common in Livy) is added to *comi fronte*: perhaps both should be considered as a gloss to explain *blande* and *benigne*.

celebrant] 'attended in state': the word implies the formality of a festival.

24 **priores**] 'first' (πρότεροι).

25 **in**] 'for,' 'to begin on' (like εἰς τρίτην ἡμέραν): cf. 28. 1 *in diem posterum*. **tricesimum**] i.e. a month's notice: cf. 32. 9.

28 § **6**. **purgando**] 'in explanation': their statements follow in *or. obl.*

quicquam] This pronoun follows naturally the negative notion contained in *invitos*. For further extensions of its use cf. 18. 1, 35. 3.

p. 29. 1 **ni reddantur**] 'failing such restitution.' The tense, like *placeat*, reproduces the original statement.

3 § **7**. **uter**] This is either (1) relative, answering to *eum*, 'that one of the two, who...,' in which case *ut* follows directly after *facere testes*: or (2) indirect question, governed by *facere testes*, 'appeals to the gods to witness which of the two...,' in which case *ut* is final, 'that so....'

4 **aspernatus**] 'with disdain.'

5 **expetant**] The word is found intransitively in Plautus with the sense of 'light upon' as of a punishment: here it seems to be transitive (as in 23. 4 below), *di* being understood as the subject, with the sense of 'visit upon,' i.e. take vengeance on him for the war.

CHAPTER XXIII.

9 § **1**. **Lavinium**] Cf. 1. 11. **Alba**] Cf. 3. 3.

11 § **2**. **dimicationem**] 'the struggle.' The word implies that it was decisive: cf. 15. 2 *dimicatio ultima*.

nec...et] The two clauses thus introduced are of similar character, but the first is cast in a negative form.

12 **tectis dirutis**] See 29. 6.

15 § **3**. **plus**] Often, as here, without *quam*, like *amplius*: cf. 32. 12 *non minus*. **milia**] The acc. (regular in such expressions as this) seems to denote that the mind crosses the intervening space. **passum**] for *passuum*: the form is supported by the evidence of the MSS., and *magistratum*, *dumvir* also occur.

16 **fossa Cluilia**] (Plut. *Coriol.* 30 Κλοιλεῖαι τάφροι) ran, roughly speaking, N.E. and S.W., across the Via Appia of a later date.

18 **re]** 'occasion,' 'event.'

vetustate abolevit] 'lapsed with length of years,' 'after long years. This intransitive use of *abolere* is found elsewhere in Livy.

19 § **4. dictatorem]** Probably the word has not its technical Roman significance here, but means 'governor,' 'commander.' The chief magistrates at Lanuvium, Tusculum, and elsewhere were so called. It is not quite clear, however, whether Mettius is intended to be king of the Albans, or merely a *dux gerendo bello* (§ 8), like a Roman Dictator.

Mettium] See n. on 12. 2. **Fufetium]** is prob. another form of the name which appears in the Roman gens *Fufidia*, and elsewhere as *Fuficia*. Cf. note on *Marcius* 20. 5.

20 **ferox]** 'emboldened.'

21 **ab ipso capite orsum]** 'beginning with the chief in person.'

22 **in...expetiturum]** See n. on *expetant*, 22. 7 above.

nomen Albanum] See n. on *nomen Caeninum*, 10. 3 above.

23 **impium]** 'unnatural' (so *civili simillimum* above), contrary to *pietas*, 'proper feeling.'

infesto] 'on the offensive': cf. 25. 3.

24 § **5. stativis]** 'stationary camp,' 'camp of occupation': it was what the Greeks called ἐπιτείχισμα, a fort on or within the enemy's frontier, intended to be a base of aggressive operations.

27 **dimicent]** *or. obl.* for *dimicemus*, probably, as Livy affects subj. with *priusquam* even in cases where little or no anticipation is expressed.

opus esse colloquio] 'a parley was advisable.'

31 § **6. tamen...adferantur]** *tamen* ('still') points the contrast between *haud aspernatus* and *in aciem educit*, and is itself explained by *si vana afferantur*, 'in case idle statements were proffered,' the thought in T.'s mind at the time. *vana* implies a lurking suspicion of falsehood: cf. *haud vana attulere*, IV. 37. 6. With the reading of MSS., *tametsi vana adferebantur*, we must take the clause as explaining *haud aspernatus*, 'even though idle statements were likely to be proffered,' a question of fact, not of feeling.

32 **instructi]** So Madvig and others: MSS. have *structi* (cf. XLII. 51. 3).

p. 30. 2 § **7.** Into this short speech of the Alban king, Livy compresses a historical summary and forecast, in order to indicate the dangers to which the conflicts of the Latin tribes exposed them.

iniurias] 'outrages'—the peasant-raids mentioned in 22. 3 above.

non redditas res...sint] 'a refusal to satisfy claims made according to treaty': *ex foedere* goes with what immediately precedes and follows.

3 **et...nec]** See n. on § 2 above. **regem...audisse videor]** 'I believe I have heard our king affirm....' To complete the sense of *audisse* something like *prae se ferentem* (or *ferre*) must be supplied from *prae te ferre* in the second clause.

5 **potius]** 'by preference': the word always implies a choice in which the speaker is interested.

8 § **8. perperam]** 'wrongly,' lit. 'heedlessly.' The form was originally a fem. acc., cf. *clam*, *palam*.

fuerit] 'let that have been,' 'that must have been': the pf. is used because the reference is to the dead Cluilius. The subj. is concessive: cf. Virg. *Aen.* VI. 62 *hac Troiana tenus fuerit fortuna secuta.*

9 **gerendo bello]** dat. of work contemplated, cf. *sacris faciendis*, 21. 5.

10 **illud]** Verbs like *moneo*, which can take two accusatives in the active, retain one (the internal accusative) in the passive, as here.

monitum velim] This use of the pf. partic. pass. is common after verbs of wishing: we say 'I wish it done' with the same omission of 'to be.' Cf. XXV. 20. 5 *Hannibal non Capuam neglectam, neque desertos volebat socios.* Cic. *Q. Fr.* III. 9. 3 *domestica cura te levatum volo.*

11 **Etrusca res]** See n. on 2. 5 above.

circa nos] Literally true, if the Etruscans occupied Volscian territory.

14 § **9. iam cum]** 'at the moment when.' **pugnae]** dat. of work contemplated, cf. Cic. *Phil.* 13. 7 *receptui signum.*

15 **spectaculo]** i.e. for the Etruscans.

17 **in dubiam...aleam]** 'to a hazardous uncertainty—sovereignty or servitude.' The two genitives define *aleam*.

18 **utri utris imperent]** 'which race is to rule which'; governed by *decerni possit*, impersonal—'the issue may be decided.'

21 § **10. cum...erat]** 'he was the bolder in heart of grace and in hope of glory.' The first gen. is subjective, the second objective.

22 **quaerentibus]** dat. of person judging. See note on 8. 5 *descendentibus.*

CHAPTER XXIV.

24 § **1. trigemini]** 'three born at one birth,' 'triplets.'

26 **Curiatios]** The word is perhaps connected with *curia*, and belonged afterwards, like *Horatius*, to a Roman gens.

28 **in re tam clara]** 'in spite of (notwithstanding) the renown of the affair.' For the use of *in* see n. on Praef. 3 *in tanta turba.*

30 **auctores...trahunt]** 'the authorities make claims for both sides': cf. 7. 1 *regnum trahebant.*

32 **cum trigeminis agunt**] 'urge each trio': the *oratio obliqua* follows, giving the argument.

p. 31. 1 § **2.** **ibi**] 'on that side.' **fuerit**] pf. subj., rendering fut. pf. of *oratio recta*, and implying that the victory must precede the sovereignty. Cf. 48. 2 *apparebatque regnaturum qui vicisset.*

3 § **3.** **dimicarent**] The subjunctive after *priusquam* (like the optative after πρὶν in Greek) properly denotes that an action is not only preceded, but intentionally anticipated, by another (cf. 14. 11 *obicerentur*); but here and elsewhere in Livy (cf. 26. 1 *digrederentur*) scarcely any intention seems to be implied, so that the subjunctive becomes practically equivalent to the indicative—a familiar tendency in Silver Latin.

4 **cuius**] Most MSS. read *cuiusque*, which must then be regarded as equivalent to *cuiuscumque*: except in Plautus, *quisque* is exceedingly rare in this sense.

5 **cum bona pace**] 'in peace and quiet'—a common phrase in Livy. For the formal epithet, cf. *dolo malo* below.

6 **foedera**] The word is formed from the root *fid-*, and implies a basis of *fides* or 'honour' between the parties: this 'honour' is confirmed by formal actions, which are obviously earlier than the formal words which prescribe them. Livy considers that the conditions of treaties differ according to circumstances, but that the formalities of treaty-making have been the same from time immemorial; he therefore applies, by a pardonable anachronism, the conventional terms of historical times to a prehistoric occasion.

9 § **4.** **fetialis**] (most probably connected with *fari*, so, like *orator*, =) 'speaker,' 'spokesman,' 'herald,' 'commissioner.' The college of *fetiales* were guardians of the public faith: their duties are summed up in a law quoted by Cicero (*de Legg.* II. 9. 21) *foederum, pacis, belli, indutiarum oratores fetiales iudicesque sunto: bella disceptanto.* Their official acts in connection with the declaration of war are described in c. 32. 5—14 below. See Wordsworth, *Fragments and Specimens of Early Latin*, p. 551 and foll.

10 **patre patrato**] 'executor in chief,' 'king's commissioner.' It was usual for two or three *fetiales* to be sent on a mission such as this: they chose one to act as their chief (see § 6 below). *patratus* may be (1) passive (so Wordsworth), 'made father,' i.e. deputed to act paternally for the king, and so 'deputy chief': or (2) deponent (so Weissenborn, who compares *cenatus*, *iuratus*), = 'that hath ratified,' so 'plenipotentiary.'

ferire] 'strike a treaty'—i.e. strike the victim sacrificed to solemnize the treaty: cf. 1. 9.

11. **sagmina**] 'handfuls' of sacred herbs, to secure the envoys from violation; taken from the Arx on the Capitoline, and carried by one of the *fetiales*, called from his office *verbenarius*.

12 **puram tollito**] sc. *herbam*, *verbenam*, 'thou shalt take it fresh': or perhaps *puram* implies that no knife was to be used = 'untainted.'

14 § **5. Quiritium**] See n. on 13. 5 above. 'The Roman nation of the Quirites' seems to denote the composite community in which the Sabines (*Quirites*) had a dominant share, though the form *Quirites* may be non-Sabine. *populo Romano Quiritibus* also occurs.

vasa comitesque] 'my badges (symbols) and retinue.' The former refers to the *verbenae*, *silex*, and *sceptrum*: the latter to the other *fetiales* sent on the mission. The *sceptrum* was naturally carried by the *pater patratus* as king's deputy.

15 **quod**] Often used to introduce a prayer: cf. 28. 1 *quod bene vertat*.

sine fraude...Romani] 'without hurt to myself or the R. nation.' The gen. *populi* is objective, and likewise the gen. implied in *mea*.

17 § **6. Valerius...Fusium** (archaic for *Furium*)]. Two more Roman *gentes* are thus introduced.

18 **verbena**] (=*sagmina*) 'slip,' 'sprig': cf. Servius on Virg. *Aen.* XII. 120, *verbenas vocamus omnes frondes sacratas, ut est laurus, oliva, vel myrtus.*

19 **ad ius iurandum...foedus**] 'Is elected to execute the oath, i.e. ratify the treaty.' Possibly in the two expressions we may trace a double form, part Roman, part Sabine.

20 **effata**] passive, 'pronounced,' 'recited.'

carmine] 'strain,' 'form,' perhaps in Saturnian metre, in which the earliest religious and legal forms were commonly composed. Cf. 26. 6 *lex horrendi carminis erat*: 32. 8.

non operae est] 'it is not worth while.' *operae* is interpreted sometimes as a gen. (as it certainly is in the phrase *operae pretium*, cf. Praef. § 1 above), but is more probably a dative in predicate, lit. 'it is a matter for trouble, attention.' Cf. Roby, § 482 (*a*), 516.

21 **referre**] 'quote,' 'repeat.' **peragit**] Cf. 18. 10; 32. 8.

§ **7. legibus**] as above, 'conditions.'

23 **audi tu**] It seems unnecessary to read *audito* (3rd pers.) which has been suggested as an emendation (Schenkl), on the ground that the third clause of such a formula usually applies to the third person: cf. 32. 6 *audiat fas*.

prima postrema] 'from first to last.' Connecting particles are frequently omitted in forms: cf. 32. 13 *fecerunt deliquerunt;* ib. *censuit, consensit, conscivit.*

24 **tabulis cerave**] 'tablets or wax,' i.e. bare boards inscribed, or waxed boards scratched with a style—the two usual forms of writing: cf. Gaius, II. 104 *haec ita, ut in his tabulis cerisque scripta sunt, ita do, ita lego, ita testor.* If these words belong to the original formula (which some editors doubt), this is an early evidence of writing at Rome.

sine dolo malo] 'without malice prepense,' a familiar term in Roman Law.

27 § **8.** **defexit**] For the form see n. on *ausim*, Praef. 1.

publico consilio] 'by formal resolution' or 'in the name of the state.'

ille Diespiter] 'that my lord Diespiter'—another form for *Juppiter*, not uncommon in old formulas. The text is uncertain here: *illo die Juppiter* is the reading of some editions (adopted by Seeley), *tum illico Diespiter* is suggested by Weissenborn.

28 **porcum**] Pigs were not infrequently used as victims in preliminary sacrifices (hence the term *hostia praecidanea*) such as this, performed in order to avoid possible pollution. Iron was avoided, as here, for the same object. Cf. Wordsworth, *Fragments etc.*, pp. 388–9.

29 **potes pollesque**] 'avail and prevail.'

30 § **9.** **saxo silice**] 'flint-stone,' i.e. a stone knife. *silex* is often similarly joined with *lapis*: cf. Plautus, *Poen.* I. 2. 77 *nam tu es lapide silice stultior.*

31 **sua...suum...suum...suos**] Notice emphatic position.

CHAPTER XXV.

p. 32. 2 § **1.** **sui**] 'their brothers in arms': the main armies were seating themselves for the spectacle.

utrosque] 'the two teams.'

deos...intueri] The *or. obl.* gives the *adhortatio.*

3 **quidquid civium**] Cf. 8. 4 *quod tum hominum erat*; 12. 1 *quod campi est.*

5 **manus**] 'swordsmanship,' 'power of fence.' **et...et**] Both clauses explain *feroces* ('emboldened,' cf. 23. 4).

6 **in medium...acies**] = the Gk. μεταίχμιον.

8 § **2.** **periculi...expertes**] 'relieved rather from immediate danger (they would not all be risking death) than from anxiety (about the issue)': *magis...quam* = μὲν...δ' οὔ.

9 **quippe...agebatur**] 'seeing that the sovereignty at stake depended on the fortitude and the fortune of so few champions.'

10 **erecti suspensique**] 'in the excitement of suspense.' **in**] 'to watch,' 'in view of' (ὡς πρὸς θέαν).

11 **animo incenduntur**] 'their fancy was aflame.' This, the reading of the MSS., is so awkward a phrase that H. J. Müller has suggested *animos intendunt*: cf. *Praef.* 9 *intendat animum.*

12 § **3**. **infestis**] 'in rest,' 'at the "ready"' as we might say. The word (cf. 23. 4 above) means 'ready to attack': in 47. 1 it has a passive sense.

13 **animos**] 'courage' (as of great armies).

14 **publicum...fecissent**] 'the thought of national sovereignty or servitude hovered before them, and the future fate of their country, which must hereafter be such as *they* had shaped it'; lit. 'what they should prove to have made it.' *publicum* is in strong contrast to *suum* immediately preceding. The clause *futura...fecissent* is really a re-statement of its predecessor: the tense of *fecissent* (in direct speech fut. pf. *fecerimus*) controls the time of the clause *futuraque...fortuna.*

18 § **4**. **perstringit**] 'seized,' 'paralysed.' **torpebat**] 'began to sink.' Notice the difference of tense.

20 § **5**. **agitatioque...armorumque**] 'twofold activity (double play) of weapon and shield.' *anceps* seems to mean that each side and each man was plying weapon and shield at once: or perhaps it should be translated 'indecisive.' *telorum*, strictly 'spears,' but used to include other weapons of offence: the combatants had both spears (cf. *pila et spolia*, 26. 11) and swords (*gladium*, § 12 below), like Roman legionaries of Livy's day.

24 § **6**. **legiones**] 'troops,' 'levies'—in a general sense. There were no 'legions' yet.

25 **cura**] 'interest.'

deseruerat...circumsteterant] These pluperfects seem to convey that the next stage of the fight was in progress before the effect of the first was realised by the spectators.

exanimes] 'in deathly terror.' **vicem unius**] (*vicem* is probably right: the MSS. give *vice*, which is a later usage in this sense) 'on account of the one': so 9. 15 *suam vicem*, 'on his own account.'

27 § **7**. **universis**] 'for the three at once.' **ferox**] 'ready,' 'bold enough.'

28 **ut segregaret pugnam eorum**] 'to break up their assault,' i.e. take them one by one. The historic tense *segregaret* suits the hist. present *capessit.*

p. **33.** 4 § **9.** **qualis**] 'as supporters will, when the unexpected happens.' **solet**] sc. *fieri.*

5 **defungi**] 'finish off.'

6 § **10.** **itaque**] as second word, is very rare before Livy's time: cf. XXXIV. 34. 9 *versis itaque subito voluntatibus.*

nec procul] i.e. 'not far off either'—any more than the first.

alter...et alterum] i.e. before one of the remaining pair could come up, he despatched the other: *et*, in addition to his first victim.

9 § **11.** **alterum**] acc. masc., with *ferocem.* **ferocem dabat**] 'emboldened.' *dare* has here the force of 'make' (i.e. it represents the root *dhe*, not *do*) which is seen in some of its compounds (*addo, condo*); cf. Virg. *Aen.* IX. 323 *haec ego vasta dabo*: *ib.* X. 870 *sic cursum in medios rapidus dedit.*

intactum...victoria] i.e. the fact that he was unhurt and victorious.

12 **victus**] 'beaten' (in spirit), 'broken.'

13 **proelium**] is emphatic, 'a real battle.'

14 § **12.** **fratrum Manibus**] 'to the shades of my brethren.'

16 **arma**] 'shield,' as above in § 5. **superne**] 'downward': Horatius was standing over his wounded foe.

20 § **13.** **alteri**] 'one army.' **aucti**] 'in proud possession of,' 'blessed with.'

21 **dicionis alienae facti**] 'brought under a foreign sway,' a genitive of secondary predicate: cf. 8. 3 *eorum sententiae esse.*

§ **14.** **exstant**] 'remain,' 'may be seen.'

23 **distantia locis**] 'in separate places.' The ablative expresses the thing in point of which the separation exists (Roby § 497): cf. Quintilian *I. O.* XII. 10. 4 *non multum aetate distantis.*

CHAPTER XXVI.

(This chapter, in which the trial of Horatius for *perduellio* is related, serves to connect the *provocatio* ('right of appeal') with the Regal period. See also Introduction, § 5.)

25 § **1.** **digrederentur**] See n. on *dimicarent*, 24. 3.

26 **iuventutem**] 'fighting men,' i.e. men of military age, 16—40.

29 § **2.** **princeps**] 'at the head.'

31 **fuerat**] This tense denotes that the betrothal was now a thing of the past: cf. 2. 1, 45. 3.

ante portam Capenam] i.e. due S. of the Palatine, W. of the Caelian Hill. The spot where Horatia was slain and buried (see § 14 below) was thus near the main road from Latium, which in historical times (*via Latina*) entered the city by the *porta Capena.*

32 **paludamento**] 'the martial cloak': the word is technically used for a general's cloak.

p. 34. 1 **solvit crines**] This, as monumental evidence shows, was a customary act for female mourners.

3 § **3. animum**] (like θυμός) 'anger'; or 'stirred his soul,' as we say.

5 § **4. immaturo**] 'unseasonable,' and therefore to a conqueror 'unreasonable.'

9 § **5. obstabat**] 'was likely to counteract,' 'tell against': cf. Sallust, *Cat.* 52 *cetera vita eorum huic sceleri obstat.*

raptus...ad regem] 'haled for trial before the king.'

11 **ad vulgus**] 'in the popular view': cf. 9. 16 *ad muliebre ingenium efficaces.*

secundum iudicium] 'resulting from the trial': the preposition implies succession both in time and in effect.

12 **concilio**] In the case of Manlius (see next note) the process was conducted by the tribunes before a *concilium plebis.*

duoviros] These officials are mentioned in three cases only—here, in that of Manlius (Livy, VI. 20) and in that of Rabirius (Cic. *pro C. Rabirio perduellionis reo*). In the case of Horatius, they seem to have been special deputies, appointed by the king, perhaps in order to make an appeal to the people possible (cf. *clemente legis interprete* in § 8) in a difficult case: there was no such appeal from the king's own sentence. Or perhaps we may suppose that, in early cases of acts regarded as specially hurtful to the state, existing methods of justice were superseded by a *privilegium* or special statute, prescribing a special procedure. Cf. Maine, *Ancient Law* (14th ed.), pp. 372—3; and for the whole case E. C. Clark, *Early Roman Law*, §§ 11—16, and W. E. Heitland, Introduction to Cicero's *Pro C. Rabirio.*

13 **perduellionem**] This word is made up of *per* in a sinister sense (cf. *perfidus, periurus*) and *duellum*, i.e. *bellum*: it means therefore an act of war against one's own country, 'treason' (Dionysius translates it by προδοσία), for which *minuta maiestas* and *crimen maiestatis* were afterwards used. The act of Horatius in this case was in itself a *parricidium* (see n. on 13. 2): but by killing his sister he assumed the right of punishment, and so committed a crime against the state, and was guilty of *perduellio.* If the case were tried as *perduellio*, an appeal could be

permitted, and motives or extenuating circumstances considered: if as *parricidium*, the facts were undeniable, and there could be no appeal.

Horatio...iudicent] 'pass judgment on H. for treason.'

14 § **6. carminis**] 'strain': cf. 24. 6. The *lex* has been arranged in Saturnian metre.

15 **provocarit**] 'appeal'—from the *duoviri* to the people, the *concilio populi advocato* mentioned above.

16 **certato**] 'he shall join issue,' 'shall contest'—fight the case, in fact.

vincent] i.e. the *duoviri*, acting as public prosecutors in the popular trial of the appeal.

obnubito] '(the constable) shall veil': the same subject is to be understood with *suspendito* and *verberato*.

infelici arbori] locative (in § 11 the form *arbore* occurs), 'on a barren tree.'

18 **pomerium**] 'bounds.' See notes on 44. 3—4. The words *vel intra ...pomerium* anticipate the terms of the *ius provocationis* established in 509 B.C., which required that the sentence appealed against should have been given in Rome or within a mile of the *pomerium*.

19 § **7. qui...posse**] 'who believed themselves unable under that ordinance to acquit even an innocent person,' i.e. a case of justifiable homicide. This looks as if the *duoviri* assumed the prisoner to be guilty (cf. *Horatio perduellionem iudicent* above), and left the case to be fought on the appeal. But in Livy VI. 20 (the case of Manlius) we read *per duoviros qui de perduellione anquirerent creatos*.

20 **cum condemnassent**] i.e. declared him guilty (as public prosecutors).

22 § **8. accesserat**] before the order. **iniciebat**] directly after it.

23 **auctore**] 'at the instance of.'

clemente...interprete] i.e. because he encouraged an appeal throughout.

24 **certatum...est**] 'issue was joined (the case was discussed) before the commons.' Cf. *certatio multae*, the discussion on a fine, XXV. 4. 8.

27 § **9. patrio...fuisse**] 'would have punished his son by his right as a father,' i.e. would have treated the case as a *parricidium*, when there would have been no appeal (see note on *perduellionem* above). Originally the *paterfamilias* had the right of punishing with death (*ius vitae necisque*) the *filiifamilias*, but this would generally be after condemnation by the family tribunal (*iudicium domesticum*).

31 § **10. Pila Horatia**] This was in the Forum. It is not clear whether *Pila* was originally meant to be fem. sing. ('a column to which the spoils were fixed') or neut. pl. ('javelins'): Livy (cf. *pila et spolia*,

§ 11) takes the latter view, but Dionysius the former. Cf. Seeley, Introd., p. 43.

p. 35. 1 **decoratum...incedentem**] 'trophy-laden and triumphant, in victorious progress.' *victoria* probably belongs to all three words. *ovantem* here (as in II. 2, 25. 13) has a general sense: in later times it was generally used for the lesser triumph (πεζὸς θρίαμβος), in which the victor entered the city on foot.

3 **sub furca vinctum**] 'tied up to a yoke (fork),' i.e. a piece of wood V-shaped, to which the criminal's arms were tied for scourging.

4 **quod...spectaculum**] The apposition gives a reason for the rest of the clause—'so foul were the scene.'

5 § **11** **i, lictor**] The father's appeal quotes once more the words of the law, with a certain irony, to which the word *i* lends itself. Cf. Martial, II. 6. 1, *i nunc, edere me iube libellos.*

11 **sua decora**] 'the distinctions he himself has won': *sua* is emphatic. See n. on *sua*, 7. 15.

13 § **12.** **parem**] 'even,' 'consistent.'

14 **admiratione...causae**] abl. of cause. The reason for the acquittal was subjective, not objective; patriotism, not justice.

15 **manifesta**] 'undisputed,' 'flagrant' (cf. n. on *manifestae reum caedis*, 7. 9). The *tamen* which follows implies a contrast between the openness of the murder, prohibiting compensation, and the compensation which in spite of all was allowed.

16 **pecunia publica**] 'by a sum paid to the state.' *publica* practically = *publicata*, 'confiscated': cf. *censeo publicandas eorum pecunias*, Sall. *Cat.* 51. 43.

17 § **13.** **sacrificiis**] to *Juno Sororia* and *Janus Curiatius* (or *Jupiter Tigillus*) (Festus, p. 297): referred to in Tac. *Ann.* XII. 8, *sacra ex legibus Tulli regis piaculaque.* 'Perhaps the whole legend of Horatius, or at any rate its connexion with this spot [the *sororium tigillum*] arose out of this gentile worship of two deities, of which the cult-titles were respectively *Curiatius* and *Sororia.*' Fowler, *R. F.* p. 239.

19 **tigillo**] 'a beam in miniature': it was let into houses on both sides of a street leading from the Carinae to the Vicus Cuprius. See n. on *sepulcrum*, below.

velut sub iugum] 'under the fiction of a yoke.' What the yoke meant is not clear. Weissenborn thinks that Horatius was made thus to indicate that as an enemy he had forfeited his life: Roscher (*Lex.* s. v. *Ianus*) that evil was got rid of by passing through split wood, of which the *iugum* was a symbol.

20 **publice**] 'officially,' 'ceremonially': not 'publicly.' **semper refectum**] 'by unbroken renewal'—of the beam and the ritual.

21 § **14**. **sepulcrum**] In the *sacer campus Horatiorum*, near the Porta Capena. The rites of the *gens Horatia* were originally performed on a part of the *Septimontium* near the Forum; then, on account of the growth of the city, they were transferred to a place outside the *porta Capena*.

CHAPTER XXVII.

24 § **1**. **invidia vulgi**] 'the popular resentment.'

25 **fuerit**] The *mood* expresses the thought of the people, the *tense* takes us back to their point of view.

27 **pravis**] dative, sc. *consiliis*.

31 § **2**. **per speciem societatis**] 'under cover of confederacy.'

32 § **3**. **Fidenates, colonia Romana**] i.e. after the conquest mentioned in c. 14 above: cf. Plut. *Rom.* 23. 12.

p. 36. 1 **pacto...Albanorum**] 'by an undertaking to desert on the part of the A.'

4 § **4**. **exercitu**] The army of Alba had been ordered (26. 1) to remain embodied.

6 **confluentis**] sc. *fluvios*. Antemnae was situated at this junction of the Tiber and the Anio.

10 **legionem**] The word is here used of a non-Roman force: see n. on 25. 6.

11 **Albano**] i.e. the A. general, Mettius: so Virgil, *Aen.* VIII. 643 *at tu dictis, Albane, maneres*.

14 § **6**. **subisse**] For the contracted form cf. *mugissent*, 6. 7: *petisse*, 11. 9.

erigit] 'led them up hill.'

16 **explicat**] 'deployed,' 'extended.'

17 § **7**. **esse**] historical inf.

20 **Salios**] It is not clear whether these *Salii* are to be assigned, with the temples, *Pallori ac Pavori* ('to Pallor and Panic'), or to be regarded as the second twelve *Salii*, belonging to Quirinus and his shrine on the Quirinal, and called *Collini*, *Agonales*, or *Agonenses* as opposed to *Palatini*. See n. on 20. 4.

22 § **8**. **nihil...opus esse**] Probably a colloquial use—'not the slightest need'; cf. Plaut. *Merc.* 394 *nihil opust nobis ancilla*.

27 § **9. id...rati]** 'believing the case to be what they had heard from the king.'

30 **ut qui]** (like *quippe qui*, and ἅτε, ὡς with participles in Greek) expresses a reason from the point of view of the speaker or writer: cf. *ut quae* Praef. 4.

coloni...essent] 'had been attached to the R. as colonists,' whether in the actual settlement of the city after the previous war (see c. 14), or subsequently. Livy seems to have thought that the Fidenates would otherwise, as Etruscans, understand no Latin: but there may well have been a community of language between Fidenae and Rome before the Etruscan occupation of the town.

p. 37. 1 § **10. Veientem]** i.e. the whole V. army: cf. *Romanus*, 15. 2; 25. 12; 29. 6.

alieno...perculsum] 'paralysed by the panic of others.'

2 **nec...arcebat]** The idea of flight is implied in *nec...impetum*, and qualified by the second clause. In Greek μέν...δέ would have been used.

3 **effusa]** 'disorderly,' 'indiscriminate.'

6 § **11. inter...consilium]** Cf. 14. 8.

oppressi] 'caught.'

alia ante Romana] See note on *novi semper scriptores*, Praef. 2.

CHAPTER XXVIII.

9 § **1. devictos]** There is a touch of flattery in the completeness of the victory implied.

11 **quod...vertat]** 'with a prayer for success': the actual words pass unchanged into indirect narration. Cf. III. 35. 8 *ille enimvero, quod bene vertat, habiturum se comitia professus*: III. 62. 5 (also in ind. narr.).

12 **sacrificium lustrale]** For the details of *lustratio* see n. on 44. 2.

13 § **2. paratis omnibus]** Livy makes the oblique cases of the neuter plural of adjectives (and especially of pronominal adjectives like *omnes*) do duty as substantives: cf. § 11 *in aliis*; 45. 1 *formatis omnibus*.

ut adsolet] sc. *fieri*: it may refer here both to what immediately precedes and to what immediately follows.

15 **ab extremo]** 'from the outermost station,' where the Albans were. They were summoned first, and also most interested, so that they naturally stood nearest (*proximi*) to the speaker.

17 § **3. ex composito]** Cf. 9. 10.

18 **centurionibus]** 'captains': the word (like *legio* here and elsewhere) is not used in a technical sense.

20 § **4. si umquam...ageretis]** 'if ever there was a reason why you

should return thanks.' The subj. is consecutive: cf. Cic. *Lael.* 17 *est quatenus amicitiae dari venia possit*: id. *ad Att.* 16. 5. 2 *magis est quod gratuler tibi.*

22 **ipsorum**] accentuates the gen. pl. contained in *vestrae*: cf. V. 38. 7 *suomet ipsorum certamine*, and the Greek τἀμὰ δυστήνου κακά. Livy is fond of the nom. in similar cases, e.g. *ipsi* here.

24 **cum proditione ac perfidia**] 'against treachery and disloyalty': the first word applies rather to act, the second to feeling.

26 § **5**. **iniussu meo**] abl. of circumstances, the negative of *meo iussu.* Cf. 17. 9.

nec imperium...consilium] 'nor was that utterance of mine a command but a stratagem.'

28 **nec...et**] Cf. note on 23. 2. **ignorantibus**] 'if you were kept in ignorance,' answering to *ratis* on the other side.

30 **terror ac fuga**] 'a run-away panic.' So Δεῖμος and Φόβος (cf. *Pallor* and *Pavor* above) are associated as the steeds of the war-god in *Il.* XV. 119.

§ **6**. **arguo**] 'censure.'

32 **fecissetis**] Notice the use of *facio* in Latin exactly corresponding to our 'do,' avoiding the repetition of a verb.

p. 38. 3 **audeat**] 'let another dare.' This use of an exclamatory wish, confirming a statement by protesting against its opposite, is fairly common: cf. Catullus 92. 4 *dispeream nisi amo*, which = *amo.* So here the real statement is *dedero.*

nisi...dedero] 'unless I impose (execute) upon him a lesson notable at once among mankind.' For *dedero* cf. n. on 25. 11.

6 § **7**. **quod bonum...sit**] Cf. 17. 10 above.

9 **legere**] 'select for,' 'appoint to be': cf. XXIII. 22. 4 *civium e quibus in patres legerentur*, and 30. 2 below.

10 **ut ex uno**] See 6. 3 above.

12 § **8**. **in variis voluntatibus**] 'in spite of divers opinions.' The same phrase is found in 17. 3 above (see note on *in*), where also it gives point to a following *tamen.*

15 § **9**. **fidem ac foedera**] 'troth and treaty.'

ea disciplina] 'that piece of learning,' 'instruction therein': *ea* refers to *fidem...servandi*, and *disciplina* harks back to *discere. insanabile* below changes the metaphor.

17 **at**] 'still,' 'at least'; found especially in conditional or quasi-conditional clauses: cf. 41. 3 *si tua re subita consilia torpent, at tu mea sequere*; Catull. 30. 11 *si tu oblitus es, at di meminerunt.*

20 **rem]** may be translated either 'state' (=*res publica*) or 'fortune,' 'cause': for the former cf. 6. 3 *Albana re*, 54. 10 *Gabina re*; for the latter 54. 3 *quibus plerumque Gabina res superior esset.* In such cases *res* with an adjective corresponds exactly to the Greek use of a neuter adjective with the definite article.

ancipitem] with *animum*, 'distracted.'

21 § **10. admotis quadrigis...earum]** This use of an ablative absolute connected by a demonstrative to another participial clause is an irregularity of style, but it serves to make clear the successive stages of an action, or to avoid an involved expression. There are many instances of it in Livy, e.g. 43. 12 *post expletas quinque et triginta tribus, duplicato earum numero.*

22 **in diversum iter]** 'in opposite directions.' So Virgil, *Aen.* VIII. 642 *haud procul inde citae Metum in diversa quadrigae distulerant.*

23 **lacerum...corpus]** 'fragments of flesh.'

26 § **11. supplicium]** The word seems to suggest that originally the capital punishment of an offender was regarded in the light of a sacrifice of expiation to the deity offended by his act. **exempli]** 'type,' 'pattern.'

27 **in aliis]** 'in other cases': **placuisse]** 'were approved.' The gradual loss of power by the *Comitia Centuriata* (which, as a half-military body, could inflict capital punishment), and the gradual acquisition of power by the *Comitia Tributa* (which could only impose a fine), indicates a tendency towards leniency in Roman *judicial* punishments: cf. Cic. *pro Rabirio perduellionis reo*, 10, *vestram libertatem non acerbitate suppliciorum infestam, sed lenitate legum munitam esse voluerunt.* The absence of the death-penalty in the *Quaestiones Perpetuae* was an important factor in the revolutionary struggles of the dying Republic (cf. Maine, *Anc. Law*, pp. 388—90). From exile, again, the early Romans shrank with horror: as a punishment it was practically unknown for centuries, and eventually came to be regarded only as a means of escaping worse penalties. On the other hand, Roman *military* punishments, of which this may be regarded as an instance, were cruel enough, e.g. *fustuarium*, *decimatio.*

CHAPTER XXIX.

p. 39. 3 § **2. omnia...miscet]** 'spreads general confusion.'

4 § **3. tacita maestitia]** 'subdued sadness': *tacita* has a notion of 'unprotesting' about it, and this phrase refers rather to persons, *silentium triste* to things.

5 **quid relinquerent...ferrent]** Intention is implied—'what they were to leave, take'—i.e. this is a deliberative subjunctive, indirectly reported in a past tense. Cf. 20. 7 *edoceret, quae prodigia susciperentur.*

6 **deficiente...alios]** amplifications of *obliti.*

8 **ultimum...visuri]** 'for the one last look.' *ultimum illud* is an acc. of extent, like *primum, iterum, aeternum,* cf. II. 15. 1.

10 § **4.** **ultimis]** i.e. the demolition began at the outside edges.

11 **distantibus]** probably not 'distant' but 'separate': so 25. 14 *distantia locis.*

12 **quibus...elatis]** The relative is attracted, in Greek fashion, to the case of the (unexpressed) antecedent, i.e. *rebus.* Cf. IV. 39. 9 *quibus poterat sauciis ductis secum*; Hor. *Sat.* I. 6. 15 *notante iudice quo nosti populo.*

13 **larem ac penates]** 'the sanctities of hearth and home'—the spirits of dead ancestry and guardians of the store-chamber—whose worship had been one of the treasures of their home-life; just as below the sight of the temples suggested memories of their state-life.

17 § **5.** **obsessa...captos]** Notice the emphasis.

19 § **6.** **Romanus]** Cf. 15. 2; 25. 12.

21 **quadringentorum]** i.e. 300 years before the foundation of Rome, and 100 since.

22 **quibus]** The abl. = period in which, suggesting rather the limits than the extent: cf. Cic. *Rep.* I. 37 *ergo his annis quadringentis Romae rex erat.*

excidio ac ruinis] 'demolition and desolation.' The two words are intended to be close-coupled, one expressing the process, the other the result.

templis] dative.

23 **deum]** gen. pl. **temperatum]** 'were left untouched.'

CHAPTER XXX.

25 § **1.** **crescit Albae ruinis]** Cf. XXXI. 29. 10 *quarum ruinis crevit urbs Roma.*

civium] Cf. 28. 7 *civitatem dare plebi.* It is not clear what was the civil status of the *plebs* at this time.

26 **Caelius mons]** the S.E. eminence of Rome—the point nearest Alba, in fact.

28 **regiae]** probably dat.: see n. on 5. 6 *Numitori.*

29 § **2.** **in patres...legit]** i.e. for the Senate, in fulfilment of what was

announced in 28. 7. The king, as chief magistrate, chose his own councillors: so under the Republic the *lectio senatus* belonged to the consuls first, then to the censors. Romulus (see 8. 7) created 100 senators: Tullus now added an Alban contingent: Tarquinius Priscus (see 35. 6) raised 100 heads of *minores gentes* to the honour. By this reckoning Livy obtains a total of 300, which was the regular complement until Sulla's time.

30 **Tullios**] *Iulios* has been suggested, in order to make Livy agree with Dionysius (III. 29). The uncertainty here, in the case of a most important *gens*, suggests that all these heroic origins must be regarded with suspicion.

31 **ordini**] Cf. *ordinum* below. Livy, mindful of the three *ordines* ('estates') of his own day—senatorial, equestrian, plebeian—makes Tullus distribute the Alban immigrants according to a similar division.

templum] 'a close,' 'enclosure': cf. n. on 18. 9. **curiam**] in apposition to *templum* (cf. 10. 6 *templum...sedem*); 'as a court-house.' It was situated N. of the Forum and Comitium. The building, having been restored by Sulla, was burnt with the body of Clodius (52 B.C.), restored again by Sulla's son, and then demolished by Julius Caesar, who set on the same site a temple to Felicitas.

32 **Hostilia**] There were besides the *Curia Iulia* (built by Julius Caesar and Augustus) and the *Curia Pompeia* (where Caesar was assassinated), in which also the Senate met.

patrum] i.e. the last generation before Livy: not used for *maiorum*. The name *Hostilia* lasted apparently till the burning of 52 B.C.

p. 40. 3 § **3**. **turmas**] 'troops.' Properly *turma* = 30 men, $\frac{1}{10}$ of an *ala*: so the Alban contribution was just one *ala*, 300 men. Romulus (13. 8) had enrolled 3 *centuriae*, so (according to Livy) this Alban contingent doubled the cavalry. For the separate organisation of *turmae*, which this passage seems to support, see note on 13. 8.

eodem supplemento] 'with a reinforcement (draft) from the same source.' **scripsit**] = *conscripsit*.

5 § **4**. **hac fiducia virium**] 'then, relying on his forces': *hac* = 'thus given.'

8 **res repetitae**] Cf. 22. 4—7, 32. 6—14.

9 § **5**. **ad Feroniae fanum**] Feronia was essentially an Italian (rather than a Roman) goddess, associated from early times with the working classes—plebeians, freedmen, slaves. Her chief shrine was at Trebula Mutusca (in the S. of the Sabine territory), and here during her festival was held a great fair (so *mercatu frequenti* 'at a crowded

mart'). Fowler, *R. F.*, p. 253. We may compare the fairs formerly held in the Isle of Ely on St Awdry's day (17 Oct.), and in Paris on and after the feast of St Denys (9 Oct.).

10 § **6. suos...retentos**] It is not quite clear what substantive is to be supplied with *suos*. (1) Dionysius (III. 32) has *ὅτι τοὺς Σαβίνων φυγάδας* ('exiles') *ὑπεδέχοντο κατασκευάσαντες ἄσυλον ἱερόν*, which suits the sense here. (2) Perhaps it should be 'slaves,' as Madvig thinks, believing that the word *servos* has dropped out from similarity to *suos*. It is possible that *servos* and not *suos* is the right reading. *lucum* is probably to be referred (cf. Dion. H., *l.c.*) to a refuge like that of Romulus (see 8. 5—6 above): runaway slaves were a frequent cause of quarrels between primitive nations.

12 **ferebantur**] 'were alleged, brought forward.'

haud...memores] 'not disposed to forget.' **locatam...auctam**] sc. *esse*.

15 **et ipsi**] 'in their turn,' 'like their opponents': see n. on Praef. 3.

§ **7. Etruria erat vicina**] Attention was drawn to this in 23. 8 above.

16 **residuas bellorum**] 'remaining from the wars.' Gen. of remoter object, i.e. the verbal construction would be such as Livy has in XL. 7. 5 *iram, si qua ex certamine residet*.

18 **traxere**] i.e. *ad se*, 'attracted.' *traho* is a favourite word with Livy: cf. 7. 1; 24. 1.

19 **publico**] 'formal,' 'official': cf. 26. 14.

20 **minus mirum**] Probably because most of the lesser states concerned had more to gain than to lose by friendship with Rome: the Veientines, as Etruscans, were less likely to be true.

21 **pacta...fides**] 'the bond of the truce arranged with Romulus'—after the struggle mentioned in c. 27.

23 § **8. occupat...transire**] For this usage of *occupo* cf. 14. 4.

25 § **9. Malitiosam**] Dionysius (III. 33) calls it *ὕλη κακοῦργος*. Both epithets mean 'crafty,' 'cunning,' so *Silva M.* may be translated 'Wily Wood.' Did the battle name the wood, or the wood the battle? We do not know. If the former, then perhaps a successful stratagem (as in c. 14) was executed by the Romans: if the latter, we must trace the title back to a primitive belief in the deceitful or destructive powers of wood-spirits. It is worth noticing in this connection that Dionysius (V. 16) says that the Romans attributed to Faunus the same power of causing sudden panic which the Greeks ascribed to Pan.

quidem...ceterum] 'to some extent'...'for the rest' or 'mainly.'

28 § **10. deinde...potuit**] 'could have been re-established.' **explicari**] *fuga* is probably nominative—'nor could a line of retreat have been cleared.' If *fuga* is ablative, we may translate 'nor could the battle have resolved itself by their flight.'

CHAPTER XXXI.

32 § **1. lapidibus pluisse**] So again in XXI. 62. 5, XXXV. 9. 4: with acc. XXVIII. 27. 16. In XXVII. 37. 1 the phrase is *de caelo lapidaverat.*

p. 41. 1 § **2. missis**] either dative, expressing the persons affected by *in conspectu...cecidere*: or ablative absolute.

4 **lapides**] put last for emphasis.

5 § **3. ex summi...luco**] This grove (probably of oak-trees) on a hill-top indicates that the deity belongs to a very early time, before the period of temples and statues in human shape—the pre-Roman Jupiter, in fact, who continued to be worshipped on the Alban Mount at the *Feriae Latinae* every year till the end of the third century A.D., as the presiding genius of the Latin communities: cf. Fowler, *R. F.* pp. 95—7, 227—8.

6 **patrio ritu**] 'in ancestral fashion'—by representatives of all the Latin cities, with a sacrifice of a white bull, the flesh of which was afterwards distributed as a symbol of communion.

7 **dis...relictis**] Cf. 29. 5 *cum...velut captos relinquerent deos.* See also § 4.

9 § **4. Romanis**] 'with the Romans.' The dat. denotes both agents and persons affected. Livy is fond of putting a dat. thus at the head of the sentence.

quoque] i.e. separately from the ex-Albans.

10 **ab**] 'in consequence of': cf. 8. 3; 17. 6.

novendiale sacrum] 'a nine days' celebration.' There are frequent mentions of this observance in Livy, which invariably followed a stone-shower: it was a form of *supplicatio* or expiation, intended to appease the anger of heaven indicated by the shower.

11 **seu voce...seu monitu**] the prompting cause.

12 **aruspicum monitu**] In most cases of prodigies in historical times the sacred books (of Etruscan origin) supplied rules of expiation; in doubtful cases the *aruspices* (='diviners,' 'soothsayers'), Sibylline books, or Delphic Oracle (cf. 56. 5 below) were consulted as to the proper steps of expiation (*supplicatio*). The *aruspices* themselves seem to have been of Etruscan origin; their art dealt with the interpretation of the entrails in sacrifice, and of extraordinary phenomena in nature; cf. 55. 6, 56. 5.

13 **sollemne**] predicative; '(it continued to be) a ritual practice.'

quandoque...nuntiaretur] With relative adjectives and adverbs, where repeated occurrence is to be expressed, Livy and later writers use the subjunctive (historic tenses), like the Gk. optative of indefinite frequency: Cicero and the earlier writers use perf. or pluperf. ind. Cf. *ubi dixisset* 32. 13 (Roby, § 720). The indic. occurs in 9. 11 *in quem quaeque inciderat.*

14 **feriae**] Under the Republic holidays were (1) *stativae*, regular and recurring: (2) *conceptivae*, settled every year: (3) *imperativae*, ordained by consuls on account of particular occurrences. The last class would cover the present instance.

18 **§ 5. militiae...domi**] For the contrast see note, Praef. 9.

19 **corpora**] 'physique.'

21 **§ 6. qui...ratus esset**] 'though he had held.'

23 **superstitionibus obnoxius**] 'the slave of superstitious fancies.'

24 **religionibus**] 'religious scruples,' implying actions as well as thoughts: cf. XLI. 16. 6 *plenis religionum animis.*

26 **§ 7. requirentes**] 'seeking to restore,' 'regretfully craving for.'

unam opem...si] 'the sole resource left was the chance of obtaining.' The tense *impetrata esset* (for *erit* of *oratio recta*) shows that the condition must be realised before the result can ensue. For *unam si*, cf. 17. 9 *sic ratum esset, si....*

28 **§ 8. volventem**] A Roman book (in Livy's time) usually consisted of a long, continuous strip of papyrus, rolled round a rod: thus the process of unrolling (*evolvere*), and re-rolling (*volvere*) meant much the same as our 'turning over (the pages).'

29 **quaedam...sacrificia**] For the accumulation of adjectives see note on 14. 7 *densa...virgulta.*

30 **Elicio**] See note on 20. 7.

operatum] The partic. has a present (or rather, aorist) signification—'in performing': so Virg. *Georg.* I. 389 *sacra refer Cereri laetis operatus in herbis.*

32 **caelestium speciem**] 'manifestation from heaven' or 'of heavenly secrets.'

p. 42. 1 **sollicitati...religione**] (so *prave cultis*, 32. 2 below), 'provoked by a fault of ritual, a ritual irregularity.' Cf. Pliny, *Nat. Hist.* XXVIII. 14 *L. Piso primo annalium auctor est Tullum...ex Numae libris eodem, quo illum, sacrificio Iovem caelo devocare conatum, quoniam parum rite quaedam fecisset, fulmine ictum.* For the significance of such a death see n. on 15. 6 above.

CHAPTER XXXII.

(For the reign of Ancus Marcius see Introduction, § 5.)

4 § **1. res...redierat]** 'the control had reverted to the Fathers, according to the original ordinance.' The pluperfect *redierat* implies that the procedure (for which see 17. 5—10 above) was now established.

6 **comitia]** sc. *curiata*: cf. 35. 1.

7 **populus...auctores]** Cf. 17. 9, 22. 1.

9 **Ancus Marcius]** The first name (from a root *ank*=bend) is interpreted to mean 'server,' i.e. priest, and was thought by Varro to be of Sabine origin: the second (cf. *Pompilius*, *Hostilius*, and many others in this book) was borne by a Roman *gens*, and has already been assigned to Numa Marcius in 20. 5.

10 § **2. cetera egregium]** (so again in 35. 6) 'in all else excellent': cf. Virg. *Aen.* III. 594 *cetera Graius*; Hor. *Ep.* I. 10. 50 *excepto quod non simul esses, cetera laetus*; Sophocles, *Ajax*, 551 *τὰ δ' ἄλλ' ὁμοῖος.*

11 **ab una parte]** See n. on 17. 2.

12 **religionibus]** 'religious duties,' 'offices': cf. 31. 6 above.

antiquissimum] 'of chiefest importance.' Only the comparative and superlative of *antiquus* are so used: cf. *πρεσβύτατον*.

14 **ex commentariis]** Cf. 20. 5 above. **pontificem]** 'a priest': cf. 20. 5.

15 **in album relata...in publico]** 'to copy them on a white block (tablet) and display them in public.' Cf. Lys. 114. 40 *ἐς λεύκωμα γράφειν*: Cic. *Att.* VIII. 9. 2 *epistulam in publico proponere.* Certain MSS. have *data* (set out) for *relata*, and this is perhaps right: there is a similar uncertainty (noted by Seeley) of text in Cic. *de Orat.* II. 12. 52 *efferebat in album.*

17 **abiturum]** 'would adopt the habits and ordinances.'

§ **3. igitur]** as first word in a sentence, gives a special instance or amplification of the preceding statement: cf. *nempe*, *αὐτίκα*.

20 **repetentibus res]** Cf. 22. 4—7, and §§ 6—14 below.

21 **desidem]** (coupled with *imbellem* in XXI. 16. 3)=*ἡσυχάζοντα* 'in his inactivity': the sense is further expressed by *inter sacella...regnum.* The adjective is put first to give it a predicative force.

22 § **4. medium]** 'a mean.' **memor]** 'which recalled.'

23 **praeterquam quod...credebat]** 'over and above his conviction' (cf. XXXV. 25. 11 *praeterquam quod ita Quintio placeret*): answered by *etiam* ('also') below.

25 **in novo...populo]** 'in the case of a young and impetuous nation.' Cf. 17. 1 *in novo populo.*

illi] i.e. Numa.

contigisset] The subjunctive is due to *oratio obliqua*, expressing the feelings of Ancus Marcius.

26 **sine iniuria**] 'free of outrage': i.e. neighbouring states would be sure to commit outrages on a peaceful Rome.

se habiturum] sc. *credebat*. Ancus Marcius was as sure that peace was impossible for him as he was sure that it had been necessary for his grandfather.

temptari...temptatam] See note on 5. 3 *cepisse, captum*.

27 **patientiam**] i.e. his own, and perhaps that of the State also.

contemni] a prophetic present.

28 **Tullo regi**] 'for a Tullus as king,' 'for the reign of a Tullus.'

29 § **5.** **religiones**] See § 2 above. **instituisset**] The subjunctive expresses the view of Ancus.

p. 43. 1 **ritu**] 'formality': not necessarily religious, though probably based on primitive religion.

ius...descripsit] Cf. C.I.L. I. 564 *Erresius rex Aequeicolus. is preimus ius fetiale paravit: inde populus Romanus discipleinam excepit.* The *fetiales* appear to have been an institution in most Italian tribes: cf. Wordsworth, *Fragments and Specimens of Early Latin*, p. 553.

2 **Aequiculis**] the N. section of the Aequi, inhabiting a hilly region S.E. of the Sabines, N.E. of Latium.

fetiales] See n. on 24. 4.

5 § **6.** **capite velato**] Cf. 18. 7, 36. 5. For other details of fetial equipment and procedure see c. 24.

filo] i.e. *apiculum* (στέμμα), a fillet of wool wound round the upper part of the priestly cap (*apex*). **velamen**] 'covering.'

7 **audiat fas**] In a triple appeal such as this (to *Iuppiter*, *fines*, *fas*) the third item is usually in the third person; cf. 24. 7 note on *audi tu*.

8 **publicus**] 'official': cf. 30. 7 *publico auxilio*.

iuste pieque legatus] 'rightly (acc. to law) and duly (acc. to religion) commissioned.'

11 § **7.** **illos...illas**] 'the persons and objects aforesaid.'

dedier...siris (=*sieris*, pf. subj. of *sino*)...**suprascandit**] archaisms, occurring in the formula from which this passage is reproduced.

12 **compotem...esse**] 'to be partaker in.'

13 § **8.** **haec**] repeated four times, showing the different stages of the pronouncement.

14 **obvius**] i.e. after the *fetialis* has crossed the boundary, and so the first enemy whom chance offers.

15 **paucis...mutatis**] 'with a few verbal changes in the form (strain) and style (setting) of the oath,' i.e. to suit the different cases. For *carminis* see n. on 24. 6. This formality of seeking satisfaction (*quo res repetuntur*), i.e. of declaring war, was known as *clarigatio*, perhaps from the loud cry of the *pater patratus*.

16 **peragit**] Cf. 18. 10.

17 § **9. sollemnes**] 'customary,' 'conventional': in 22. 5 the thirtieth day is mentioned.

19 § **10. Iane Quirine**] an emendation for *Iuno Quirine*. *Quirine* = Ianus as guardian of the completed state (cf. Fowler, *R. F.*, p. 290), or 'Sabine' (from *Cures*), or 'of the oak' (from *quercus*). See notes on 15. 6 above. In any case the appeal to Juppiter and Janus—probably duplicate deities—and to all the *di caelestes, terrestres, inferni*, is in accordance with the practice of archaic worship, which feared to omit any epithet or agency that might lend assistance.

21 **iniustum**] 'against right,' of thought. **neque...persolvere**] of deed.

22 **maiores natu**] 'elders'—i.e. the Senate (γερουσία), who formed the King's council.

25 § **11. quarum rerum litium causarum**] 'as concerning the objects, claims, and considerations, whereof.' These genitives are a difficulty. (1) We may suppose that they express the sphere of action contemplated in the formula, and affected by the formal term *condixit* (i.e. *condictionem fecit* or *dixit* = *denuntiavit*) 'has given notice.' Such a genitive is not unfamiliar in legal forms, and is found occasionally in connection with the *legis actiones* (cf. Gaius, IV. 21) of which *condictio* became one. In this case *rerum l. c.* are attracted into the case of the relative, like *in quem primo egressi sunt locum Troia vocatur*, in c. 1. 3 above. Or (2) the genitives may depend on *quid censes?* (like our 'what think you of...?'); in which case the relative is attracted from accusative (i.e. *earum rerum...quas* governed by *condixit*) into the case of its nouns, after the Greek fashion. Cf. 29. 4, 40. 5.

26 **pater patratus**] See n. on 24. 4.

populi...Quiritium] See n. on 24. 5.

27 **Priscorum Latinorum**] See n. on 3. 7. Hitherto the formulae have been left open: now a particular people is inserted, with reference to the war which immediately follows in the next chapter.

dederunt...solverunt...fecerunt] 'rendered...fulfilled...discharged': the three words recall the three specifications *res, lites, causas*, which are here expressed in *res* alone.

31 § **12. puro pioque duello**] 'by a war of justice and duty.' Cf. Cic.

de Off. I. 11. 36 *ex quo* (i.e. *ius fetiale*) *intellegi potest nullum bellum esse iustum, nisi quod aut rebus repetitis geratur, aut denuntiatum ante sit et indictum.*

quaerendas] sc. *res*: the omission of *esse* in gerundival clauses with *censeo* is common, especially in Plautus.

32 **consentio consciscoque**] 'agree and by vote approve.'

p. 44. 2 **in eandem...ibat**] Livy describes a 'division' (*discessio*) according to the usage of the later Republic. After the individual opinions had been asked for (*perrogatio sententiarum*) the 'ayes' moved (*discedo*) to that side of the Senate-House on which sat the author of the opinion (*sententia*), the 'noes' to the other.

3 **fieri solitum**] 'the usual procedure was.'

sanguineam praeustam] 'fire-hardened and blood-stained' (or 'blood-red'): i.e. a wooden substitute for a real spear. In both cases the weapon seems to symbolize fire and slaughter.

4 **non minus**] For the omission of *quam* cf. 23. 3.

5 § **13**. **quod**] 'whereas,' 'forasmuch as.'

populi] 'tribes,' 'communities')(*homines* 'individuals.'

7 **fecerunt deliquerunt**] 'have acted and sinned,' 'committed act and offence.' Such omissions of connecting particle are not uncommon in old forms, cf. 24. 7 *prima postrema.*

9 **censuit consensit conscivit**] 'affirmed, agreed, and by vote approved.'

13 **dixisset**] The subjunctive denotes frequency: see n. on 31. 4 *nuntiaretur.*

CHAPTER XXXIII.

16 § **1**. **demandata**] 'delegated.' His enemies had expected (see 32. 3) that he would devote his personal attention to religious observances.

19 **morem**] Instances are to be seen in 11. 4, 30. 1.

22 § **2**. **veterum**] 'original': cf. 17. 2, 54. 1.

23 **Capitolium atque arcem**] i.e. the S. and N. ends of the Capitoline.

24 **implessent**] For the contracted form cf. 7. 7 *mugissent*, 11. 9 *petisse*, 27. 6 *subisse.*

25 **eodem**] 'to the same quarter.'

Tellenis] Tellenae, about 10 miles S. of Rome. **Ficana**] near the mouth of the Tiber.

30 § **4**. **Medulliam compulso**] 'concentrated at M.': N.E. of Rome, near Crustumerium: the exact position is not known.

Marte...victoria] 'with indecisive issue and alternating victory': the second expression is merely a more definite restatement of the same fact. For the pair of ablatives see note on 12. 10.

31 **et...et**] i.e. there was fighting round about the walls and in the open. *comminus* in the second clause implies that a good deal of the fighting in the other case was carried on *eminus*, at long range.

p. 45. 2 § 5. **omnibus...conisus**] 'with a supreme effort of his whole force.'

6 **ad Murciae**] i.e. *ad aram* (*sacellum*) *Murciae*, in the valley afterwards occupied by the Circus Maximus, between the Palatine and the Aventine. The name *Murcia* may belong to the valley itself (i.e. 'swampy,' cf. *marceo*); or to an old name of the Aventine; or to an ancient goddess of 'Ease' (cf. *mulcere*, *Mulciber*, and *murcidus* 'indolent'), perhaps brought thither by the Latin immigrants on this occasion, and then applied as an epithet to Venus (cf. *Libentina* and *Volupia*). The variant spellings *Murtia*, *Myrtea* led some antiquarians (e.g. Varro, *L. L.* v. § 154) to connect the word with the myrtle. In any case, this became the most important shrine of Venus in Rome. Cf. Preller, *R. M.*, I. pp. 438—9.

§ 6. **Ianiculum**] i.e. the abode of Janus, who was supposed to have reigned there in the prehistoric age. The oak woods on this hill may supply the explanation for the connection of the god with it.

8 **muro**] i.e. the spot selected as an outwork was enclosed. But it is by no means probable that the Janiculum was fortified thus early: perhaps Livy is repeating a mistake contained in his authorities.

• **ob commoditatem itineris**] 'for convenience of transit.'

9 **ponte Sublicio**] 'the bridge of piles' (*sublicae*). It was originally made of wood throughout (perhaps lest the use of iron might offend the river-god), and had often to be repaired in consequence.

in Tiberim] 'over the Tiber.' The abl. with *in* is more usual in this phrase, and is read here by Madvig: but the acc. may be defended on the ground of the motion implied in the actual construction.

10 § 7. **Quiritium quoque fossa**] *quoque* here refers not to the word immediately preceding, but to *Quiritium fossa*, taken together as a single notion. Cf. 36. 1 *muro quoque lapideo...parabat.* The position of the *Quiritium fossa* is not known. Such dykes might well precede more definite fortification of the city. Festus (p. 254) mentions *Quiritium fossae* dug in the reign of Ancus Marcius round Ostia; another authority (*de Vir. Ill.* VIII. 1. 3) applies the same term to the sewers dug by the order of Tarquinius Superbus.

11 **a planioribus...locis**] 'on the side of localities more level in approach': cf. 12. 2 *ab Sabinis*, 17. 2 *ab sua parte*, 37. 3 *ab cornibus*.

12 **§ 8. ingenti...confuso]** A long series of ablatival expressions leads up to *facinora...fierent*. For this accumulation see n. on 12. 10.

13 **discrimine...confuso]** 'the distinction between right and wrong action was blurred.' *an* is used because the word *discrimine* implies an act of choice—has a subjective sense, in fact: cf. 8. 6. It is a substantival form of *discerno recte an perperam factum sit*.

17 **ager]** See note on 15. 5 above. **silva Mesia]** now the Bosco di Baccano. The possession of the woods on the right bank of the Tiber would make it possible for an enemy to contrive ambushes for the Roman merchants and inhabitants on the other side; and this actually occurred (Dion. Hal. III. 45).

19 **Ostia]** really a nom. pl., i.e. 'mouths,' but as a place-name treated as a fem. sing.

salinae] 'salt-pits,' 'salt-works': cf. VII. 19. 8. According to Dionysius (II. 55) the Romans got possession of the salt-pits after the defeat of the Veientines by Romulus: cf. c. 15. 5 above. But this statement may be due to the fact that the *tribus Romulia* occupied land in that district.

20 **aedis...Feretrii]** It was built by Romulus (see c. 10 above). The singular form *aedis* is commoner than *aedes*.

CHAPTER XXXIV.

(For the reign of Tarquinius Priscus see Introduction, § 6.)

21 **§ 1. Lucumo]** =Etruscan *Lauchme*. The word is derived from a root *luk* 'light,' and denotes 'man of light,' 'chief,' 'grandee' (cf. *Luceres*, *splendidus*); it is therefore a mark of rank, and not strictly a proper name.

23 **honoris]** 'position,' 'station': cf. *honoratum*, § 5 below.

24 **peregrina]** 'alien.' Lucumo was born (*oriundus*) at Tarquinii, but of half-alien parentage: his mother was a native.

25 **facultas non fuerat]** 'had found no chance,' on account of the intrigues described below.

§ 2. Demarati] Dionysius (III. 46) says that Demaratus had established trading connections with the Etruscan cities for some time before he actually migrated from Corinth: the immediate cause of his departure from thence was the tyranny of Cypselus (about 650 B.C.), which threatened destruction to the clan of the Bacchiadae, of whom Demaratus was one. From a critical point of view we may regard Demaratus as playing the same mythical part in the tale of Etruria which Aeneas and

Evander play in the tale of Rome—i.e. the Greek character represents early Greek, or Pelasgian, influence.

28 **Arruns**] (=Etr. *Arunth*) perhaps comes from root *ar*, i.e. 'able,' 'excellent.'

32 § **3. ventrem ferre**] 'was with child.'

immemor...nepotis] 'without mention of a grandson in his will.'

p. 46. 2 **Egerio**] mentioned again in 38. 1, 57. 6. The name is connected by Livy with *egēre* (*ab inopia*): possibly it should be referred to the same sources as *Egeria* (cf. 19. 5), and regarded as a regular epithet of the kingly house.

With such phrases as *nomen indere*, *facere* the name given is regularly put in the dative, by attraction to the dative of the person to whom the name is given: cf. Plautus, *Men.* II. 1. 37 *huic urbi nomen Epidamno inditum est*, *Trin.* IV. 2. 1 *huic ego diei nomen Trinummo faciam*. For the usage with *nomen est* see n. on 1. 3 *Troiano*.

§ **4. Lucumoni**] For the dat. and position cf. n. on 5. 6 *Numitori*.

4 **auxit**] sc. *animos*.

ducta...Tanaquil] 'his marriage with Tanaquil.' The name (=Etr. *Thanchvil*) is said to be derived from a root *tag* 'know,' 'think.'

5 **quae...sineret**] 'not the woman lightly to allow': the subj. is consecutive.

6 **ea quo innupsisset**] 'the sphere into which she married': cf. Plautus, *Aul.* III. 5. 15 *quo illae nubent divites*. Livy is fond of using pronominal adverbs instead of pronouns in such cases: cf. 47. 3 *istic*, 49. 5 *unde*, and the English use of 'whereby,' 'thereto.'

8 § **5. ingenitae**] 'inherited.'

10 **ab Tarquiniis**] Cf. § 6 *a Curibus*. Livy usually inserts the preposition with names of towns, in expressing 'place whence.'

11 § **6. repentina...virtute**] 'a creation of the moment and of merit': cf. Cic. *Brut.* 69. 242 *ignoti homines et repentini*; *Phil.* II. 27 *modo egens*, *repente dives*.

12 **sit**] The subjunctive is due to *or. obl.*, expressing the view of Tanaquil.

forti ac strenuo] These two epithets are frequently joined to denote a strong character; cf. XXI. 4. 4 *ubi quid fortiter ac strenue agendum esset*, Hor. *Ep.* I. 7. 46 *strenuus et fortis*, *causisque Philippus agendis clarus*.

14 **et Ancum**] 'even Ancus.'

15 **nobilem...imagine**] 'ennobled by the single portrait of Numa': cf. 47. 4. The custom of keeping *imagines* (i.e. portrait-masks, originally

funeral-masks of dead men, prepared at the time of burial) was a most ancient one with the Romans: at first it was a privilege of patrician families, as being the only true *gentes*, then gradually it came to be regarded as an ensign of nobility (*ius imaginum*) for those who had held office. In this sense Livy uses it here, by an anachronism.

16 § **7**. **ut**] (= ὡς, ἅτε) belongs both to *cupido* and *cui*, expressing Tanaquil's view of her husband's case. Cf. n. on *Praef.* 4 *ut quae*; 54. 7 *ut re imperfecta.*

19 § **8**. **carpento**] abl. of place where, after *sedenti*. The *carpentum* was a two-wheeled vehicle, with an arched covering or hood: the word occurs again in 48. 5.

20 **aquila**] Is it possible that the bird and the omen were suggested by the name *Tan-aquil*?

suspensis...alis] 'drooping gently on poised pinions.'

21 **pilleum**] a close-fitting cap of felt, in shape like half an egg (= Gk. πῖλος), and so akin to the *apex*. It is frequently seen in Etruscan monuments, on the heads of men and women.

22 **ministerio**] 'for that office,' dat. of predicate, expressing purpose after a verb of motion: rare except in the case of *auxilio*, *praesidio*, *subsidio*.

23 **apte**] 'neatly,' 'deftly.'

24 § **9**. **accepisse**] 'grasped,' 'understood': so again in 55. 4.

ut vulgo Etrusci] Cf. 55. 6, where seers are summoned from Etruria.

26 **eam...ea...eius**] 'the proper' bird—quarter—god, for sovereignty (*excelsa et alta*). *regio* is a word of augury: cf. n. on 18. 7. The *or. obl.* follows the sense of *sperare iubet*.

27 **circa**] seems to indicate both place and reference.

28 **culmen**] The word is significant, for it denotes 'summit': cf. XLV. 9. 7 *a summo culmine fortunae*.

auspicium fecisse] 'gave a token' as detailed in the next clauses, *levasse...redderet*. The word *auspicium* properly denotes divination from the flight of birds.

31 § **10**. **L. Tarquinium**] Latin equivalent of *Lauchme Tarchnas*. According to one tradition Tanaquil was naturalized in Rome as *Gaia Caecilia*, who came to be regarded as the ideal and patron of married women, and was held in such reverence that a bride was formally asked before her husband's door what was her name, and replied 'Gaia.' Cf. Pliny, *Nat. Hist.* VIII. 48. 4, Festus, s.v. *praedia*.

Priscum] i.e. 'eldest,' 'senior': cf. *Prisci Latini*.

32 **edidere nomen**] 'they gave out his name as.'

p. 47. 2 § **11. comitate...beneficiis**] 'by courteous entertainments and kindly actions': both expressions are supplemented by, and united in, *conciliando*. Cf. 8. 4 *crescebat urbs munitionibus...appetendo*: 14. 7 *minaci genere pugnae adequitando*.

6 § **12. ut**] 'till,' as we should say.

7 **bello**] Not common for *militiae* in this connection: cf. IX. 26. 11 *domi belloque*.

per omnia expertus] passive, 'tried (proved) in every particular.'

8 **liberis**] For the dat. cf. n. on 5. 6 *Numitori*. We say likewise 'guardian to,' 'secretary to' and (in play-bills) 'son to.'

testamento] So we find in the XII Tables, *pater familias uti de pecunia tutelave rei suae legassit ius esto*. It is doubtful whether, under the Kings, a *tutor* could be so appointed by will, because it tended to give a person (like Tarquinius here) outside the *gens* a charge which belonged to the *gens*.

CHAPTER XXXV.

3 § **1. comitia...creando**] dat. of 'work contemplated.' Livy assumes that Ancus was now dead, and that the process of electing a successor (i.e. the *interregnum*, see c. 17) had already reached the stage at which the *populus*, assembled in *comitia curiata*, designated a king, subject to the ratification of the *patres*: cf. 17. 9 and 10, 22. 1, 32. 1.

14 § **2. indictis**] 'advertised.' The phrase occurs again in III. 35. 1 in regard to the election of the *decemviri* for the second year.

15 **petisse**] The same form occurs in II. 9: see note on 7. 7 *mugissent*.

ambitiose] 'by regular canvass' (*ambitio*), of which one item in Republican times was the *oratio in toga candida*, apparently alluded to in this instance.

16 **plebis**] i.e. that part of the *populus* which was not connected with the *patres*. In § 5 we have *populus Romanus*.

17 § **3. cum**] sc. *memoraret*, to be supplied from *haec eum...memorantem* in § 6, where the narrative is resumed.

18 **quisquam**] Livy extends the regular use of *quisquam* with negatives or quasi-negatives (cf. 18. 1, 22. 6 above) to cases like this, where a negative notion is remotely represented, if at all, by *non* preceding. The meaning here seems to be 'at which one could have expressed indignation or surprise' (but one cannot as things are).

posset] reproduces the actual phrase and tense of the *or. recta*.

9 **Romae**] is probably connected with both *peregrinus* (as a locative) and *regnum* (as an objective genitive).

ex peregrino] 'from the position (status) of an alien': cf. Sophocles, *Oed. Tyr.* 454 τυφλὸς ἐκ δεδορκότος.

1 **ultro**] 'unexpectedly': almost a summary of *ignarum urbis* and *non petentem*.

2 § **4**. **sui potens**] 'his own master,' i.e. by his father's death: see 34. 2, 3. For the phrase cf. 38. 2 *in sua potestate*. **fuerit**] reproduces *fui* of *oratio recta*.

6 § **5**. **haud paenitendo**] 'not unsatisfactory,' 'not to be regretted': cf. XXIII. 28. 8 *Hannibali, vix per se ipsi tolerando Italiae hosti*; XXV. 6. 10 *pudendae clades*. The gerundive of impersonal verbs like *paenitet*, *pudet* is scarcely to be regarded as passive, but rather as a reversion to the primary notion of a verbal adjective, in which the sense of voice is indefinite: e.g. *homo amandus* = a man for the loving, i.e. lovable; *magister paenitendus* = a master for the shaming, i.e. shameful.

7 **obsequio et observantia**] 'adulation and attention' or 'compliance and courtesy.'

p. **48**. 2 § **6**. **ingenti consensu**] 'emphatic unanimity.'

3 **iussit**] Cf. 17. 9, 22. 1.

cetera egregium] Cf. 32. 2.

4 **ambitio**] 'studied purpose': an echo of *ambitiose* above.

6 **centum...legit**] See note on c. 30. 2.

minorum...appellati] sc. *patres*: 'designated Fathers (i.e. heads, chiefs) of secondary clans.' It would seem that Tarquin, though accepted as king by the people, was not acceptable to the Patres (who were naturally jealous of a foreigner), and did not receive their confirmation (*auctoritas*). To strengthen himself, then, and increase the body-politic, he chose 100 new senators, who became *ipso facto* Patres: this new creation (*factio haud dubia regis*) doubled, according to Cicero's account, the number of Patres (cf. Cic. *Rep.* II. 20 *duplicavit pristinum patrum numerum*), and thus served to neutralise the opposition of the old nobility.

That certain patrician *gentes* were called *minores* is a historical fact: Livy (like Cicero) attributes their creation to Tarquin. See n. on 36. 2 *addere alias constituit*.

8 **in curiam**] i.e. 'into the House,' the Curia Hostilia.

9 § **7**. **oppidum ibi Apiolas**] 'the Latin township of Apiolae': somewhere near Aricia, perhaps (so Strabo) a Volscian town.

12 **ludos**] probably vowed (*votivi*) during the war to Jupiter, and therefore *magni* (see § 10).

opulentius instructiusque] 'with greater magnificence and elaboration': this also is an instance of Tarquin's *ambitio*. The expression does not imply that *these* games had been celebrated before, but that Tarquin, in introducing them, improved upon the games instituted by previous kings, e.g. the *Consualia* of Romulus (9. 6 above).

13 **§ 8. circo**] It was situated immediately between the Palatine and the Aventine. For the dative see n. on 5. 6 *Numitori*.

14 **designatus**] 'traced,' 'marked out': cf. 10. 5. **loca**] 'sites.'

patribus equitibusque] Livy anticipates the distinction of *ordines* which existed in the later Republic. According to Suetonius (*Claud.* 21) the allotment of special seats in the circus properly belongs to Augustus.

15 **spectacula**] 'places,' 'seats.' **facerent**] i.e. by means of the wooden structures described below.

fori] 'benches,' 'rows' of seats: cf. 56. 2, where the younger Tarquin employs forced labour for making *fori*.

16 **§ 9. spectavere...pedes**] 'their view was obtained by the use of piers supporting seats twelve feet up above the ground-line.' The distributive numeral *duodenos* implies that each block was constructed on the same general plan.

17 **equi**] Horsemanship—chariot-driving and riding—was always a characteristic feature of the *Ludi Romani*.

ex Etruria] Tarquin was able to introduce Etruscan performers in virtue of his connection with that country, as a means of amusing his new subjects—another instance of his *ambitio*.

18 **§ 10. sollemnes, deinde annui**] 'periodical (lit. customary), subsequently annual': perhaps they developed out of a festival celebrated each year when the army returned from its summer manœuvres, whether these had included active service or not.

19 **Romani magnique**] The first epithet insists on the national character, the second on the religious priority of the festival, as dedicated to Jupiter. Although Livy gives the two epithets as interchangeable, it is probable that *magni* should really be applied to any games performed in fulfilment of a vow to Jupiter, *Romani* to these particular games when they became regular (*annui*): but there was a certain similarity in the programme. Eventually the *Ludi Romani* extended over many days (4—19 September), and included an important sacrificial banquet, the *epulum Iovis*.

20 **et**] 'also.' **aedificanda...loca**] 'building-sites': *aedificanda* = 'to be built upon.'

21 **porticus**] 'colonnades.' **tabernae**] Probably the *tabernae veteres*, on the S. side of the Forum: see plan of Rome.

CHAPTER XXXVI.

21 § **1.** **muro quoque lapideo**] This was eventually built by Servius Tullius; cf. 44. 3. For *quoque* see note on 33. 7.

26 **posset**] subjunctive, because of anticipation implied.

27 § **2.** **dubia...caede**] For the accumulation of circumstances see note on 12. 10.

29 **ad comparandum...bellum**] 'for fresh war-preparations.'

31 **centurias**] 'squadrons,' 'corps': see note on 13. 8.

scripserat] = *conscripserat* (the verb used in 13. 8) 'had enrolled.'

32 **addere alias constituit**] It is probable that Livy here restates in another aspect (using the lack of cavalry as a pretext) the increase which Tarquin introduced in the privileged clans: in other words, the doubling of the Patres by the new creation mentioned in 35. 6 above is intimately connected with a doubling of the old *centuriae* of cavalry. So the new nobility were known as *Ramnes Tities Luceres secundi* (as opposed to *primi*), and their cavalry as *equites Ramnenses Titienses Lucerenses posteriores* (see § 7 below). The total of *sex centuriae* (twice 3) thus formed was included in the Servian system (see 43. 9).

It is difficult to see in this case (as in that of the Patres) what has become of the Alban reinforcement mentioned in 30. 3: perhaps in that chapter Livy was following a different authority from that adopted in 13. 8 and here, and did not trouble to reconcile his statements. The gradual increase of the Equites is as obscure as that of the Patres.

p. 49. 1 § **3.** **id quia...fecerat**] 'because that action of Romulus had waited upon augury.' *inaugurato* is the emphatic word of the sentence. It occurs again in 44. 4: for the ablative see n. on 18. 6 *augurato*.

negare (historic infinitive)...**neque...neque**] The first negative is here emphasized by the two alternatives.

2 **Attus Navius**] The first name is perhaps connected with *atta* 'father,' the second probably with *navus* 'knowing': the two together make up the augur-character, which is supposed here to represent the religious opposition of the older Patres to the innovation of Tarquin. The name *Attus* appears again (Livy II. 16) in the Sabine Attus Clausus, Romanized as Appius Claudius.

4 **addixissent**] 'had proved propitious'—a technical word of bird-omens: cf. 55. 3. The tense represents fut. perf. of *oratio recta*.

5 § 4. **eludens**] 'mocking': so in 48. 2.

6 **divine tu**] 'sir prophet.'

8 **futuram**] 'possible.' **atqui**] 'ah, but,' 'well now.'

10 **haec**] i.e. the razor and whetstone. **tuae**] somewhat contemptuous, 'your precious birds.'

12 § 5. **capite velato**] 'with his head covered' (not 'veiled'): augurs are commonly represented in sculpture with a fold of the robe drawn over the head, and with the crook (*lituus*) in the right hand; cf. 18. 7, 8.

in comitio] The rectangular enclosure, at the N.W. end of the Forum, within which was the Curia Hostilia. See the plan of Rome.

13 **cotem**] 'the whetstone.' **sitam fuisse**] This seems to imply that it was no longer there: see n. on 2. 1 *fuerat*.

14 **ad posteros**] Cf. 3. 8.

17 § 6. **belli domique**] 'in matters military or civil': locatives. Cf. Praef. 9 n. *domi militiaeque*.

18 **exercitus vocati**] 'mobilization of armies.'

summa rerum] 'supreme administration': cf. 17. 5.

19 **admisissent**] a technical term of augury = *addixissent*; cf. 55. 3. The subjunctive is consecutive.

21 § 7. **numero**] 'strength.'

23 **posteriores**] 'secondary': see n. on § 2 above.

sub isdem nominibus] Servius (see 43. 9) accepted in his turn the same classification.

CHAPTER XXXVII.

29 § 1. **missis qui...conicerent**] This clause explains *dolus*. The participle, used absolutely, has here no substantive in agreement: cf. XXXI. 45. 3 *missis, qui tentarent oppidanorum animos*. The usage, not uncommon in Livy, finds a parallel in such examples of the Greek genitive absolute as Thucydides VII. 48. 2 *θαλασσοκρατούντων*.

vim] 'quantity,' as in 51. 2 below; cf. Caesar, *B. C.* II. 26 *vis magna pulveris*.

31 **ventoque...incendunt**] The sentence is awkwardly arranged. The wind fanned the smouldering logs into flame: as most of them were aboard rafts, they were driven by the stream against the piles of the bridge and set light to it. The historic tense in *cum haererent* corresponds with the historic sense of *incendunt*.

p. 50. 1 § **2. in pugna**] 'during the action,' in opposition to *effusis*, 'in their disorder.'

4 **arma**] (=*scuta*) 'shields,' which, being made of wood or wicker-work, would float down the Tiber, and be recognized (*cognita*) by their shape or badges as they passed the city.

6 § **3. ab cornibus**] The preposition here expresses the point of formation, and base of operation: cf. 12. 1 *n. ab Sabinis*, 33. 7 *a planioribus locis*; XLIV. 42. 4 *phalanx a fronte, a lateribus, ab tergo caesa est.*

9 **cedentibus**] i.e. the Roman infantry.

11 § **4. tenuere**] 'gained them.'

14 § **5. spoliis**] (as distinct from *praeda*) means the arms, clothing, and personal effects taken from the enemy.

votum Vulcano] In historical times the dedication of spoils to Vulcan was not infrequent: and it was especially appropriate where, as here and in the destruction of Hasdrubal's camp by Scipio (XXX. 6. 9), fire had played an important part in the conflict.

17 § **6. gesturos**] sc. *se*.

18 **tumultuario milite**] 'emergency troops': in colloquial English 'a scratch army.'

19 **perditis iam prope rebus**] 'as their cause was well-nigh ruined.'

CHAPTER XXXVIII.

20 § **1. Collatia**] about 13 miles E. of Rome, and 3 or 4 N.W. of Gabii.

citra] 'on the near side' from the Roman point of view, i.e. west.

21 **Egerius**] Cf. 34. 3 n.

23 **deditionis**] The formula of *deditio* here given should be compared with that used by the Campanians in VII. 31. 4 *populum Campanum urbemque Capuam agros delubra deum divina humanaque omnia in vestram, patres conscripti, populique Romani dicionem dedimus.* Postumius, after the disaster of the Caudine Forks, refers to the same formula (IX. 9. 5).

24 § **2. rex**] Notice that the king received the *deditio* himself, as it probably took place at Rome.

legati oratoresque] 'ambassadors and spokesmen': the latter word (used similarly in 15. 5. above) seems to be equivalent to *fetiales.*

27 **in sua potestate**] 'a free agent'—competent to act on its own behalf: cf. 35. 4 *sui potens.*

28 **agros**] See note on 15. 5 above.

30 **at**] 'then,' introduces the answer, which is as it were an apodosis to a protasis implied in the question '*deditisne?*'

31 § **3. triumphans**] Although this is Livy's first actual mention of a triumph, he has already (10. 5) described something similar in Romulus' reign, and Dionysius (II. 34) assigns the first triumph to the earlier time.

32 § **4. Priscis Latinis**] See n. on 3. 7.

p. 51. 1 **ad universae rei dimicationem**] 'to an absolutely decisive battle.'

3 **nomen Latinum**] See note on 10. 3 *nomen Caeninum.*

Corniculum...Nomentum] all situated N. of the Anio, and E. of the Tiber, from five to fifteen miles N.E. of Rome.

5 **de**] used, as often, with a whole from which something is taken.

8 § **5. animo**] 'zeal.'

9 **mole**] 'exertion,' 'effort': cf. XXV. 11. 17 *plaustris transveham naves haud magna mole.*

14 § **6. quia ex planis...aquas**] sc. *cives*: the imperfect expresses a recurrent difficulty, 'could not carry off.'

15 **cloacis...ductis**] 'by sewers run on a down grade (i.e. with a fall) into the river.' This sense of *fastigium*, 'slope,' naturally developed from its original meaning of 'gable,' is not uncommon in Caesar, e.g. *B. C.* I. 45. 5 *ab oppido declivis locus tenui fastigio vergebat*; II. 24. 3 *iugum paulo leniore fastigio.* The attribution of these *cloacae* to Tarquinius Priscus is parallel to, perhaps a duplication of, the attribution of the *cloaca maxima* (c. 56) to Tarquinius Superbus.

16 § **7. aream ad aedem**] 'site for the temple.' This use of *ad* is not uncommon in Livy, but otherwise chiefly poetical: cf. XXXIV. 6. 13 *servos ad remum*, XXII. 61. 2 *servos ad militiam emendos*; Virg. *Aen.* X. 253 *ad frena leones.*

quam voverat] This vow is referred to in 55. 1 below, when Tarquinius Superbus took the work in hand.

17 **futuram olim**] 'in the distant future': cf. 7. 10 *opulentissima olim.*

18 **occupat fundamentis**] 'laid foundations to secure': *occupare* has the double sense of anticipation and appropriation.

CHAPTER XXXIX.

(For Servius Tullius see Introduction, § 7.)

19 § **1. eventu**] 'in its sequel,' 'fulfilment.'

20 **puero**] For this dative of close relationship and its position see n. on 5. 6 *Numitori.*

Servio Tullio] For the dat. see n. on 1. 3 *Troiano*. The surname *Tullius* associates Servius, like Numa, Tullus, and Ancus, with a Roman gens.

21 **caput arsisse**] This legend may imply that the mother of Servius Tullius was a Vestal, and his father the fire-god. Plutarch (*Romulus*, 2) repeats a similar tale about the birth of Romulus. Cf. Frazer, *Early History of the Kingship*, p. 219.

23 § **2**. **ad...miraculum**] 'at this stupendous marvel': for *ad* cf. 7. 7 *ad desiderium*.

24 **reges**] 'their Majesties.' The construction continues in *or. obl.* after *ferunt*.

familiarium] 'attendants'—a natural, but not frequent, use of the word: cf. Seneca, *Ep.* 47 *maiores nostri servos* (*quod etiam in mimis adhuc durat*) *familiares appellaverunt*.

26 **vetuisse**] sc. *eam*, which some editors read here instead of *iam*.

27 **experrectus esset**] The tense represents future perf. of *or. recta*.

abisse] For the contracted form cf. 7. 7 *mugissent*, 11. 9 *petisse*, 27. 6 *subisse*.

29 § **3**. **cultu**] 'style,' 'fashion.'

30 **lumen...futurum**] 'a light foreordained for our dark days to be.' Tanaquil's prophecy is twofold—distinction for Servius, distress for the Tarquins.

31 **regiae**] 'royal house,' 'court,' in the personal sense, not the local (as in § 1): so in 46. 3.

32 **materiam...decoris**] 'the cause (means) of great distinction for our state and our house.'

p. 52. 1 § **4**. **liberum loco**] 'like a child': *liberum* is gen. pl. (Livy affects the shorter form in proper names and words of common use), as in 9. 14 above; cf. the phrase *in parentis loco*.

2 **coeptum haberi**] *or. obl.* after a verb of narration understood. The past tense of *coepi*, if the infinitive governed be in the passive, may be passive also in form: Cicero always so uses it, and Livy inclines to the construction in his earlier books (cf. 57. 3 below), but in some cases adopts the active form; whether he does so to indicate a slight difference of meaning, or from a neglect of the stricter idiom, is not clear.

quibus...excitantur] 'whereby persons are encouraged to adopt the demeanour of lofty estate.'

4 **cordi esset**] a predicative dative, 'was pleasing': cf. 47. 9 *fraudi. esset*, if read, must express the feeling of those who watched the development of Servius: in this case *evenit* is the perfect tense. Madvig

reads *est*, in which case the statement becomes a general proposition, and *evenit* is present.

7 § 5. **quacumque de causa**] with *habitus*, 'on whatever grounds conferred.' For the independent use of the pronoun, cf. 3. 3 *is Ascanius, ubicumque et quacumque matre genitus.*

10 **sententiae sum**] See n. on 8. 3.

13 **prohibitam...servitio**] 'preserved from slavery.'

15 **domo**] not *domi*, because a notion of origin is implied.

17 § 6. **in caritate**] The preposition expresses the circumstances; cf. Cic. *pro Roscio* 28 *ei servi apud Chrysogonum sunt in honore et pretio.*

18 **venerit**] i.e. *venit* of direct statement, represents the view held at the time. **crederetur**] a historic tense, as directly dependent on the historic *fecisse*. See note on 1. 8 *audierit.*

CHAPTER XL.

23 § 2. **tum**] This is repeated and the construction modified, after the parenthetic clauses *etsi...stirpis. etsi...tum* are equivalent to *μέν...δέ.*

24 **pro indignissimo habuerant**] 'had considered it a downright indignity.'

26 **non modo**] for *non modo non*, as often.

ne Italicae quidem stirpis] because he was of Corinthian extraction; see 34. 2 above.

27 **impensius...crescere** (hist. inf.) **si**] 'felt their indignation the more fiercely increased by the prospect.' For *si* cf. the Greek use of *εἰ* after words of surprise or emotion: other instances occur in 47. 6, 53. 10. *rediret...caderet* represent *redeat, cadat* of direct narrative, i.e. a future possibility.

29 § 3. **servitia**] 'a slave': the plural is put for the singular, a type for a person.

post centesimum...quam] *postquam* is here divided, *post centesimum annum* ('a hundred years after') forming a phrase similar to those used in expressing dates (e.g. *ante diem tertium Kalendas Ianuarias*), while *quam* marks the extent of the interval. Cf. Cic. *pro Milone* 16 *post diem tertium gesta res est, quam dixerat*; Sallust, *Iug.* 102 *post diem quintum, quam iterum barbari male pugnaverant, legati a Boccho veniunt.*

31 **tenuerit...fuerit...possideat**] The tenses represent the *tenuit, fuit, possidet*, of direct narration, the mood gives the view of the sons of Ancus. See note on 1. 8 *audierit.*

32 **serva natus**] For them there was no doubt of the servility of Servius.

p. 53. 4 **§ 4. sed et...privatus**] They had two incentives to an attack on the person of Tarquin in preference to Servius; their indignation at the insult, and the moral certainty that the king, if he survived, would prove more severe than a subject in avenging the murder.

8 **tum**] i.e. in the other event = *Servio occiso.*

delegisset] sc. the king. The tense indicates that this clause, in point of time, precedes the next (*facturus videbatur*): the *or. recta* would have had *delegerit* (fut. perf.) and *faciet.*

11 **§ 5. quibus...ferramentis**] 'with the rustic implements of their daily use.' Dionysius (III. 73) says δρεπάνοις ὑλουργοῖς. The construction is a case of attraction of the Greek pattern, *quibus* standing for *iis, quibus* (dat. or abl.). Cf. 29. 4 *raptim quibus quisque poterat elatis*; Lucceius in Cicero, *Fam.* V. 14. 1 *cum aliquid agas eorum, quorum consuesti, gaudeo.*

13 **apparitores**] See n. on 8. 3.

16 **§ 6. certatim...obstrepere** (hist. inf.)] 'strove to shout each other down.'

19 **dum...averteret**] 'waiting until the king was concentrating his whole attention upon him.' For *totus* cf. Cic. *pro Cluentio*, 26. 72 *qui esset totus ex fraude et mendacio factus.* Hor. *Sat.* I. 9. 2 *nescio quid meditans nugarum, et totus in illis.* The subj. *averteret* is due to the intention implied on the part of the conspirators.

20 **§ 7. securim**] 'hatchet': the word is commonly used to denote a domestic implement, and so suits *agrestibus ferramentis* above.

CHAPTER XLI.

25 **§ 1. mirantium**] The genitive plural expands the sense of *populi*: 'while men wondered.' For the substantival use of the participle see n. on 25. 9 *faventium.*

quid rei esset] The genitive expresses an indefinite whole—here, all the vague possibilities: cf. 48. 1 and Plautus' phrase *quid negotist?*

26 **arbitros**] See n. on 21. 3.

27 **quae...opus sunt**] 'all things needful for treating a wound.' *curando vulneri* is a dat. of 'work contemplated.' For this use of *opus*, with a phrase expressing purpose, cf. XXXVII. 18. 10 *parari, quae ad transitum Hellesponti opus essent*; Cicero *ad Atticum* V. 8. 2 *si quid opus erit in sumptum.*

28 **sedulo**] 'diligently,' almost 'designedly.'

si...molitur] 'devised other expedients by way of safeguard, in case her hope should fail.' *praesidia* really contains an apodosis to the protasis *si destituat spes*, wherein the tense of *destituat* represents the actual condition in the mind of Tanaquil: cf. 23. 6 *tamen, si vana adferantur, in aciem educit.* Similarly *sinat* below reproduces the actual tense of her prayer (*sinas*). On the other hand *subesset* and *ostendisset* both belong to the narrative, not to the personal feeling of the chief character, and both accordingly take the historic form, to suit the sense of the historic presents in these sentences. See n. on 1. 8 *audierit.*

p. 54. 2 § **2. inimicis ludibrio esse]** The second dative is predicative, the first expresses the persons concerned.

4 § **3. eorum]** i.e. the sons of Ancus.

5 **hoc]** She touches the head of Servius in her appeal.

9 **tua]** emphatic, with *consilia*: *mea* is emphatic also. The whole passage brings out the virility of Tanaquil's character—*γυναικὸς ἀνδρόβουλον ἐλπίζον κέαρ.*

at] 'still,' 'then': frequently so used to emphasize, after a qualifying clause, a possible or advisable line of action: cf. 28. 9.

12 § **4. in novam viam versus]** 'looking over the New Street,' which ran round the N.W. edge of the Palatine. See the plan of Rome.

13 **ad Iovis Statoris]** 'near the temple of Jupiter the Stayer,' situated at the bottom of the N. slope of the Palatine. Tradition (see c. 12. 6) attributed its origin to a vow of Romulus; history (see X. 37. 16) assigned the building to the year 294 B.C.

14 § **5. sopitum]** 'stunned': so in XLII. 16. 2 *sopitum vulnere.*

18 **dicto audientem]** 'obedient': the two words form one notion, *dicto* retaining no special significance.

20 § **6. trabea]** 'state robe.' According to Servius (on *Aeneid* VII. 612) there were three varieties thereof: (1) all purple, for religious uses; (2) purple and white, for kings; (3) purple and scarlet, for augurs.

23 **fungendae vicis]** *fungor* (cf. *fruor, utor*) in old Latin took a direct object; and in clauses like the present one the gerundive (not the gerund) construction continued to be the regular idiom.

25 **comploratione]** The word implies a loud lamentation of many persons; its use in 26. 3 is exceptional.

praesidio] an echo of the *praesidia* mentioned in § 1.

26 **iniussu populi]** 'without the nomination of the people': cf. 17. 9.

voluntate patrum] 'with the consent of the Patres': the phrase does not imply formal confirmation (*auctoritas*), but merely absence of opposition.

27 § 7. **iam tum**] i.e. before this, at the time of the murder (see § 1).

29 **Suessam Pometiam**] in the country of the Volsci, according to 53. 2 below. Its position is not known: it is thought by some authorities to have been at the N. end of the Pomptine marsh.

exsulatum] Such retirement into exile (i.e. into the territory of a state having certain relations with Rome), for the purpose of avoiding possible condemnation and punishment, came to be regarded as a right (*iūs exsulandi*) in the republican period. As Cicero says (*pro Caecina* 34) *exsilium enim non supplicium est, sed perfugium portusque supplicii: ...confugiunt quasi ad aram, in exsilium.* So in c. 54. 9 some of Tarquin's prospective victims seek safety in exile. The infliction of exile (with loss of *civitas* and sometimes of *bona*) as a penalty belongs to the latter days of the Republic.

CHAPTER XLII.

p. 55. 1 § 1. **filias**] i.e. the two Tulliae. The elder is generally assigned to Lucius, the younger to Arruns: but Livy's account (see 46. 9) is not clear on this point.

iuvenibus regiis] They may have been sons or grandsons of Tarquin: if the former (as Livy in 46. 4, 48. 2 is inclined to consider them), they married their nieces on this occasion, an alliance held in historic times to be illegal.

3 § 2. **fati necessitatem**] 'the inevitable course of destiny': this idea of a jealous Fate resembles the Nemesis which occasionally appears in the narrative of Herodotus.

qui in] The relative clause gives the circumstances ('inasmuch as'), from the writer's point of view. Most texts, however, read *quin* here. *quin* regularly follows verbs of prohibition and prevention, when they are in the negative, and is here attached (with the meaning of *ut non*) to a phrase of the same character: so in V. 45. 7 *vix temperavere animis, quin extemplo impetum facerent*; and in Horace, *Sat.* II. 3. 42 *nil verbi, pereas quin fortiter, addam.*

4 **invidia regni**] 'ill-feeling against his kingship.' *regni* is objective genitive: *invidia*, if *quin* be read, is either nominative, or ablative of cause.

infida...infesta] 'general insincerity and animosity': or perhaps *infestus* has its other meaning here (cf. c. 47. 1) and should be rendered by 'insecurity.'

6 **ad...status]** explains *peropportune*, giving at once the reference and the object: 'for the tranquil maintenance of the existing order.'

8 **sumptum]** The word implies that Servius deliberately began it.

9 § **3. haud dubius rex...periclitaretur]** 'with his kingship indisputable, no matter whether he put the feelings of Patres or populace to the test': a commentary on *iniussu populi voluntate patrum* in 41. 6.

12 § **4. divini iuris]** 'religious law,' i.e. the code of regulations ('canon law,' one might almost say) concerning priestly offices and ritual observances: see chapters 20 and 21.

fuisset] The subjunctive expresses the view of Servius.

14 **ordinum]** close coupled with *discriminis*: 'distinctive classification'—one is almost tempted to translate 'class-distinction.'

15 **aliquid interlucet]** 'a clear line is drawn': the whole clause is a general statement on the part of the historian, not part of Servius' intention.

fama ferrent] 'might glorify.'

§ **5. censum]** 'registration,' of persons and property.

17 **non viritim...pecuniarum]** 'not personally, as aforetime, but according to financial estate.' In other words, the property of the citizen was to determine his place in the legion as well as the value of his vote in the *comitia*. Hitherto the citizens (i.e. Patricians, *Quirites*) had discharged all duties of war and peace, and the non-citizens had doubtless benefited by immunity.

19 **classes centuriasque]** Both words have a military significance to begin with. *classis* (Dionysius renders by σύνταξις, 'contingent') means the force 'called out' as a whole: *centuria* (λόχος) a 'company' of the same.

ordinem] The *arrangement* of the classes and centuries was the most important feature, as well from a military as from a political point of view.

20 **discripsit]** See n. on 19. 6.

CHAPTER XLIII.

There can be no doubt that the classification which is described in this chapter (and by Dionysius, IV. 16—21, and Cicero, *de Re Publica*, II. 22. 39—a fragment) was originally intended for military purposes. The Roman king found it necessary, for the defence of the city and for campaigns in the field against jealous neighbours, to raise a larger and a better-equipped army; and therefore to increase the recruiting area by admitting others besides the patrician burgesses to service.

Military equipment, if the panoply of the Greek or Graeco-Etruscan man-at-arms was to be encountered in the field, involved a considerable outlay, which none but wealthy citizens could afford: and it was logical therefore to base the new qualification and liability for service upon a property-valuation.

The subjoined plan indicates the distribution and rating of units, as attributed to Servius Tullius.

From the military point of view, the centuries were 'establishments' which contributed each its quota to make up the total required at each levy: and the four districts contributed, from the numbers in each century and class, a quarter of the levy. The total force available was four legions, two of *seniores* and two of *juniores*: and each legion was drawn up in a phalanx of Dorian pattern, a close-order formation of six ranks, 500 in each, with 1200 light-armed troops on the flanks or in rear, and 300 cavalry. The first three classes composed the phalanx, but in what proportions is disputed: the fourth class, according to the equipment assigned to it by Dionysius, seems to have been used either as a supernumerary rank if required, or as skirmishers (*rorarii*): the fifth class fought only with missiles. The association of the centuries of *fabri* with the first or second class is obviously due to the frequent need of such artificers for the repair of arms and armour: and the quota of *fabri* required in each levy would depend immediately on the proportion of *juniores* called out for active service in the first two classes. The association of the trumpeters (by Dionysius) with the fourth class seems to suggest that they also had definite duties to perform with the phalanx, the movements of which might well depend upon regular trumpet-calls.

The scales of property-qualifications given by Livy and Dionysius involve difficulties which have long exercised the ingenuity of scholars, but have never been—perhaps cannot be—completely solved. It is clear that the various ratings—*centum milia aeris*, and the rest—are based on a more definite system of monetary values than is believed to have been in existence in Rome under the kings.

It is generally agreed that pieces of copper or bronze (*aes*) were in use from 1000 B.C. as the lowest units of reckoning in a system of which the ox was the highest unit, and the sheep the intermediate unit: these pieces were called *asses*, and were reckoned by bulk (*aes rude*), not even by weight, in the first stage. It may be admitted, on the authority of Timaeus, Pliny (*H. N.* XXXIII. 3. 13) and Festus (*s.v. infra censum* p. 113 Müller), that in the reign of Servius Tullius, i.e. towards

Class	Centuries: Livy	Centuries: Dionysius	Rating: Livy	Rating: Dionysius	Arms	Equipment
Equites	18	18	6 'patrician' 12 *ex primoribus civitatis*	ἐκ τῶν ἐχόντων τὸ μέγιστον τίμημα καὶ κατὰ γένος ἐπιφανῶν	—	—
Pedites: I	80* [Cic. 70] 2 (*fabri*) [Cic. 1]	80	100,000 *asses* [Pliny 120,000]	100 *minae* [10,000 *drachmae*]	*hasta*, *gladius*	*galea*, *clipeum*, *ocreae*, *lorica*
II	20	20 2 (χειροτέχναι)	75,000 *asses*	75 *minae* [7500 *dr.*]	*hasta*, *gladius*	*galea*, *scutum*, *ocreae*
III	20	20	50,000 *asses*	50 *minae* [5000 *dr.*]	*hasta*, *gladius*	*galea*, *scutum*
IV	20	20 2 (musicians)	25,000 *asses*	25 *minae* [2500 *dr.*]	*hasta*, *verutum* (Livy) ξίφη καὶ δόρατα (Dion.)	none (Livy) θυρεοί (Dion.)
V	30 ? 3 {*accensi*, *cornicines*, *tubicines*}	30	11,000 *asses*	12½ *minae* [1250 *dr.*]	*fundae*, *lapides* (Livy) σαυνία (=*veruta*) καὶ σφένδοναι (Dion.)	none
—	1 (*immunis militia*)	VI Class 1 (ἄποροι)	*hoc minor census*	less than 12½ minae	—	—
	? 194	193				

* i.e. half *seniores*, and half *iuniores*, in all the classes.

the end of the regal period, these pieces were stamped (*aes signatum*) with figures of animals (*nota pecudum*, *pecore notatum*), and hence known as *pecunia*. The use of *aes signatum* seems to have given place to a definite currency of bronze weights (*aes grave*), with the *as* of 12 ounces as unit, in the fifth century, between 452 and 430 B.C., and this innovation is by some authorities attributed to the Decemvirs. The coinage of *asses librales* (i.e. of weight equal to their value) was introduced considerably later, perhaps not till 338 B.C.

Now we know by a *Lex Tarpeia* of 451 B.C. that an ox was then reckoned as equivalent to 100 *asses*: and if we apply this standard by way of experiment to the Servian classification as recorded by Livy, we get 1000 cows (= 100,000 *asses*) as the minimum of property required for the first class—or 1200 cows, if Pliny's figure of 120,000 *asses* is correct. This is surely far too high a standard of wealth for the regal period: and most scholars are accordingly of opinion that the ratings given by Livy cannot refer to *asses librales*, but must represent some depreciation.

It is recorded that in the course of the First Punic War (264—241 B.C.) the coined *as* which had already been depreciated in weight from 12 (or, as most specimens show, 10) to 4 ounces, was reduced to 2 ounces, or ⅙ (*sextans*) of a pound, and in the Second Punic War to one *uncia*. That is to say, the original or libral *as* was equivalent to 5 or 6 *asses sextantarii*, and to 10 or 12 *asses unciarii*. There had been also a certain reduction in the weight and value of the silver *denarius*, or 10-*as* piece, until by 241 B.C. or thereabout it was practically equivalent to the Attic *drachma*.

Dionysius assigns 100 *minae*, or 10,000 *drachmae*, to the first Servian class, and this (as 10,000 *drachmae* = 10,000 *denarii*) is equivalent to 100,000 *asses* of 241 B.C. If then Livy is expressing the original qualifications in terms of the currency of 241 B.C., we ought to divide his totals by 6 (or 5). This gives us roughly 16,600—12,500—8,300—4,150 (or, dividing by 5, 20,000—15,000—10,000—5,000) for the first four classes; or, in terms of oxen, 160, 120, 80, 40 (or, 200, 150, 100, 50). These figures do not appear unreasonable for the regal period.

On the other hand, 100,000 *asses sextantarii* is held to be too low a figure for the first class in the *comitia centuriata* as reformed *about* 241 B.C. 400,000 *sestertii* (i.e. 1,000,000 *asses*) became after this time the standard of qualification for the *equites*, and therefore presumably of the first class. Now 100,000 *asses librales* would yield just about 1,000,000 *asses unciarii*, and therefore we may be justified in considering that Livy's totals, reckoned as *asses librales*, supply a clue to the reformed ratings.

Mommsen considers that land was the basis of the Servian assessment —the hide for the first class, and proportional quantities for the others. But *res mancipi* (real property) on which the assessment was made, included not only land in fee simple, but oxen, at any rate those broken to the yoke. So Cicero (*de Rep.* II. 9. 16) says, in regard to the age of Romulus, *tum erat res in pecore et locorum possessionibus, ex quo pecuniosi et locupletes vocabantur.* It is then quite possible that the Servian rating of all *res mancipi* was expressed first in terms of oxen: rating by cattle, not land, was actually practised in Sicily (cf. Ridgeway, *Origin of Currency and Weight Standards*, p. 393). The reckoning by *aes signatum*, if we ascribe the introduction thereof to Servius, would provide a subsidiary means of valuation, suitable to smaller properties and to the cases of *incensi.*

In the centuries between the reign of Servius Tullius and the reform of the *comitia centuriata*, the value of real property in and near Rome must surely have increased: and it is reasonable to suppose that the introduction of changes in currency necessitated revisions of the *census*-ratings. For instance, the year 338 B.C., in which according to some authorities *asses* were first coined at Rome, was the beginning of the Roman supremacy, commercial as well as political, over the Latins. The value of Roman *res mancipi*, we may well believe, was greatly enhanced at this time: and the *census*-ratings may have risen then to a standard which, though not equal to that adopted after the great Punic Wars, was altogether different from that of the Servian era.

20 § **1. centum milium aeris**] *assium* is to be understood, and the whole phrase is dependent on *censum*, 'rating.'

22 **centurias**] i.e. 'hundreds' or units of organization, varying necessarily according to the number of citizens contained in each *classis*: there would obviously be more poor citizens than rich, and conversely fewer members of a *centuria* in the higher *classes* of the Servian constitution than in the lower. Each *centuria* or unit would be required to furnish for the military levy (*dilectus*) a certain quota, a *centuria* for service.

23 **seniorum ac iuniorum**] The *seniores* were men between 45 and 60 years of age: the *iuniores* between 17 and 45 (inclusive).

§ **2. classis**] Originally this term denoted an army, i.e. a body of men called (cf. *calare*) to the colours. The five *classes* thus consisted of *classici*, and the remainder of the body-politic was *infra classem*: but certain authorities (e.g. Aulus Gellius, VI. 13) state, perhaps owing to a confusion between different reckonings of the *as*, that the terms *classis*, *classici* belonged properly to the first *classis* alone, and that *infra classem* included all the rest.

26 **arma**] 'armour,' for defence (*tegumenta*), as opposed to *tela in hostem*, for offence.

imperata] 'required,' 'requisitioned' (so in XL. 34. 9 *arma imperata a populo Romano*). It was part of the *munus* of each citizen to provide himself with the arms and equipment of the *classis* to which he belonged.

clipeum] (the neuter form is found more often in Livy than the masculine) a round shield, like the Greek *ἀσπίς*. Its use by the first *classis* and by the *equites* alone suggests that it belongs to the distinctive armour of a dominant part of the state. Cf. Ridgeway, *Early Age of Greece*, I. p. 469.

27 **omnia ex aere**] i.e. the regular bronze armour of a hoplite, which would naturally be suggested to the Roman king by intercourse with Greek colonies, or rather with the Etruscans who had copied their armament. Cf. Ridgeway, *ib.* p. 470.

28 **hasta**] This pike could probably (like that of a Greek hoplite) be used either for throwing or for thrusting. It was longer and more slender than the *pilum* of the legionary in later times.

29 § **3**. **fabrum**] The shorter form of the gen. pl. occurs chiefly, as would be expected, in words of common use, e.g. *liberum*, *socium*.

Of the two centuries of *fabri* ('artificers,' 'engineers') here mentioned together (as also by Dionysius) one consisted of *tignarii*, the other of *aerarii* or *ferrarii*. In addition to the task which Livy assigns them they would have to repair armour (hence their association with the first and second *classes*) and to make bridges. They had no definite place in the order of battle, and thus there is some difference of opinion as to which *classis* they voted with in the *comitia*.

stipendia facerent] 'were to do their service': the subjunctive expresses the intention of the organization.

30 **machinas**] 'engines,' e.g. battering-rams, and other siege-appliances: but there is danger of anachronism here, for few, if any, of such engines became familiar in Greek and Roman warfare until a later date.

31 § **4**. **intra centum usque ad**...**censum**] So Dionysius (IV. 16) says *οἷς ἦν ἐντὸς μὲν μυρίων δραχμῶν, οὐ μεῖον δὲ πέντε καὶ ἑβδομήκοντα μνῶν τὸ τίμημα*. Both writers wish to show that the rating of the second class did not include 100,000 *asses*.

p. 56. 2 **scutum**] This shield (called *θυρεός* in Greek, from its resemblance to a door) was made of wood, covered with leather: in shape it was oblong, rectangular, and bent so as to envelop the body of the warrior. It is possible that in the *scutum*, which in some respects resembled the *ancile* (see note on c. 20. 4 above), we have a survival of an old Pelasgian or Aboriginal pattern, as opposed to the round *clipeus* of the Umbro-Latins.

praeter loricam] The use of the *scutum* made a breastplate unnecessary.

3 § 5. **tertiae classis...voluit**] If the reading is right, the sense is 'he wished those to be of the third class who ranged [from a rating of less than 75,000 *asses*] to a rating of 50,000': as Dionysius has it, *ὅσοι τίμησιν εἶχον ἐλάττονα μὲν τῶν ἑπτακισχιλίων καὶ πεντακοσίων δραχμῶν, οὐ μείονα δὲ μνῶν πεντήκοντα*, it is inclusive, 'to and including 50,000': the whole prepositional phrase is regarded (as a Greek prepositional phrase with the article might be) as the object of the verb.

It is not necessary to bracket *in*, as some commentators have done. The sense becomes simpler ('he wished the rating of the third class to be a 50,000 rating'), but the stage in the rating—the *terminus ad quem* of the third class—is not so well marked.

4 **et haec**] i.e. 'this class also was (consisted of) the same number of centuries.' *et hae* is read by some editors, for the sake of simplicity.

discrimine aetatium] 'distinction of ages,' between *seniores* and *iuniores*.

7 § 6. **mutata**] means, not an actual change on the part of this class from one armament to another, but a change in Livy's description—not 'were changed' but 'represented a change.'

nihil praeter hastam et verutum] i.e. they were *rorarii*, skirmishers. The *verutum* was a dart, three or four feet long, used by light infantry: with the *hasta* this fourth class could join, if need were, in the heavier fighting, and Dionysius, who gives its armament as *θυρεοὺς καὶ ξίφη καὶ δόρατα*, and its place as the last rank, evidently supposes that this was the case.

8 § 7. **aucta**] not 'were increased,' but 'represented an increase' (on the last three classes): cf. *mutata* above.

10 **in his accensi...in tres centurias distributi**] This is the reading of the MSS., and as it stands it means that the *accensi*, *cornicines* and *tubicines* formed three centuries, attached to, and counted in with, the fifth class. This gives a total of 193 centuries, which is the same as that given by Dionysius. But if we regard the *una centuria* mentioned

in § 8 as additional to the three mentioned here, Livy's total is 194, an even, and therefore unlikely, number.

Various solutions of the difficulty have been suggested. It should be remembered first that *accensi* may be considered (*a*) as a substantive, = 'supernumeraries,' intended to replace casualties; (*b*) as a participle, = 'rated with,' 'reckoned among.'

(1) It is thought that the *una centuria* of § 8 refers again to the *accensi*, and thus identifies these with the *proletarii*, as the body of citizens without rating came to be called, in distinction from the name *assidui*, applied to the *equites* and the five classes;

(2) *accensi* may be taken as a participle, and *duas* read for *tres* (*II* for *III*);

(3) *accensi* may be taken as a substantive, and *duas* read for *tres*; i.e. *cornicines tubicinesque* may have formed one century (they formed one *collegium* in later days);

(4) *accensis...duas* may be read; i.e. the term *accensi* is applied to the fifth class, not to the *proletarii* (the *una centuria* of § 8).

For the term *tubicines* in this connection Cicero has the older word *liticines* (i.e. clarion-players). The *tuba* was straight, the *lituus* curved at the bell-end, the *cornu* semicircular.

11 § 8. **undecim milibus**] 'at 11,000': ablative as of price. Dionysius says *οἷς ἐντὸς εἴκοσι καὶ πέντε μνῶν ἄχρι δώδεκα καὶ ἡμίσους μνῶν ὁ βίος ἦν*, i.e. from less than 25,000 *asses* to 12,500.

12 **hoc minor census**] 'the rating below this' (*hoc*), i.e. the *proletarii* (*ἄποροι* in Dionysius).

multitudinem] 'population': so in c. 29. 1, 33. 1.

13 **inde**]=*ex ea.*

immunis militia] 'exempt from military duty': Dionysius says more explicitly *στρατείας τ' ἀπέλυσε καὶ πάσης εἰσφορᾶς ἐποίησεν ἀτελεῖς*. *immunis* has here its literal meaning 'that performs no duty' or 'pays no tax' (*ἀτελής, ἀνείσφορος*), and so 'exempt.' The ablative expresses separation; Livy's use of the case for this purpose, without a preposition, is considerably freer than that of Cicero and Caesar.

14 **ornato**] 'equipped,' 'accoutred,' i.e. in the scheme of Servius now described, not as yet in actual fact.

15 **ex primoribus...centurias**] i.e. he enrolled (*scripsit* for *conscripsit*) 12 centuries of knights from among the leading citizens of first-class rating (Dionysius says *ἐκ τῶν ἐχόντων τὸ μέγιστον τίμημα καὶ κατὰ γένος ἐπιφανῶν*). It would seem that this part of the cavalry was recruited in conformity to the general scheme of property-qualification, while the

remainder represented a re-organization (*sex...centurias...fecit*) of an existing establishment.

16 § 9. **alias**] 'separate.'

sex...centurias] These consisted of Patricians (Cicero, *Or.* 156, calls them *centuriae procum patricium*), and came to be known as the *sex centuriae* (cf. 36. 8), or the *sex suffragia*, perhaps because their votes were taken first separately from those of the other 12 centuries, in the earliest meetings of the *comitia* for political purposes.

The total establishment of 1800 knights may have belonged to the pre-Servian epoch. (See c. 36. 7 above.) Cicero (*de Rep.* II. 20. 36) says of L. Tarquinius, *equitatum ad hunc morem constituit qui usque adhuc est retentus, nec potuit Titiensium et Ramnensium et Lucerum mutare cum cuperet nomina...sed tamen prioribus equitum partibus secundis additis MDCCC fecit equites numerumque duplicavit.* But here as in c. 36. 7 *M ac CC* may be the right reading. In any case the effect of the Servian organization was to rearrange the cavalry into 18 centuries, and to reserve six, with the old names doubled, to the patricians. It seems scarcely possible, in view of the previous increases mentioned by Livy, that Servius Tullius doubled the establishment to a total of 3600 *equites*.

tribus ab Romulo institutis] See c. 13. 8.

17 **quibus inauguratae erant**] 'which they had received inaugurally' (under augural sanction), and so unalterably: cf. 36. 3 *id...inaugurato Romulus fecerat.*

18 **• dena milia aeris ex publico data**] i.e. *aes equestre.* If the valuation of the *as* given above (§ 1) be correct, we are to suppose that each *eques* received a sum equivalent to 2000 libral *asses* (= 20 oxen) from the state-chest (*publicum*) for the purchase of a horse—or of two horses, for himself and his squire (Paulus, p. 221). It does not appear whether the allowance was renewed as occasion required, or made once for all; if two horses cost 2000 libral *asses*, the sum here agrees with Varro's statement (*L. L.* VIII. 71), *equum publicum mille assarium esse.* The *equites* proper were said *equo publico merere*, as distinguished from *equites equo privato*, who provided horse and forage at their own expense.

19 **quibus...alerent**] This clause is final, depending on *bina milia.*

viduae attributae] i.e. 'unmarried women,' whether widows or not, whose property was rateable. Cicero (*de Rep.* II. 36) says *orborum* (i.e. orphans, or perhaps childless men as well) *et viduarum tributis* in this connection. *attributae* either means 'were laid under contribution,' in other words, paid *tributum* in this form; or, as *attribuere* is a technical term for assigning a sum from the treasury for a public purpose, here the *viduae* were 'assigned'—as an account to be drawn on—for this maintenance.

bina milia aeris in annos singulos] i.e. a yearly allowance of 400 libral *asses* (= 4 oxen), raised by requisition according to the number of the levy on each occasion. It came to be known as the *aes hordearium* (*hordeum* = barley, corn for horses).

20 **in dites a pauperibus inclinata**] 'diverted from the poor to the rich,' i.e. from poor patricians to wealthy citizens, whether patrician or plebeian. Dionysius (IV. 20) says that Servius, seeing the indignation so caused, proceeded to make political privileges proportional to financial (and therefore military) obligations, in other words, to use the new *exercitus* as a political organization: *καὶ τοῦτο διαπραξάμενος ἔλαθε τοὺς δημοτικούς*.

21 § **10. additus**] to the rich, in compensation for the new obligations.

22 **ut...reges**] 'in accordance with the tradition established by Romulus and maintained by the other kings.'

23 **viritim**] 'individually': the meaning is emphasised by *promisce omnibus* 'to all citizens without distinction.' In the *comitia curiata* the vote of a *curia* was determined by a majority of the votes given by its individual members. So the poor citizen 'had as much power and privilege.' *vis* and *ius* are likewise found together in XXVI. 12. 8 *qui indignitate sua vim ac ius magistratui...dempsisset*.

25 **ut neque...videretur**] Every citizen had a vote, though its individual importance, e.g. in the fifth class and in the *una centuria* of *proletarii*, would be insignificant or infinitesimal.

26 **primores**] i.e. the citizens of first-class rating (see note on *ex primoribus* above), in other words the 18 centuries of *equites* and the first class, or 98 centuries in all, a substantive majority (if they agreed) in a total of 193.

27 § **11. vocabantur**] i.e. to vote in the *comitia*.

primi...primum peditum] After the reform of the *comitia* the right of voting first (*centuria praerogativa*) belonged to one of the centuries of the first class, chosen by lot on each occasion.

29 **si variaret**] 'if there were a difference of opinion.' Livy uses the word elsewhere in this sense, with or without a personal subject: cf. VII. 22. 10 *nec variatum comitiis est*.

ut...vocarentur...descenderent] The construction presupposes some such idea as *constitutum est*, in other words, the intention of Servius.

30 **infra**] 'lower' (in the list of classes).

31 § **12.** **nec...non convenire**] The other *locus classicus* alluding, but with no greater certainty than Livy, to this reform of the *comitia centuriata*, is Dionysius, IV. 21: *ἐν δὲ τοῖς καθ' ἡμᾶς κεκίνηται χρόνοις, καὶ μεταβέβληκεν εἰς τὸ δημοτικώτερον, ἀνάγκαις τισὶ βιασθεὶς ἰσχυραῖς, οὐ τῶν λόχων* (centuries) *καταλυθέντων, ἀλλὰ τῆς κλήσεως* (classification) *αὐτῶν οὐκέτι τὴν ἀρχαίαν ἀκρίβειαν φυλαττούσης, ὡς ἔγνων ταῖς ἀρχαιρεσίαις αὐτῶν πολλάκις παρών.*

It is not told by any ancient authority when this change of the Servian *comitia* took place, nor what was the exact arrangement adopted. It may well have been connected with the completion of the 35 tribes (in B.C. 241), and it was clearly based upon a co-ordination of tribes and centuries. Pantagathus, in the 16th century, proposed a solution of the problem which has been confirmed by inscriptions and generally accepted.

According to this view, each of the 35 tribes contained a century of *seniores* and of *iuniores* in each of the 5 classes, i.e. 10 centuries, making a total of 350 centuries, i.e. 70 centuries in each class. It is not possible to say with certainty what arrangement was adopted in regard to the *equites equo publico*—whether they were included (as Livy XLIII. 16 [169 B.C.] includes them) with the *pedites* in the first class in each tribe (as those citizens would be who had the equestrian property-qualification but not the *equus publicus*) or remained distinct as 18 centuries. The latter alternative, if we include in the reformed classification, as in the Servian, 4 centuries of supernumeraries (*fabri*, *accensi*, *liticines*, *cornicines*) and one of *capite censi* (= *proletarii*), gives the new total as 350 + 18 + 5 = 373 centuries: the former gives 355.

Livy's phrase *duplicato earum numero centuriis iuniorum seniorumque*, in reference to the classification existing in his own day (*hunc ordinem*, *qui nunc est*), is difficult. *earum* most naturally refers to *tribus*: and the sense is 'their number being doubled (i.e. reckoned twice over, as 70 instead of 35) by—in respect of—the centuries of *iuniores* and *seniores*.' Or it is perhaps possible to take *earum* as referring to *centuriae*, and *centuriis* as referring to the Servian classification: in this case the sense is 'the present classification...in view of their (the centuries') duplication does not agree with the centuries of *iuniores* and *seniores* to make the total instituted by Servius.' The first of these renderings alludes to the reform which co-ordinated tribes and centuries: the second is merely concerned with the numerical discrepancy between the old and the new arrangement.

Now if, in the new arrangement, there had been in each tribe a single, instead of a double, reckoning of centuries, we should have had a total of (35 × 5 =) 175 centuries, i.e. one century of each class in each tribe. This (if we disregard the 18 centuries of *equites* in both cases) is the same as the Servian total of 170 centuries of infantry + the 5 centuries of supernumeraries and *proletarii*: and therefore the double reckoning of 350 centuries (10 to a tribe) might well seem to be a duplication of the Servian 175, and so to suggest some reference to the Servian classification, and some connection between it and the Servian tribes.

Livy then desires to refute such a supposition; first, by stating incidentally that the *number* of centuries in the reconstituted *comitia* does not agree with the Servian total; and secondly, by the statement next following, that the tribal divisions of Servius had nothing to do with the centuriate arrangement, although tribes and centuries were afterwards combined for this purpose.

p. 57. 3 § 13. **quadrifariam**] sc. *partem*: 'in four parts.' *trifariam* is similarly used several times by Livy. **enim**] shows that this sentence is intended to explain the preceding: see note above.

regionibus collibusque] may be taken (1) as in apposition to *urbe* (so Weissenborn-Müller), or (2) as indicating the lines of division 'according to the districts and hills.' The latter seems the better interpretation. One of the 'tribes' concerned was named (*Sucusana*, later *Suburana*) from a district, the other three from hills (*Palatina*, *Exquilina*, *Collina*): or, if the word *collibus* is to be regarded here (so W.-M.) as distinct from *montes*, it applies to the Viminal and Quirinal (*regio Collina*), and *regionibus* to the rest.

In any case, the four 'regions' represent in all probability a pre-Servian division, which was now utilized for a definite purpose—the *census* and the collection of the *tributum*: the area actually included within the Servian rampart was considerably larger.

4 **tribus...a tributo**] This derivation cannot be accepted, for *tributum* surely comes from *tribus*. There is some reason to doubt the conventional derivation of *tribus* from *tres*, which may have been suggested by the coincidence that the three chief partners in the earliest state of Rome were so called.

The prevalent connotation of *tribus* is 'part' or 'district,' without regard to number (cf. *tribuo*): and here Servius is represented as applying the term, for administrative purposes, to the fourfold division which he created or recognized.

The *tributum* was, as this passage indicates, a property-tax (cf. εἰσφορά). It was levied as required from time to time, chiefly for war-purposes; and occasionally it was repaid, after a successful campaign. It continued till the conquest of Macedonia (167 B.C.), when the treasury was enriched by so much booty that there was no further need to tax the citizens for the maintenance of the armies.

6 **aequaliter**] 'equably,' (not 'equally') 'proportionally.' **ex censu**] 'according to (as the result of) the rating.'

ratio] 'method,' 'system.'

7 **neque...pertinuere**] See note on § 12 above. The tribes were administrative units for military and financial purposes, without political significance at this era.

CHAPTER XLIV.

10 § **1. incensis**] 'unregistered persons,' i.e. those who refused to return the necessary information about themselves and their property. Dionysius (IV. 15) gives a more detailed description of the penalties imposed by this law of Servius: *τῷ δὲ μὴ τιμησαμένῳ τιμωρίαν ὥρισε τῆς τ' οὐσίας στέρεσθαι καὶ αὐτὸν μαστιγωθέντα πραθῆναι.* To be sold thus—as a slave, *trans Tiberim*—meant disfranchisement (*capitis deminutio maxima*): cf. Dion. H. V. 75, where the penalty of non-registration, in the census taken by the first dictator, T. Lartius, is given as deprivation of property and of citizenship. Cicero (*pro Caecina* 99) mentions the selling of census-defaulters as slaves.

12 **in campo Martio**] This parade-ground was situated outside the *pomerium*, as it was improper for an army to assemble (and in historical times illegal for a general to bring his army back) within that ritual boundary.

14 § **2. exercitum**] This word, here used in its ordinary sense, served also as a designation of the *Comitia Centuriata*, showing that the military origin of that assembly was not forgotten.

suovetaurilibus] 'the sacrifice of a pig, a sheep, and a bull.' The victims were probably carried on spears thrice round the army (just as in other purificatory rites they were carried round estates or fleets); the form of prayer on such occasions was: *Mars pater lustri faciendi ergo macte hisce suovetaurilibus lactentibus esto.* (Cato, *de Re Rustica*, 141. 3.)

lustravit...conditum lustrum] 'purified'...'the close of the purification.' In historical times this rite was performed by the censors every five years (hence the secondary meaning of *lustrum*, a period of five years), when the census was finished.

17 **Fabius Pictor**] belongs to the period 250—200 B.C.: he wrote in Greek (there was afterwards a Latin version also) a history of Rome from Aeneas' time to his own. His account of the foundation of Rome was used by Dionysius; Livy refers to him not infrequently (e.g. in 55—8 below), and sometimes quotes him, but it is not clear whether he regarded him as his chief authority.

19 **§ 3. ad**] 'in view of,' 'to meet': cf. 8. 4.

20 **Quirinalem Viminalemque**] These two hills (the term *mons* is never applied to them) and the Esquiline are separate at the southern end, but towards the north-east form a continuous plateau, along which the *agger* of Servius was now thrown up. See the plan of Rome. The name *Quirinalis* is variously derived: cf. Varro, *L. L.* v. 51 *collis Quirinalis ob Quirini fanum: sunt qui a Quiritibus, qui cum T. Tatio Curibus venerunt Romam, quod ibi habuerunt castra*. See also the note on *Quirinus*, 20. 2 above. *Viminalis* is derived from *vimina* (osiers), of which there were large quantities in this region.

21 **auget Esquilias**] 'enlarged (i.e. developed) the Esquiline,' as a centre of habitation. *Esquiliis*, which has been suggested as an emendation, would mean 'increased (the city) by including the Esquiline.' The Esquiline formed one of the four *regiones* into which Servius (cf. 43. 13) was believed to have divided the city. The name *Esquiliae* (originally *Exquiliae*) is generally taken to indicate 'out-district,' 'suburb,' whose inhabitants were *esquilini* 'outlanders,' i.e. not *inquilini*.

22 **aggere**] This term came to denote both mound and ditch. In the case of the 'Servian' fortifications it applies especially to that portion, about a mile long, which ran over the plateau to the N.E., the side on which the city was best defended by nature.

23 **fossis**] probably carried all round outside the wall, according to the ancient custom, by which a plough was driven, in the direction of the sun's course, round the circuit of a proposed town: the furrow so made marked the ditch, the up-turned clods the line of wall inside it. Varro says (*L. L.* v. 143) *terram unde exsculpserant fossam vocabant et introrsus iactam murum: post ea qui fiebat orbis, urbis principium, qui quod erat post murum, postmoerium dictum, eoque auspicia urbana finiuntur.*

muro] The date of the 'Servian' wall now remaining is much disputed: perhaps it is of two periods (1) of the second half of the sixth century B.C., (2) shortly after 390 B.C. See the article *Topography of Rome*, in the *Companion to Latin Studies*.

24 **pomerium**] According to the general interpretation of the passage from Varro in the last note, this word seems to mean first of all the 'boundary line' itself, marked off (see Tac. *Ann.* XII. 24) by stones at intervals. Then (cf. Gell. VIII. 14. 1) it is the 'circuit-space' inside the wall, important for defensive communication. See Introduction, § 4.

profert] 'extends.' Such extension was a sovereign's prerogative: after Servius Tullius there was no instance thereof till Sulla became dictator, and even the Aventine (though within the Servian Wall) was not included within the *pomerium* till the reign of the Emperor Claudius.

§ 4. **verbi vim solam**] 'the mere etymology.'

postmoerium] 'inner passage'—'behind' the wall from the enemy's point of view, protected by it: whereas **circamoerium** means 'double passage,' i.e. the circuit-space on both sides of the wall. *ambitus* is similarly used in the case of private houses. Livy is probably wrong in his statement here, as the other authorities invariably refer *pomerium* to the inner side only. For the form *pomerium* cf. *pomeridianus*.

26 **Etrusci**] The *pomerium* is attributed, like many other ancient ordinances mentioned in this book, to the Etruscans; but it is probably wiser to suppose that in this and other cases the Latins and Etruscans followed a common tradition.

27 **certis...terminis**] 'with definite limit-marks on either side' (of the wall): the circuit-spaces were defined by stones (*cippi*, *lapides*) at intervals, and the area thus enclosed formed a *templum*, within which auspices could be taken. *circa* is adjectival: cf. 17. 4 *multarum circa civitatium*, and see n. on Praef. 2 *novi semper*.

inaugurato] Cf. 36. 3 above.

29 **continuarentur**] 'carried up to': **coniungunt**] 'build into.' The subject is easily understood from *vulgo*.

30 **puri...cultu**] 'free from human occupation': cf. Ovid, *Met.* III. 709 *purus ab arboribus campus*.

31 § 5. **habitari**] refers to the inner, **arari** to the outer circuit. **esset** expresses the feeling of the Romans.

p. 58. 3 **termini...proferebantur**] See note on § 3 above.

CHAPTER XLV.

4 § 1. **magnitudine**] 'by the enlargement': the increase of the city necessarily follows the increase of citizenship.

omnibus] 'all arrangements': for this substantival use of *omnia* see note on 28. 2.

6 **armis**] is emphatic, 'by force of arms,' as opposed to **consilio**, 'by policy': cf. 8. 7 *consilium deinde viribus parat.*

8 § **2. Dianae Ephesiae**] Information about this temple and its significance was perhaps received directly from Greeks. Massilia was founded in 600 B.C., a little before the legendary date of Servius' reign; the statue (ξόανον) set up by Servius was like that of Artemis at Massilia, which in its turn was like that at Ephesus, cf. Strabo, IV. 1. 4, 5 (p. 180).

9 **communiter...factum**] 'built by contribution (or, for a common purpose) by the city-states of Asia (Minor).' There were many similar centres of Greek worship: e.g. the temples of Poseidon in Calauria and at Mycale, of Apollo at Cnidus and in Delos. Livy uses *Asia* here in its Roman sense.

10 **deos consociatos**] 'religious communion,' 'associated worship.'

11 **publice privatimque**] 'officially and unofficially.'

13 **fanum**] not a *templum*, nor within the *pomerium*. The cult of the Sabine Diana—for the goddess was closely associated with the Sabines, see n. on Egeria, c. 19. 5 above—was brought to Rome very early: Varro (*L. L.* V. 74) says by Tatius. And this temple on the Aventine, like that at Aricia, certainly did form the focus of a federal cult like that of Jupiter Latiaris. The rules (*lex arae Dianae in Aventino*) for the feast and the fair of Diana (on the Ides of August), together with the names of the participators, were graven in ancient Greek characters on a bronze pillar, which survived to Dionysius' day: ὃ καὶ αὐτὸ ποιήσαιτ' ἄν τις οὐ μικρὸν τεκμήριον τοῦ μὴ βαρβάρους εἶναι τοὺς οἰκίσαντας τὴν Ῥώμην (D. H., IV. 26).

The temple of Diana on the Caelian Hill was also a Latin sanctuary for *gentilicia* on the Ides of August; and, like the Dianium (c. 48. 6) on or near the Esquiline, was among oak-trees. Other centres of Diana-worship (Mount Algidus, Mount Tifata for example) were among oak-woods: so that the temple on the Aventine was doubtless set in an oak-wood.

15 § **3. caput...esse**] because they agreed to a Roman proposal and a Roman site.

16 **fuerat**] i.e. the strife was now a thing of the past; cf. note on 2. 1 *pacta fuerat.*

omissum...ex cura] 'dismissed from the attention.'

18 **uni**] in contrast to *omnium* above, 'a single Sabine.'

20 § **4. patri familiae**] 'head of a house.'

miranda...specie] Cf. 7. 4 *boves mira specie.*

22 **monumentum**] We should say (as also in 36. 5) that they were rather the cause, than the evidence, of the marvel. The nailing up of the horns of the victims seems to have been part of the ceremonial of sacrifices to Artemis, e.g. in Taurica. Plutarch (*Q. R.* 4, quoted by Seeley) says, διὰ τί τοῖς ἄλλοις Ἀρτεμισίοις ἐπιεικῶς ἐλάφων κέρατα προσπατταλεύουσι, τῷ δ' Ἀβεντίνῳ βοῶν; For the dat. *ei miraculo* see n. on 5. 6 *Numitori.*

23 § 5. **prodigii loco**] Cf. 39. 4 *liberum loco.*

cecinere vates] The seers, who would be consulted as to the treatment of the prodigy, delivered their reply (*responsum* below) in rhythmic form (*cecinere*): cf. 7. 10 *cecinit.*

24 **immolassent**] = fut. perf. of *or. recta.*

25 § 6. **antistitem**] 'the prior': cf. 7. 14, 20. 3.

28 **Romanus**] The epithet seems to hint that there was a suspicion of Sabine sympathies in the case of the seers.

31 **inceste**] 'in sin,' 'uncleansed.'

32 **vivo...flumine**] 'in a running stream.'

p. 59. 1 § 7. **religione tactus**] 'stirred by religious scruple' (one might almost say 'conscience-stricken'): the reason is given in *qui... facta.* For the use of *tactus* cf. Propertius, III. 5. 34 *materno tacta dolore Thetis.* For *cuperet...facta* see n. on 23. 8 *monitum velim.*

3 **Romanus**] According to Plutarch (*Q. Rom.* 4) Servius planned the trick, and sacrificed the cow.

4 **mire**] Livy is fond of this word as an emphasis (see § 2 above), as is Pliny in his letters: Cicero uses *mirifice* in the same way. Both are probably colloquial.

CHAPTER XLVI.

6 § 1. **haud dubie**] After the war with Veii he had become *haud dubius rex* (see 42. 3).

8 **iniussu populi**] This was literally true; see 41. 6.

10 **agro...diviso**] Servius (as Weissenborn points out) adopts the same method of catching the popular vote as the tribunes of later days.

viritim] is here opposed to all distinctions and Patrician privileges; the distribution, which included the *plebs*, would naturally incur the displeasure of the nobler and wealthier citizens. *viritim* implies 'in fee simple,' i.e. as individual property. See n. on 15. 5 above.

11 **ferre ad populum**] 'submit to the people the question'...

vellent iuberentne] the regular formula for introducing a *rogatio*. The two verbs (*velitis iubeatisne*) are as it were hyphened, and thus the interrogative particle is attached to the second. Asyndeton is not uncommon in formulae: cf. 24. 7 *prima postrema*: 32. 13 *fecerunt deliquerunt*.

14 § 2. **impensius**] 'more vehemently'—to be taken with *criminandi*. The same word occurs in 40. 2.

quia...agi] 'because he had realised that the Act relating to land for the populace was opposed to the feeling of the Patres,'—and knew also that to the *patrum voluntas* (see 41. 6) Servius had originally owed his succession.

17 **crescendi**] 'of gaining power': cf. *crescere* below, 47. 7.

18 **et ipse**] For the usual meaning see n. on Praef. 3. In the present case it helps to give *iuvenis ardentis animi* a quasi-participial force (in Greek we should have had *καὶ αὐτὸς ὢν νεανίας*), by way of balancing the participial clause *uxore...stimulante*.

19 § 3. **tulit**] 'produced.'

20 **et Romana regia**] i.e. no less than the house of Atreus or of Oedipus. For *regia* see n. on 39. 3.

sceleris tragici exemplum] 'its type of tragic outrage,' i.e. 'of tragedy and crime.'

ut...foret] Here again (as in 42. 2) Livy speaks with an air of fatalism which reminds us of Herodotus.

23 § 4. **filius neposne**] See n. on 42. 1.

24 **pluribus...auctoribus**] ablative absolute. **ediderim**] a subjunctive of polite assertion, equivalent to the Greek aor. optative + *ἄν*: cf. 55. 8 *crediderim*, Cic. *Brut.* 83 *sic ego istis censuerim novam istam orationem fugiendam*. Roby, § 644.

27 § 5. **et ipsae**] See n. on Praef. 3.

28 **ne...iungerentur**] expresses the purpose, not the consequence, of *fortuna* (which is best taken as an ablative, not as nominative to *inciderat*): *quo...possent* adds a second purpose. *fortuna populi Romani* has here something of a personal character, as elsewhere in Livy (e.g. II. 40. 13 *ibi fortuna populi Romani duos hostium exercitus...confecit*; XXXVIII. 46. 4 *magna fortuna populi Romani, magnum et terribile nomen*). This is not surprising when it is remembered that Fortuna was included in the Roman Pantheon. *credo* then gives a touch of scepticism on the part of the author.

30 **constitui...possent**] 'that the character of the community might become settled.'

31 § **6. ferox**] not 'spirited Tullia' but 'the Tullia who had spirit,' as distinguished from the gentler sister.

nihil...ad audaciam] 'no stuff for ambition or enterprise.'

p. 60. 3 **muliebri...audacia**] 'was wanting in enterprise as a woman'—she had not the γυναικὸς ἀνδρόβουλον ἐλπίζον κέαρ of a Clytaemnestra.

6 § **7. alieni**] 'the other's.' **parcere...contendere**] historic infinitives. **de viro...virum**] 'about her husband to his brother, about her sister to her sister's husband.'

8 **se...viduam...caelibem**] 'without a husband'...'without a wife.'

9 **iungi**] In this apparently irregular sentence the meaning is clear enough. Tullia is unsuitably married: she feels that she would have been better off unmarried. The construction as it stands is an elaboration, best explained step by step. *rectius* may be taken as an adjective or an adverb: if an adjective it is equivalent to *magis rectum*, and supplies a predicate to the two infinitive phrases *se...futurum fuisse, cum impari iungi*; if an adverb, it has a predicative force ('it would have been juster that'...) which, properly belonging to *se...futurum fuisse*, is extended to *cum impari iungi*. On the whole, it seems preferable to take it as an adjective. As a direct statement then the sentence might run *rectius* [*est*] *caelibem fuisse quam cum impari iungi*. *futurum fuisse* gives the first infinitive a potential force (cf. ἂν with aor. infin. in Greek), expressing a possibility now past: *iungi* is present, not perfect, because the effect of the marriage continues into the present. Then *contendere* ('she would maintain') turns the whole expression into *oratio obliqua*: we might render it—'she would maintain it as fairer for herself and him to have had the chance, now past, of being unmarried, than to be in fact wedded to an inferior.'

12 § **8. videat**] For the tense see n. on I. 8 *audierit*.

13 **suae...implet**] With *implere* Livy uses the genitive (to express the thing supplied, as a secondary object, cf. Roby, § 530) rather than the ablative.

§ **9. Arruns**] So the MSS. *Lucius*, which seems to be required for the sake of consistency, may be the correct reading, lost by a copyist's confusion of words or persons. If we retain *Arruns* we must suppose either (1) that Livy has made a slip in detail: or (2) that the clause *Arruns...fecissent* refers to the victims, a view which scarcely suits the meaning of the words, disagrees with Dionysius (who says that the younger Tullia was the violent one), and requires a very awkward change of subject for *iunguntur*.

14 **prope continuatis funeribus**] 'by deaths in almost immediate succession.'

vacuas novo matrimonio] The dat. expresses the object in view: cf. Sallust, *Cat.* 15 *necato filio vacuam domum scelestis nuptiis fecisse*; Hor. *Ep.* II. 2. 94 *vacuam Romanis vatibus aedem*. *vacare* frequently takes a dat. in this sense.

CHAPTER XLVII.

17 § 1. **infestior**] 'more threatened,' 'more precarious': cf. 42. 2, and for a different sense of the word 25. 3.

20 **gratuita**] 'unrewarded' and so 'ineffectual.'

21 **parricidia**] See n. on 13. 2.

§ 2. **non sibi defuisse...serviret**] She refers to her life with her first husband.

22 **tacita**] 'without protest,' 'inactive': cf. 50. 9.

25 § 3. **si tu is es...virum...appello**] The whole appeal is similar to that of Tanaquil in 41. 3.

27 **istic**] 'in your case.'

quin accingeris?] The interrogative *quin* (i.e. *qui-ne*, 'how not?' 'why not?') never introduces a real inquiry, but only a rhetorical question, i.e. an exhortation: cf. 57. 7 *quin conscendimus equos?*

28 § 4. **ab Corintho**] 'starting from Corinth,' or 'as a man of Corinth': cf. 50. 3 *Turnus Herdonius ab Aricia*, and see n. on 34. 5.

29 **di...penates patriique**] It is not clear whether these two epithets are intended for distinction or for emphasis: if they are to be distinguished, *penates* seems to refer to the *household* gods of Tarquin in Rome, *patrii* to the *ancestral* gods that connected him with Tarquinii and Corinth.

30 **imago**] See n. on 34. 6. **domus**] It was on the Mons Oppius. See 48. 6, and the plan of Rome.

31 **creat...regem**] Notice that Tullia gives to family considerations the right (*creare*) that belonged to the sovereign people (cf. 17. 10 *Quirites, regem create*).

p. 61. 1 § 5. **civitatem**] She identifies her own party—the disaffected citizens—with the state at large.

2 **facesse**] 'retire': here, as in 48. 6 and elsewhere, this word denotes a withdrawal from public into private life. In the imperative it has a colloquial bluntness.

devolvere (imperative passive) **retro ad stirpem**] 'sink down again to your stock.' The phrase seems to allude to the premature decline of young and promising branches, which, for want of nurture, shrink down to their starting-point from the parent stock.

3 § **6. his aliisque increpando**] See n. on 8. 4 *munitionibus...appetendo.*

4 **ipsa**] in contrast to Tarquinius: the second **ipsa** (l. 7) is in contrast to Tanaquil.

5 **si...faceret**] See n. on 40. 2.

7 **nullum momentum...faceret**] 'should bring no weight to bear.' *momentum* = weight that turns the scale, the Greek *ῥοπή*.

9 § **7. circumire et prensare**] *circumire* ('canvass') and *prensare* ('solicit') are both electioneering terms. Tarquin's conduct recalls that of Absalom, II. Samuel XV. 2—6.

10 **minorum...gentium patres**] Cf. 35. 6.

12 **cum...crescere**] See 46. 2, of which passage this is a recapitulation. *regis* is objective genitive after *criminibus*, 'by slandering the king.' In his fondness for accumulating ablatives to express the means and circumstances of an action, Livy uses freely the ablative of the gerund, sometimes as a supplement to others (see note on 8. 4 *munitionibus... appetendo*), sometimes as an equivalent, as here.

14 § **8. agendae rei**] either dat. of work contemplated, or explanatory genitive, after *tempus*: see n. on 1. 8 *condendae urbis locum*, and cf. 48. 9 *liberandae patriae consilia.*

stipatus agmine armatorum] Here, as always (cf. 15. 8), the preliminary step to despotism.

16 **pro curia sedens**] *pro* is either 'in front of,' i.e. outside (so Dionysius says of Tarquin πρὸ τοῦ βουλευτηρίου στάς), or 'in the forefront of,' i.e. inside, as in the phrases *pro rostris*, *pro aede*, *pro tribunali.* In any case Tarquin delivered his denunciation inside.

17 **ad regem Tarquinium**] 'before Tarquin as king': he assumed at once the kingly prerogative of convening the council.

18 § **9. ne non venisse fraudi esset**] 'lest non-appearance might do them harm.' For *fraudi* see n. on 39. 4 *cordi.*

20 § **10. ab stirpe ultima**] 'from the very beginning, his birth.'

21 **servum**] All the following clauses, to the end of the chapter, are in *or. obl.* after the denunciation contained in *maledicta.*

23 **non per suffragium populi**] See 41. 6 and 46. 1.

non auctoribus patribus] See n. on 41. 6 *voluntate patrum.*

26 § **11. honestatis**] 'honourable estate,' 'rank.'

27 **ereptum primoribus**] It is part of Tarquin's policy, in opposition

to that of Servius, ostensibly to approve the exclusiveness of the 'nobility.'

divisisse] Cf. 46. 1.

29 § **12. insignis ad invidiam...largiretur**] 'a mark for envy, and a ready means of largess to the neediest persons, whenever he chose.'

CHAPTER XLVIII.

For the localities mentioned in this chapter, the map of Rome should be consulted.

32 § **1. trepido nuntio**] 'a message of alarm.'

p. 62. 1 **quid hoc...rei est?**] Cf. 41. 1.

4 § **2. cum ille**] sc. *dixisset.*

6 **potiorem**] 'preferable' (from the point of view of the nobles): yet in the adoption and the succession of Tarquinius Priscus himself there were many points of similarity to the case of Servius.

illum] i.e. Servius.

7 **per licentiam eludentem**] 'with the mockery that impunity gave': *per licentiam* explains *eludentem*, which is in agreement with *illum.*

9 **regnaturum qui vicisset**] 'that the conqueror would be king.' *vicisset*=fut. perf. of *or. recta*: cf. 45. 5 *cuius civitatis eam cives Dianae immolassent, ibi fore imperium.*

10 § **3. necessitate**] i.e. as well as his own ambition, and his wife's instigation.

13 **ad cogendum senatum**] *cogere* is the technical term for collecting the senate: in the present instance it seems to convey a certain notion of force, for the senators were not all of Tarquin's party.

14 § **4. apparitorum**] See n. on 8. 3.

ipse prope exsanguis] After these words the MSS. have *cum semianimis regio comitatu domum se reciperet pervenissetque ad summum Cyprium* (?) *vicum*, a duplication (with the exception of three words, *semianimis regio comitatu*) of a sentence found in § 6, to which context it clearly belongs. Of the three words which are not doubled we may dismiss *semianimis* as superfluous with *exsanguis*: *regio comitatu* ought perhaps to be retained as a genuine survival from some such clause as *cum regio comitatu domum se reciperet*, which caused the confusion by its similarity to a clause in § 6.

17 § **5. carpento**] See 34. 8.

18 **reverita...virorum**] She had no compunction in entering a formal assembly of men—a breach of matronly decorum.

20 § 6. **facessere iussa**] See n. on 47. 5.

22 **ad summum Cuprium vicum**] *summum* = 'at the highest part of' a sloping street. *Cuprium* is explained by Varro (*L. L.* v. 159) as connected with a Sabine occupation: *nam cuprum Sabine bonum.* It would thus be named in direct contrast to the *Sceleratus Vicus.* The spelling *Cyprium* is surely incorrect in a word not derived from the Greek: and we know that there was an old Italian deity named *Cupra* (more or less identical with Juno) who might well give her name to a *vicus.*

23 **Dianium**] a Greek form, due probably to the fact that Livy is using a Greek authority.

nuper fuit] A *sacellum Dianae in Caeliculo* had been removed by L. Piso in Cicero's day (cf. Cic. *de Harusp. Resp.* 32), but this can scarcely be identified with a *Dianium* on the Esquiline, unless Livy's topography is altogether faulty. The sentence *ubi...fuit* is inserted parenthetically by Livy, and is independent of its context.

flectenti] 'as she turned,' i.e. bade the driver turn.

in Vrbium clivum] This incline seems to have led up the western slope of the Oppian spur, and so to the plateau of the Esquiline. The meaning of *Vrbius* is doubtful: some scholars connect it with, or correct it into, *Virbius*, a King of the Wood, coupled with Diana at Aricia and thus also here in Rome.

24 **in collem Esquiliarium**] This adjectival form occurs nowhere else, and Madvig accordingly emends to *Esquiliarum.* On the Esquiliae, as we were told in 44. 3, Servius had built his palace, perhaps as a kind of fortress: cf. Dion. Hal. IV. 13 ἐν τῷ κρατίστῳ τῆς Ἰσκυλίας τόπῳ.

27 § 7. **traditur**] sc. *factum esse.*

monumento] The name of the street was evidence of a crime, but not necessarily of this crime, with which it may have been connected subsequently; cf. 36. 5, 45. 4.

28 **Sceleratum vicum**] The 'Street of Crime' is probably identical with the *Vrbius Clivus.*

29 **amens**] 'maddened': so *ferox* means 'emboldened' in 23. 4. The adjective in such cases is no mere epithet, but has a participial force: cf. *inscia*, 54. 3.

furiis] 'avenging spirits,' a touch of Greek tragedy applied to a Latin legend: cf. 59. 13.

31 **sanguinis ac caedis paternae**] 'the blood of her murdered father'; or, if *caedis* means 'gore' (cf. Catullus, 64. 181 *respersus fraterna caede*, Prop. II. 8, 34 *sparsae caede comae*) the phrase emphasizes a single notion, 'her father's life-blood.'

cruento vehiculo] with *tulisse*.

32 **contaminata ipsa respersaque**] The first participle expresses the moral, the second the physical, result of the foul deed: *ipsa*, like *αὐτός*, points the distinction between the person and the environment.

p. 63. 1 **quibus iratis**] 'by whose indignation' at the crime the ultimate developments 'were to follow' (*sequerentur*): the subjunctive expresses at once the consequence of the action, and the purpose of divine vengeance.

malo...principio] dat. governed by *similes*.

4 § 8. **bono etiam difficilis aemulatio**] and therefore, for a king who was the reverse of *bonus moderatusque*, 'competition' with the record of Servius was impossible.

6 § 9. **iusta ac legitima**] 'regular and constitutional,' as opposed to arbitrary and tyrannical. Cf. 46. 3 *ut...ultimum regnum esset, quod scelere partum foret*.

8 **quia unius esset**] 'because it was vested in one person': the subjunctive expresses the feeling of Servius himself.

9 **intestinum**] 'domestic,' 'family.'

liberandae patriae] See note on 47. 8 *agendae rei tempus*.

CHAPTER XLIX.

(For Tarquinius Superbus, see Introduction, §§ 6, 8.)

11 § 1. **Superbo**] 'the Proud,' i.e. 'the Tyrant': for the dat. see n. on 1. 3 *Troiano*.

13 **sepultura prohibuit**] as Creon in the legend of Oedipus sought to prevent the burial of Polynices.

16 § 2. **male quaerendi regni**] 'of usurpation.'

17 **armatis...circumsaepsit**] Cf. 15. 8, 47. 8.

§ 3. **neque...ad ius regni quicquam**] 'no sort of claim to the crown': *ad*, as often, = 'towards,' 'by way of,' implying an object.

18 **ut qui**] See n. on Praef. 4 *ut quae*.

19 **populi iussu...auctoribus patribus**] the two essentials for legitimate kingship (cf. 17. 9, 22. 1, 32. 1, 35. 5, 41. 6, 46. 1, 47. 10), for the lack of which Tarquin had denounced Servius.

20 § 4. **eo accedebat**] impersonal, a periphrase for 'moreover.'

in caritate...reponenti] (sc. *Tarquinio*) is opposed to **metu...tutandum esset**. *metu* = 'intimidation' (as in 44. 1). The contrast between love and fear is familiar enough.

22 **cognitiones...exercebat**] For the cognizance of capital cases, i.e.

those involving the *caput* (freedom, franchise, life) of a citizen, the king was not compelled (any more than a *pater familias* judging a son in a capital case: cf. 50. 9 below) to hold 'consultations' (*consilia*) with competent advisers; but the custom of seeking such assistance grew with the growth of the state.

23 § 5. **perque eam causam**] 'with that as a pretext.' *per causam* is common in this sense.

24 **bonis multare**] 'punish by confiscation': the abl. *bonis* expresses the sphere of punishment. Cicero has the same phrase in *Tusc.* v. 37. 106.

suspectos...invisos] 'the objects of his suspicion or animosity.'

25 **unde**] i.e. 'persons from whom.' See note on 34. 4 *ea quo innupsisset.*

26 **posset**] The subjunctive implies that a general class, not special individuals, were contemplated.

§ 6. **praecipue**] applies to *patrum*: the members of that order would be the chief, but not the only, sufferers.

28 **minus**] either 'less'—because the rest would be deterred by the punishment of the victims; or 'less effectively'—because their opposition would be weaker numerically.

per se nihil agi] 'that no state business passed through their hands.'

p. 64. 1 § 7. **senatum**] The proper function of the Senate was to advise the king in matters of state: Tarquin intended to act independently in political as well as judicial affairs, and dispensed with the formal 'consultations' (*consilia*) customary in both cases, seeking merely the advice of his own private council of friends. There is a clear contrast between *domesticis* and *publicam* in the next sentence.

2 **foedera societates**] 'treaties and alliances.' See note on 19. 4 *societate ac foederibus.*

5 § 8. **conciliabat**] 'tried to win over.'

peregrinis] natural enough, for Tarquin himself was the descendant of *peregrini.*

9 § 9. **Circa**] Circeii was mythologically connected with Circe.

ei Mamilio] For this resumptive use of *is* cf. 19. 1 *urbem...eam,* 58. 11 *cultrum...eum.*

10 **nuptum dat**] The supine implies motion, i.e. to the husband's house; so Terence, *And.* 301 *daturne illa Pamphilo hodie nuptum?*

CHAPTER L.

13 § 1. **in diem...indicit**] The use of *indicit* with *ut* is not elsewhere found, but the subordinate clause is really equivalent to *concilium*, and the phrase *concilium in diem certam indicere* occurs in Caesar, *B. G.* I. 30: cf. Livy III. 35. 1 *comitia in trinum nundinum.*

14 **Ferentinae**] The form of the word suggests an epithet rather than the actual name of a goddess: it may be that we have here the equivalent of the Diana mentioned in c. 45 as the goddess associated with the league of Romans and Latins. The *lucus Ferentinae* stood at the source of the *aqua Ferentina* (so in 51. 9 *ad caput aquae Ferentinae*, II. 38. 1 *caput Ferentinum*), on the north shore of the Alban Lake: the mention of grove and spring denotes a primitive cult.

esse] The *or. obl.* indicates the terms of the *indicium*.

15 **agere**] 'discuss': cf. our use of 'agenda' in a notice of meeting.

16 **frequentes**] 'in full muster': so again in 52. 5.

18 § 2. **occideret**] The subj. after *ante quam* implies something more than a mere statement of fact—some thought or intention of anticipating the sunset on the part of Tarquin. The *concilium* could do no business after sunset.

toto die] expresses the time *within* which (not *during* which) the general discussion had gone on.

concilio] This word is regularly used by Livy to denote the assemblies or meetings of confederate communities (*populi*)—e.g. Aequi, Samnites, Achaeans, Aetolians—attended by delegates or by any citizens able to come. It is thus appropriate here as applied to a meeting of the *Latinorum proceres*, convened by the head of the league. The gradual prohibition of such *concilia* was one feature of the Roman progress towards supremacy in Italy and Greece.

19 § 3. **Turnus**] See n. on 2. 1. **ab Aricia**]=*Aricinus* (51. 1). Livy often uses the preposition *ab* with the name of a town to denote the origin of a person: cf. II. 22. 2 *a Cora atque Pometia liberos*. Aricia was S. of the Alban Lake, S. W. of Alba: it was the centre of the most famous cult of Diana.

21 **haud mirum esse**] This is the beginning of the *or. obl.*, which continues to *observet* (end of § 6).

Superbo] See n. on 34. 3 *Egerio*. Here (as in 4. 7) *ei* is to be supplied.

22 **clam...tamen**] 'in secret undertones, but still commonly enough.' This use of *quidem...tamen* in antithesis corresponds to the Greek μὲν... δέ, or to καίπερ...ὅμως (with participles).

26 § **4. indixerit**] For this and the following tenses of the subjunctive see n. on 1. 8 *audierit.*

27 **obnoxios**] (explained by *si iugum acceperint*) 'at his mercy.'

28 § **5. adfectare**] (the word used of Tarquin before in 46. 2) 'aim at.'

in] seems to imply both extent and opposition—'over' and 'against' the Latins.

quod...illud] sc. *imperium.*

29 **sui**] See note on 7. 1 *sua.* **bene crediderint**] 'had done well (had proved right) in entrusting': cf. 13. 3 *melius peribimus.*

30 **parricidio**] 'by outrage': see n. on 13. 2. The word here combines its literal and applied senses, for Tarquin was guilty both of kindred murder and of treachery. It is to be noticed that he applies the same word (in c. 52. 1) to the conduct of Turnus.

31 **alienigenae**] So in 40. 2 the sons of Ancus called the elder Tarquin *advenam non modo vicinae sed ne Italicae quidem stirpis.*

§ **6. paeniteat**] 'were dissatisfied with'; cf. 35. 5 *haud paenitendo.*

p. 65. 2 **se**] i.e. Turnus.

4 § **7. eodem pertinentia**] 'of the same purport': for the use of *eodem* (=*ad idem*) cf. 33. 2 *additi eodem*, and see note on 34. 4 *quo innupsisset.*

seditiosus...homo] 'the turbulent mischief-maker.'

6 **cum maxime**] 'just when,' 'at the moment when.'

9 § **8. id temporis**] a loose accusative of time; cf. *id aetatis* (Roby, § 460).

11 **exemisset**] 'had taken up, wasted': the regular word of occupying time unworthily or unsuitably, cf. Cic. *ad Att.* IV. 3. 3 *Metellus calumnia dicendi tempus exemit.*

12 § **9. ne id quidem...ferunt**] 'They say that neither was this remark of Tarquin passed without comment by Turnus.' *tacitum* in this phrase has the sense of a perfect participle, 'left in silence': cf. 47. 2.

14 **cognitionem**] 'cognizance,' 'judgment,' as in 49. 4.

15 **habiturum** (sc. *filium*) **infortunium esse**] 'the young man would catch it': *infortunium* is a colloquial word, found in Plautus and Apuleius.

CHAPTER LI.

17 § **1. increpans**] As there is no past participle active in Latin, the present participle, which properly denotes an action concurrent with that

of the principal verb, is sometimes used (as here) with the sense of an aorist: cf. XXIV. 7. 11 *Romam veniens comitia edixit.*

21 § 2. **pro imperio**] 'in virtue of his authority': cf. III. 49. 5 *iam pro imperio Valerius discedere a privato lictores iubebat.* The *ius vitae necisque*, implied in the *imperium* of Tarquin, could not be exercised beyond the *pomerium* of Rome.

24 **vim magnam**] 'a large quantity,' as in 37. 1 above.

25 **sineret**] a mild form of jussive, introduced by the general sense of the previous clause. So in IV. 45. 4 *Tusculanis negotium datum, adverterent animos ne quid novi tumultus Lavicis oriretur.*

27 § 3. **re nova**] 'strange occurrence': cf. 60. 1 *re nova trepidus.* The plural, *res novae* (cf. 52. 1 *novantem res*), denotes change and connotes revolution, like *νεωτερισμός*: the singular is but rarely found in this sense, which is not intended here.

30 § 4. **dici**] 'he was told, he said'—an *or. obl.* within an *or. obl.*: so again in § 6.

31 **teneat**] For the subjunctives in this *or. obl.* see n. on 1. 8 *audierit.*

32 **adgressurum fuisse**] 'meant to have made his attack'; *adgressus esset* in direct narration.

p. 66. 1 **auctor concilii**] 'the convener of—the person responsible for—the council.'

3 § 5. **morando**] 'by the delay' (caused by Tarquin), not 'by delaying.' Livy thus extends the use of the ablative of the gerund to denote a circumstance over which the speaker has no control, rather than an instrument. This is in effect a reversion to the neutral sense of the verbal noun, which appears in Lucretius I. 312 *anulus in digito subter tenuatur habendo.* The more personal sense is seen in *comparando*, c. 5: 6, above.

5 **instructus**] 'duly equipped': the phrase *cum...manu* (which ought perhaps to be taken with *venturus sit*) amplifies the sense, to lay stress on the point—the armed preliminaries of tyranny.

8 § 7. **suspectam...rem**] 'the case was rendered suspicious by....'

11 **quidem...tamen**] See note on 50. 3 above.

12 **nisi**] The ablative phrase which follows itself implies a condition (*si gladii deprehensi erunt*), with which, expressed in finite form, *nisi* would be pleonastic (*nisi si* for *nisi*). But with the condition only implied *nisi* is a help to clearness. The use is common enough in Livy, cf. VI. 35. 1.

existimaturi] may express both what they *meant to think*, and what they were *likely to think*. The future participle in Livy becomes (like μέλλω in Greek) a convenient means of indicating all shades of intention and futurity: cf. III. 60. 8, V. 43. 1.

16 § 8. **enimvero**] 'then of a truth,' like *καὶ κάρτα*. This corroborative force of *enimvero* appears likewise in V. 25. 6 *enimvero illud se tacere suam conscientiam non pati*.

19 § 9. **indicta causa**] 'without a hearing.' *indictus* (=*non dictus*) must be distinguished from *indictus*, the pf. part. pass. of *indīco*, which occurs in 35. 2.

ut...mergeretur] This sentence is a striking instance of Livy's fondness for accumulation: six separate items are worked into the description. See note on 12. 10.

20 **ad caput**] 'at the well-head': cf. *Digest*, XLIII. 20. 1 § 8 *caput aquae illud est, unde aqua nascitur*. **aquae Ferentinae**] See n. on 50. 1.

CHAPTER LII.

23 § 1. **Turnum novantem res**] 'the revolutionary attempt of Turnus': see n. on 51. 3 *re nova*.

pro manifesto parricidio] amplifies *merita*, 'in view of his flagrant treason.' For this meaning of *parricidium* see n. on 13. 2: the word was used of Tarquin by Turnus in 50. 5.

24 **adfecissent**] The subjunctive is used to express the view of Tarquin.

25 § 2. **quidem**] answered by *ceterum* in § 3, =*μὲν...δέ*.

vetusto iure agere] 'act upon an ancient right.'

26 **ab Alba**] See n. on 34. 5 *ab Tarquiniis*.

in eo...teneantur] not 'were bound by that treaty' (unless we accept the reading *eo* for *in eo*), but 'were included in that treaty.' The substance of the treaty is given in c. 24. 3, but no mention is made there of colonies. Perhaps Livy is using, without regard to historical accuracy, the phrase usual in historical times.

29 **cesserit**] almost has the sense of a passive, 'was handed over,' with which *ab Tullo* would be natural.

§ 3. **utilitatis...causa**] The order of words throws a stress upon *utilitatis*. Livy not infrequently separates words (e.g. *omnium* here) from their immediate connections.

32 **urbium...agrorum**] See cc. 29. 6 and 33.

p. 67. 3 § 4. **superior...erat**] This was felt also at the time of the foundation of the confederate temple of Diana; see 45. 3.

4 **nominis Latini**] See n. on 10. 3 *nomen Caeninum*.

stare ac sentire] 'sided and sympathized.'

sui cuique] See note on 7. 1.

si adversatus esset] = fut. perf. of *oratio recta*: the apodosis to the condition is contained in *periculi*.

7 § **5. iunioribus**] So, according to the Servian classification at Rome (see 43. 2 above), the *iuniores* were liable for field-service. See also 59. 12 below.

8 **ad lucum Ferentinae**] See n. on 50. 1.

frequentes] Cf. 50. 1.

12 § **6. manipulos**] 'bands,' 'companies': the word implies the smallest tactical unit which had a separate standard. In the later organization of the Roman army, associated with Camillus, the *manipulus* consisted of two *centuriae*, each under a *centurio*, and thus represented a sort of 'double-company' (to use a modern military phrase), commanded by the senior centurion. In the present passage Livy probably identifies *manipulus* and *centuria*.

ut singulis] i.e. he took a Latin half-company and combined it with a Roman half-company to make a new company. What had been two (Latin and Roman) became one, what had been one (a whole company, Latin or Roman) became two (i.e. a part of two companies).

CHAPTER LIII.

17 § **1. degeneratum in aliis**] 'his degeneracy in other respects.' This use of the perf. part. by itself to denote a state of things is very rare. It seems to have been developed from such impersonal phrases as *nuntiatum est*, *auditum est*, treated participially, and so substantivally (e.g. XXVII. 37. 5 *liberatas religione mentes turbavit rursus nuntiatum*). A few other instances occur in Livy (e.g. VII. 8. 5 *diu non perlitatum tenuerat dictatorem*), and there is one well known in Virgil, *Aen.* V. 7 *notumque furens quid femina possit*. The Greek formations in which the neuter article with perf. part. or perf. infin. passive produces a substantive may have suggested the construction in Latin.

18 § **2. Volscis**] dat. of indirect object. **in**] 'which was to last for'; the preposition in such cases usually contains some idea of intention, e.g. IX. 37. 12 *indutias in triginta annos impetraverunt*. **ducentos amplius**] See n. on 23. 3 *haud plus quinque milia*.

20 **Suessam Pometiam**] See n. on 41. 7.

21 § **3. quadraginta talenta argenti**] If the talent here be taken as a sum equivalent to about £220 (the value of the Euboic talent), this means about £8800: if the calculation be made according to weight, the result is about £8100. The word *talenta* here suggests that Livy is using an authority who wrote in Greek, probably Fabius Pictor.

The ancient authorities differ as to the date of the first coinage of silver in Rome. Varro (*de R. R.* II. 1. 9.) attributes it to Servius Tullius: Livy (*Epit.* 15) and Pliny (*N. H.* XXXIII. 44) to the year 269—8 B.C.

refecisset] 'had realised,' 'got in return.'

24 **captivam pecuniam**] 'the price of the spoil,' 'prize-money.'

26 § **4.** **excepit**] 'engaged,' 'occupied,' = κατέλαβεν. The word is not often so used with an inanimate subject: Caesar, however, supplies several examples.

27 **propinquam**] It was just 15 miles E. of Rome.

29 **minime...Romana**] The good faith of a Roman, like the word of an Englishman, was proverbial. For the reverse of the picture we have such expressions as XXV. 39. 1 *Punica ars*, Virg. *Aen.* II. 152 *dolis instructus et arte Pelasga.*

30 **fraude ac dolo**] = *dolo malo.* Cf. Caesar, *B. C.* II. 14. 1 *hostes sine fide tempus atque occasionem fraudis ac doli quaerunt.*

31 § **5.** **velut**] 'ostensibly,' 'apparently,' like ὡς, δῆθεν.

p. 68. 2 **ex composito**] 'according to the plan': the phrase occurs in 9. 10 above. The treacherous trick here described has its original in Herodotus (III. 153—158), where Zopyrus similarly contrives the capture of Babylon from the Persians.

3 § **6.** **iam ab alienis**] The sentences from this point down to *inventurum* (§ 9) are in *or. obl.*, introduced by *conquerens.* For the subjunctives see note on 1. 8 *audierit.*

vertisse] is intransitive. **superbiam**] sc. *patris.*

5 **in curia solitudinem**] See c. 49, §§ 6, 7.

7 § **7.** **inter...patris**] 'from the fence of spear and sword set by his father.'

9 **nam ne errarent...**] This sentence explains *hostes*: 'enemies... For, make no mistake, you have a war to come, although in pretence it is abandoned.'

11 § **8.** **supplicibus**] In Italy, as in Greece, the obligation of hospitality was recognised and safe-guarded from the earliest times: a host was bound to protect his guest, as a patron his client. The *ius hospitii* was under the special protection of *Iuppiter Hospitalis*, in whom we see the Latin counterpart of Ζεὺς Ξένιος. Cf. Apollonius Rhodius, *Argon.* III. 192—3 πάντες ἐπεὶ πάντῃ, καὶ ὅτις μάλα κύντατος ἀνδρῶν, ξεινίου αἰδεῖται Ζηνὸς θέμιν ἠδ' ἀλεγίζει.

13 **Hernicos**] This is the first mention in Livy of that tribe which, because of its strategical position between the Volsci and the Aequi, became important in the triple alliance with the Romans and the Latins.

14 **impiis**] 'unnatural,' offending against the *pietas* of father to son.

15 **§ 9. forsitan**] Cf. *Praef.* 12.

ardoris aliquid] 'an element of zeal': i.e., in addition to the obligation to defend a suppliant, some nation might feel a positive desire to fight against a bitter tyrant (*superbissimum regem*).

17 **§ 10. si nihil morarentur**] 'if they did not care at all': this is part of the reflection of the Gabines. *nihil morari* in this sense is mainly a poetical usage, but cf. III. 54. 4 *nihil ego quidem moror, quominus decemviratu abeam*. The phrase is found in a literal and transitive sense (=not to detain at all), e.g. in the words with which a consul dismissed the Senate (*nihil amplius vos moramur*) or an accuser withdrew his charge (cf. IV. 42. 8 *C. Sempronium nihil moror*): it is possible that the literal meaning is intended in the present case.

19 **vetant** (sc. *Sextum*) **mirari, si**] See note on 40. 2.

20 **socios**] e.g. Turnus of Aricia.

CHAPTER LIV.

25 **§ 1. veteribus**] 'senior,' i.e. established residents, as distinguished from himself, a *peregrinus*; cf. 17. 2, 33. 2.

27 **auctor esse**] 'advocated.' The historic infinitive is here introduced by a subordinate clause: cf. 58. 3.

29 **nosset...sciret...potuissent**] These subjunctives all imply that the views of Sextus himself are given.

32 **§ 2. praedatum**] The supine—the acc. of a verbal noun—expresses the object aimed at, with verbs of motion or kindred sense: it is thus not inappropriately coupled with such a phrase as **in expeditiones**] 'on expeditions'—for training or reconnaissance: cf. XXXIV. 62. 5 *simul ad purganda crimina et questum de se Romam eos ituros comperit*.

p. 69. 2 **vana...fides**] 'their false confidence' in him.

3 **§ 3. inscia**] The adjective is in sense a participle here ('not knowing') and takes a dependent clause: cf. Caesar, *B. G.* VII. 77 *inscii quid in Aeduis gereretur*, Horace, *Odes* III. 5. 37 *unde vitam sumeret inscius*. See n. on 48. 7 *amens*.

multitudine] 'the rank and file,' 'the general public.'

5 **Gabina res**] 'the cause (fortunes) of Gabii': see note on 28. 9 *rem*.

12 **§ 5. sciscitatum**] supine.

14 **ut omnia unus per se Gabiis posset...dedissent**] 'heaven had granted to him the power to act in everything as master of Gabii.' As a solution of the $\bar{p}$ or *p* found in the MSS. before *Gabiis* I have suggested the reading *per se*, which seems to satisfy the text and the sense. Or *pro*

might be read, to give the necessary ambiguity: to a Gabine Sextus would then seem to say that he was plenipotentiary 'in the interests of Gabii,' to Tarquin that he had the complete control, while the messenger (*dubiae fidei videbatur*) would not have his suspicions aroused.

18 § 6. **summa papaverum capita**] Herodotus' account (V. 92) of the conduct of Thrasybulus, tyrant of Miletus, when Periander of Corinth had sent a messenger to ask what policy was safest, is so much like what is here related, that it may well have been borrowed by Greek or Roman writers for the present purpose. See note on 53. 5 *supra.*

19 § 7. **interrogando...responsum**] For the use of the abl. of the gerund see n. on 5. 6. The gerund-construction *exspectando responsum*, not infrequent in Livy in similar cases, here serves to avoid assonance, and to keep the two ideas (*interrogando, exspectando responsum*) apart.

20 **ut re imperfecta**] *ut* gives the personal feeling of the messenger: the Greek equivalent would be ὡς ἄπρακτος ὤν. Cf. 34. 7 *facile persuadet ut cupido honorum.*

22 **eum**] i.e. Tarquin.

24 § 8. **ambagibus**] 'enigmas': the word occurs again in 55. 6, 56. 9.

25 **sua ipsos invidia opportunos**] 'through the chances afforded by personal unpopularity.' Cf. VI. 24. 3 *Romanus cedentem hostem effuse sequendo opportunus huic eruptioni fuit.* For the position and force of *ipsos* see n. on 11. 9 *sua ipsam peremptam mercede.*

26 **multi palam...interfecti**] This sentence amplifies its predecessor.

27 **in quibus**] 'in whose case.' **futura**] 'likely to be,' 'sure to be': the participle expresses the possibility as viewed by Tarquin.

28 § 9. **patuit**] 'was allowed': besides these voluntary exiles were those who had no choice (*acti sunt*). On the question of exile see n. on 41. 7.

30 **divisui fuere**] 'stood for distribution.' This predicative dative, in which the action is directed towards a point, resembles the dative of 'work contemplated' elsewhere noticed. Other verbal nouns so used by Livy are *risui, usui, sumptui: divisui erant* occurs in XXXIII. 46. 8.

§ 10. **largitiones**] 'grants,' from the point of view of Sextus: **praedae**] 'spoils,' from that of the recipients.

32 **adimi**] historic infinitive.

Gabina res] Cf. 6. 3 *Albana re.*

CHAPTER LV.

p. 70. 4 § 1. **foedus...renovavit**] It does not appear when this treaty *cum Tuscis* was first made: perhaps it is implied in the family connection between the Tarquins and Etruria. Peaceful relations must have been interrupted for a time by the war mentioned in c. 42. 2. Or are we to suppose that *Tusci* here means something different from *Etrusci*?

6 **Iovis templum**] The temple was dedicated to Jupiter, Juno and Minerva, the great trinity of Etruscan deities, whose statues in terra-cotta occupied the three chambers of the *cella*. Its *dies natalis* was observed on the Ides (13th) of September; on this day took place also the *epulum Iovis*, the sacred feast held in honour of the three deities, and graced by the presence of their statues. The original building, which was dedicated (according to tradition) in the first year of the Republic, lasted till 83 B.C., when it was burnt to the ground: the second building (which Livy saw) was raised on the same plan. Detailed measurements indicate that the early Italic foot, not the later Roman, was the unit, and that the *cella* was 100 feet square: in front were three rows of six columns each, and on either side a single row, the whole forming a larger square.

in monte Tarpeio] According to Dionysius (XI. 8) this was the earlier name of the Capitoline hill. Subsequently the epithet *Tarpeius* was usually applied to the S.W. side: but see note on c. 11. 6.

8 **Tarquinios...perfecisse**] These clauses are dependent on the idea contained in *monumentum*. The vow of the elder Tarquin is mentioned in 38. 7.

9 § **2**. **a ceteris religionibus**] 'all other claims of religion.' **libera**] has practically the force of *liberata*, 'freed,' 'released.'

10 **tota**] perhaps to be taken adverbially with *esset*, 'entirely': cf. Hor. *Sat.* I. 9. 2 *nescio quid meditans nugarum, et totus in illis.*

exaugurare] 'withdraw from dedication,' opposed to *inaugurata* below. *inauguratio* means the dedication by augurs of places (*templa*) to be used for the taking of auspices, or for meetings held, or actions done, *auspicato*. *consecratio* means the dedication of sites or buildings (e.g. *fana*, *sacella*), whether *templa* or not, for religious uses. See note on c. 18. 9 *templo*.

11 **sacella**] 'shrines,' i.e. small unroofed places containing an altar sacred to some deity.

a T. Tatio] This name gives the clue for an explanation of the *exauguratio*. The Sabine, i.e. the Patrician, cults on the Capitol were dispossessed, at least in part, to make room for Tarquin's (i.e. the Etruscan, anti-Patrician) reformation.

12 **in ipso discrimine**] 'just at the crisis.'

13 **fuerant]** denotes a state of things now past: cf. 2. 1, 45. 3.

§ 3. **inter principia...operis]** For the use of *inter* cf. 6. 1, 10. 7.

14 **movisse numen]** 'exerted their influence.'

16 **admitterent...addixere]** The two words have the same meaning in augury—'favour,' 'approve'; both occur in c. 36.

in Termini fano] 'in the case of the temple of Terminus.' It would seem that there was on this spot a prehistoric stone, identified with a *numen*, perhaps the great Jupiter of the Latins, and representing a cult distinct from that which Etruscan influences introduced. The stone in question was left open to the air by a hole in the roof of the temple. The personality of Terminus is probably a later development. The conflict between the old Terminus and the new Jupiter is told by Ovid, *Fasti* II. 667—676. On the whole question see Fowler, *Rom. Fest.*, pp. 326—7.

17 § 4. **id...omen auguriumque]** The two words *omen* and *augurium* seem to form a single notion ('the significance of that augury'), and are followed by a verb in the singular. Strictly speaking, *omen* had nothing to do with bird-augury, for Festus (p. 195, Müller) defines it as follows: *omen velut oremen, quod fit ore augurium, quod non avibus aliove modo fit.* Varro (*L. L.* VI. 76, VII. 97) says that *osmen* is the original form, and this may be derived from *ausmen*, i.e. something heard. But, as *aves* only are mentioned in § 3 here, it is best to give *omen* a general sense, to represent the prophetic value or importance attached to the *augurium*.

18 **ita acceptum est]** (so in 34. 9) 'was taken (understood) as follows.'

non motam Termini sedem]=τὸ μὴ κεκινῆσθαι, 'the non-removal.' Translate 'that because the abode of T. had not been removed'...

19 **evocatum]** In V. 21. 5 this word is used of the gods of Veii, 'called forth' from their proper abode by Roman prayers.

20 **cuncta]** Sallust is somewhat fond of this use of *cuncta* (=τὰ πάντα) as a substantive, e.g. *Jugurtha* 92. 2 *deorum nutu cuncta portendi.*

22 § 5. **caput]** Cf. V. 54. 7 *hic Capitolium est, ubi quondam capite humano invento responsum est eo loco caput rerum summamque imperi fore: hic cum augurato liberaretur Capitolium, Iuventas Terminusque maximo gaudio patrum vestrorum moveri se non passi.* The Capitolium was intended to be the visible head and centre of the state: the name belonged originally to an earlier temple on the Quirinal, dedicated to the same triad of divinities, and known hereafter as *Capitolium vetus*, to distinguish it from the greater foundation of Tarquin.

integra facie] 'with the features intact.' **aperientibus]** For this quasi-Greek usage (=τοῖς with a present participle) see notes on 8. 5 *escendentibus*, 41. 1 *mirantium*.

24 § **6. haud per ambages**] 'in no enigmatical fashion.' See 54. 8, 56. 9 for other instances of this word.

25 **cecinere**] See n. on 7. 10, and cf. Virg. *Aen.* VI. 98, 99 *talibus ex adyto dictis Cumaea Sibylla horrendas canit ambages.*

26 **ex Etruria**] These would be *haruspices*. In 34. 9 Tanaquil is described as *perita, ut volgo Etrusci, caelestium prodigiorum mulier.*

27 **augebatur...animus**] 'the king's inclination for outlay was increasing.'

28 § **7. Pomptinae manubiae**] The spoliation of Suessa Pometia is mentioned in 53. 3. *manubiae*='prize-money' realised by the sale of *praeda*, spoils in kind.

29 **in fundamenta**] The preposition expresses the object contemplated; so *in eam rem* in § 9.

30 § **8. Fabio**] See note on 44. 2 above. This instance of a discrepancy between early Roman historians is interesting. **crediderim**] See n. on 46. 4 *ediderim*.

31 **quadraginta...talenta**] See note on c. 53. 3 above. Livy uses *talenta* when his authority is Fabius Pictor, who wrote in Greek: *milia pondo* when his authority is Piso, who wrote in Latin.

32 **Pisoni**] This is L. Calpurnius Piso Frugi, who was consul in 133 B.C., censor in 120. He wrote seven books of annals (*sane exiliter scriptos*, according to Cicero, *Brut.* 27. 106), from the beginning of Rome to his own day.

§ **9. quadraginta...argenti**] *pondo* is an old ablative, 'by weight': as *librarum* (which must be supplied here) was often omitted, *pondo* became the ordinary accompaniment of an expression denoting weight in pounds. The sum represented here seems to be about £105,000 of our money, i.e. about 12 times as much as the *quadraginta talenta.* Dionysius (IV. 50) follows Piso here.

p. 71. 1 **quippe**] The corroborative force of the particle (='undoubtedly,' 'obviously') gives additional certainty to the notions contained in *sperandam...exsuperaturam*; cf. III. 63. 2 *quippe fuso validiore cornu*; Phaedrus, III. 2. 4 *quidam contra miseriti, periturae quippe.* *quippe* is the emendation of I. Becker for the *quia* of the MSS.

3 **nullius...exsuperaturam**] The general sense is 'which would surpass in magnificence the foundations even of any of our present buildings.' Most MSS. read *magnificentiae*, which makes so cumbrous a construction with *nullius...operum* that Reiz reads *nullorum ne huius*

quidem magnificentiae operum. The reading *magnificentia* (ablative) of the Medicean MS. has been adopted, as the simplest expedient, though it leaves the sentence almost as clumsy as before.

The *opera* which Livy has in his mind are the public buildings at Rome which he had seen begun or completed before the date of this book (i.e. about 27 B.C.). Such were the *Basilica Aemilia* (54—46 B.C.), which cost about £500,000; the *Forum Iulium* (54—46 B.C.), which cost about £800,000; the *Forum Augustum* (43—2 B.C.); the Imperial Palace, including the *Domus Augustana* and the Temple of Apollo, in building from 28 B.C. onwards: and the *Mausoleum*, built in 27 B.C.

CHAPTER LVI.

5 § **1. undique ex Etruria**] 'from every part of Etruria': the second expression limits the first.

6 **pecunia...publica**] Presumably a part of the *tributum*, to which since the institution of the *census* by Servius each citizen contributed according to his income.

7 **operis...ex plebe**] 'labourers drawn from the populace': *ex plebe* answers *publica*. For the whole statement cf. Cic. *Verr*. V. 48 *Capitolium...publice coactis fabris operisque imperatis gratis exaedificari potuit*. Tarquin's use of forced labour recalls the corvées of ancient Egypt.

8 **militiae**] dative.

10 § **2. specie minora**] 'less pretentious.'

11 **traducebantur**] 'were transferred': the imperfect (as in the case of *gravabatur* above) implies a common occurrence.

foros...faciendos] See 35. 8, where the introduction of these 'rows' is assigned to the older Tarquin. The gerund and gerundive are occasionally used thus in apposition: cf. 14. 7, and II. 47. 12 *neque immemor eius, quod initio consulatus imbiberat, reconciliandi animos plebis*. [W.-M.]

12 **cloacam maximam**] 'main drain.' The extant remains of this (which date in all probability from the third century B.C., with alterations and restorations made in Imperial times) show that it ran from the E. end of the Subura in a W. S. W. direction across the Forum, under the Vicus Tuscus and Velabrum, and so into the Tiber. There is no reason to doubt that the original structure belonged to the Regal period: and the existence of similar structures in Etruria, dating from that era, shows that it may well have been made under Etruscan influence. Its

crookedness is probably due to the fact that it followed originally the direction, and regulated the flow, of a natural stream, perhaps the Spinon.

14 **quibus...potuit]** This sentence refers to the buildings recently erected by Augustus: see note on c. 55. 9 above, and cf. VI. 4. 12.

16 § **3.** **usus]** 'employment.'

oneri] predicative dative.

18 **Signiam]** among the mountains in the N. of the Volscian territory.

Circeios] on the coast in the S. of the same.

praesidia futura] 'to serve as safeguards'—the key-note of Roman colonization.

20 § **4.** **anguis...elapsus]** These words, really an explanation of *portentum*, are so placed as to form also the basis for a fresh statement *cum...curis*.

24 § **5.** **ad publica...adhiberentur]** 'were called in to treat portents of state.'

25 **Etrusci]** Cf. 31. 4 and 55. 6.

26 **Delphos ad maxime...oraculum]** At this time—the end of the sixth century B.C.—the Delphic temple had been restored by the Alcmaeonidae, and the oracle, in general sympathy with their political ambitions, exercised an important influence on the affairs of Greece. The Etruscans had a treasury at Delphi: Herod. I. 169, Strabo, p. 220.

28 § **6.** **sortium]** 'oracle,' lit. 'tablets,' on which the oracular utterances were written: so Virg. *Aen.* IV. 346 *Italiam Lyciae iussere capessere sortes.*

per ignotas...maria] This is surely a rhetorical exaggeration, for the journey to Delphi would be chiefly by sea, and by a route that must at this time have been familiar.

30 § **7.** **Arruns]** For the name see n. on 34. 2.

32 **longe alius...induerat]** 'of a very different temperament from that which he had adopted in pretence.'

p. 72. 1 **cum primores...interfectum audisset]** The sentence is irregular, though easily intelligible; *fratrem suum*, as a particular instance of *primores*, attracts *interfectum* to itself: *inter primores*, without *in quibus*, would have been more natural, but less graphic.

2 **neque...statuit]** 'determined to leave the king nothing to fear in his disposition, nothing to covet in his estate.' For the whole expression cf. Tacitus, *Hist.* IV. 42 *nihil quod ex te concupisceret Nero, nihil quod timeret.*

4 **contemptu...esset]** 'to win safety in neglect, where there was but

scant protection in privilege.' *ubi esset*, subj. because it expresses the view of Brutus, not of Livy: *ubi*=ὅτε, 'in a case where.'

5 § **8. ex industria...stultitiae**] 'in studied counterfeit of idiocy.'

7 **Bruti...cognomen**] 'the surname Dullard,' 'Stupid': the name is probably the cause, not the effect, of the story.

8 **liberator ille...animus**] 'that spirit destined to deliver.'

9 **tempora sua**] 'its proper opportunities.'

10 § **9. ludibrium...comes**] 'assuredly more for sport than company.'

11 **corneo cavato...baculo**] 'in a wand of cornel-wood hollowed for the purpose.'

12 **per ambages effigiem**] 'an enigmatical counterpart.' For other instances of *ambages* see 54. 8, 55. 6.

16 § **10. ex infimo specu**] 'from the depth of the cave.' The Pythian priestess (who is not mentioned here) was supposed to derive her inspiration from a sulphureous vapour emitted from a hole in the earth.

imperium...tulerit] Perhaps Livy is paraphrasing here two hexameters from an early annalist, e.g.:

imperium Romae summum, nisi fallor, habebit,
qui vestrum, o iuvenes, tulerit prior (or prima?) oscula matri.

19 § **11. expers**] 'without share.'

20 **summa ope**] 'with all possible care.'

21 **sorti permittunt**] 'left it to chance' (to decide): historic present, after which the historic tenses *redissent*, *daret* follow naturally.

22 § **12. alio...spectare**] 'had another bearing,' 'had something else in view.' *alio* is an adverb, like *eo*, *quo*.

25 **esset**] 'was, as he believed.'

§ **13. Rutulos**] See note on 2. 1.

CHAPTER LVII.

27 § **1. Ardeam**] The city was in the centre of the territory of the Rutuli (see map) about three miles from the coast, in a district so unhealthy that even in the time of the Empire it was avoided on account of malaria.

ut in ea...aetate] 'considering the district and the period.' For this restrictive use of *ut*, giving the author's view, cf. notes on *Praef.* 4 *ut quae*, 34. 7 *ut cupido*.

30 **ditari**] sc. *studebat*.

32 § **2. praeter aliam...infestos** (sc. *animos*)...**indignabantur**] 'for over and above the general arrogance, they had a further ground of animosity against the kingdom because the king (as they protested) had

kept them so long at the work of carpenters and the labour of slaves.' *praeter* is found several times in Caesar with the inclusive sense which it has here, 'besides,' 'in addition to.' *aliam* = 'in other matters,' i.e. 'in general,' and so is almost equivalent to *ceteram*: like *praeter* it is used here in an inclusive sense, that is to say, it joins *superbia* in general (as the reason for the public animosity) with the special form of *superbia* implied in the words *in fabrorum...ab rege.* This expression of a general notion followed by a special case is best illustrated by the Greek idioms ἄλλα τε καὶ..., τά τε ἄλλα καὶ..., ἄλλως τε καὶ.... *alius* in this sense is not uncommon in Livy, but it usually *follows* the special case or instance which it is intended to emphasize: e.g. XXII. 5. 7 *nec ut pro signis antesignani, post signa alia pugnaret acies.*

regnum and *rex* in the present passage are intended to suggest that, in the minds of most Romans, Tarquin had turned a kingdom into a despotism.

p. 73. 4 § 3. **obsidione munitionibusque**] 'blockade-works.'

coepti] See n. on 39. 4.

5 § 4. **stativis**] 'permanent camp,' 'cantonments.'

6 **commeatus**] 'periods of furlough,' 'grants of leave.'

7 § 5. **quidem**] = γοῦν, 'at any rate.'

8 **comissationibus**] 'carousals.' The word *comissor* (= the Greek κωμάζω) is used primarily of a festive procession, then (as the holiday-makers usually retired to the house of one of their number for entertainment) of a revel, drinking-party: thus *comissationibus* here serves appropriately as an introduction of *potantibus.*

10 § 6. **Egerii**] See 38. 1.

11 **miris modis**] probably a colloquial or provincial phrase for 'exceedingly' (cf. 'wonderfully' in English): it is common in Plautus. See note on *mire* 45. 7 above. Or it may be a translation from a Greek authority who wrote θαυμασίως ὡς: cf. 16. 8 *mirum quantum.*

12 § 7. **accenso**] The metaphorical use of this word is not uncommon in Livy (who rarely employs *conflare*, a word of similar sense affected by Cicero) and Tacitus: cf. XXXV. 10. 5 *certamen accendebant fratres candidatorum*, II. 29. 8 *accendi magis discordiam quam sedari.* *exardere* (which denotes the result of *accendere, conflare*) is a common metaphor.

paucis...horis] Collatia was about 25 miles (across country) from Ardea.

id] i.e. *quantum...sua.* **sciri**] 'known' as opposed to 'disputed.'

14 **quin**] See note on 47. 3.

15 **praesentes**] 'in person': **nostrarum ingenia**] 'the tempers of our own wives.'

16 **id...sit**] 'that would be (must be) an indisputable proof.'

19 § **8.** **Romam**] about 30 miles, if they went by Aricia, which seems the most probable route. Strabo (p. 229) gives the distance as 160 stades, probably by the *Via Ardeatina.*

20 **Collatiam**] about 13 miles E. of Rome.

23 § **9.** **lanae**] 'wool-spinning.' Diligence in such work was ever the mark of an honourable matron: Gaia Caecilia (=Tanaquil, see note on 34. 10), the ideal Roman wife, was said to have excelled in spinning, and in Livy's own day Augustus made his daughter and granddaughters attend to the same (cf. Suet. *Aug.* 64. 4). So, in the Proverbs, XXXI. 13, 19 the good wife *seeketh wool, and flax, and worketh diligently with her hands....She layeth her hands to the spindle, and her hands hold the distaff.*

lucubrantes] 'late at work,' 'at their night-work.'

in medio aedium] i.e. in the *atrium.* This substantival use of a neuter adjective, with a genitive dependent on it in a partitive or quasi-partitive sense, is found with plurals in Lucretius and the Augustan poets: in prose Sallust employs it fairly often (in both singular and plural), but Livy has it at every turn, e.g. V. 41. 2 *medio aedium eburneis sellis sedere,* II. 33. 7 *in proximo urbis,* XXVI. 40. 9 *in media urbis ac forum,* VI. 32. 6 *ad subita belli.*

§ **10.** **muliebris certaminis**] The adjective has the force of an objective genitive, i.e. 'about the wives.'

spectata] 'approved' and therefore 'excellent.'

§ **11.** **ab nocturno iuvenali ludo**] For the accumulation of adjectives cf. 14. 7 *n. densa obsita virgulta,* 31. 8 *quaedam occulta sollemnia* *acrificia.*

CHAPTER LVIII.

4. 1 § **2.** **ab ignaris consilii**] 'by a household unaware of his ent.'

cubiculum] probably in the front part of the house, and so as far ay as possible from the apartment of Lucretia.

§ **3.** **versare...animum**] 'tried every way to twist a woman's will.'

§ **5.** **violatrix**] This emendation for the *velut victrix* of the MSS. ich is suggested by Seeley, and occurred independently to myself), as exactly to satisfy the sense of the passage.

ut...veniant] Lucretia's request.

ita facto...opus esse] 'they needs must do so, and with speed': *oratio obliqua*, as part of the message. This construction of the perf. part. with *opus* is probably colloquial: it occurs frequently in Plautus and Terence.

21 § **6.** **Valerio Volesi filio**] *Volesus* or *Volusus* seems to be a collateral form (cf. *Clausus* and *Claudius*) of Valerius: its presence here may serve to indicate the antiquity—perhaps the Sabine origin—of the Valerii. P. Valerius became *Publicola* soon after this (see II. 8. 2): and the family is associated *ab initio* with the liberty of the citizens.

23 **conventus**] 'met,' 'confronted.'

24 **suorum**] See note on 7. 1 *sua*.

25 § **7.** **'satin salve?'**] With the adverb *salve* some word such as *agis*, *agitur* is to be supplied. *salvi* refers at once to health and to chastity. 'Is all well with thee?' 'Nay, how can it be well with a woman...?'

28 **corpus**] sc. *mihi*.

29 **dexteras fidemque**] 'your hands in pledge,' a hendiadys.

30 **fore**] sc. *rem*, *factum*.

§ **8.** **hostis pro hospite**] 'giving enmity for amity,' 'fiend and no friend': cf. 12. 9 *perfidos hospites, imbelles hostes*.

32 **pestiferum**] 'fatal,' 'to my destruction and his own.'

p. 75. 1 § **9.** **aegram animi**] See n. on 7. 6 *incertus animi*.

2 **ab coacta**] 'from the victim of violence,' 'from a helpless woman.'

mentem peccare] *mentem* is the emphatic word: 'sin is of the mind, not of the body, and where there has been no previous intention, there is no guilt.'

4 § **10.** **vos videritis**] perf. subj., 'it shall be for *you* to see': so Virg. *Aen.* X. 743 *nunc morere: at de me divom pater atque hominum rex viderit*; and 23. 8 above *fuerit*.

§ **12.** **eum**] For this resumptive use cf. 19. 1 *urbem...eam*, 49. 9 *ei Mamilio*.

8 **in vulnus**] 'over the wound.'

conclamat] It was the custom after death and before burial to call often and aloud (*conclamare*) the name of the departed (cf. 26. 2). Here it is rather the cry of horror that is intended: but *conclamatio* is implied in the next sentence by *illis luctu occupatis*.

CHAPTER LIX.

12 § **1.** **ante...iniuriam**] 'until a prince did outrage it'—the phrase qualifies *castissimum*.

14 **scelerata**] 'infamous,' 'impious.'

15 **ferro...possim**] This formula of utter destruction occurs again in II. 10. 4 and 6. 9.

exsecuturum] This is the only known case where this verb takes a personal object in the sense of 'visit,' 'punish': *persequor* is common with the same sense and construction.

17 § **2**. **cultrum...tradit**] he handed the knife, that each in turn might take the oath, not by the knife, but by the life-blood on it, which was nearest and dearest to them.

18 **unde...ingenium**] explains *miraculo*: *ingenium* ('power') is meant to contrast with *Bruti* ('Dullard').

19 **praeceptum**] 'prescribed': an oath was usually administered by a formula (*conceptis verbis*).

20 **toti**] not 'all' but 'altogether': cf. 40. 6.

iam inde] 'straightway,' 'unhesitatingly.'

21 § **3**. **elatum**] This verb (like *ἐκφέρειν*) is used technically in connexion with burial.

22 **forum**] the 'square' or market-place of Collatia.

23 **miraculo...atque indignitate**] 'surprised, as ever, by the strange event, but shocked as well.'

24 **pro se quisque**] In this case a plural verb follows these words, to denote that the individual complaints make up one whole: in Praef. 9 the verb is in the singular.

25 § **4**. **castigator**] 'who reproved.' **auctorque**] 'and advocated, urged.'

26 **quod...deceret**] 'as men and Romans should'; the subjunctive implies that this was part of Brutus' harangue.

27 **hostilia**] So Lucretia had called Sextus *hostis pro hospite* (58. 8).

29 § **5**. **pari**] So the MSS., but the meaning is not quite clear; does it mean 'equal' to the detachment which marched on Rome—half the force, in fact; or 'equal' to the task, 'suitable'? Heerwagen reads *parte...relicta*, in which case *praesidio* is a dative of purpose.

30 **Collatiae ad portas**] Cf. *undique ex Etruria*, 56. 1.

custodibus] 'sentries,' 'piquets,' furnished from the *praesidium* for this special purpose.

31 **regibus**] 'king and queen': cf. 39. 2.

p. 76. 1 § **6**. **rursus**] 'then again,' in contrast to the *pavor* and *tumultus*. **anteire**] 'took the lead,' in person and purpose. **vident**] i.e. the people in Rome.

2 **quidquid...rentur**] 'decided that the movement, whatever its nature,

was not without design.' The different stages in popular feeling are clearly outlined in successive sentences: (1) panic, (2) reconsideration, (3) indignation, (4) communication.

6 § 7. **praeco**] It was the duty of the *praecones*, as state-heralds, to attend (*apparere*) certain magistrates, to summon the people (as here) to *contiones* or *comitia*, to summon senators to the Senate House (see c. 47. 8, and cf. Suetonius, *Claud.* 36).

ad tribunum Celerum] Whatever the origin of the *Celeres* (see c. 15. 8)—some authorities are inclined to connect their origin and their disappearance with the rise and fall of Etruscan influence—it would seem that by their close association with the king's person their commandant became a sort of king's deputy: his relationship towards the king was (or was supposed to be) analogous to that of the *magister equitum* towards the *dictator* (*magister populi*) of Republican times. The *tribunus Celerum* therefore combined military and civil functions—the command of the cavalry (or even of the whole army), and the presidency (if deputed by the king) of *comitia* and senate (i.e. of *concilium* and *consilium*).

8 § 8. **eius...ingeniique**] 'characterised by the feeling and capacity.' Here the particular kind (*eius*) is of so inferior a degree as almost to express absence of real 'feeling' and 'capacity.' *fuerat* denotes a state of things which has ceased to exist, cf. 2. 1, 55. 2.

11 **Tricipitini**] a surname in the *gens Lucretia*: cf. III. 8. 2, IV. 30. 4.

12 **esset**] subjunctive to denote Brutus' statement.

13 § 9. **in fossas...demersae**] 'buried alive (kept underground) for the excavation of channels and sewers.'

14 **Romanos...factos**] The *oratio obliqua* follows easily from the previous clauses describing the speech of Brutus.

15 **opifices ac lapicidas**] 'mechanics and masons.'

16 § 10. **memorata**] i.e. by Brutus, and likewise *invocati* below. **caedis**] So the best MSS., and the form is justified by a good many parallels, e.g. I. 11 *stirpis*.

17 **invecta...filia**] 'the act of the daughter in driving her chariot of crime over her father's body.'

18 **di**] either gods in general, or the special powers presiding over vengeance for parents, the *parentum furiae* mentioned below.

19 § 11. **quae...subicit**] 'suggested by the palpable iniquity of the position, but by no means easy for the historian to reproduce.' *praesens rerum indignitas* certainly refers to the immediate surroundings of Brutus, not of Livy, who had, so far as we know, no grounds of censure

against the administration of Augustus: *subicit* is merely a vivid variation from the past tenses around.

22 **abrogaret**] Tarquin had acquired the kingdom *neque populi iussu neque auctoribus patribus*, so that this formal suspension was not strictly necessary: but the author wishes to lay stress on the deliberate attitude and action of the people in thus preparing for a constitutional reconstruction.

exsules] In c. 41. 7 the sons of Ancus *exsulatum ierant*, withdrawing from the possible consequences of the assassination of Tarquin, just as Roman citizens withdrew from condemnation under a capital charge in Republican times. But here the people exercised its sovereignty to enforce the exile of certain persons, a form of punishment which was adopted in the last era of the Republic (e.g. in the case of Cicero), and continued under the Empire.

23 **§ 12. iunioribus**] See note on c. 52. 5 above.

24 **inde**] may belong to *exercitum*, 'the army there,' or merely indicate with *profectus* the change of scene.

26 **praefecto urbis**] The special duty of this official was to take charge of the city, and to deal with law business and emergencies, in the absence of the king (cf. Tac. *Ann.* VI. 11). In the early days of the Republic, a similar deputy was appointed when both consuls were absent from the capital.

27 **§ 13. inter hunc tumultum**] Cf. 6. 1.

CHAPTER LX.

(See Introduction, § 8.)

30 **§ 1. re nova**] See n. on 51. 3.

32 **senserat**] 'had anticipated'—felt by instinct.

p. 77. 5 **§ 2. Caere in Etruscos**] See n. on 56. 1. Caere was about 25 miles W. N. W. of Rome, near enough to be effective as a base of operations. The Tarquins naturally retired to Etruria, as their ancestral home.

11 **§ 3. regnatum**] 'there was a king.'

13 **§ 4. consules**] The derivation of this word is disputed. The Romans themselves referred it to *consulere*, e.g. Varro, *L. L.*, V. 80, *qui recte consulat consul fuat* (*cluat*): Dionysius XIV. 76 agrees—κωνσούλας· τοῦτο μεθερμηνευόμενον εἰς τὴν Ἑλλάδα γλῶτταν τοὔνομα συμβούλους ἢ προβούλους δύναται δηλοῦν, κωνσίλια γὰρ οἱ Ῥωμαῖοι τὰς συμβουλὰς

καλοῦσιν. Nettleship, however (*Journal of Philology* IV. 272—274), is inclined to derive it from a root *sal* meaning 'abide,' 'remain': so *consules* are 'those who stay together,' 'colleagues,' *exsul* 'one who lives away,' *consilium*, 'a staying together,' 'meeting.'

comitiis centuriatis] 'at a meeting of the court of centuries.'

a praefecto urbis] This officer thus acted as *interrex*, and such is the name given to Lucretius in the account of Dionysius (IV. 84). Perhaps Livy avoids the mention of an *interrex* in this case where, in contrast to the other *interregna* of the book, no king was to be elected.

14 **creati**] 'returned as elected': *creo* is used here of the presiding officer.

ex commentariis] 'according to the memorandum (schedule).' The *comitia centuriata* had lapsed into abeyance during the tyranny of Tarquin, and it is quite possible that the classification and procedure attributed to Servius were not yet definitely complete, but tentative only.

LIST OF READINGS

ADOPTED IN CERTAIN PASSAGES WHERE THE TEXT IS DISPUTED

(The reading of this edition is given first, then the alternative or alternatives, in MSS. or editions. An asterisk shows that the question of reading is considered in the general notes *ad loca.*)

Praefatio 9. **dissidentis*. So MSS.: *desidentis*, a later MS.
13. **tantum*. So MSS.: *tanti*, editors.
c. **4.** 5. *alluvie*. So MSS.: *eluvie*, Gronovius.
7. 7. *morte*. So MSS.: *mortem*, Madvig.
8. 5. **escendentibus*, H. J. E.: *descendentibus*, MSS.
9. 13. **violati hospitii foedus*. So MSS.: For *foedus* Grunauer suggests *scelus*: or perhaps *violatum* (so Perizonius) should be read for *violati*.
14. 7. **densissima ob virgulta*, H. J. E.: *densa obsita virgulta*, MSS.
17. 1. *ad singulos*, Graevius: *a singulis*, MSS.
19. 6. *intercalariis*, Heerwagen: *intercalares*, MSS.
22. 5. **comi fronte*, Madvig: some MSS. have *comiter*, some *comi fronte comiter*.
23. 6. **tamen*, J. H. Voss: *tametsi*, MSS.
24. 3. *cuius*, 2 later MSS.: *cuiusque* (?=*cuiuscumque*), MSS.
24. 8. **ille Diespiter*, Alschefski and Hertz: *ille dies Iuppiter*, MSS.
43. 7. **accensi*. So MSS.: *accensis*, Lange.
48. 4. **ipse prope exsanguis ab iis*, Weissenborn-Müller, following Drakenborch and Heerwagen. The words after *exsanguis* contained in the MSS. are discussed in the note *ad loc.*
54. 5. **unus per se Gabiis*, H. J. E.: *p̄* or *p Gabiis*, MSS.
55. 9. *quippe*, I. Becker: *quia*, MSS.
**magnificentia*, Medicean MS.: *magnificentiae*, the rest.
58. 5. *violatrix*, Seeley, H. J. E.: *velut victrix*, MSS.

INDEX.

A. LATIN WORDS.

[*The figures give chapter and section of text and notes.*]

B. PROPER NAMES.

C. SUBJECTS.

D. LANGUAGE.

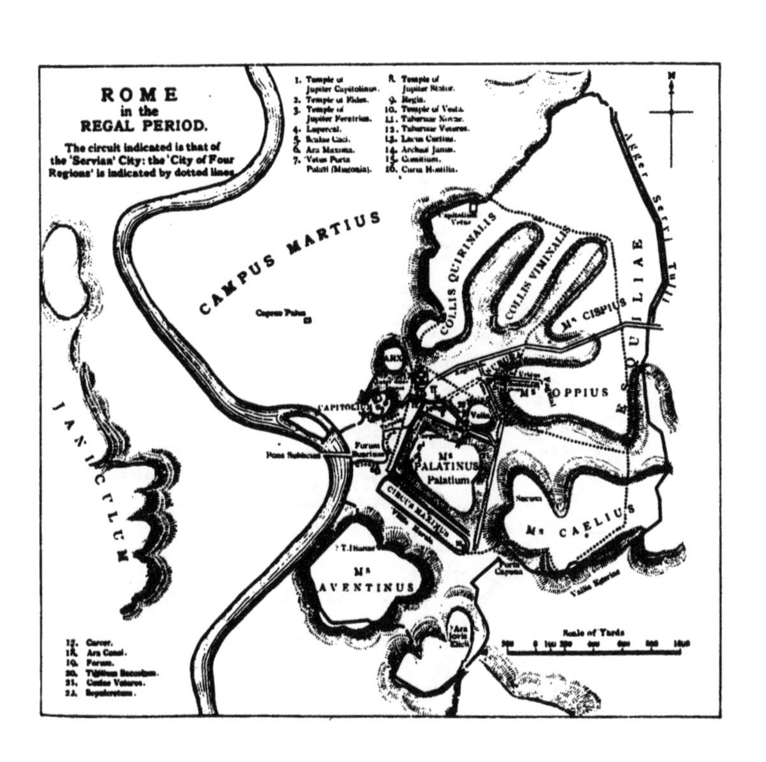
ROME
in the
REGAL PERIOD.
The circuit indicated is that of the 'Servian' City: the 'City of Four Regions' is indicated by dotted lines
1. Temple of Jupiter Capitolinus.
2. Temple of Fides.
3. Temple of Jupiter Feretrius.
4. Lupercal.
6. Ara Maxima.
7. Vetus Porta Palatii (Mugonia).
8. Temple of Jupiter Stator.
9. Regia.
10. Temple of Vesta.
11. Tabernae Novae.
12. Tabernae Veteres.
13. Lacus Curtius.
14. Archaic Janus.
15. Comitium.
16. Curia Hostilia.
17. Carcer.
18. Ara Consi.
19. Forum.
21. Curiae Veteres.
22. Sepulcretum.
CAMPUS MARTIUS
COLLIS QUIRINALIS
COLLIS VIMINALIS
Mˢ CISPIUS
ESQUILIAE
Agger Servi Tullii
ARX
CAPITOLIUM
Mˢ OPPIUS
Velia
Mˢ PALATINUS
Palatium
CIRCUS MAXIMUS
Vallis Murcia
Mˢ CAELIUS
Porta Capena
Mˢ AVENTINUS
JANICULUM
Pons Sublicius
Forum Boarium
Scale of Yards
N

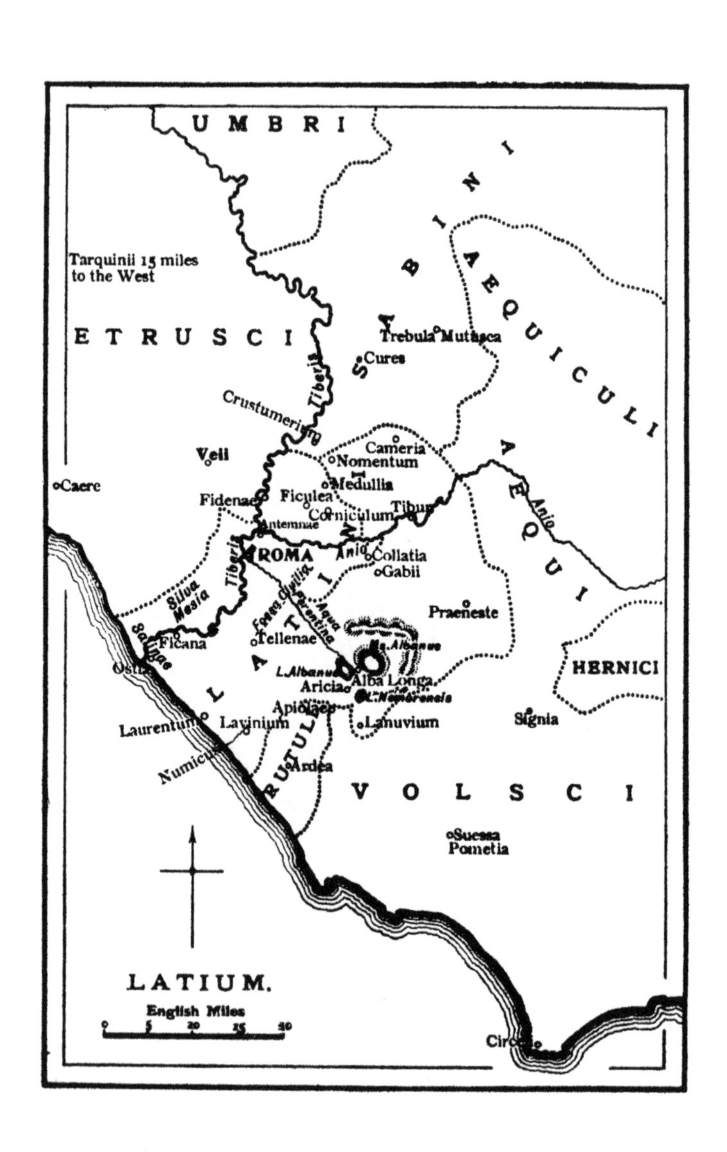
UMBRI
SABINI
AEQUICULI
AEQUI
Tarquinii 15 miles to the West
ETRUSCI
Trebula Mutusca
Cures
Tiberis
Crustumerium
Cameria
Nomentum
Veii
Caere
Medullia
Fidenae
Ficulea
Corniculum
Tibur
Antemnae
Anio
ROMA
Collatia
Gabii
LATINI
Silva Mesia
Fossa Cluilia
Aqua Ferentina
Praeneste
Salinae
Ficana
Tellenae
Ms. Albanus
HERNICI
Ostia
L. Albanus
Alba Longa
Aricia
L. Nemorensis
Apiolae
Lanuvium
Signia
Laurentum
Lavinium
RUTULI
Numicus
Ardea
VOLSCI
Suessa Pometia
Circei
LATIUM.
English Miles
0 5 20 25 30

For EU product safety concerns, contact us at Calle de José Abascal, 56–1°, 28003 Madrid, Spain or eugpsr@cambridge.org.

www.ingramcontent.com/pod-product-compliance
Ingram Content Group UK Ltd.
Pitfield, Milton Keynes, MK11 3LW, UK
UKHW020320140625
459647UK00018B/1946

* 9 7 8 1 1 0 7 6 2 1 2 2 0 *